Immersion

Immersion

The Experience of Literary Reading

EDITED BY NAOMI ADAM,
JESSICA NORLEDGE, PETER STOCKWELL
AND MATTHEW VOICE

EDINBURGH
University Press

Edinburgh University Press is one of the leading university presses in the UK. Publishing new research in the arts and humanities, EUP connects people and ideas to inspire creative thinking, open new perspectives and shape the world we live in. For more information, visit www.edinburghuniversitypress.com.

Edinburgh University Press Ltd
13 Infirmary Street, Edinburgh EH1 1LT

Typeset in 9 on 12pt Noto Serif
by Cheshire Typesetting Ltd, Cuddington, Cheshire and
Printed and bound in the UK using 100% renewable electricity by
CPI Group (UK) Ltd

A CIP record for this book is available from the British Library
ISBN 978 1 3995 4956 1 (hardback)
ISBN 978 1 3995 4958 5 (webready PDF)
ISBN 978 1 3995 4957 8 (epub)

EU Authorised Representative:
Easy Access System Europe
Mustamäe tee 50, 10621 Tallinn, Estonia
gpsr.requests@easproject.com

MIX
Paper | Supporting responsible forestry
FSC® C013604
FSC www.fsc.org

This book is printed using paper from well-managed forests, recycling and other controlled sources

Contents

List of contributors

Naomi Adam is a researcher in literary linguistics on staff at the University of Liverpool (UK) and the University of Nottingham (UK). Her research interests span award-winning and/or contemporary fiction, fictolinguistics, narrative ontologies, popular culture, and postcolonial fiction. Her work has been published in outlets including *English Text Construction*, the *Journal of Language and Pop Culture*, and *Language and Literature*. She is currently preparing the monograph *Metaperspectives in Contemporary Literary Fiction*, scheduled for publication in 2026. Naomi is also the editor of the Poetics and Linguistics Association's biannual newsletter, *Parlance*.

Miranda Anderson is an Honorary Fellow of the University of Edinburgh (UK) and an Associate Lecturer at the Open University. She has led the development of distributed cognition as a theoretical framework, and is the author of *The Renaissance Extended Mind* (2015), as well as co-editor of *The Book of the Mirror* (2007) and four volumes on distributed cognition between classical antiquity and modernism (2018–20). She is currently developing the fission-fusion concept of the mind and self through her work on articles focusing upon contemporary and historical literature and culture.

Harry Cooper is a postgraduate researcher at the University of Liverpool (UK), where he also completed a Master of Research in Arts. His research interests include cognitive poetics and ecostylistics, and his doctoral project focuses on the readerly experience of projection and immersion in a selection of cross-cultural texts.

Andrew Currie is a postgraduate researcher at the University of Strathclyde (UK), where he also completed a Master of Research in English Studies. His doctoral project, funded by the Scottish Graduate School for the Arts and Humanities, focuses on literary narrative processing in autistic adult readers and explores their engagement with literary fiction. In particular, he is interested in whether the cognitive traits associated with autism may lead to a unique reading experience.

Gaetano Fiorin works as a Research Fellow in the Department of Humanities at the University of Trieste (Italy). His research spans theoretical linguistics, experimental linguistics, and philosophy of language, and he is particularly interested in model-theoretic semantics and the syntax-semantics interface, language development and language impairments, the metaphysics of meaning, and the connection between language and other cognitive domains. His work has been published in *Intercultural Pragmatics* and *Social Semiotics*, among other journals, and he is co-author of the monograph *Harmony Effects Across Language and Perception* (2021, with Denis Delfitto).

Polina Gavin works as a Teaching Fellow of English Language and Literature at the University of Aston (UK). Her research interests lie in the areas of cognitive poetics and literary linguistics, most especially the readerly experience of ekphrasis, intermediality, and intertextuality. Polina's most recent publication is the chapter 'Creative writing practice of ekphrastic intervention: a case study of literary responses to *A Blind Girl Reading* by Ejnar Nielsen' in the collection *Style and Sense(s)* (2024, edited by Linda Pillière and Sandrine Sorlin).

Alice Haines is a Research Fellow at the University of Nottingham (UK), where she specialises in literary linguistics. She has also held posts at the University of Derby and De Montfort University. Her research on the stylistics of humour has been published in *Language and Literature* and the *Journal of Literary Semantics*, and her popular regular column, 'Kill the Joke', appears in *Babel: The Language Magazine*. Outside of academia, Alice has previously worked in healthcare, advertising, and film production. She is currently working on a monograph on the stylistics of humour.

Suzanne Keen is a Professor of English at Scripps College (USA), where she specialises in narrative empathy. Her interdisciplinary work draws on literary and narrative theory, neuroscience, developmental and social psychology, and affective science. Her books include *Thomas Hardy's Brains: Psychology, Neurology, and Hardy's Imagination* (2014), *Empathy and the Novel* (2007), *Romances of the Archive in Contemporary British Fiction* (2001), *Victorian Renovations of the Novel* (1998), and the textbook *Narrative Form* (2003, revised and expanded second edition 2015). A volume of her selected essays, titled *Empathy and Reading*, was published in 2022.

Jessica Mason is a Senior Lecturer in English Language at Sheffield Hallam University (UK). As an interdisciplinary researcher, Jessica specialises in linguistics and education, with her research focusing upon the cognition and discussion of reading in different contexts, including online, in school classrooms, and in book clubs. In particular, she studies how readers make intertextual connections between the stories they read, hear, watch, or experience over time, considering how the texts we read and our responses to them can shape our identity. She is author of *Studying Fiction: A Guide for Teachers and Researchers* (2021) and *Intertextuality in Practice* (2019).

Jessica Norledge is Assistant Professor in Stylistics at the University of Nottingham (UK). She is a stylistician and discourse analyst with a particular expertise in the cognitive poetics of emotion, and worlds theories in dystopian fiction. She is the author of *The Language of Dystopia* (2022) and co-author of *Digital Pedagogies for Linguistics* (2022). She has co-edited *Reading Fictional Languages* (2024) and is currently working on a book on *Contemporary Feminist Stylistics*.

Ralf Schneider is Professor and Chair of English Literature at RWTH Aachen University (Germany) as well as co-founder of the Aachen Centre for Cognitive and Empirical Literary Studies (ACCELS). His main research interests are cognitive narratology and cognitive reception theory, and he has also published widely on several areas of British literary and cultural studies, including the relationship between literature and war, literary representations of masculinities, migration and literature, and literary constructions of childhood. He is co-editor of the *Handbook of British Literature and Culture of the First World War* (2021, with Jane Potter).

Peter Stockwell is Professor of Literary Linguistics at the University of Nottingham (UK), and a Fellow of the English Association. He has published twenty books and more than 100 articles in stylistics, sociolinguistics, science fiction, and applied linguistics, including *Digital Teaching for Linguistics* (2022), *Cognitive Poetics* (2020), *The Language of Surrealism* (2017), *Texture: A Cognitive Aesthetics of Reading* (2009), and *The Poetics of Science Fiction* (2000). He co-edited *Reading Fictional Languages* (2024), *The Cambridge Handbook of Stylistics* (2014), *The Language and Literature Reader* (2008), *Contemporary Stylistics* (2007), and *Impossibility Fiction* (1996).

Piergiorgio Trevisan is an Associate Professor of English Language and Translation in the Department of Humanities at the University of Trieste (Italy). His research interests include stylistics, systemic functional linguistics, corpus linguistics, and critical discourse analysis. He is the author of the books *Characterisation through Language: Perspectives from Stylistics* (2019) and *Towards a Stylistic Approach to Character in Literature* (2008), as well as co-author of *Cultures on the Screen. Family, Identity, Gender, and Language in Television Series* (2022, with Leonardo Buonomo).

Matthew Voice is an Assistant Professor in the Department of Applied Linguistics at the University of Warwick (UK), where he teaches courses on linguistic research methods, sociolinguistics, and language and power. His research, published in journals including *Language and Literature* and *Discourse Studies*, covers topics ranging across military memoir, multiverse fiction, pop song lyrics, and forensic linguistics, all connected through cognitive approaches to language and style. He is currently preparing a contribution to the *Cambridge Elements in Cognitive Linguistics* series, on the critical and literary analysis of agency in discourse.

Ella Wydrzynska is a Visiting Research Fellow at Aston University (UK), where she specialises in literary linguistics and narratology. Her research concentrates on the language of contemporary children's fiction and the use of metafictive devices as a source of readerly engagement and interactivity. She co-authored Routledge's *Researching Stylistics* (2026) and is currently preparing a monograph that will explore the style, structure, and storytelling strategies of postmodern children's books. Ella also works at the University of Nottingham as an Educational Developer and leads the implementation of student co-creation strategies to enhance curricula and assessment design.

Acknowledgements

We would like to thank the Midlands 4 Cities (M4C) doctoral training partnership and the Arts and Humanities Research Council (AHRC) for financial support for the symposium at the University of Nottingham that was the origin of this book. The symposium was also supported by the Centre for Research in Applied Linguistics (CRAL) at the University of Nottingham, and the Poetics and Linguistics Association (PALA): <www.pala.ac.uk>

The editors and Polina Gavin would like to thank John Milkereit for kindly granting permission to reprint his poem 'Lost Dream for my Unvaccinated Lover'. The poem appears in *Lost Sonnets for My Unvaccinated Lover* (Kelsay Books, 2023).

The editors would like to thank the following for permission to reproduce the lyrics of Tom Waits' 'The Piano has been Drinking (Not Me)':

CHAPTER 1

Introduction: immersion – the experience of literary reading

Naomi Adam, Jessica Norledge, Peter Stockwell, and Matthew Voice

The fact of immersion

Immersion is a common experience of literary reading. At its most simple, it can be understood as the feeling while reading of being so engaged in the world that is described by a text that this imagined world fills much of the consciousness of the reader. Effects of this engagement include a sense that the imagined world is vivid and rich, that the reader's ordinary-world capacities for anticipating action and event can be applied in the imagined world, that characters in the imagined world can be engaged with as if they were people with consciousness and emotions of their own. Though of course this sense of the real-ness of the imagined world is an illusion, it is one that cannot be simultaneously conceived as an illusion while it is being enacted. As Gombrich (1959: 5) says, in a discussion that locates the sense of artistic engagement in ancient Greek discussions of representation and mimesis, 'though we may be intellectually aware of the fact that any given experience *must* be an illusion, we cannot, strictly speaking, watch ourselves having an illusion'.

This sense that the experience of immersion involves a shift in the attentional end-point of consciousness makes it hard to study. How can a researcher gather information about what a reader is experiencing, when that reader's conscious awareness is located elsewhere at the time, and as soon as you ask them about it, that intervention itself breaks the illusion? It is the observer's paradox in its most catastrophic form. We are reliant on retrospection, then, for any sort of direct account of the experience; or we are reliant on indirect evidence from empirical, reader-response methods; or we are reliant on our existing insights into the effects of certain textual and narratological patterns. All of these approaches are represented in this book.

This volume does not set out to prove whether immersion exists as a phenomenon or not: we take it as given that it does. This is not to say that all researchers agree on our understanding of immersion. Several chapters in this book take issue with different conceptualisations of the phenomenon, and one key feature of the work represented here is that the chapters are in dialogue with each other. Neither does the fact of immersion deny the equal fact that different readers experience immersion in different ways, with some people never or very rarely having this sort of fully engaged experience. This resonates with work in cognitive literary studies, which has suggested that there are various distinct ways of processing narrative, tied to differences in the visualising of verbal language, which may impact the reading experience (Otis 2015a, 2015b). Ultimately, the prevalence of immersion across readers is variable; the depth of the experience is variable; and of course the experience of different readers engaging with the same specific text might also be highly diverse. These are matters for exploration.

Approaches and perspectives

Many current discussions of immersion locate their origins in Samuel Taylor Coleridge's (1817: ch.XIV) endeavour in literary writing 'to transfer from our inward nature a human interest and a semblance of truth sufficient to procure for these shadows of imagination that willing suspension of disbelief for the moment, which constitutes poetic faith'. It should be noted that the phrase 'willing suspension of disbelief' has since been taken by many as a general principle of all literary fiction, whereas in fact Coleridge had immediately prior to this only been talking about writing 'directed to persons and characters supernatural, or at least romantic'. He was contrasting this with his friend Wordsworth's view that poetry (= literature) should take natural topics and make the reading of them meditative. Coleridge wrote of the supernatural in a way that would engage the reader as if it were realistic (as in his 'The Rime of the Ancient Mariner', for example). He uses the word 'disbelief' because this would be the default disposition for a reader encountering a tale of the supernatural, and this is why he has to cast the immersive engagement doubly negatively as a suspension of (the default) disbelief (see Paige 2024). Indeed, Coleridge's more interesting comment comes in the *Marginalia*, where he writes, 'the fact [is] that we know the thing to be a representation, but that we often feel it to be a reality' (Coleridge 1992: 405–6). Here, he distinguishes the cognitive awareness that the fiction is an illusion from the simultaneous *feeling* that it is engaging, involving, immersive. In essence, this enacts the proverbial 'head vs. heart' dichotomy.

In more recent cognitive psychological work, Gerrig (1993, and see Gerrig and Rapp 2004) reformulates Coleridge's phrasing as 'the willing construction of disbelief'. Observing that it is difficult to will beliefs into and out of existence, Gerrig suggests that readers must expend psychological effort in engaging with what is plainly an illusory world being presented to them in fiction. Gerrig and Rapp suggest that the effort invested in building and immersing in this world is sustained during that immersion, but then the return back to the reader's actual own level of consciousness – as the 'disbelief' is once again set aside – is the mechanism which allows readers to make thematic, ethical, or insightful connections from the imagined world to the actual world. This is what Raghunath (2020: 47ff.) discusses as the process of 'reciprocal feedback'. The consequence of this view is that the experience of immersion is a key factor that gives literature its potential for powerful impact and significance.

Immersion is also a key concept in theatre studies. 'Immersive theatre' was first a reaction to the realism of early cinema in the 1920s, emphasising the physicality of the dramatic space, and the interaction of actors' and audiences' bodies (Artaud 1971, Jamieson 2007). The staged world is imagined as a border space between the actual and imagined worlds of the performance (see Dove 1994, Machon 2013), with the audience's engagement in that liminal space being a matter of immersion. Contemporary theatre often continues in this tradition, assisted by the immersive technology of lighting, sound, and staging, but also by multimodal digital, virtual, and online technology. Gibbons (2014), for example, has explored the immersive experiences of mobile theatre on location using phone and mapping technology (see also Bell and Ensslin 2011, Bouko 2014).

Similarly, immersion is a key design factor in the videogaming industry, with the objective being a seamless sense of 'gameflow' (Cowley et al. 2008, van Eck 2010). In so-called 'hedonic software' like videogames, gameflow is regarded as an ideal state of player-participation, where the gaming experience is felt to be more intense than the distracting world outside (van der Heijden 2004, Sweetser and Wyeth 2005). This notion of 'flow' derives from work in psychology by Csikszentmihalyi (1990, 1996), where the concept is defined as a state of mind in which the engaged activities are felt as being automatic, with an illusory sense of agency, a distorted idea of the passage of time, and a temporary distraction away from self-consciousness (see also Agarwal and Karahanna 2000). The features of flow are:

- Extreme focus on a task;
- Loss of self-awareness;
- Distractions are excluded from consciousness;
- Automatic balance between challenges and skills;
- Immediate feedback to actions;
- Merging of action and awareness;
- Activity becomes an end in itself;
- No worry of failure;
- Intrinsic motivation;
- Distortion of the experience of time.

(from Csikszentmihalyi 2014)

The central, defining characteristic of immersion is the sense of whole or partial self-effacement: a neglect of physical reality which is most obviously observable to others as a participant's lack of responsiveness to physical distraction. A gamer has become 'carried away' by the game; an athlete is 'in the zone'; a reader has become 'lost in a book' (see Nell 1988). These flow states feel automatic, with the gamer or reader feeling as if they have an agency in the immersed world, and the objects and characters within those worlds feeling richer and more engaging than their relatively flimsy textual traces might suggest (see Chen 2007). In gaming, the avatar becomes the player; in driving, the car becomes an extension of the driver's body; in remote drone warfare, the operator is deictically placed in the distant sky above the target (see Yamamoto and Kitazawa 2001, Voice 2022). In gaming and immersive theatre, there is of course an environmental, haptic, and physical setting for the feeling of immersion. In literary reading, the engagement is more symbolic and representative, accessed through text. In all situations, though, the experience is comparable, and immersion has been studied across different art forms (see Grau 2003, Dyson 2009, Liptay and Dogramaci 2015).

Immersion has been of particular interest in relation to literary engagement. Different researchers of the literary phenomenon and effects of immersion have adopted different terms to characterise the experience: Kuijpers and Hakemulder (2017: 2) wryly note that 'each research group, or even individual researchers used their own concepts when referring to phenomena that looked suspiciously similar'. Though these terms are indeed all broadly synonymous, they convey subtly different perspectives on the notion. Gerrig (1993) is clearly describing the feeling of immersion when he characterises it as a *transportation* that often occurs with compelling fictional narratives (see also Green and Brock 2000). Elsewhere, transportation is characterised as a mere facet of immersion, rather than a synonymous alternative (Atencia-Linares and Sebastián 2023). Stockwell (2009) notes that readers most commonly describe their reading process using the metaphors of *transportation* (as outlined by Gerrig 1993), but also as *investment* of emotional psychological work, and as a sense of *control* by the book. Nuttall and Harrison (2020) explore the transportation metaphor in terms both of text-as-agent and reader-as-agent. Holland (2008) adopts a hypnotic perspective in describing readers as being *entranced*. These different shades of thinking about immersion make different aspects prominent – principally that of the relative agency assigned to the text and to the reader. Senses of transportation, control, and entrancement appear to give agency to the textual patterning, while a reader's sense of their own psychological investment in a fiction is figured as a more reader-empowered perspective. (Keen, this volume, returns to the concept of transportation and argues for it as the vehicle for empathy-potential through immersion).

Kuiken et al. (2004) describe the experience of *self-implication* in a fictional world, linking a sense of immersion of the self with a feeling of personal identification (see also Miall and Kuiken 2002). Hakemulder (2013) labels the phenomenon as *absorption*, and adopts *narrative absorption* as the title of an important collection of work on the effect (Hakemulder et al. 2017, see also Kuijpers et al. 2014). Here, the same liquid metaphor underlying *immersion* is adopted, redolent of the term's etymology, as it was originally understood to denote the action of dipping or plunging into liquid, and later, by analogy, the administration of Christian baptism. However, *absorption* perhaps conveys more of a connotation of the fiction 'soaking into' the reader, rather than the reader becoming enveloped in the world of the text. There is a slightly different conceptual dynamic at work here. Ryan (1999, 2001), in the context of a worlds-based and deictic model of fictionality, terms the experience an *imaginative recentering*, which further privileges the spatial modelling around her approach.

In another wide-ranging tradition, immersion is discussed as *aesthetic illusion* (Wolf 2004, see also Burwick and Pape 1990, Wolf et al. 2013, Wolf 2017). Wolf (1998) is one of the few researchers to explore immersion without assuming it is a feature of narrativity, describing its effects around lyric poetry, and returning the discussion closer to the concerns set out by Coleridge above. Bilandzic and Busselle (2017) conclude by asserting that *narrative absorption* can only be a matter of narrative:

> The text needs to be a narrative. [. . .] A text that does not contain representations of events and/or inner states of characters does not prohibit deep experiences; however, they will not be narrative in nature: if the text is not a narrative in form, there can be no narrative engagement in the audience.
>
> (Bilandzic and Busselle 2017: 24)

Of course, their focus is on *narrative* absorption, and so this restriction is pre-defined by their own parameters. However, it does demonstrate that *immersion* is the more all-encompassing concept. While we might think that immersion is a long-form and gradually accumulating experience most suited to extended narrative texts, it still seems apparent to us that immersion can be sometimes very swift, and this can thus encompass other, non-narrative encounters, such as with the lyric. Voice (this volume) deals with a song lyric and its performative immersion; Mason and Gavin (both in this volume) also explore multimodal non-narrative texts; and Anderson (this volume) includes examples from lyric poetry.

Most of the chapters in this book explore immersion as a cross-world transition from everyday life to the imagined situation of the fiction, lyric, painting, song, or other immersible object. As Haines (this volume) points out, however, the key fact that allows a sense of immersive displacement to happen at all is that we are by default immersed in our own conscious reality. Our own natural immersion is unmarked because it is our own foundational condition, and it is this very fact that makes artificial immersion marked and remarkable. This insight also alerts us to the fact that immersion – while involving a textural transition if it is to be noticed – does not necessarily require that transition to be an ontological crossing between worlds. Author-reader engagement, absorption in skilled, flow activities such as driving, playing sports, meditating, and even the basic decoding visuals of literacy all occur in the participant's own world without involving a world-transition. Despite this, we would still describe these activities as immersive.

Ultimately, immersion is a matter of the tip of conscious attention. Just as a tool that we might use feels as if we have extended our reach to the tip of the implement (Yamamoto and Kitazawa 2001, Kitazawa 2002), so texts that we encounter extend our cognitive sensorium through the process of immersion.

Throughout all of the work outlined above, several distinctive or characteristic stylistic patterns and textual strategies have been presented as being good drivers of an immersive experience. You might expect to find, for example, pronouns of involvement (first and second person), proximal deictics, a strong point of view or focalisation, and an identifiable sense of mind-style (articulated through prominent evaluations, modalisations, and observations). There might be an emotional resonance and empathetic alignment. There might be complicit presumptions of shared cultural knowledge, such as intertextual familiarity. Immersive texts might be thought to have vivid descriptions that are likely to be carried in adjectival and adverbial phrases, especially concerning sensory inputs. The world being presented is likely to amount to a coherent world, described with a great deal of stylistic repetition and parallelism that reinforces cohesion. There will be clear and imaginable locatives, mainly expressed in prepositional phrases denoting time and space. There will be minimal disruptions to the world-building, and the avoidance of metafictional discourse markers. There will be, in the narrative arc, a general inwards trajectory of text-world creation, rather than constant emergence back towards the level of the reader's own world. And immersive texts might often feature symbolic or emblematic features of their own immersiveness, such as a literal transportation, travel, displacement, memoir-embedding, confession, or tales within tales, for example. This simple list of features might be regarded as a template stylistic profile for immersive texts, but of course – as several of the chapters in this book demonstrate – they are often breached, contradicted or differently patterned.

Immersion and its contraries

There are various ways in which a reader can terminate their immersive experience: reaching the end of a text and closing the book or screen; pausing mid-reading to engage in some action or thought back in their everyday life; being distracted during a reading; encountering clunky or jarring writing that draws attention to the authorial rather than fictional level, for example. These might all be thought of as external distractions that are not part of the intended design within the text itself. Of course, a text can build in its own immersive manipulations as well. The manner with which a text ends can manipulate the texture of the disengagement, from a sudden, abrupt ending to one that signals its own closure explicitly and returns the reader to their actual world. Such endings can be formulaic, such as variations on the early literacy 'and they all live happily ever after' phrasing. Often, texts will gesture outwards deictically, or will end with a sort of panoramic spatial withdrawal from the world of the text, so that the emergence is effected as a gradual transition (see Toolan 2016). The thematic effect of such outward gestures can be to indicate a linkage between the fiction and the actual world for the reader to take away. The most direct and explicit form of this would be to finish with 'The moral of this tale is . . .', though modern texts tend not to be so direct, rather implying their 'message' by a more subtle or ambivalent means.

The movement out of an immersed state has been termed *emergence* (Stockwell 2019), which can be abrupt or gradual. Emergence allows for the conceptualisation that the process is a transition with these possibly variable speeds. A book can in one sentence throw you out ('And that was the story of Beauty and the Beast'), or it can develop slowly over several paragraphs or pages (as a memoirist reflects on the story they have just narrated, and returns their and the reader's attention gradually to the present moment, for example).

Emergence is only one of the contraries of immersion, however, and like the term *immersion* itself, the possible variants can connote different aspects of the concept. Ryan (1999: 18) simply calls it 'de-immersion', as if the process is the mirror-image, or reverse of the initial immersion. However, immersion and emergence are not merely inversely equivalent: aside from being directionally opposite, the destination of each process is radically different. Immersion takes the reader into another world that is as yet unknown; the reader emerging from an imagined world knows exactly where they will finally, familiarly end up. Similarly – as the empirical psychological work mentioned above attests – immersion requires active readerly agency to construct and maintain disbelief and sustain the immersivity, whereas emergence seems altogether more passive and less effortful. (In Duchan et al.'s (1995) deictic shift theory, the movements into and out of imagined deictic levels are termed *pushes* and *pops*, in recognition of their directionally asymmetrical properties.) Indeed, it seems that a relaxation into shallow processing in reading would by default result in the end of immersion.

A text that fails entirely to immerse a reader can be conceived of as *non-immersive*. In this case, emergence never gets a chance to occur. Non-immersive texts are probably more numerous than immersive ones (encompassing the vast majority of non-literary works, as well as many literary texts that are not immersive) – so it is important to note that immersion is a special case of literary reading. That said, immersion cannot be exclusively literary, nor exclusively narratorial, nor even exclusively fictional. We can also differentiate forms of emergence that are ascribable to the textual patterns in the work from those that are matters of the reader's actions. A bored, distracted reader can *disengage* from the world of the text simply as a matter of choice and agency. Putting the book down or leaving the cinema breaks immersion by such disengagement. Other texts are deliberately anti-immersive by design. Much of the work in the 'epic theatre' tradition, by Erwin Piscator, Vladimir Mayakovsky, and Bertolt Brecht among others, aims deliberately to remind the audience that they are watching a play that has resonance with their own political realities, where characters are written so that the audience cannot empathise nor engage with them, and where the fourth wall is regularly transgressed (see Schall 2015). The distancing effect (*Verfremdungseffekt*, which may also be translated as *estranging* or *defamiliarising*) in such theatre can be seen as a resistance to immersion.

Defamiliarisation itself might be considered as a potentially anti-immersive device. If the reader is constantly forced into a dialectic realisation and comparison of their own familiar world and the estranging figuration of the imagined world, you might think that this would work against an immersive experience. However, research on the readerly effects of metafiction in particular cast doubt on whether this is the case (see Macrae 2019, and Wydrzynska, this volume). It seems a paradox that metafictional and metaleptic moves by a narrator or by the implied author in fact seem to enhance immersion, in some cases. For example, the author-narrator interventions in *The French Lieutenant's Woman* (Fowles 1969) or *Atonement* (McEwan 2001) are widely regarded as enriching their emotional immersive power, in spite of the fact that the reader is toggled back and forth between the imagined and their own worlds.

Immersion is generally regarded as positively in literary fiction as it is in gameplaying. However, novels that are regarded as *escapist* are often so named either pejoratively or classed as a guilty pleasure of formula fiction, in spite of the fact that escapist fantasy, science fiction, romances, thrillers, and action adventures are often highly immersive. It is clear that immersion alone cannot be considered as an inherently valued feature of a literary work, but must be considered in the context of its genre expectations and as a matter of readerly experience and judgement.

The current volume

This collection of work on immersion began as a symposium held at the University of Nottingham in April 2024. We were keen to include established figures in the field as well as new researchers, and we held the event both on campus and online to allow as large a participating audience as possible.

We accepted full traditional papers for presentation, as well as short 'videograms' in the form of animated digital posters which played around the conference room. We are pleased to have been able to preserve both the ethos and the innovation of the event in this edited collection of work arising from the dialogues of the day.

The volume is divided into three parts. In the first part are collected those chapters that focus primarily on immersion as a theoretical concept, though of course every chapter even in this section includes examples and illustrations from actual texts, to a greater or lesser extent. The second part comprises cross-modal explorations of immersion, for example in online social media, in paintings, and in song lyrics. The final part brings together diverse discussions of different literary immersions. Each chapter is prefaced with a short introductory abstract, written by the editors.

If there is an overarching approach, it is very broadly literary-linguistic. This is a field that we regard as incorporating elements of both narratology and literary criticism. Given the nature of immersion as an experience that requires a readerly encounter with a text, many of the approaches taken in the following chapters are cognitive poetic in orientation. The centre of gravity is in literary works, though our contributors have indeed ranged beyond the literary, both to explore adjacent modes and to illuminate in retrospect the experience of literature itself.

The chapters in the first part offer new perspectives on immersion, with their literary examples presented as case studies for illustration. Schneider begins the collection by challenging the prevailing or default view that immersion tends to focus on readerly engagement with a single character or involved narrator. Instead, he presents the concept of a *multiple-character scenario* primarily as a means of understanding more complex narratives, but suggests that this approach can also provide insight even into single-character focused immersive texts. The potential for immersion to enrich and sustain a feeling of empathy is the topic of Keen's chapter. She teases out distinct empathetic effects, and argues for the feeling of transportation as a key feature of immersion, and as a mode of empathy in its own right. Anderson's chapter realigns the immersive experience as the integrated combination of processes of *fission-fusion* – a concept drawn from anthropology and ethology. Her approach is a critical reminder that immersion is a process, and one that is protean and dynamic. In the final chapter of the book's first part, Stockwell proposes a means of thinking about the ways that subliminal effects during a reading – at both a local textual and diffused textual level – are the accumulated building blocks for immersion.

The second part of the volume presents cross-modal studies of immersion. Mason explores the nature of conspiracy belief in social media texts, presenting immersion as an increasing pathology on the part of some readers and participants. Cooper presents empirical research on reading groups, reading cross-cultural literary texts, to explore immersion. Their responses are framed by drawing on the psychological feature of *simulation* within the presumption of a Theory of Mind. Gavin explores cross-modal immersion and its relationships directly by tracing responses to an encounter between a painting and its poetic response. She finds that these responses are complex rather than straightforwardly descriptive, suggesting a rich form of immersion which she terms an *entanglement*. This part of the book finishes with Voice's stylistic analysis of the textual lyric and performance of a song, in which both aspects of the experience are integrated as a means of understanding the mimetic power of the metaphors throughout a lyrical immersion.

Literary explorations of immersion are the focus of the chapters in the book's final part. Haines offers a unified theoretical approach to both humour and immersion, applied to a comic novel by P.G. Wodehouse. Wydrzynska explores metafiction and its paradoxical power to sustain immersion, taking as her case studies works of children's literature, and demonstrating immersion as a feature of early literacy. Trevisan and Fiorin take a combined text-worlds and addressivity approach to the immersive layering in the Fredrik Backman novel *Anxious People*. The status of belief in ghosts is the subject of Adam's stylistic and worlds-based account of recent Booker Prize-winning literary novels. She notes that a readerly discarding of belief in ghosts does not seem to affect a temporary belief while immersed, and explores the specific linguistic features that may facilitate this cognitive dissonance. Currie adopts an experimental method in generating two idealised readers in order to explore neurodivergent immersions in Samuel Beckett's stylistically experimental novella *Worstward Ho*. Finally, Norledge closes the volume with another narratologically and stylistically challenging text, N.K. Jemisin's *Emergency Skin* – where immersion is a necessary reading strategy enabling the reader to experience the posthuman and a non-human mind.

Almost every chapter begins with its author's own view of immersion. These often vary subtly from each other, and we have left them in their nuanced states, thus in dialogue with each other, rather than trying to forge them into a single unified definition or account. Each chapter is prefaced with our editorial introduction, which further emphasises the dialogic nature of this collection, and tries to draw out the key insight or innovation of that chapter. We hope that the reader of this book emerges from it with an enhanced sense of immersion, a greater curiosity about the topic, and even more questions than our contributors have addressed here for its feeling, phenomenon, and experience.

References

Agarwal, R. and Karahanna, E. (2000) 'Time flies when you're having fun: cognitive absorption and beliefs about information technology usage', *MIS Quarterly* 24 (4): 665–94.

Artaud, A. (1971) *Collected Works of Antonin Artaud* (trans. V. Corti). London: Calder and Boyars.
Atencia-Linares, P. and Sebastián, M.Á. (2023) 'Narrative immersion as an attentional phenomenon', *Inquiry* 66 (5): 885–902.
Bell, A. and Ensslin, A. (2011) '"I know what it was. You know what it was": second-person narration in hypertext fiction', *Narrative* 19 (3): 311–29.
Bilandzic, H. and Busselle, R. (2017) 'Beyond metaphors and traditions: exploring the conceptual boundaries of narrative engagement', in F. Hakemulder, M.M. Kuijpers, E.S. Tan, K. Bálint and M.M. Doicaru (eds) *Narrative Absorption*. Amsterdam: John Benjamins, pp.11–27.
Bouko, C. (2014) 'Interactivity and immersion in a media-based performance', *Participations: Journal of Audience and Reception Studies* 11 (1): 254–69.
Burwick, F. and Pape, W. (eds) (1990) *Aesthetic Illusion: Theoretical and Historical Approaches*. Berlin: de Gruyter.
Chen, J. (2007) 'Flow in games (and everything else)', *Communications of the ACM* 50 (4): 31–4.
Coleridge, S.T. (1817) *Biographia Literaria*. London: Rest Fenner.
Coleridge, S.T. (1992) *The Collected Works: Marginalia, Vol. 12, Part 3* (eds H.J. Jackson and G. Whalley). Princeton: Princeton University Press.
Cowley, B., Charles, D., Black, M. and Hickey, R. (2008) 'Toward an understanding of flow in video games', *Computers in Entertainment* 6 (2): 1–27.
Csikszentmihalyi, M. (1990) *Flow: The Psychology of Optimal Experience*. New York: Harper and Row.
Csikszentmihalyi, M. (1996) *Creativity: Flow and the Psychology of Discovery and Invention*. New York: Harper Perennial.
Csikszentmihalyi, M. (2014) *Flow and the Foundations of Positive Psychology: The Collected Works of Mihaly Csikszentmihalyi (Volume 2)*. Dordrecht: Springer.
Dove, T. (1994) 'Theater without actors – immersion and response in installation', *Leonardo* 27 (4): 281–7.
Duchan, J.F., Bruder, G.A. and Hewitt, L.E. (eds) (1995) *Deixis in Narrative: A Cognitive Science Perspective*. Hillsdale: Lawrence Erlbaum.
Dyson, F. (2009) *Sounding New Media. Immersion and Embodiment in the Arts and Culture*. Ewing: University of California Press.
Fowles, J. (1969) *The French Lieutenant's Woman*. London: Jonathan Cape.
Gerrig, R.J. (1993) *Experiencing Narrative Worlds: On the Psychological Activities of Reading*. New Haven: Yale University Press.
Gerrig, R.J. and Rapp, D. (2004) 'Psychological processes underlying literary impact', *Poetics Today* 25 (2): 265–81.
Gibbons, A. (2014) 'Fictionality and ontology', in P. Stockwell and S. Whiteley (eds) *The Cambridge Handbook of Stylistics*. Cambridge: Cambridge University Press, pp.408–23.
Gombrich, E.H. (1959) *Art and Illusion: A Study in the Psychology of Pictorial Representation*. Oxford: Phaidon.
Grau, O. (2003) *Virtual Art: From Illusion to Immersion*. Cambridge: The MIT Press.
Green, M.C. and Brock, T.C. (2000) 'The role of transportation in the persuasiveness of public narratives', *Journal of Personality and Social Psychology* 79 (5): 701–21.
Hakemulder, F. (2013) 'Travel experiences: a typology of transportation and other absorption states in relation to types of aesthetic responses', in J. Luedke (ed.) *Wie*

gebannt: Aesthetische Verfahren der affektiven Bildung von Aufmerksamkeit. Berlin: Freie Universität, pp.163–82.
Hakemulder, F., Kuijpers, M.M., Tan, E.S., Bálint, K. and Doicaru, M.M. (eds) (2017) *Narrative Absorption*. Amsterdam: John Benjamins.
Holland, N.N. (2008) '"Spider-man? Sure!" The neuroscience of suspending disbelief', *Interdisciplinary Science Review* 33 (4): 312–20.
Jamieson, L. (2007) *Antonin Artaud: From Theory to Practice*. London: Greenwich Exchange: London.
Kitazawa, S. (2002) 'Where conscious sensation takes place', *Consciousness and Cognition* 11: 474–7.
Kuijpers, M.M. and Hakemulder, F. (2017) 'Narrative absorption: introduction and overview', in F. Hakemulder, M.M. Kuijpers, E.S. Tan, K. Bálint and M.M. Doicaru (eds) *Narrative Absorption*. Amsterdam: John Benjamins, pp.1–7.
Kuijpers, M.M., Hakemulder, F., Tan, E. and Doicaru, M. (2014) 'Exploring absorbing reading experiences: developing and validating a self-report scale to measure story world absorption', *Scientific Study of Literature* 4 (1): 89–122.
Kuiken, D., Miall, D.S. and Sikora S. (2004) 'Forms of self-implication in literary reading', *Poetics Today* 25 (2): 171–203.
Liptay, F. and Dogramaci, B. (eds) (2015) *Immersion in the Visual Arts and Media: Studies in Intermediality*. Leiden: Brill.
McEwan, I. (2001) *Atonement*. London: Jonathan Cape.
Machon, J. (2013) *Immersive Theatres: Intimacy and Immediacy in Contemporary Performance*. Basingstoke: Palgrave Macmillan.
Macrae, A. (2019) *Discourse Deixis in Metafiction*. London: Routledge.
Miall, D.S. and Kuiken, D. (2002) 'A feeling for fiction: becoming what we behold', *Poetics* 30: 221–41.
Nell, V. (1988) *Lost in a Book: The Psychology of Reading for Pleasure*. New Haven: Yale University Press.
Nuttall, L. and Harrison, C. (2020) 'Wolfing down the *Twilight* series: metaphors for reading in online reviews', in H. Ringrow and S. Pihlaja (eds) *Contemporary Media Stylistics*. London: Bloomsbury, pp.35–60.
Otis, L. (2015a) *Rethinking Thought: Inside the Minds of Creative Scientists and Artists*. Oxford: Oxford University Press.
Otis, L. (2015b) 'The value of qualitative research for cognitive literary studies', in L. Zunshine (ed.) *The Oxford Handbook of Cognitive Literary Studies*. Oxford: Oxford University Press, pp.505–24.
Paige, N.D. (2024) 'The "willing suspension of disbelief". The long history of a short phrase', in A. James, A. Kubo and F. Lavocat (eds) *The Routledge Handbook of Fiction and Belief*. London: Routledge, pp.28–40.
Raghunath, R. (2020) *Possible Worlds Theory and Counterfactual Historical Fiction*. Cham: Palgrave Macmillan.
Ryan, M.-L. (1999) 'Immersion vs. interactivity: virtual reality and literary theory', *Substance* 28 (2): 110–37.
Ryan, M.-L. (2001) *Narrative as Virtual Reality: Immersion and Interactivity in Literature and Electronic Music*. Baltimore: Johns Hopkins University Press.
Schall, E. (2015) *The Craft of Theatre: Seminars and Discussions in Brechtian Theatre*. London: Bloomsbury.
Stockwell, P. (2009) *Texture: A Cognitive Aesthetics of Reading*. Edinburgh: Edinburgh University Press.

Stockwell, P. (2019) 'Immersion and emergence in children's literature', in B. Neurohr and L. Stewart-Shaw (eds) *Experiencing Fictional Worlds*. Amsterdam: John Benjamins, pp.15–32.

Sweetser, P. and Wyeth, P. (2005) 'GameFlow: a model for evaluating player enjoyment in games', *Computers in Entertainment* 3 (3): 1–24.

Toolan, M. (2016) *Making Sense of Narrative Text: Situation, Repetition, and Picturing in the Reading of Short Stories*. London: Routledge.

van der Heijden, H. (2004) 'User acceptance of hedonic information systems', *MIS Quarterly* 28 (4): 695–704.

van Eck, R. (ed.) (2010) *Gaming and Cognition: Theories and Practice from the Learning Sciences*. Hershey: Information Science Reference.

Voice, M. (2022). 'Distance, proximity, and authenticity in the point of view of US military drone operator autobiographies', *Discourse Studies* 24 (6): 781–97.

Wolf, W. (1998) 'Aesthetic illusion in lyric poetry?', *Poetica* 30: 251–89.

Wolf, W. (2004) 'Aesthetic illusion as an effect of fiction', *Style* 38: 325–51.

Wolf, W. (2017) 'Illusion (aesthetic)', in P. Hühn, J. Pier, W. Schmid and J. Schönert (eds) *The Living Handbook of Narratology*. Hamburg: Hamburg University Press, available at <http://www.lhn.uni-hamburg.de/>

Wolf, W., Bernhart, W. and Mahler, A. (eds) (2013) *Immersion and Distance: Aesthetic Illusion in Literature and Other Media*. Amsterdam: Rodopi.

Yamamoto, S. and Kitazawa, S. (2001) 'Sensation at the tips of invisible tools', *Nature Neuroscience* 4: 979–80.

Part I

Theoretical innovations

CHAPTER 2

Immersion and the challenges of character constellations and multiperspectivity

Ralf Schneider

Many studies of immersion have focused on readers' full involvement in a storyworld, mostly through adopting a single character's perspective. This chapter argues that in the context of extended narratives, such as novels, this results in an understanding of immersion that is overly optimistic and too narrow. Not only are novels read intermittently, which may impede immersion, they also present a range of perspectives to readers. In this chapter, Schneider introduces the concept of the 'Multiple-Character Scenario' to better understand how readers navigate contrasting and often conflicting narrative perspectives, suggesting it to be the backbone of a particular kind of immersion which occurs when reading extended narratives with complex character constellations.

Introduction: the concept of immersion needs to be (further) differentiated

Two connected aspects of readers' engagement with narrative fiction have been at the centre of interest in cognitive and empirical studies of literature for some time: the experience of witnessing storyworlds from 'within', and that of being cognitively, emotionally, and perceptually close to fictional characters. For the former aspect, the term 'immersion' (see Ryan 2001: 14–15) has been used, but also, and mostly interchangeably with it, the notions of 'absorption' (see Kuijpers et al. 2021) or 'transportation' into fictional worlds (Gerrig 1993, Green 2004, Green et al. 2004). For the latter, differentiations between 'empathy' and 'identification' have been discussed (Cohen 2001, Coplan 2004, Koopman and Hakemulder 2015; see Forster Tukachinsky 2021 for an overview). The two reading experiences are usually seen in close conjunction, immersion referring to an intensive engagement with the storyworld *in general*, involving a 'feeling of absolute involvement in the world of the text' (Stockwell 2020: 197), whereas empathy and identification are considered particular *character-related* varieties of that state, in which the reader shares a character's perspective (see Sestir and Green 2010: 276). Although some narratives foreground spatiotemporal and material characteristics of the fictional world (for instance, varieties of speculative fiction, including science fiction and mystery), which suggests that readers can get immersed in character-less fictional surroundings, David Herman's definition of the storyworld as a dynamically updated mental representation of 'who did what to and with whom, when, where, why, and in what fashion' (2002: 570) highlights the importance of characters with their interrelated actions and motivations, so that the involvement is most likely to focus on characters. Some scholars have even argued that stories become narratives mainly by virtue of rendering human (or human-like) experience (Fludernik 1996, Caracciolo 2014); this suggests that character-related kinds of immersion profit particularly from the presence of characters and/or narrators *as experiencers*, whose perspectives readers can share.

The broad scholarly attention that immersive-identificatory (or empathic) reading has received certainly highlights the importance of this kind of readerly engagement with fiction. However, the definitions of, and differentiations between, these concepts vary considerably, since explanations have come from different disciplines, including cognitive psychology, philosophy (of mind), film and (mass) media studies, cognitive linguistics, and cognitive narratology; volumes like the present one continue to explore the various facets of the phenomenon. Federico Pianzola has formulated a caveat concerning the use of the immersion concept, pointing to the many aspects of the phenomenon and suggesting that

> narrative immersion is best conceived as just one dimension among the interconnected phenomena of spatial presence, social presence, and flow. Additionally, intrinsic traits of the medium, literary work, or narrative, such as style, characters' likeability, or the suspenseful delay of information, cannot be univocally associated with stronger or weaker narrative immersion. This is because immersion-like experiences are strongly dependent on extrinsic factors, such as individual personality traits, experiential background, media literacy, familiarity with literary conventions, and the reading situation itself, which should favor focused attention.
>
> (Pianzola 2025: 126)

In a similar spirit, notions of narrative engagement have already been diversified and differentiated. For instance, while narratives that foreground their own artificiality – through particular language use or metafictional devices – would seem to hinder the reader's feeling of getting 'into' the narrative world, such features are now argued to present no obstacle to immersive reading (Anderson and Iversen 2018, Polvinen 2022, Wydrzynska, this volume), since the immersion concept can be split into *storyworld* absorption and *artefact* absorption (Doicaru 2016). Another differentiation refers to engagement with characters: the theory of Storyworld Possible Selves (Martínez 2018) suggests that quite different qualities of relating to characters exist, depending on which perceived aspects of a character and which aspect of their self-concepts readers integrate into self-character blends (as in future-oriented desired or feared versions of the self, or in readers' past and present self-concepts triggered by characters). As I have argued elsewhere, acknowledging the fact that most extended narratives feature many characters, there is no logical reason to exclude the possibility that readers recognise aspects of their self-concept in *any* of the characters that people the fictional world, and that these characters need not be protagonists nor even focalisers for readers to be able to create self-character blends for them (Schneider, 2025).

In this chapter, I argue that we also need an immersion concept that is further differentiated by reaching beyond reader engagement with *single* characters, which previous approaches have focused on. I go so far as to claim that in the reading of extended narratives, such as novels, the single-character-oriented forms of immersion are unlikely to be the dominant, or even very frequent, modes of engagement. While I do not claim that single-character related forms of engagement do not occur, I aim to demonstrate that there is a form of immersion which is more complex, relational, and multiperspectival than has been theorised so far. In what follows, I will pursue three lines of argumentation for this view of immersion. First, the nature of novel reading speaks against strong forms of immersion in general; second, the nature of the novel itself suggests that there must be more kinds of immersion than single-character related ones; third, the nature of human cognition suggests that narrative engagement makes use of the human ability to easily cope with multiple perspectives. I propose the concept of the 'Multiple-Character Scenario' (MCS) to denote the mental correlate of multiplicity in characters and perspectives in a narrative (a proposal I develop in detail elsewhere; see Schneider, 2026). I infer that if MCSs are created, we need to differentiate between perspective construction on the one hand, and perspective-taking on the other. In that context, general and marked forms of perspectivisation and multiperspectivity ought to be differentiated. I consider perspective construction in the face of general multiperspectivity central to the formation of MCSs, and alternative types of immersion.

Strong forms of immersion are the exception: the nature of novel reading

Victor Nell (1988) famously provided the study of immersive narrative engagement with the key phrase of 'getting lost in a book' – but how intensive and extensive can this feeling of losing oneself in a whole book's fictional world be? The reading of a novel is usually distributed over various sittings, which may span many days, and sometimes weeks. Consider that when reading an average novel of ca. 300 pages in length at a speed of 2.5 to 3 minutes per page, a reader will need between 12.5 and 15 hours to finish the book, and even if someone's reading speed is quicker than that, they are still extremely unlikely to read a novel in one go, unless they are under some time pressure and/or have to do so for professional purposes. The most likely reading scenario for extended narratives is therefore not the single sitting – which plays such a big role in the effects that short stories are supposed to achieve (see, e.g., Edgar Allan Poe's poetological considerations of the impact of short narratives; 2006: 525–69). Rather, novel reading will occur in interrupted and irregular intervals embedded in the reader's everyday routines, so that distractions will be unavoidable. If – as most definitions either imply or state explicitly – focused attention is a central feature of the immersive experience, these conditions would seem to at least decrease the chance of immersion of a strong and identificatory variety. Among the potential distractors from narrative engagement that Busselle and Bilandzic describe, some are located in the reading situation or the reader, such as 'noise, hunger, job stress' (2009: 326). I would be surprised to find readers of this chapter who have lived with young children denying that concentrating on a book was possible only in very few blissful moments in that phase of their lives. The kind of convenient sampling frequently used in empirical literary studies, which tends to recruit study participants from literature and language degree programmes, might lead to an overestimation of the concentration and time other readers have available in their lives. We need more empirical studies on actual novel-reading practices among different groups of readers. In any case, results gained from studies conducted on short texts ought to be transferred to extended narratives with some caution. It has also been argued that mind wandering (Smallwood and Schooler 2015) occurs in reading (Fabry and Kukkonen 2019), which provides another hint that the full concentration required for getting lost in a book is not necessarily the default mode of reading, or, alternatively, that the getting lost is less focused on the storyworld and its characters than is generally assumed. Beside such reader-related factors, textual ones may stand in the way of immersion. Busselle and Bilandzic go on to point to hindrances to engagement found in the story, including 'a plot flaw, a behaviour that is inconsistent with a character's motivations, or a portrayal that is inconsistent with real world knowledge or familiar genre conventions' (2009: 326). Both storyworld and artefact absorption are likely to be affected by such factors.

To counter my scepticism towards full immersion, one could of course argue that immersion, if interrupted by short and intermittent sittings, is quickly and fully resumed whenever the book is taken up again, but I would not expect that to be guaranteed or automatic. If the difference between short story and novel reading is as significant as I have claimed, we may question the transfer of results corroborating the importance of immersion, which many empirical investigations have produced using very short narratives, to the novel. Representatives of this type of empirical work have recently conceded this point:

> The ways in which we are currently investigating narrative absorption necessarily leave *gaps in our knowledge* about the nature of absorption and its effects. So far, the effects of (absorbed) literary reading have only been investigated *using brief stimulus materials* (i.e., short stories, poems, or fragments of novels), often selected or manipulated by the experimenter to isolate the effects of specific text features on specific outcomes. [. . .] Future research *should look into reading long form narratives*, such as complete novels.
>
> (Kuijpers et al. 2021: 298; emphasis added)

To summarise, it looks as if we have overwhelming evidence for the importance of immersion and its effects in the reading of short texts, but that we still lack a good understanding of the quality and intensity of immersion in the reading of extended narratives. Having pointed out differences in the temporal framework and reading situations of novels vs. short stories, which are likely to affect the concentration required for immersion, the presence of many characters in novels, in contrast to the usually reduced personnel of short stories, makes a difference in the kinds of immersion that are possible, as I will argue in the next section.

There must be more to immersion than the single-character related kind

Novels come equipped with complex constellations of many characters. Although an exact count of all characters in all novels does not exist, it is important to me to highlight this apparently banal fact. I therefore randomly selected ca. every tenth novel from my bookshelves (ca. 800 novels), on which I keep the English-language prose narratives dating from the Elizabethan period to today, which I have read and taught over the last ca. thirty-five years, as a student, lecturer, and professor of British Literature, and I counted the characters in 100 of them. The average number of characters in these 100 novels is slightly over twenty. I included characters who never appear in the storyworld if they were mentioned by other characters and seemed relevant enough for that character to make it into the reader's mental representation. Such characters as the parents of orphan characters and other lost relatives, partners, or close friends, and former lovers who still haunt protagonists, are cases in point. Since I disregarded characters who are not named, or appear only as part of a group, the actual figure is likely to be higher. The count is admittedly non-representative, subjective, and unsystematic. There are also internal differentiations in the figures, whose effects would have to be considered: the Victorian period, for instance, yields the highest numbers, with novels sometimes reaching up to fifty characters, whereas contemporary fiction displays a tendency to use fairly reduced constellations, some with only five to seven characters. Still, I believe this gives an impression of what we are talking about: If there are always many characters around, how likely is it that a reader's immersion is related to only *one* out of these characters throughout? In that case, the reader's mind would have to employ deliberate strategies to overlook and *not* notice the many-headed fictional population of the storyworld. Even if we assume that readers follow the shifting perspectives of varying focalisers, which feature in many of the texts, so that the impression of the fictional world is not restricted to only one character, the majority of characters in novels simply are neither focalisers nor protagonists but still need to be accounted for as elements of readers' narrative engagement.

From the work of Bakhtin in the 1920s and 1930s to contemporary narratology, literary scholars have pointed out that the multiplicity of characters and viewpoints (or 'voices') is a defining criterion of the novel. In Bakhtin's phrasing, the genre is fundamentally 'polyphonic', 'dialogic', or 'heteroglossic', since it gives expression to the fact that in our modern world individual socioeconomic positions, opinions, beliefs, and evaluations of individuals – in short, their viewpoints – differ, and that one authoritative world-view cannot exist (see Bakhtin 1981, 1984). Thus, every single character in a novel has the potential to be regarded as a representative of a perspective of their own; I will return to this condition below and call this a case of 'general multiperspectivity'. Functionalist approaches (Propp 1928, Greimas 1966) were less interested in such ideological complexities but they emphasised that the characters in a narrative tend to fulfil functions *in relation to* other characters – a narrative's hero, according to Greimas, is usually found in a constellation with both a helper and a preventer, and the object the hero desires involves a sender and a receiver; the hero can therefore not be thought of in isolation, but is involved in a basic constellation of at least four other parties. Woloch (2003) has proposed a sophisticated analysis of how the many main and minor characters in the novel form systems of relatedness that also negotiate the thematic spectrum of the narrative, and Palmer (2008, 2010) has taken narratology to task for concentrating too much on single minds in the novel, overlooking the fact that characters' minds in prose fiction are usually active in relation to, and sometimes even in unison with, other characters' minds. He therefore speaks of 'social minds', which can amount to a group of persons sharing *one* thought. All of this points to the fact that, according to literary scholarship, readers can expect to find in novels complex constellations of characters with different interests and functions in the narrative, whose meaning never emerges from a single character's view of things, but from the ensemble of characters and perspectives.

Beside narratology, literary psychology has also maintained that 'literary narratives fundamentally deal with relationships among individuals and the navigation of conflicting desires' (Mar and Oatley 2008: 174), and that readers engage with precisely these social entanglements. Although not every single character in a novel is connected with every other character, I claim that the mental representation or embodied response to a single character – what has been called a 'mental character model' (Schneider 2001, Vaeßen 2021) or the 'mind-modelling' of characters (Stockwell 2020, ch.11; 2021a) – will always contain the presence of *other* characters, too. If the reader's mental representation of a character 'involves imputing to them not only a physical experience of their surroundings, but also a perspective, ideological outlook, self-regard, stream of thoughts, aspirations and emotions, and dramatising for ourselves their likely actions, intentions, desires, and dispositions' (Stockwell 2020: 179), it is necessary to acknowledge that a large part of these internal processes are triggered by, interfered with, helped by, directed at, or in any other way related to, *other characters* in the narrative, and that they must enter our character modelling in one way or another.

To take a classic example with which many readers will be familiar: it will strike most readers as a platitude if I say that to think of Elizabeth Bennett, in Jane Austen's *Pride and Prejudice*, involves thinking of Mr Darcy, too – their connection, or the way towards it, is the novel's main theme, after all. But the Elizabeth-Darcy dyad is only the start: on Elizabeth's side, the influence of the motivations, opinions, and actions of her mother and her sisters (Lydia and Jane probably more than Mary and Kitty) have a direct influence on her opinions and actions, also in relation to Mr Darcy; and on Darcy's side, George Wickham and Charles Bingley are also likely to linger in the mental representations of the central couple, being a negative and a positive foil to Darcy, respectively. Lady Catherine de Bourgh, with her disapproval of the relationship between Elizabeth and Darcy, might very well be looming in the mental background, too, as might Mr Collins, with both his unwanted attention to Elizabeth and his toadyism towards Lady Catherine. (All in all, I counted twenty characters in *Pride and Prejudice*.) If this is the case, though, theories that focus on the reader's adoption of an individual character's perspective do not seem to suffice. Even if we assume that readers predominantly take the protagonist-focaliser's perspective (Elizabeth's, in this case, because she is the dominant focaliser), we must at least factor in the presence of complex social relations pertaining to that character and their view of the fictional world. That idea, however, does not solve all problems but appears to create new ones. Discussing potential hindrances for perspective-taking, Dixon and Bortolussi have recently stated that:

> [i]n most fiction, characters interact with each other and with their surroundings, form inferences to produce assessments and judgments, including of themselves, and attribute motivations, desires, feelings,

> and causality. Such complexities place *enormous cognitive demands* on readers, who *must not only track all shifting perspectives* but also remember who said what to whom when and for what reason, a *potentially overwhelming task* of perspectival bookkeeping. [. . .] How such complex fiction affects our elaboration of the story world requires further empirical attention.
>
> (Dixon and Bortolussi 2023: 165; emphasis added)

The question here, in my opinion, is how we conceptualise the perspectivisation involved and its effects, i.e., whether readers really 'must [. . .] track all shifting perspectives', what this 'tracking' implies, and whether this 'task of perspectival bookkeeping' really needs to be thought of as 'potentially overwhelming'. I suggest that we need not only more empirical work on this but also more theoretical explanations. I propose an explanation by differentiating between kinds of perspectivity, and by speaking of 'multiple-character scenarios' as readers' mental correlates of innerfictional networks of character constellations. On this basis, I suggest thinking of immersion as containing, as a central element, the reader's establishing an MCS that feels satisfactory for their understanding of the story.

Minding constellations: perspectivisation, multiple-character scenarios, and immersion

Cognitive theories have provided evidence suggesting that the mind has no problems coping with the presence of multiple persons and their viewpoints. For instance, in theorising embodied cognition, it is implied – although not always made explicit – that what is called 4E cognition really refers to the mind as being *socially* embodied, *socially* embedded, *socially* extended, *socially* enactive (for more on immersion and embodiment, see Anderson and Norledge, both this volume). Mark Johnson, in an important article on the body as a source of cognition, wrote:

> The human environment of which the body partakes is not just physical or biological. It is also composed of *intersubjective relations and coordinations of experience*. [. . .] The key idea here is that the body does not come fully formed prior to entering into relations with social others; rather, the character of those relations is crucial in shaping bodily modes of comportment. The brain and the entire bodily organism are being *trained up through deep interpersonal transactions*.
>
> (Johnson 2008: 165; emphasis added)

Just as we can characterise the novel as 'social', in the Bakhtinian sense of always offering complex constellations of characters inhabiting different viewpoints, the quote from Johnson suggests that the mind, too, is fundamentally 'social'. Given this fundamental interpersonal relationality of the body-mind, Eve Sweetser summarises a position held by some cognitive linguists:

> We are not just capable of multiple viewpoints; *we are in fact incapable of keeping to one single viewpoint of space, or of cognitive structure, when other humans are present.* [. . .] We are constantly aware of our bodily proximity to objects around us, but when another human being is present, we are also *unavoidably aware not only of our own bodily affordances, but of (his or) hers as well,* what she can reach, what she can see, and so on.
>
> (Sweetser 2012: 12; emphasis added)

There is no reason to believe that this embodied social or interpersonal awareness is somehow 'switched off' when reading fictional narratives. It therefore seems that mentally engaging with multiple perspectives is not an unsurmountable obstacle to readers but employs their very basic intersocial cognitive skills. I propose to call such a mental correlate to the character constellation offered by a text the readers' MCS. It is also likely that there is a kind of immersion that consists in mentally and emotionally managing multiple perspectives and social relations, a feeling of absolute involvement in the world of the text, which is then grasped as a vibrant network of social relations, viewpoints, and multiple, potentially conflicting, desires, plans, and strategies, and so on.

These deliberations require some further distinctions. First, it makes sense to differentiate between *marked* and *general cases of perspectivisation* (see also Schneider, 2025). Marked perspectivisation is usually found in passages in which a character (or character-narrator, in the case of homodiegetic narration) is a focaliser, i.e., when we are given access to their perceptions, thoughts, feelings, and memories (see Niederhoff 2013a, 2013b for a narratological approach, and Zeman 2016 and 2017 for cognitive-linguistic ones). The wealth of theoretical and empirical studies of perspectivisation and its effects – in narratology, linguistics, and empirical literary studies – strongly suggests that marked perspectivisation invites perspective-taking in the sense of a reader's strong cognitive and emotional alignment with a character, and an engagement which enacts the character's perspective. This is most likely to give rise to the kind of empathic or identificatory immersion experience that is related to a single character. As Dixon and Bortolussi (2023) have recently shown in detail, the reader's construction of an analogy of situation and evaluation between themselves and the target character underlies this kind of engagement with a character. Even in this mode, however, I claim that the reader will also retain an awareness of the social entanglements of that character. General perspectivisation, in contrast, refers to all available hints at characters' or narrators' perceptual, cognitive, emotional, evaluative dispositions and activities, be they focalisers or not. As theoreticians of Theory of Mind in literature (Zunshine 2006, Palmer 2008, 2010) have argued, this is a basic human ability that we apply to our fellow humans and to fictional characters, interpreting their behaviour, utterances, and external appearance as indicative of states of mind – or perspectives. We therefore have no problem assigning such a perspective also to characters who are not in the foreground of a narrative as protagonists, and who are not even focalisers, as long as their actions, habits, looks, and speeches are rendered through narratorial or figural description.

This leads to the second differentiation, namely that between *marked* and *general multiperspectivity*. Many narratologists focus on marked cases of multiperspectivity, i.e., narratives which highlight epistemological complexities or incompatibilities by presenting two or more contrasting and conflicting perspectives of the same event (see Hartner 2014). In contrast to that, I side with Bakhtin, Woloch, and Mar and Oatley in considering the mere presence of many characters' potentially diverging world-views to be important, and I propose treating constellations of characters in extended narratives as cases of general multiperspectivity, of which the MCS is the reader's mental correlate. In both the Bakhtinian and the literary-psychological sense, every single character with their plans and motivations, fears and desires, habits and opinions is a potential representative of a perspective on, or view of, the world that includes particular perceptual, cognitive, emotional, and evaluative stances. Nothing will prevent the reader from stopping to consider any character's world-view, motivations, relation to other characters, etc., even if they are only minor, non-focalising actors in the fictional world. As readers, we see multiplicity the moment we understand the fictional world to be inhabited by a number of characters, and we expect the story to unfold on the basis of the potential tensions between their opinions, motivations, and actions. Although we are likely to ascribe perspectives to minor and non-focalising characters in less elaborate fashion than to main characters – and many of the minor ones are presented in such ways that the reader's attention is likely to remain focused on the protagonists – all of the characters are there to furnish the fictional world with meaning through the relationships of their perspectives to other characters. This is precisely what keeps readers of novels involved – or immersed. Whether the experience of a multiple character kind of immersion in reading a novel with three or four dozen characters is different from novels with just a handful is an interesting question for empirical research. I would expect the difference to consist in the degree to which attention is directed at the presence of other groups than the central constellation.

I argue that the MCS is readily available at all times in reading, even if the text currently foregrounds only one character, or constellations in which very few characters of the full ensemble are present. Cognitive linguistics, and cognitive poetics in particular, have considered the dynamic process of mentally keeping track with a narrative in terms of 'windows' or 'frames' of attention in which the current contexts of the fictional world, including the characters acting in it, are represented and then fade into the background when the text focuses on other scenes, characters, and events (Emmott 1997: chs 4–6, and 2003, Stockwell 2020: ch.12). But not only does not every item disappear from a frame immediately once a new frame follows, since some linger on – see Stockwell's (2009: ch.2) discussion of 'resonance' – but I contend that even characters who have not been mentioned for a very long time can form part of an MCS, if the reader attributes relevance to them or the text has suggested they might return to be important because their perspective stands in some vital relation to that of the main character(s). On this view, the world of the text that a reader is immersed in is not restricted to a single character's perspective but yields a mental scenario in which the reader maintains and continuously updates their awareness of relational complexities between characters. Understanding and evaluating the meaning of the constellations of characters is a major aspect of the experience of reading extended narratives.

This awareness of the relations, contrasts, and correspondences between characters' perspectives is what the MCS maps. According to cognitive literary and linguistic scholarship, readers have strategies of dealing with viewpoint complexity by mentally forming networks, hierarchical embeddings, and blends of different perspectives (Hartner 2012, Dancygier and Vandelanotte 2016, Zeman 2016). This implies that not every single viewpoint a text offers needs to be *adopted* – that would certainly overstrain mental capacities, as Dixon and Bortolussi have suggested. I consider general perspectivisation, and general multiperspectivity to require no perspective-taking but perspective construction, i.e., the ascription of a viewpoint to a character, or, rather, potentially all characters in a narrative. If the multiperspectivity is marked, the reader is likely to actually adopt the contrasting perspectives by turns and come up with a blended space in which both the contrasts and the individual positions are available. In the case of general multiperspectivity, however, the reader can have an immersive experience that rests on the awareness of complex constellations of characters and their perspectives.

Concluding remarks and some open questions

Readerly engagement with narrative is often described metaphorically. The use of such terms as *immersion*, *absorption*, *transportation*, and *presence* is likely to capture the phenomenological qualities of that experience quite well. However, we need to specify the cognitive-emotional processes underlying these experiences, first, to better understand different varieties of immersion, in the sense that I have proposed to do above; and, second, we have to operationalise them for empirical testing. The introspective qualities of a literary experience are always a perfectly legitimate starting point for further theorising (see Stockwell 2021b). However, as critical discussions of central terms such as empathy and others used in narrative engagement research have shown (see, e.g., Dixon and Bortolussi 2023: 26, 58–62, and ch.4, and Martínez 2018: ch.1), more frequently than not a broad range of distinct and only partly overlapping cognitive-emotional operations are lumped together that had better be kept apart if we want to understand the interaction of textual features and reader constructs in literary reading.

Insisting on a more specific theorisation of the cognitive-emotional operations of narrative engagement brings some open questions to light that my short discussion has not been able to address. For instance, my differentiation between a single character-related, empathic, or identificatory form of immersion on the one hand, and one that centrally involves an MCS on the other, raises the question whether these immersive modes can be active at the same time, or whether a reader 'zooms into' one and has to 'zoom out of' it again to make room for the other. Also, there may be subgenres of the novel or textual strategies that prompt the reader to favour one type of immersion over the other. Finally, empirical scholarship will have to explicate also the potential influence of reader variables: Are there some readers who routinely engage with a fictional world more in the 'social' mode, i.e., who are particularly interested in the complex relationships between the many characters that people a fictional world, whereas others might want to focus only on the protagonist and wish to disregard the other characters? More questions are sure to come up in the discussion of different modes, processes, and effects of immersion, to which I hope to have contributed with this chapter. My main point has been that the presence of complex constellations of many characters and the availability of multiple perspectives with which a reader can engage in extended narratives are likely to trigger other kinds of immersion than those usually described in the research on short texts that present the experiences of only one or few central characters.

References

Anderson, M. and Iversen, S. (2018) 'Immersion and defamiliarization: experiencing literature and world', *Poetics Today* 39 (3): 569–95.

Bakhtin, M.M. (1981) *The Dialogic Imagination: Four Essays by M.M. Bakhtin* (ed. M. Holquist, trans. C. Emerson and M. Holquist). Austin: University of Texas Press.

Bakhtin, M.M. (1984) *Problems of Dostoevsky's Poetics* (ed. and trans. C. Emerson). Minneapolis: University of Minnesota Press.

Busselle, R. and Bilandzic, H. (2009) 'Measuring narrative engagement', *Media Psychology* 12 (4): 321–47.

Caracciolo, M. (2014) *The Experientiality of Narrative: An Enactivist Approach*. Berlin: de Gruyter.

Cohen, J. (2001) 'Defining identification: a theoretical look at the identification of audiences with media characters', *Mass Communication and Society* 4 (3): 245–64.

Coplan, A. (2004) 'Empathic engagement with narrative fictions', *The Journal of Aesthetics and Art Criticism* 62 (2): 141–52.

Dancygier, B. and Vandelanotte, L. (2016) 'Discourse viewpoint as network', in B. Dancygier, W. Lu and A. Verhagen (eds) *Viewpoint and the Fabric of Meaning: Form and Use of Viewpoint Tools across Languages and Modalities*. Berlin: Mouton de Gruyter, pp.13–40.

Dixon, P. and Bortolussi, M. (2023) *The Analogical Reader: A Cognitive Approach to Perspective Taking*. Cambridge: Cambridge University Press.

Doicaru, M.M. (2016) *Gripped by Movies: From Story-World to Artifact Absorption* (unpublished doctoral thesis). University of Amsterdam.

Emmott, C. (1997) *Narrative Comprehension: A Discourse Perspective*. Oxford: Clarendon Press.

Emmott, C. (2003) 'Constructing social space: sociocognitive factors in the interpretation of character relations', in D. Herman (ed.) *Narrative Theory and the Cognitive Sciences*. Stanford: CSLI Publications, pp.295–321.

Fabry, R.E. and Kukkonen, K. (2019) 'Reconsidering the mind-wandering reader: predictive processing, probability designs, and enculturation', *Frontiers in Psychology* 9: 26–48.

Fludernik, M. (1996) *Towards a 'Natural' Narratology*. London: Routledge.

Forster Tukachinsky, R. (2021) 'Character engagement and identification', in D. Kuiken and A.M. Jacobs (eds) *Handbook of Empirical Literary Studies*. Berlin: De Gruyter, pp.251–75.

Gerrig, R.J. (1993) *Experiencing Narrative Worlds: On the Psychological Activities of Reading*. New Haven: Yale University Press.

Green, M.C. (2004) 'Transportation into narrative worlds: the role of prior knowledge and perceived realism', *Discourse Processes* 38 (2): 247–66.

Green, M.C., Brock, T.C., and Kaufman, G.F. (2004) 'Understanding media enjoyment: the role of transportation into narrative worlds', *Communication Theory* 14 (4): 311–27.

Greimas, A.J. (1983 [1966]) *Structural Semantics: An Attempt at a Method*. Lincoln: University of Nebraska Press.

Hartner, M. (2012) 'Constructing literary character and perspective: an approach from psychology and blending theory', in R. Schneider and M. Hartner (eds) *Blending and the Study of Narrative: Approaches and Applications*. Berlin: de Gruyter, pp.85–120.

Hartner, M. (2014) 'Multiperspectivity', in P. Hühn, J.C. Meister, J. Pier and W. Schmid (eds) *The Living Handbook of Narratology*. Hamburg: Hamburg University, available at <https://www-archiv.fdm.uni-hamburg.de/lhn/node/37.html>

Herman, D. (2002) 'Storyworld', in D. Herman, M.-L. Ryan and M. Jahn (eds) *Routledge Encyclopedia of Narrative Theory*. London: Routledge, pp.569–70.

Johnson, M. (2008) 'What makes a body?' *Journal of Speculative Philosophy* 22 (3): 159–69.

Koopman, E. and Hakemulder, F. (2015) 'Effects of literature on empathy and self-reflection: a theoretical-empirical framework', *Journal of Literary Theory* 9 (1): 97–111.

Kuijpers, M.M., Douglas, S. and Bálint, K. (2021) 'Narrative absorption: an overview', in D. Kuiken and A.M. Jacobs (eds) *Handbook of Empirical Literary Studies*. Berlin: de Gruyter, pp.279–304.

Mar, R.A. and Oatley, K. (2008) 'The function of fiction is the abstraction and simulation of social experience', *Perspectives on Psychological Science* 3 (3): 173–92.

Martínez, M.A. (2018) *Storyworld Possible Selves*. Berlin: Mouton de Gruyter.
Nell, V. (1988) *Lost in a Book: The Psychology of Reading for Pleasure*. New Haven: Yale University Press.
Niederhoff, B. (2013a) 'Focalization', in P. Hühn, J.C. Meister, J. Pier and W. Schmid (eds) *The Living Handbook of Narratology*. Hamburg: Hamburg University, available at <https://www-archiv.fdm.uni-hamburg.de/lhn/node/18.html>
Niederhoff, B. (2013b) 'Perspective – point of view', in P. Hühn, J.C. Meister, J. Pier and W. Schmid (eds) *The Living Handbook of Narratology*. Hamburg: Hamburg University, available at <https://www-archiv.fdm.uni-hamburg.de/lhn/node/26.html>
Palmer, A. (2008) *Fictional Minds*. Lincoln: University of Nebraska Press.
Palmer, A. (2010) *Social Minds in the Novel*. Columbus: Ohio State University Press.
Pianzola, F. (2025) 'The phenomenon of narrative immersion', in J. Alber and R. Schneider (eds) *The Routledge Companion to Literature and Cognitive Studies*, London: Routledge, pp. 126–37.
Poe, Edgar Allan (2006) 'On unity of effect [1836]', in J.G. Kennedy (ed.) *The Portable Edgar Allan Poe*. London: Penguin.
Polvinen, M. (2022) *Self-Reflective Fiction and 4E Cognition: An Enactive Approach to Literary Artifice*. London: Routledge.
Propp, V. (1968) *Morphology of the Folk Tale* (trans. L. Scott, 2nd rev. edn [1928]). Austin: University of Texas Press.
Ryan, M.-L. (2001) *Narrative as Virtual Reality: Immersion and Interactivity in Literature and Electronic Media*. Baltimore: Johns Hopkins University Press.
Schneider, R. (2001) 'Toward a cognitive theory of literary character: the dynamics of mental-model construction', *Style* 35 (4): 607–39.
Schneider, R. (2025) 'Multiple perspectives in the novel and storyworld possible selves: an alternative approach to narrative engagement', in M.A. Martínez (ed.) *Storyworld Possible Selves and Narrative Intersubjectivity*. Berlin: de Gruyter, pp. 133–51.
Schneider, R. (2026) *Character Constellations in Cognitive and Empirical Literary Studies: A New Approach to Readerly Engagement*. London: Routledge.
Sestir, M. and Green, M.C. (2010) 'You are who you watch: identification and transportation effects on temporary self-concept', *Social Influence* 5 (4): 272–88.
Smallwood, J. and Schooler, J.W. (2015) 'The science of mind wandering: empirically navigating the stream of consciousness', *Annual Review of Psychology* 66 (1): 487–518.
Stockwell, P. (2009) *Texture: A Cognitive Aesthetics of Reading*. Edinburgh: Edinburgh University Press.
Stockwell, P. (2020) *Cognitive Poetics: An Introduction* (2nd edn). London: Routledge.
Stockwell, P. (2021a) 'Mind-modelling literary personas', *Journal of Literary Semantics* 51 (2): 131–46.
Stockwell, P. (2021b) 'In defence of introspection', in A. Bell, S. Browse, A. Gibbons and D. Peplow (eds) *Style and Reader Response: Minds, Media, Methods*. Amsterdam: John Benjamins, pp.165–78.
Sweetser, E. (2012) 'Introduction: viewpoint and perspective in language and gesture from the ground down', in B. Dancygier and E. Sweetser (eds) *Viewpoint in Language: A Multimodal Perspective*, Cambridge: Cambridge University Press, pp.1–22.

Vaeßen, J. (2021) 'Characters: a cognitive perspective', in J. Alber and P. Wenzel (eds) *Introduction to Cognitive Narratology*. Trier: WVT, pp.43–64.

Woloch, A. (2003) *The One vs. the Many: Minor Characters and the Space of the Protagonist in the Novel.* Princeton: Princeton University Press.

Zeman, S. (2016) 'Introduction: perspectives on narrativity and narrative perspectivization', in N. Igl and S. Zeman (eds) *Perspectives on Narrativity and Narrative Perspectivization.* Amsterdam: Benjamins, pp.1–14.

Zeman, S. (2017) 'Confronting perspectives: modeling perspectival complexity in language and cognition', *Glossa: A Journal of General Linguistics* 2 (1/6): 1–22.

Zunshine, L. (2006) *Why We Read Fiction: Theory of Mind and the Novel.* Columbus: Ohio State University Press.

CHAPTER 3

Immersive transportation as a mode of empathy and narrative empathy

Suzanne Keen

Immersive transportation via fiction has been persistently associated with readers' empathy, manifesting variously as perspective-taking, accurate inference, emotional congruence, compassion/sympathy for imaginary others and real-world counterparts, and even prosocial behaviour. This chapter illustrates how distinct empathic phenomena can be disambiguated, and urges researchers to eschew value-laden judgements about immersed reading experiences. It includes a review of the relationships between transportation, empathy, and narrative empathy (and the scales used to measure them), revealing that connections among the suite of empathic experiences prompted by narrative can be confounded, and arguing for transportation to be understood as a mode of interpersonal human empathy in its own right.

Introduction

Immersion while experiencing narrative has been persistently associated with readers' empathy, appearing in lay accounts and scholarly theorising under various labels: being 'lost in a book', presence, absorption, engagement, and preeminently, transportation. I refer to it here as *transportation*, as a shorthand for immersive transportation stimulated by narrative, or a kind of immersion that is an effect of absorbed reading. Linked to the conceptual metaphor READING IS A JOURNEY (Stockwell 2009: 81), transportation's expansive tenor has been critiqued (Bortolussi and Dixon 2015); as a vehicle it typically carries empathy. Transportation has not always been recognised as a basic construct of empathy, though experiencing it constitutes an element of a subject's empathic disposition, as measured by prominent empathy scales such as the Interpersonal Reactivity Index (Davis 1980, hereafter IRI). Readers' accounts of immersion typically involve not only the experience of departing the real world to feel present in another world called up by narrative (transportation) but also other distinct modes of empathy. Transported, immersed reading is commonly understood to involve additional modes of narrative empathy: readers' perspective-taking with characters or role-taking projection; their inferences about and emotional congruence with characters' feelings; and their compassion/sympathy for imaginary others and their real-world counterparts. It has even been linked to subsequent prosocial behaviour after immersed story-reading (Johnson 2012) and to other real-world impacts, such as an increased interest in travelling after being transported by a TV series (Irimiás et al. 2021).

Immersed reading or transportation should be understood as *one of a suite of lower-order constructs that constitute empathy*, with implications for the understanding of narrative empathy. In making this recommendation I am following the advice of an interdisciplinary group of empathy scholars convened by Mark Davis and Sara Konrath to regularise the language used to denote distinct constructs of empathy, a project in which I participated (Davis and Konrath et al., under submission). Not *only* a phenomenon of textually mediated narrative empathy, when a reading subject engages imaginatively with discourse cues set out by an author to co-create a story, transportation is first a basic construct of interpersonal empathy not requiring literacy, fiction nor even reading. Immersion can be evoked by an intense memory, by oral storytelling, and by nonfiction narrative. I focus here on the nature and relations of immersive transportation spurred by fiction. To be lost in a book or immersed in a tale is to experience other-oriented replacement of one's own concerns by the situation and responses of another (real or unreal) person: a form of empathy that has been called Fantasy Empathy (Davis 1980). The unreality signalled by the term 'fantasy' emphasises the involvement of inanimate cues, as in aesthetic empathy, according to the earliest formulations of *Einfühlung* in response to artworks (Lee and Anstruther-Thomson 1897).

Writing in the 1890s about art's ability to provoke 'closer relations with the *not-ourselves*' (Lee and Anstruther-Thomson 1897: 563), Vernon Lee and her collaborator Anstruther-Thomson had yet to adopt Titchener's coinage of empathy for *Einfühlung* (Titchener 1909: 21), but Lee's theorising already associated the immersive and transportive elements of aesthetic responses to form, writing of art's 'strange power of ridding us of the sense of the passage of time [. . .] we are safe and serene in what seems like a little railed off or mysteriously guarded circle of existence' (Lee and Anstruther-Thomson 1897: 559). In her later work *The Beautiful*, writing of empathy with line and shape as a matter of mimicry, Lee describes the aesthetic absorption as a contrast to 'scattered or hustled' real life (Lee 1913: 83). The key elements of an empathic construct are already present: immersion absorbs us, takes us away from real life, brings us into contemplative presence of something other than ourselves, changes our sense of time passing, and provokes inner mimicry of sensations. It is worth dwelling on Lee's early insights because they highlight the intensity of responses to inanimate cues, like the marks on a page or screen that readers activate when they get lost in a book. Because immersive transportation is one sort of empathic experience, it is often linked by readers to other, more human-centred modalities of narrative empathy and their supposed outcomes. Though the association of immersive transportation with emotional congruence, perspective-taking, or projection recurs in readers' experiences, whether immersion reliably *causes* those other empathic experiences in many or all immersed subjects is not known.

It is not surprising to find empathy and transportation as co-present when queries about empathy appear in transportation scales and queries about transportation appear in empathy scales such as Davis' IRI (Davis 1980). Immersed reading constitutes empathic experience, but how does it relate to other common forms of emotional resonance and cognitive recognition with representations that are also labelled empathic? Entangled definitions of empathic constructs can confound causal relations between and among them. For example, when the term 'empathy' is measured by the ability to recognise emotions through facial expressions, high empathy individuals are those especially good at recognising others' emotions through facial expressions (or renderings of them). Low empathy individuals by this usage would include people suffering from prosopagnosia, or face blindness. However, performing well or badly on this one construct of empathic awareness is an entirely different matter from being good or bad at perspective-taking (understanding how another is likely to be feeling) or projection (imagining oneself in the position of another, or role-taking), or getting lost in a book (immersion). It isn't the same, and it isn't even predictive. The use of the single term 'empathy' for all four of the phenomena mentioned in this example can cause confusion about what might be leading to a desirable outcome such as mature sympathy and compassion (yet another empathic construct). When Paul Bloom (2016) argues that he is 'against empathy' and in favour of rational compassion, he actually means that he is against over-valuing experiences of emotional congruence (one form of empathy) and prefers another ('compassion'). Why does this matter to our topic of immersed reading? It matters because terminological blurring of differing phenomena under the single term 'empathy' occludes complexities of readers' experiences and can imply causal relations when associations or correlations would be more accurate. One may be immersed and also resonate with a character's feelings; one may be lost in a book without also feeling sympathy (antagonism is as legitimate a response to narrative as fellow-feeling). Fiction can be thoroughly engrossing without generating compassion or inviting altruistic action in the real world. Transportation *can* operate in tandem with perspective-taking, accurate inference, emotional congruence, and compassion, for fictional or nonfictional targets, but it should not be employed as a proxy for these other versions of empathy, nor assumed reliably to cause them. If we tease the different constructs apart, we are more likely to be able to see how they interact, rather than assuming that one form of empathic response brings along all the others.

Transportation deserves distinct treatment in the study of narrative empathy, for beyond its role in relation to separate constructs of narrative empathy transportation is a mode of interpersonal human empathy in its own right. A causal connection between this one form of empathy, transported reading, and other empathic experiences stirred by narrative is often assumed but cannot be regarded as predictable or inevitable. Furthermore, much depends upon the underlying dispositions of subjects co-creating narrative: Are they low or high empathy individuals? How transportable are they? Are they capable of mental visualising, or are they aphantasiacs?

The complications begin with transportation's status as a discrete mode of human interpersonal empathy, where the stimulus is narrative that invites the reader or listener to replace their here-and-now with what Thomas Hardy metonymises as 'visioning on the air' in 'The Roman Road' (Hardy 1909: 144). Transportation need not begin with reading; it can be stimulated by memory, by recounting events of the past, or by another's oral storytelling. The walkers on the Roman Road neither witness nor remember the passing soldiers in Hardy's poem; they see what has not been there for more than 1,000 years. Hardy's 'visioning on the air' captures a form of imagining that replaces outer reality with the figurations of an inward mental visualising, which is understood by psychologists today as both more emotional and more realistic than purely verbal thought (Matthews et al. 2013). Hardy was an acute observer of behaviour, here capturing the common (though not universal) capacity of humans to experience visual mental imagery while awake. In his poem 'One We Knew (M.H., 1772–1857)', Hardy describes what a transported individual looks like from the outside:

> With cap-framed face and long gaze into the embers –
> We seated around her knees –
> She would dwell on such dead themes, not as one who remembers,
> But rather as one who sees.
> She seemed one left behind of a band gone distant
> So far that no tongue could hail:
> Past things retold were to her as things existent,
> Things present but as a tale.
>
> (Hardy 1909: 164–5)

He slips the poem's focus from a report of the speaker's tale-telling (about country dances and the location of the old maypole) to a consideration of her inward experience, a visioning of the past that the poem itself replicates. The effective replacement of '[t]hings present' with '[p]ast things retold' in Hardy's grandmother's attention speaks to her experience of mental imagery, gazing into the fireplace, seeing the 'dead themes' of a 'band gone distant,' and reliving traumatic memories:

> She said she had often heard the gibbet creaking
> As it swayed in the lightning flash,
> Had caught from the neighbouring town a small child's shrieking
> At the cart-tail under the lash . . .
>
> (Hardy 1909: 164; original ellipsis)

The strain of the gallows loaded with the weight of an executed criminal and the cry of a child punished by public flogging yield to an ellipsis that suggests the old woman's absorption in further recollections that have transported her far from those she educates, back in time, merged with a younger self marked by witnessing such suffering. At the same time Hardy's report summons his poem's reader to share in the painful sights and sounds of the past, potentially to flinch with empathy for the victims or their witness or both. Transportation is contagious, spreading from teller or narrator to listener to reporter to reader. It is a phenomenon of communication, even when the parties involved in eliciting and experiencing it are not present at the same time.

I come to this work as a theorist of narrative empathy. In my approach to these broad subjects of empathy, reading, and transportation, I am aligned with both embodied, enactive theories of language, cognition, and emotion (Caracciolo 2014, Caracciolo and Kukkonen 2021, Kuzmicova 2012, Zwaan 2004, Zwaan and Taylor 2006) and also the neuroscientific account of a shared manifold for intersubjectivity as contributing to embodied narratology (Wojciehowski and Gallese 2011). My sense of transportation has roots in both psychology (Gerrig 1993) and transmedial theorising (Ryan 1991, 2001), and my own theorising is informed by rhetorical narratology (e.g., Booth 1983, Phelan 1996, Rabinowitz 1987) and contextual cognitivist narratology (e.g., Schneider 2021, Zunshine 2014). Interdisciplinary pursuits are aided by terminological clarity, and, as it turns out, parsing interrelationships at the level of basic vocabulary gets at some of the conundrums of the subject. To that end, the following sections define terms and explore them in relation to one another.

Immersive transportation as one mode of empathy

As distinct from private reveries or daydreaming, transportation is 'immersion in a storyworld, during which one experiences absorption in the narrative physically, cognitively, and emotionally, as if one were present, with an accompanying distancing from one's actual surroundings' (Davis and Konrath et al., under submission). Experiences of transportation are described by Green and Brock as 'an integrative melding of attention, imagery, and feelings, focused on story events' typified by empathy (Green and Brock 2002). Other scholars and some of the most revealing experimental evidence about transportation emphasise both mental visualising and storyworld absorption, suggesting that readers respond both to the artistry of language creating the world as well as the spaces and places evoked (Kuijpers et al. 2014). Transportation can be fleeting or of significant duration; interrupted, it can be resumed, but it only ever offers a temporary relocation from the reader's actual surroundings (Ryan 1991). Though its sensory richness or 'thickness' may be experienced as envisioning (Caracciolo and Kukkonen 2021), it is neither hallucinatory nor an involuntary psychotic break from reality. Though the narratives eliciting transportation are often fictional works such as novels and short stories, immersive storyworlds may be nonfictional, as in history, life-writing, or in truthful relations of experience told aloud (Bal and Veltkamp 2013). A narrative format may be more influential than a text's fictional or nonfictional status in stimulating transportation and empathy (Savitri and Farah 2021). Neither textuality nor fictionality is a required component of transportation, but narrative communication must occur to stimulate transportation, and facticity evokes a more logic-driven reading process. Fiction is processed with less concern for verification or obligation to respond, a circumstance which has been hypothesised to enhance empathy (Keen 2006) and transportation itself (Bal and Veltkamp 2013).

Transportation has been shown to impact belief and attitude change (Fitzgerald and Green 2017), improve social abilities (Calarco et al. 2017), reduce bias and prejudice (Johnson 2012), and increase openness to persuasion (Green and Brock 2002). From keeping company with some of the outcomes also associated with the cultivation of empathy, transportation and empathy have been drawn into parallel, as when transportation into a narrative world is positively associated with higher levels of sympathy or compassion (Bal and Veltkamp 2013).

According to a recent compact regarding vocabulary, 'empathy' designates diverse phenomena: emotional congruence, mimicry/synchrony, sympathy/compassion, personal distress, perspective-taking, accurate inference, projection, and transportation, which should be individuated (Davis and Konrath et al., under submission). Transportation differs from the other empathic constructs in the delimited situation of its stimulus: it occurs in the co-creative reception of narrative. Whether a part of rapt listening, absorbed viewing, or entranced reading, transportation requires attention, involves imaginative projection, and often results in the sensation of presence. It bridges the real-world/storyworld divide without ontological elisions, for every other empathy construct which occurs both in the real world and as narrative empathy requires a caveat in its narrative alternative, acknowledging the representational/fictive status of a narrated target (see Pianzola et al. 2021). In contrast with other constructs of empathy, transportation fundamentally attends to subjects' responses to narrated, often fictional, targets of attention. Even when the represented persons have real-world correlates, as in life-writing, the transported/immersed empathiser responds imaginatively to narrative cues, not directly to a fellow creature in the real world.

The social *sensation* of transportation shows in some of the alternative terms for it, such as *presence* (Kuzmicova 2012, Lee 2004, Pianzola et al. 2021), *absorption* (Kuijpers and Hakemulder 2017), and *engagement* (Busselle and Bilandzic 2009), which alludes to the parasociality of the experience. The paradoxes of transportation come through in each of its alternative labels: *immersion* both surrounds and distances the empathiser without going anywhere; *absorption* trains the attention on unreal targets that temporarily replace awareness of real surroundings; *engagement* involves the reader with non-existent persons and things who cannot reciprocate; *presence* casts an illusion in the reader's mind's eye, invisible to others who share space and time with that reader. An ability to get lost in a book does not imply incapacities in the real world; to the contrary, trait absorption has been related to readiness to engage in real-world experiences and to identify and respond richly to objects of attention (Wild et al. 1995). Powerful communal experiences of transportation occur in storytelling and theatre audiences and in movie theatres, and may set off intensities of shared emotional response, but the central paradox of transportation is its activation of intersubjectivity and even intercorporeality (Wojciehowski and Gallese 2011) in the absence of real others.

Because transportation is a form of empathy, closely related to *Einfühlung* and imaginative projection, it can be bundled with neighbouring forms of empathy, to be dignified by association with more virtuous modes, such as sympathy or compassion. Some kinds of immersion, particularly submergence in popular genre fiction and role-taking fantasising, have been denigrated as less worthy than, for example, expressions of sympathy for marginalised out-groups elicited by realistic fiction making justice-oriented appeals. The exceptions to this trend are noteworthy, as when Andrew Elfenbein dignifies transportation as an aspect of nineteenth-century 'easy reading': 'scorned as the shallowest of occupations and respected as the source of the deepest memories' (Elfenbein 2018: 164). For every major claim that has been made about the positive influence of novel reading – such as compassionate character formation, ethical practice in understanding people different from ourselves, and the training of empathetic, conscientious citizens – a matched set of concerns can be found. Wasting time, ignoring duties, entertaining falsehoods, and indulging in immoral fantasies are among the milder criticisms of the novel-reading person.

Though immersed fiction reading has been disparaged for centuries by worthies such as John Stuart Mill (1833: 204), I am not weighing in here on transportation's affordances or failings with respect to ethical outcomes of reading. I offer instead a refinement of the relations among transportation, interpersonal human empathy, and narrative empathy. Two positions in particular, the initiator (teller, writer) of a transportive communication, and the transported receiver (listener, reader), exist in all three of these phenomena, each of which also requires a narrative communication of some sort. Though the storyworld called up in that narrative communication almost inevitably includes represented persons, transportation does not mandate any particular relation to those figures, despite its strong association with readers' perspective-taking, their inferences, or their emotional congruence.

Transportation deserves a central position in accounts of readers' empathy. The empathic phenomenon of being 'lost in a book' (Nell 1988) should be elevated to at least the same level of dignity as perspective-taking, emotional congruence, compassion, imaginative projection, and other forms of interpersonal human empathy, and it should be distinguished both from the versions of those constructs stimulated by reading narrative and also from the techniques and representational strategies which evoke them. Then the following six proposals could be evaluated: (1) as a phenomenon of immersed reading, transportation likely precedes character identification (which may not occur at all), but (2) it may only be noticed when and if connection with a character occurs. (3) It involves more than emotional fusion with fictional characters. (4) It can be focused on the spatiality of a fictive setting, for example, through sensations of orientation or enclosure. (5) Though connection with characters' situations and resonance with their thoughts and feelings are often a part of immersed readers' reports, other facets of transportation (feeling 'there'; moving through a space or landscape; perceiving settings perspectivally) loom large in the experience of getting lost in a poem, a story, or a novel. (6) It may be most noticed when interruption breaks its spell.

Absorbed reading that temporarily blots out awareness of readers' surroundings, trains their attention on storyworld features of setting and atmosphere, evokes mood through imagery and verbal tones, and engages their minds with accounts of events and circumstances also qualifies as transportation. Indeed, as David Herman has established, narrative's capacity to employ transportive techniques of world creation is part and parcel of its bid to communicate and be comprehended by readers (Herman 2002: 9–22). In Herman's account (following Ryan 1991, Gerrig 1993), transportation as a response to narrative worldmaking makes understanding possible. Intrinsic to fictionality, transportation marks fiction as a type of discourse 'in which participants are transported, through a more or less immersive experience, to a STORYWORLD assumed to be imaginary' (Herman 2009: 186).

However, a reader's report of immersed engagement in a fictional world need not be validated by expressions of sympathy or compassion for characters or their real-world counterparts; a sensation of the presence of figures and spaces need not attach readers ethically through character identification or obligate them to a rooting interest for a particular plot outcome. I agree with Marisa Bortolussi and Peter Dixon that 'the lack of one feature of transport does not preclude other forms of engagement [. . .] neither imageability nor emotional reactions of sympathy or empathy are necessary features of a transport-like experience' (Bortolussi and Dixon 2015: 528). Transportation is no more a unitary phenomenon than narrative empathy or empathy itself. Just because some of the most intense experiences of transportation layer or swiftly alternate different varieties of empathic response to fiction does not require that all such possibilities must be realised for readers' immersion to count as transported reading. I propose that comprehension (validating attention) is a better test of whether transportation has occurred than empathic resonance with a character.

Entangled terms: empathy, narrative empathy, and transportation

Empathy, defined in Merriam Webster's dictionary as 'the action of understanding, being aware of, being sensitive to, and vicariously experiencing the feelings, thoughts, and experience of another', is constituted by a suite of overlapping phenomena of shared emotions and understanding. It has long been understood as an umbrella term that covers – variously – cognitive, emotional, neurological, involuntary, effortful, moral, ethical, and/or prosocial responses. Writing about interpersonal human empathy, the psychologist C. Daniel Batson enumerates eight different concepts that travel under the shared label of empathy:

1. Knowing Another Person's Internal State, Including His or Her Thoughts and Feelings
2. Adopting the Posture or Matching the Neural Responses of an Observed Other
3. Coming to Feel as Another Person Feels
4. Intuiting or Projecting Oneself into Another's Situation
5. Imagining How Another is Thinking or Feeling
6. Imagining How One Would Think of Feel in the Other's Place
7. Feeling Distress at Witnessing Another Person's Suffering
8. Feeling for Another Person Who is Suffering

(Batson 2009: 4–8)

Perhaps because Batson embeds the historical original of empathy (*Einfühlung*) as 'aesthetic projection' under his concept 4, he does not create a separate category for either empathic aesthetic responses nor those mediated by artistic representations – the operative types involved in narrative empathy. Nor does he refer directly to transportation, though it can be inferred to be involved in concept 4, 'Intuiting or Projecting Oneself into

Another's Situation' (Batson 2009: 6). Transportation would make a ninth distinct empathy concept, different from the other eight because it is evoked not by the *other person* so prominent in Batson's definitions, but by narrative. Indeed, when your approach to empathy foregrounds interpersonal empathy, you are likely to de-emphasise the non-human targets of aesthetic empathy that are involved in the original conception of *Einfühlung*, though they are historically and physiologically related (Ganczarek et al. 2018).

To fill the gap in Batson's taxonomy, Mark Davis' theorising of empathy (Davis 1983) and his widely adopted Interpersonal Reactivity Index (Davis 1980) provide a place for Fantasy Empathy. A subject's IRI score includes transported experiences of fictional stories, as queries about study subjects' 'tendencies to transpose themselves imaginatively into the feelings and actions of fictitious characters in books, movies, and plays' constitute the Fantasy subscale (Davis 1980: 10). Key phrases in Davis' queries include imagining one's own reaction to a fictional situation, getting 'involved with the feelings of the characters', daydreaming and fantasising, putting oneself in the place of a character, 'becoming extremely involved in a good book', feeling as if one were one of the characters afterwards, and (for a reverse score) staying objective and avoiding emotional involvement with a story (Davis 1980: 10). While the Fantasy subscale of the IRI can be used to measure the general disposition to become engaged in narratives, it also gets at subjects' experiences of emotional congruence, aesthetic projection, perspective-taking, immersion, role-taking, and character identification as elements of a subjective and emotionally engaged reading experience. The Fantasy subscale has been validated as a measure of general empathy, especially in correlations between Perspective-Taking and Fictional Perspective-Taking, Empathic Concern and Fictional Empathic Concern, and Personal Distress and Fictional Personal Distress (Nomura and Akai 2012: 310–11). Being transportable makes a higher overall empathy score likely.

The reverse is also true: higher empathy also involves the capacity to be transported, though not necessarily predicting a fondness for fiction (Nomura and Akai 2012: 312). Nomura and Akai's finding of positive correlation between Fictional Perspective-Taking and Fictional Personal Distress (in contrast to a weak negative relation of those responses with respect to real people) emphasises that transportation away from a real-world context may liberate intensities of emotional response in those immersed in storyworlds known to be fictional, as I previously theorised (Keen 2007: 168).

Narrative empathy, as I have earlier defined it, involves

> the sharing of feeling and perspective-taking induced by reading, viewing, hearing, or imagining narratives of another's situation and condition. [It] plays a role in the aesthetics of production when authors experience it [. . .] in mental simulation during reading, in the aesthetics of reception when readers experience it, and in the narrative

> poetics of texts when formal strategies invite it. Narrative empathy overarches narratological categories, involving actants, narrative situation, matters of pace and duration, and storyworld features such as settings.
>
> (Keen 2013: para.1)

As this eclectic definition suggests, narrative empathy, like empathy itself, is an umbrella term encompassing diverse phenomena. There are undoubtedly many touch-points linking variants of empathic experience, such as perspective-taking, sympathy/compassion, accurate inference, emotional congruence, and even personal distress, with narrative stimuli in fictional and nonfictional texts of a variety of genres. These familiar interpersonal empathic constructs operate in rough parallels with their narrative counterparts, offering related experiences of perspective-taking or emotional congruence with fictional characters or represented subjects on the one hand and with real people apprehended dynamically in intersubjective experience on the other hand. Inhering in the process of creation, in the choice and deployment of textual features through narrative techniques, representational strategies, and evocative content, the text-based opportunities for narrative empathy are activated in and by the co-creating reader or audience member. Whether or not a reader, viewer, or audience member must be transported in order to experience narrative empathy is an open question: the opportunities for narrative empathy and avenues approaching it are sufficiently various to rule out any one phenomenon, even transportation, as necessary or prior to the experience.

However, because transportation itself constitutes an empathic response, then immersed presence in a narrative world that temporarily distances readers, listeners, or creators of narrative from the real world is also a basic form of narrative empathy. This proposition augments my earlier definition of narrative empathy. The absence from this proposal of represented persons with whom to experience emotions or share perspectives will strike some as insufficiently interpersonal, but *Einfühlung* starts as feeling into inanimate objects, and Titchener saw that the 'attitudinal feels' of empathy could be touched off by an author's arrangement of words (Titchener 1909: 181) not just people. The work of understanding narrative involves attention to artefacts, not just persons (Herman 2009). Narrative empathy, even the kind that feels intensely interpersonal, operates by animating the inanimate. The common-sense association of engaged reading with character identification and emotionally congruent responses to characters neither limits narrative empathy to empathy with characters nor requires immersed, transported reading. As I have argued since 2006 and amplify in a recent essay, 'intense experiences of narrative empathy may be attributed to the simultaneous (or rapidly interchanging) invitations of an immersive fictional world: its compelling existents; the entrancing voice of the narrator; the impulsions of narrativity; its stylistic foregrounding of wrought language; and the reader's self-recognition in, or rapport with, the implied author or implied reader' (Keen 2024: 351). In repeating this contention about the multiplicity of pathways to emotionally resonant reading experiences, I note parallel arguments about readers' potential affective or attentional engagement: with multiple characters, not just protagonists or focalisers (Schneider 2013, and this volume); with narrators and multiple aspects of narrative situation (Popova 2015); as a result of narrative omniscience (Ryan 2001); with space-time coordinates of place (Ryan 2001); and with the overt structures of storytelling (Herman 2013). The complexities obviate simple causal claims and should inspire careful experimental design in the future.

For despite its centrality to both narrative understanding and immersed engagement, transportation should not be oversold as the basis for all experiences of narrative empathy. Finer-grained accounts of the interactions of diverse readers' responses to a variety of formal cues in narrative are needed. (For attempts to tie readerly immersion to specific linguistic features, see Adam, Cooper, and Mason, all this volume.) It would be rewarding to discover not only how transportation interacts with other lower-order constructs of interpersonal empathy (some already demonstrably related, though not inevitable), but also how the complex of readers' responses to narrative involve, respond to, or stimulate transportation.

The trouble with scales (of value)

Because transportation into a narrative world is positively associated with diverse forms of narrative impact, it has been perennially linked to empathy – but to which constructs of the multidimensional phenomenon? Transportation has occasionally been studied without specifying 'empathy': for example, Hsu and colleagues use physiological measures to show how haemodynamic response in the mid-cingulate cortex correlates with transported reading of *Harry Potter* novels (Hsu et al. 2014). (Jacobs and Lüdtke (2017) provide a thorough review of experimental studies.) Empathy is never very far away when studying transportation, because of its emotional component. Pianzola et al. (2021) propose a predictive-processing model of narrative absorption, defined as a 'subjective-phenomenal state that can emerge during narrative experiences and that is characterised by a heightened sense of focused attention, transportation into the fictional world, emotional engagement with characters, and activated mental imagery' (Pianzola et al. 2021: 5 of 37). Empathy constructs come into this model through perspective-taking and the resultant interoceptive attunement of character and reader (Kukkonen 2019), both of which contribute to a sense of social presence. Melanie Green and Timothy Brock devised a scale to measure self-reported levels of transportation, defining it as: 'an integrative melding of attention, imagery, and feelings, focused on story events'

(Green and Brock 2000: 701), without directly invoking empathy constructs by name. Their focus is on aspects of mental visualising, attention, and plot engagement. In work augmenting Green and Brock's influential approach, Kuijpers et al. (2014) developed a Story World Absorption Scale (SWAS) that includes queries that invite reflection on perspective-taking, sympathy, and emotional congruence – all empathic constructs. A dispositional measure of trait transportability (Green 1996) has been used in the context of narrative persuasion to study the impact of emotional, empathic responses in contrast to rationalistic approaches (Mazzocco et al. 2010).

Alison Denham (2024) recently reviewed the interactions of transportation and empathy in a variety of studies, remarking on the overlap between the two: 'While most transportation theorists take it to denote a psychological event type distinct from empathy, even a cursory look at the self-report items on transportation scales and those on empathy measures such as the IRI [Davis 1980] suggest otherwise.' Denham is certainly correct that for many immersed readers, 'being transported by or absorbed in a narrative just *is* [. . .] a matter of resonating emotionally with its characters and events' (Denham 2024: 7), an observation that supports the idea that transportation is either a *cause* or a *kind* of empathy. They may *both* be expressions of high empathy individuals' temperaments reacting to environments that include narratives as well as other creatures, but chicken-and-egg problems crop up as soon as we start debriefing readers about their experiences. Denham calls for the distinguishing of 'the experience of transitioning into a narrative world' and empathic identification responses to characters, while recognising the common-sense conflation of the experiences. I agree that greater precision is called for.

Some trustworthy studies connect transportation with specific constructs of empathy mediated by reading. For example, Bal and Veltkamp (2013) show that higher degrees of emotional transportation into fiction corresponded with greater levels of compassion (as measured by Davis' IRI empathic concern subscale), while low level transportation in fiction reading led to lower expressions of compassion. In an experiment measuring empathy, prosocial behaviour, and perceptual bias towards fearful expressions, Dan R. Johnson demonstrated that higher degrees of transportation into a fiction, prompted by mental visualising exercises, correlated with subjects' enhanced compassionate responses. Future work in this arena should de-emphasise the general term empathy in favour of precise targets in both phenomena: transportation, emotional congruence, mimicry/synchrony, sympathy/compassion, personal distress, perspective-taking, accurate inference, and projection.

If we were to construct a scale of values for the various constructs of empathy, attending especially to experts with high hopes for the impact of empathy and reading, we might quibble about the details, but most would place *other-directed* varieties of empathic experience higher than *self-directed* constructs. (The perspective-taking of predators for their prey or the pleasures of sadists only occasionally trouble such ethical rankings.) Most theorists indebted to the moral sentimental tradition would place accurate inference about others' thoughts and feelings higher than self-directed personal distress, which tends to be aversive and makes you want to get away from the stimulus. Sympathy and compassion usually rate as more mature than motor mimicry or emotional contagion. The ascending values of types of empathic response can support a developmental model (e.g., Martin Hoffman 2000), with neonates capable of catching feelings through emotional contagion or birds flocking in motor mimicry, and adult humans maturely responding to victims of injustice by empathetically imagining their perspectives.

If, as is often the case in this tradition, the virtue of empathy is validated by ensuing altruism or prosocial action on behalf of others, the impulse to rank or prioritise its various manifestations by efficacy is understandable, though misguided. Transportation, especially when associated with escapist pleasure reading, would place low on such an ethical ranking of empathic constructs. Because transportation is strongly associated with pleasure and enjoyment (Hall and Bracken 2011), it receives a boost in worthiness when it is shown to invite emotional congruence or perspective-taking with suffering others. I have written elsewhere about how immersion reading has been criticised as wastefully eliciting expenditure of emotional responses for non-existent beings for centuries (Keen 2007: 45–7). In relation to discreditable enjoyment of narratives, characterised by immersed readers ignoring the real world around them in a trance of aesthetic absorption, transportation benefits reputationally from the proximity of empathy variants more closely associated with the inculcation of other-directed values: perspective-taking and compassion.

Conclusion

The intuition that getting lost in a book connects directly to identifying with a particular character's situation, even sharing the character's feelings, need not be cast away altogether, but we will better understand the relations between transported reading and emotional congruence or perspective-taking if we can distinguish them. If we are to grasp how fiction reading actually enriches readers' understanding and – potentially – extends the empathetic circle, we should approach transportation as already empathic in nature, but not automatically causally related to other constructs of empathy. We should avoid scales of value in discriminating among varieties of empathic reading: perspective-taking, or 'putting oneself in the shoes of another' should not rate more highly than the intensities of emotional congruence, mimicry, or distress. Transportation should neither be stigmatised as lazy or self-gratifying, nor sanctified as a path to other-orientation and righteousness.

While there are certainly better or worse readings at the level of comprehension, competent readers differ markedly in their inferences about particular fictional situations, filling gaps as they co-create. Readers' own memories, experiences, identities, and dispositions colour the fictional worlds that come to life temporarily as they read them. We should eschew value-laden judgements, both of readers who get lost in a book and also of readers who are *not* transported by ostensibly immersive fiction (potentially due to aphantasia; Zeman et al. 2016). To withhold judgement in this manner makes space to investigate the variations in readers' experiences with fiction, rather than setting up unrealistic expectations for the impact of a society's fiction-reading on the real world.

References

Bal, P.M. and Veltkamp, M. (2013) 'How does fiction reading influence empathy? An experimental investigation on the role of emotional transportation', *PLoS one* 8.1: e55341.

Batson, C.D. (2009) 'These things called empathy: eight related but distinct phenomena', in J. Decety and W. Ickes (eds) *The Social Neuroscience of Empathy*. Cambridge: The MIT Press, pp.3–15.

Bloom, P. (2016) *Against Empathy: The Case for Rational Compassion*. New York: Ecco.

Booth, W.C. (1983) *The Rhetoric of Fiction* (2nd edn). Chicago: University of Chicago Press.

Bortolussi, M. and Dixon, P. (2015) 'Transport: challenges to the metaphor', in L. Zunshine (ed.) *The Oxford Handbook of Cognitive Literary Studies*. New York: Oxford University Press, pp.525–40.

Busselle, R.W. and Bilandzic H. (2009) 'Measuring narrative engagement', *Media Psychology* 12 (4): 321–47.

Calarco, N., Fong, K., Rain, M. and Mar, R.A. (2017) 'Absorption in narrative fiction and its possible impact on social abilities', in F. Hakemulder, M.M. Kuijpers, E.S. Tan, K. Bálint and M.M. Doicaru (eds) *Narrative Absorption*. Amsterdam: Benjamins, pp.293–314.

Caracciolo, M. (2014) *The Experientiality of Narrative: An Enactivist Approach*. Berlin: de Gruyter.

Davis, M.H. (1980) 'A multidimensional approach to individual differences in empathy', *JSAS Catalog of Selected Documents in Psychology* 10: 85.

Davis, M.H. (1983) 'Measuring individual differences in empathy: evidence for a multidimensional approach', *Journal of Personality and Social Psychology* 44 (1): 113–26.

Davis, M. and Konrath, S., et al. (under submission) 'Mapping the empathy universe: toward a common lexicon of empathy-related constructs', *American Psychologist*.

Denham, A.E. (2024) 'Empathy & literature', *Emotion Review* 16 (2): 1–12.

Elfenbein, A. (2018) *The Gist of Reading*. Stanford: Stanford University Press.

Fitzgerald, K.S. and Green, M.C. (2017) 'Narrative persuasion: effects of transporting stories on attitudes, beliefs, and behaviors', in F. Hakemulder, M.M. Kuijpers, E.S. Tan, K. Bálint and M.M. Doicaru (eds) *Narrative Absorption*. Amsterdam: Benjamins, pp.49–68.

Ganczarek, J., Hünefeldt, T. and Olivetti Belardinelli, M. (2018) 'From 'Einfühlung' to empathy: exploring the relationship between aesthetic and interpersonal experience', *Cognitive Processing* 19 (2): 141–5.

Gerrig, R.J. (1993) *Experiencing Narrative Worlds: On the Psychological Activities of Reading*. New Haven: Yale University Press.

Green, M.C. (1996) *Mechanisms of Narrative-Based Belief Change* (unpublished master's thesis). Columbus: Ohio State University.

Green, M.C. and Brock, T. (2000) 'The role of transportation in the persuasiveness of public narratives', *Journal of Personality and Social Psychology* 79 (5): 701–21.

Green, M.C. and Brock, T. (2002) 'In the mind's eye: transportation imagery model of narrative persuasion', in M.C. Green, J.J. Strange and T. Brock (eds) *Narrative Impact: Social and Cognitive Foundations*. Mahwah: Lawrence Erlbaum, pp.315–41.

Hall, A.E. and Bracken, C.C. (2011) '"I really liked that movie": testing the relationship between trait empathy, transportation, perceived realism, and movie enjoyment', *Journal of Media Psychology* 23 (2): 90–9.

Hardy, T. (1909) *Time's Laughingstocks*. London: Macmillan.

Herman, D. (2002) *Story Logic. Problems and Possibilities of Narrative*. Lincoln: University of Nebraska Press.

Herman, D. (2009) *Basic Elements of Narrative*. Malden: Wiley-Blackwell.

Herman, D. (2013) *Storytelling and the Sciences of Mind*. Cambridge: The MIT Press.

Hoffman, M. (2000) *Empathy and Moral Development: Implications for Caring and Justice*. Cambridge: Cambridge University Press.

Hsu, C., Conrad, M. and Jacobs, A.M. (2014) 'Fiction feelings in Harry Potter: haemodynamic response in the mid-cingulate cortex correlates with immersive reading experience', *NeuroReport* 25 (17): 1356–61.

Irimiás, A, Mitellev, A.Z. and Michalkó, G. (2021) 'Narrative transportation and travel: the mediating role of escapism and immersion', *Tourism Management Perspectives* 38.

Jacobs, A.M. and Lüdtke, J. (2017) 'Immersion into narrative and poetic worlds: a neurocognitive poetics perspective', in F. Hakemulder, M.M. Kuijpers, E.S. Tan, K. Bálint and M.M. Doicaru (eds) *Narrative Absorption*. Amsterdam: Benjamins, pp.69–96.

Johnson, D.R. (2012) 'Transportation into a story increases empathy, prosocial behavior, and perceptual bias toward fearful expressions', *Personality and Individual Differences* 52: 150–5.

Keen, S. (2006) 'A theory of narrative empathy', *Narrative* 14 (3): 207–36.

Keen, S. (2007) *Empathy and the Novel*. Oxford: Oxford University Press.

Keen, S. (2013) 'Narrative empathy', in P. Hühn et al. (eds) *The Living Handbook of Narratology*. Hamburg: Hamburg University, available at <http://www.lhn.uni-hamburg.de/article/narrative-empathy>

Keen, S. (2024) 'Narrative empathy as animator of the inanimate', *Texas Studies in Literature and Language* 66 (4): 350–75.

Kuijpers, M.M. and Hakemulder, F. (2017) 'Narrative absorption: introduction and overview', in F. Hakemulder, M.M. Kuijpers, E.S. Tan, K. Bálint and M.M. Doicaru (eds) *Narrative Absorption*. Amsterdam: Benjamins, pp.1–9.

Kuijpers, M.M., Hakemulder, F., Tan, E.S. and Doicaru, M.M. (2014) 'Exploring absorbing reading experiences: developing and validating a self-report scale to measure story world absorption', *Scientific Study of Literature* 4 (1): 89–122.

Kukkonen, K. (2019) 'Exploring inner perceptions: interoception, literature, and mindfulness', *Journal of Consciousness Studies* 26 (11–12): 107–32.

Kuzmicova, A. (2012) 'Presence in the reading of literary narrative: a case for motor enactment', *Semiotica* 189: 23–48.
Lee, K.M. (2004) 'Presence, explicated', *Communication Theory* 14 (1): 27–50.
Lee, V. (1913) *The Beautiful: An Introduction to Psychological Aesthetics*. Cambridge: Cambridge University Press.
Lee, V. and Anstruther-Thomson, C. (1897) 'Beauty and ugliness', *Contemporary Review* 72: 544–69.
Matthews, A., Ridgeway, V. and Holmes, E. (2013) 'Feels like the real thing: imagery is both more realistic and emotional than verbal thought', *Cognition and Emotion* 27 (2): 217–29.
Mazzocco, P., Green, M., Sasota, J. and Jones, N. (2010). 'This story is not for everyone: transportability and narrative persuasion', *Social Psychological and Personality Science* 1 (4): 361–8.
Mill, J.S. (1897) 'What is poetry?' [1833], in J.W.M. Gibbs (ed.) *The Early Essays of John Stuart Mill*. London: George Bell and Sons, pp.201–17.
Nell, V. (1988) *Lost in a Book: The Psychology of Reading for Pleasure*. New Haven: Yale University Press.
Nomura, K. and Akai, S. (2012) 'Empathy with fictional stories: reconsideration of the fantasy scale of the Interpersonal Reactivity Index', *Psychological Reports* 110 (1): 304–14.
Phelan, J. (1996) *Narrative as Rhetoric*. Columbus: Ohio State University Press.
Pianzola, F., Riva, G., Kukkonen, K. and Mantovani, F. (2021) 'Presence, flow, and narrative absorption: an interdisciplinary theoretical exploration with a new spatiotemporal integrated model based on predictive processing', *Open Research Europe* 1 (28).
Popova, Y.B. (2015) *Stories, Meaning, and Experience: Narrativity and Enaction*. London: Routledge.
Rabinowitz, P.J. (1987) *Before Reading: Narrative Conventions and the Politics of Interpretation*. Ithaca: Cornell University Press.
Ryan, M.-L. (1991) *Possible Worlds, Artificial Intelligence, and Narrative Theory*. Bloomington: Indiana University Press.
Ryan, M.-L. (2001) *Narrative as Virtual Reality: Immersion and Interactivity in Literature and Electronic Media*. Baltimore: Johns Hopkins University Press.
Savitri, I. and Farah, K. (2021) 'The role of narrative format in increasing narrative transport and empathy for fiction and non-fiction readers', *Jurnal Psikologi* 20 (2): 152–62.
Schneider, R. (2013) 'The cognitive theory of character reception: an updated proposal', *Anglistik* 24 (2): 117–34.
Schneider, R. (2021) 'Time and the experience of narrative', in J. Alber and P. Wenzel (eds) *Introduction to Cognitive Narratology*. Trier: Wissenschaftlicher Verlag Trier, pp.95–117.
Stockwell, P. (2009) *Texture: A Cognitive Aesthetics of Reading*. Edinburgh: Edinburgh University Press.
Titchener, E.B. (1909) *Experimental Psychology of the Thought Processes*. London: Macmillan.
Wild, T.C., Kuiken, D. and Schopflocher, D. (1995) 'The role of absorption in experiential involvement', *Journal of Personality and Social Psychology* 69 (3): 569–79.
Wojciehowski, H.C. and Gallese, V. (2011) 'How stories make us feel: toward an embodied narratology', *California Italian Studies* 2 (1): 1–35.

Zeman, A., Dewar, M. and Della Sala, S. (2016) 'Reflections on aphantasia', *Cortex* 74: 336–7.

Zunshine, L. (2014), 'Introduction to cognitive literary studies', in L. Zunshine (ed.) *The Oxford Handbook of Cognitive Literary Studies*. Oxford: Oxford University Press, pp.1–9.

Zwaan, R.A. (2004) 'The immersed experiencer: toward an embodied theory of language comprehension', *The Psychology of Learning and Motivation* 44: 35–62.

Zwaan, R.A. and Taylor, L. J. (2006) 'Seeing, acting, understanding: motor resonance in language comprehension', *Journal of Experimental Psychology* 135 (1): 1–11.

CHAPTER 4

From literary immersion to fission-fusion aesthetics

Miranda Anderson

In this chapter, Anderson draws on the notion of *fission-fusion*, originally from anthropology and ethology, and develops the concept in relation to literary reading and immersion. The term *fission-fusion* refers to the shifting capacity of all sorts of phenomena (including people, animals, and conceptual systems) to act autonomously or come together in an integrated group, as the situation demands. It is a useful extension and corrective to the notion of distributed cognition. Anderson explores the idea in relation to literature itself and literary engagement, suggesting in the end that immersion is too passive a metaphor for the experience of literary reading and literary aesthetics, and proposes that the fluxing and dynamic nature of fission-fusion is a useful way of thinking about the experience.

Literary immersion

What happens when we become *immersed* in a literary work? Literary immersion is commonly conceived of as ‘a state of forgetting language and losing oneself in the textual world’ (Ryan 2015: 136). Traditional notions are based on an either/or mode of understanding the mind’s engagement: it is *either* in a literary world *or* this one. Yet immersion heightens perceptions of the work, oneself and the world as aspects of the immersive process (Anderson and Iversen 2018). Recent scientific research invites an understanding of mind, self and world as *fission-fusion concepts, entities, and processes* (Anderson 2015a, 2023). Literary experiences, including immersive ones, are fission-fusion phenomena too. This chapter sets out scientific evidence combined with literary examples which illustrate the insights a fission-fusion perspective offers into the nature of literary experiences. Fission-fusion aesthetics has implications for how we do literary analysis and is a means of substantiating the value of literature, as well as helping us reflect on the use of the term *immersion*.

History of the term immersion and recent cognitive theories

The term *immersion* itself demonstrates the fission-fusion nature of concepts across time and cultures. It is entwined with understandings of mind-body-world relations and emerges from experience of moving from one element to another, air to water. Etymologically, the word derives from the Latin *immergere*, to dip, plunge (or merge) into, then begins appearing in fifteenth-century descriptions of baptism, believed to enable access to another world; it is a physical enactment of a spiritual transformation. Beliefs in fusibility and separability of mind and body are borne out of our capacities to think through our bodies and environments *and* for purely intellective flights. As well as emerging in theological notions of an immortal soul and brain-in-a-vat philosophical thought experiments, ideas about separability are mediated by aesthetic and technological forms of virtualisation. Our fission-fusion mind-body-world capacity enables, and influences understanding of, experiences of literary works, including their immersive qualities.

Renaissance notions of literary immersion emerge amidst wider concerns about human immersion in the world and conversely the extent to which the mind 'inserts and mingles its own nature with the nature of things' (Bacon 2000: 19; Anderson 2015a).

That human perceptions of the world are fictional was claimed as far back as Plato, while more recently cyberspace has been described as 'an extension of our age-old capacity and need to dwell in fiction' (Nusselder 2009: 53). Fictional literary realms act as supplements to our individual life spans and evolutionary inheritances, and are distinct forms of extension to our more general 'as if' stance to reality due to our recognition of literature's *intentional* fictionality (Anderson 2015b, Anderson and Iversen 2018). These correlations and distinctions between modes of processing factual, counterfactual, and fictional realms provide a foundation for understanding the nature and value of literary experiences, including those thought of as immersive.

While imagining of any world necessarily deploys our understandings of being human in the world and our modes of processing this, such that factual, counterfactual, and fictional realms necessarily overlap and are entwined, this need not lead to positing 'minimal departure' (Ryan 2013) – the purpose of fiction is the space for play it opens through divergences as well as continuities. A distinction is that fictional literary works tend to present themselves as fictional (even while framing narratives may simultaneously evoke real-world continuities); this means that a wider range of divergences from our existing reality are less likely to impede imaginative flights, with different genres facilitating ease of immersion in different trajectories. At the same time, because imaginative play is enabled in ongoing ways by readers' bodies and environments, even when aided by literary works it has constraints. Literature itself highlights these connections and constraints: in *Richard II* when Bolingbroke's father implores that he uses his imagination as a mediatory measure against grief, Bolingbroke protests as to the limits of the imagination to transform experiences, scathingly asking who can 'wallow naked in December snow / By thinking on fantastic summer's heat?' (Shakespeare 2002: 1.3.298–9).

Fission-fusion recalibrations

The term I have adopted, *fission-fusion*, builds on distributed cognition and critical cultural theories. Distributed cognition is an umbrella term for the various overlapping and sometimes competing theories also frequently termed 4E cognition: embodied, embedded, extended, and enactive cognition (Anderson et al. 2018–20, Newen et al. 2018). 4E accounts of mind have increased awareness of the cognitive roles of embodiment and environments, yet they can also display a naïve optimism, tending to present the distribution of cognition as beneficial and in computational problem-solving terms, rather than realising the extent of the negative aspects and ethical issues that can arise (such as fascist groupthink, devaluation of sentience, systemic regimentation, and merely financial instrumentalisation), or the significance of the capacity for separability and distinctness. The emergence of distributed cognition from classical AI and functionalist concepts of 'the brain as a computer', or the 'mind as abstractable into information processes' (Turing 1950, Clark and Chalmers 1998, Chalmers 2022), is echoed by cultural theories' virtualisation of the mind and self as merely the product of sociocultural forces. Despite this, cultural theories help to foreground anxiety about a fragmentation of self, a sense of lack in representational systems and of loss of access to reality that persist alongside celebratory accounts of human cognitive distribution throughout human history. Fission-fusion encompasses the celebratory and troubled accounts of distributed cognition, and of cognitive, epistemological, and ontological separability and distinctions that emerge conceptually in, and shape the creation and interpretation of, literature (Anderson 2015a, Anderson et al. 2018–20).

Fission-fusion, a scientific term for the division of a nucleus or merging of nuclei, is also used by ethology to describe dynamic social networks that periodically merge together and divide to optimise performance of activities (Aureli et al. 2008). I initially reapplied fission-fusion to cognition, to capture the flexible and shifting nature of the cognitive clusters which constitute features of the mind across a range of temporal and spatial scales (Anderson 2015a), before expanding my use to encompass our understanding of any entity or process (Anderson 2023).

A dynamic multiplicity of factors come together to compose a mind or self at any one point in time, with experience being an evolving array of intermingling constellations, across which consciousnesses play. An instantiation of any entity or process can be composed of aspects of my brain, body, or the world, and may at times be composed by different constellations of these. So, for example, a constellation of internal and external phenomena may produce an experience of pain, though the particular nature of the composition may only be of import in certain cases, for example, in relation to ethical accountability. Each constellation resonates with or is dissonant to varying degrees with aspects of other entities. Our reformulatory capacity enables ongoing *interconnections* with and *disconnections* from aspects of others and the world. That we are neither merely separated off from one another nor form a continuous amalgam avoids the extreme of our operating either in solipsistic isolation or as an undifferentiated mass.

As with distributed cognition, fission-fusion is not merely epistemological but ontological, pervading the nature of being in the world. Fission-fusion's wider bearing is supported by the affinities it holds with a range of other theories that have arisen across the disciplines in recent decades, including Kimberlé Crenshaw's (1989) 'intersectionality', which emerged from the double marginalisation suffered by black women in legal systems, physicist Karen Barad's (2007) 'agential realism', which highlights the unceasing flux of entities, and Michaela Massimi's (2023) 'perspectival realism' in the field of philosophy of science, which examines the situated nature of our access to reality.

The multidisciplinary and cross-societal evidence for fission-fusion approaches substantiates this new theoretical approach to analysing literary and other art experiences, including immersive ones, and provides a basis for the value of literature and other arts.

Imaginative exercise

To understand what literary works do to our imaginations, we first need to understand the imagination. Try imagining the view from your window without looking out of it, or another scene close by but not in your current gaze range, close your eyes and keep them closed for a few moments. Imaginings tend to morph and mutate as we attempt to feel our way into their details. Now look out the window at chosen scene. Which is more detailed? A presumption that people experience more detail through actual world perceptual forays is a reason often given for imagination's inferiority to real life experience; Hume, for example, describes the imagination as 'weak and imperfect' (1739–40: 1.3.10.10). A rendering of 'imperfect' as unfinished invites another thought experiment. Close your eyes: imagine the view again, but this time consciously alter some aspect of it. Imagining this for most people is easier and faster than changing actual environments, hence this open-ended free play of our capacity to imagine can be beneficial: the ability to imagine the world as other than it is opens up potential for change. Artworks then supplement this special capacity of the imagination through what I have termed 'spooky cognition'.

Case study: spooky cognition in Douglas Dunn's 'Loch Music'

Artworks act as imagination enriching companions rendering us in realms beyond the constraints of our unaided imaginations, by supplementing our prior thoughts, with the experiences and perspectives of other people, places, and times. Our engagements with artworks, as with the world, involve shifting weightings across cognitive constellations rather than the either/or dynamic of conventional notions of immersion. In a poem called 'Loch Music', Douglas Dunn (1981) evokes an imagining of a loch and then a moor that his listening to Bach prompts:

> I listen as recorded Bach
> Restates the rhythms of a loch.
> Through blends of dusk and dragonflies
> A music settles on my eyes
> Until I hear the living moors,
> Sunk stones and shadowed conifers,
> And what I hear is what I see,
> A summer night's divinity.
> And I am not administered
> Tonight, but feel my life transferred
> Beyond the realm of where I am
> Into a personal extreme,
> As on my wrist, my eager pulse
> Counts out the blood of someone else.

As Bach's music transports Dunn, he embodies in his blood's beatings Bach's rhythms, a pulsing liberation from the constraints of daily existence. If described merely as immersion in a conventional sense, the implication is that Dunn is transported by Bach, and we by Dunn, to the evoked landscape. However, as Dunn himself writes, Bach's pulse composed into music is translated into Dunn's physical pulse, which then through the poem is translated into our own pulse's rhythms. Both music and poem mediate fission-fusions of conceptual associations and embodied consciousness with those of others manifested in the artworks. This is cognition at a distance, a spooky cognition to which we are so accustomed that we oft are unaware of it: the special human capacity to take intellective flights through the soaring of our own imaginations and through being borne aloft and metamorphosed by others' aesthetic endeavours. Quantum theory's 'spooky action at a distance' overturns standard physics concepts of 'locality' by positing that previously entangled particles can instantly influence each other regardless of distance (Rauch et al. 2018). Spooky cognition operates across time and space too, as artworks remain open to each unique engagement and simultaneously metamorphose us, through those same underpinning parameters: our capacity to resonate with aspects of other forms of existence, living or long dead, which is based in the entanglement of the particles that compose our constellations.

This metamorphosis is also analysable on the neurological level. The rich array of associations conjured in your mind as you read the poem were also borne out of your episodic memory. The same neural processes are applied to our own real lives and to imagining. Autobiographical memories enable us not only to recall our past, comprehend the present, and anticipate the future, but also to imagine fictional scenarios (Hassabis et al. 2007, Mullally et al. 2012). In the process the memories are recalibrated, as through their activation in concert with the literary works, a revitalising opening out of the arrays of associations occurs. Our experience of literary works therefore contains aspects particular to ourselves, as well as ones shared with other people. And as our cognitive horizons are thereby widened and made more flexible, enrichment of our imaginations entails enrichment of our selves. The ways in which literature and the arts expand the scope of our experiences in the world through building on our own life experiences and those instantiated in our bodies and environments explain three central puzzles about them: how they can evoke emotional responses and be morally persuasive, while there also remain limitations on what we can imagine (Anderson 2023). Thus, the fission-fusion nature of literary experiences, including immersive ones, are activated by entanglement, cognitive capacities, and – as discussed further in the following sections – specific features of literary works.

Literary language

The question of what constitutes a literary work or literary language has long been a topic of debate; as with the debate around the nature of the mind, I argue that this is due to its polythetic nature. Nonetheless, certain features can be foregrounded as being more pervasive to literary works. In *Uses of Literature* Rita Felski points out that 'language is not a hurdle to be vaulted over in the pursuit of pleasure, but the essential means of achieving it' (2008: 63). She continues that: 'We need only think of those moments when a reader, on opening a book, is drawn in by a cadence of tone, by particular inflections and verbal rhythms, by an irresistible combination of word choice and syntax' (63). Literary language's supplementation of our imaginative capacities is evident in distinctions between perceptual processing of mundane versus vivid language. While there is oft a discrepancy between brain regions activated by perception and mental imagery, when imagery is sufficiently rich and detailed, even early regions of activation are activated as they would be by actual perception, creating an iconic image of the absent percept as they would were it present. More generally, a wide array of cognitive scientific research shows that capacities such as motor resonance, mirror neurons, aspects of embodiment, and sociocultural phenomena enable experiential fusions across people (Anderson 2015b). On the one *hand*, commonalities grounded in shared features of embodiment lead to the easiness with which we can understand clichés. On the other *hand*, differences in bodies and wider environments can lead to diverse concepts, experiences, and readings of world and works. Divergences between our evolutionary and developmental histories and those of others, or between our own past and current states, generate fissions in our sense of what is salient in the world, our selves, and in literary works, with literary works themselves also developing our future perceptions of saliency (Anderson 2022). Daniel Casasanto and Gary Lupyan (2015) use the term 'ad hoc' to describe the linguistic conceptual flexibility that accommodates the complexities of word meanings across users and domains; their theory is yet another expression in another discipline of the fission-fusion nature of existence and our understandings of it. Fission-fusion creates a basis for understanding continuities and divergences between our readings of literary works, and the validity and value of both.

Literature itself, as with all our concepts, is a fission-fusion category. Literary works take diverse forms – including oral storytelling, manuscripts, books, audibles, graphic novels, plays, films, and sometimes even games – with which people merge and then emerge with more or less recalibrated beliefs and behaviour. As well as some literary forms using real or substitute physical domains, stylistic devices supplement the kinds of cues oft provided by physical context, taking advantage of their liberation from it. A frequent feature of literary texts, particularly poetic ones, is a recurrent use of *weak* implicatures that cause one to range widely around one's mind to make sense of a word (Wilson 2011), whereas with the strong implicatures of everyday language one oft lands more immediately on meanings – an example of the latter is saying 'it is getting cold' in the context of your being next to an open window (see Pinker 2007).

Hume's critique of imagining can again be positively recast: qualities of the imagination that are perceived as 'weak' are actually its strength, and the imagination's ability to be *diffuse* and *flickering* in quality is mimicked by literary devices. Our hypotheses of words' associations accrue a reinvigorated, deepened, and widened conceptual scope through this process too. Weak implicatures also open more space for us to bring our own thoughts and experiences to a poem, while the author via a range of literary devices nudges the reader to the meaning they intend.

The oft polyvalent nature of literary language, which leaves words particularly open to multiple interpretations, assists in widening readers' conceptual range. To illustrate this, let us try another imaginative exercise. Imagine yourself on a bus journeying into the night, and looking out the window:

> On the left, a red light
> swims through the dark:

a ship's port lantern.
Two rubber boots show,
illuminated, solemn.
A dog gives one bark. [. . .]

Moonlight as we enter
the New Brunswick woods,
hairy, scratchy, splintery;
moonlight and mist
caught in them like lamb's wool
on bushes in a pasture.

For a minute, like the mist and moonlight caught like lamb's wool in the branches, our minds were caught up by these words, from Elizabeth Bishop's poem 'The Moose' (2010: 153). The evocation of the combined mist and moonlight's qualities through the simile of the lamb's wool caught in trees, render a wonderous experience more substantial, while simultaneously the commonplace is rendered mystical. Both are transfigured in the process regardless of whether they are target or source of poetic comparison. Poetic language oft uses what Elaine Scarry (1999: 89–99) has termed 'rarity', where something rare and nebulous is made more vivid through comparison with something more substantial. In the earlier verse, the seemingly uncanny is revealed to be a commonplace: 'a red light swims through the dark' that is then recognised, rendered more definitely as simply 'a ship's port lantern'. Then more humorously in their incongruity the uncanny returns as 'Two rubber boots show, / illuminated, solemn', on which the only pronouncement is that of the dog's singular bark. Such shiftings of perspective, through literature's immersing us in worlds beyond our lived realities, can help us make a case for its relevance as a mode of decolonising our minds, as discussed in the next section.

Freedom of thought

Through such recalibrations, which expand our capacity to imagine other minds, worlds, and ways of being, literary works widen our degrees of freedom of thought. Without freedom of thought, neither freedom of speech nor of any other kind is possible. Angela Carter describes new modes of fiction, and fiction written as a woman, as modes of 'decolonising our language and our basic habits of thought' by creating 'means of expression for an infinitely greater variety of experience' (1997: 42). This has ethical consequences; rather than merely instructing people how to behave, Carter believed that by 'nudging at the edges of possible experience' fiction can 'reflect' and 'precipitate changes' (1997: 34). She adds that 'the reader is doing a lot of the work, reading a book is in a sense a recreation of it' (1997: 37). This notion of how fiction can work, by feeling its way into and beyond the edges of the known, and through a collaboration between writer and reader, suggests its ability to contribute to the creation of more critical, creative, and compassionate thinkers. These capacities are necessary in order to engage ethically with ever-evolving ideas and environments and resist the mind-shackling nature of mere observance to current ethical norms.

Aesthetic structures can take us beyond the entrenched narratives instantiated by our contemporary lifeworlds, making new modes of thinking and being possible. This opening out occurs and is evident across the personal and subpersonal levels. It relates to what occurs through social play in the young, which leads to more developed prefrontal cortexes, which are correlated with appropriate behavioural adaptivity, emotional development, creativity, and cognitive flexibility (Bell et al. 2010, Woolston 2021). Social play produces a dopamine surge (Vanderschuren et al. 2016): the significance of the surge in this neuromodulator associated with the brain reward system can be better understood in relation to research that suggests a *distribution* of value. Rather than 'a single mean' being anticipated, a dopamine *array* represents 'multiple future outcomes simultaneously and in parallel', with this weighted probability distribution recalibrated through each successive engagement (Dabney et al. 2020: 671). Combining these neuroscientific studies on social play and on value distribution affords insights into the importance of the diverse modes of playfulness that literature and the arts enable, supporting the intuitions of those working in the arts, such as Theocharis Raptis (2022: 100), who argues that the 'arts undertaken by adults perform the function of play and can prepare people for friendship and for their political and ethical life'. Playfulness is both an aspect of and an outcome of engagement with literary language, as discussed above. Other features such as functional shift lead to the emergence of new word forms, e.g., 'godded' (Shakespeare 1990: 5.3.11); such linguistic creativity, here through noun turned verb, creates new apprehensions of existence. The longer processing times and heightened cognitive activity observed in processing literary language also indicate its recalibrative nature (Davis 2007, Anderson 2018).

Literary works also deepen and strengthen freedom of thought, because they display and immerse us in situations and roles; this includes 'a *library of agencies*' which we can use 'to grow', as C. Thi Nguyen describes in his analysis of game playing (2020: 22). Nyugen presents the developmental potential offered by games as arising through encounters with unfamiliar agential modes and through a conscious narrowing and widening of them: playing immerses us in a 'narrowed evaluative attitude' with a 'narrow goal', which we may then shift out of into a more 'open-ended, sensitive' reflection (2020: 18–19, 221). Scope-narrowing in our real-life roles can be practically helpful to focus behaviours, as Nyugen observes; however it must be combined with 'agential fluidity'; development of the capacity to shift between self-aware narrowing to more subtle and complex agential modes, he adds, is a potentially positive outcome of gameplaying. A similar flexing between agential modes occurs in our literary fission-fusions, though literary works instead tend to explore the complexities and nuances of multiple value systems operating in concert. Games have fixed rules but are open-ended in terms of the outcomes; the openness in literary works is in the extent of fission-fusion sense-making that emerges via the reader's fleshing out of the literary works. Nyugen (2020: 12) describes 'a special experience of harmony between their abilities and the challenges of the world' as arising in gameplayers; this is comparable with conventional notions of literary immersion as involving a flow state. While flow has long been thought of as a no-thought state (Csikszentmihalyi 1990), it is now argued that flow states combine mastery of the basic practical dimensions and consequent liberation of the mind for more refined and complex engagements with the act in process (Montero 2016, see Currie, this volume). Immersion itself is a fission-fusion category: some forms are merely habitual, providing forms of cognitive shorthand for the performance of certain roles or activities which immediately minimise cognitive effort, and more formulaic works of literature are intellectual equivalents to the variously reassuring or tedious patterns and cycles of repetitive forms of daily life. More usually, a vicarious sense of knowledge and aptitude (sometimes revealed to be misplaced) is offered by a literary work, which enables free play of the reader's imagination as it mentally brings to life the literary work's imaginative scaffolding. Nyugen's (2020: 1–2) description of other art forms as 'recordings' implies their relative passivity, as do conventional notions of literary immersion, yet through their playing out across our minds and selves literary works generate a hybrid liveliness and polyvalency.

Players taking on of game world values Nguyen terms 'value capture', but this phenomenon might better be hybridly termed 'fission-fusion values' since, as with people reading texts, if game roles did not resonate with some aspect of a player's own beliefs and behaviours no engagement would be possible. The rationale for fission-fusion values in gameplaying or literary experience can be developed by considering its relation to the dopamine array research. While repetitive prior experiences instigate rule-following beliefs and behaviour, entrenching the weighting of certain future predictions and narrowing our cognitive range, unexpected and heightened psychological experiences of all kinds, including wonder, joy, surprise, horror, and tragedy, widen our experiential repertoires. On a subpersonal level, artworks generate a reweighting and opening out of our distributed dopamine arrays, enabling more imaginative, complex, and nuanced future predictions without involving the complexities and dangers of real-life encounters with extreme (or cognitively burdensome) phenomena (Anderson 2022). Hence a relatively safe developmental potential is offered by literary works (and gameplaying); this can counteract and supplement adults increasing resistance to imaginary play, which is oft increasingly 'administered' and co-opted by a mass of assumed roles constraining us into stagnant amalgams. As we have seen, literary techniques catalyse affective, perceptual, and intellectual imaginings beyond our everyday narratives.

These diverse strands of research together substantiate the value of engagement with literature and the arts. Another instance of the ameliorative potential of this fission-fusion dynamic is illustrated by Augusto Boal's (2022) discussion of how actors can make use of emotions by disentangling them from the intense yet narrow sphere of their personal narratives and redeploying them as a source of a character's beliefs and behaviours. Such modes of acting dynamically widen the narrowing of experiential horizons: the entrenching of emotions that occurs through their reiterative circling instead spirals open through the newly recast playing out of the emotional resonances, as not only the actors but also the spectators reverberate with the chords of another's story.

Aesthetics and ethics

Literary immersion is a means of counteracting and enriching our more general immersion in our day-to-day lives, and of developing our ethical capacities through the engaging of our minds and morals in fictional realms. Aesthetics and ethics cannot be collapsed into one another, yet the pulse that enlivens a work rendering it aesthetic rather than boring by its nature has an affective power and tends towards an increasing of cognitive reflection, reach, and flexibility, and this in turn tends to virtue. Thinking beyond the rational, the self, and the human, and moving towards the wider circuits and deeper currents that generate surface-level dynamics, artworks enable us to extend our minds beyond our current reality, to conceive distant and different realities and minds, and so to recognise our own world and selves anew.

Due to our enduringly fission-fusion composition, we have the capacity not only to resonate with aspects of other humans, but also with other living creatures and entities in this and imagined worlds. Richard Powers' *The Overstory*, itself a fission-fusion interweaving of narratives, shifts between attempts to evoke the apprehensions of humans, trees, and other life forms, in the process placing in question the species' chauvinism and narrow parameters conventionally used to define intelligence. He attempts to communicate apprehensions of other forms of intelligence, such as that of an ant colony: 'The colony possesses something; Adam doesn't know what to call it. Purpose. Will. A kind of awareness – something so different from human intelligence that intelligence thinks it's nothing' (Powers 2018: 67). Elsewhere, both through the novel's content and style, we are extended beyond a short-term mentality into the epic span manifested in the temporally and spatially extended lives of forests. This novel speaks to concerns over the limitations of John Rawls' (2005) theory of social justice, whereby the most fair and just world would be created by a human who does not know their role in it, such as their status or physical characteristics; Mark Rowlands (2008, 2016) extends this to encompass not knowing if one is human or not, while also questioning the social contract's limitations, the calculatory nature of which he argues can tend to zero-sum logic and deception, rather than heart-led love.

The cognitive flexibility that arises from playfulness and engagement with the arts helps to counteract this zero-sum logic and 'us and them' mentality along with our tendency to aggrandise ourselves and our own cultures. Such biases can occur when different cultures encounter one another, across national boundaries, within them, and on a one-to-one level (Nussbaum 2012). Our tendency to prioritise ourselves, or those close to us, above others can be a natural part of being able to survive in the world: such tendencies can be positive, affirming, and necessary, as well as manifesting in destructive ways involving prejudice, repression, and violence. At the same time, for us to exist as human beings at all it is necessary for us to hold on to the continuities that underlie such distinctions – interconnecting us all to each other and to the world. This is not merely metaphorical: just consider the accretion of physical, cultural, and social artefacts and environments that enable you to exist as the human being you are. The fission-fusion nature of our minds and selves can also help us accept or even celebrate our own mortality, given the resonances and regeneration of diverse aspects of ourselves across other people and entities. A vivid literary enactment of this fission-fusion phenomenon occurs in Shakespeare's *Sonnets* (1997). Each sonnet operates as an individually contained poem, as well as being dynamically interrelated to one another, as one self is to others, as words and images reappear across sequences, with their re-emergences igniting a shifting array of associations and indicating the open-natured reading of the work as a whole that is intended. Like 'the concord of well-tuned sounds' each string is 'sweet husband to another' and 'strikes each by each in mutual ordering' ('Sonnet 8'). What is required is the ability to shift between these modes, and literary fission-fusions help us develop awareness of and the capacity to shift our weightings across mind-self-world constellations.

Conclusion

Literature and other artworks of all kinds trace the development of the nature of human minds across time and space, and are part of the process through expressing and generating new ways of thinking and being in the world. Fission-fusion aesthetics is epistemological and ontological: it is based in scientific accounts of the merging and diverging of aspects of mind-self-world across time and space, and it resonates with ideas on the nature of knowledge and identity emerging in cultural theory.

Fission-fusion dynamics arise in the style and content of literary works, and provide a more nuanced mode of analysing our cognitive entanglements with them. Fission-fusion helps us understand how literature works and why it matters through clarifying continuities with and divergences from our processing of real, counterfactual, and literary worlds. Literary engagements offer imaginative scaffolding and alternative agential modes that limber up our dopamine arrays, expanding readers' freedom of thought and cognitive flexibility, while building on more general cognitive speculative stances and readers' embodied and experiential repertoires.

We and artworks are brought into flickering coexistences, at times with an intensity that is necessarily fleeting, and for which the term *immersion* may at times appear too passive, especially given that what is distinctive about our literary and other art experiences is our bringing of them to life and their revitalisation of us in the process. Literature expands our minds in ways that are not always possible to maintain when more caught up in the ongoing flux of our daily lives, with the many demands on attention and immediacy of requirements to function in the world. Nonetheless, literary works widen and deepen our experiential range not only in that moment but also in the future recalling, imagining and playing out of our lives. Disproportionate to the time spent in their vibrant spheres, literary works can act as lodestars amidst our constellations, qualitatively transforming our existences, and rendering them more meaningful and more full of wonder.

References

Anderson, M. (2015a) 'Fission-fusion cognition in Shakespearean drama: the case for *Julius Caesar*', *Narrative* 23 (2): 154–68.

Anderson, M. (2015b) *The Renaissance Mind*. Basingstoke: Palgrave Macmillan.

Anderson, M. (2018) 'Shakespeare and the mind', in C. Bourne and E. Caddick Bourne (eds) *The Routledge Companion to Shakespeare and Philosophy*. London: Routledge, pp.436–53.

Anderson, M. (2022) '4E cognition and the mind-expanding arts', *European Journal of Philosophy in Arts Education* 7 (2): 1–64.

Anderson, M. (2023) 'Developing the fission-fusion concept: a journey through the Arts, Humanities, Social Sciences and Natural Sciences'. The Centre for Science, Knowledge and Policy, University of Edinburgh.

Anderson, M. and S. Iversen (2018) 'Immersion and defamiliarization', *Poetics Today* 39 (3): 569–95.

Anderson, M., Wheeler, M. and Sprevak, M. (2018–20), 'Distributed cognition and the humanities', Volumes 1–4 in *The Edinburgh History of Distributed Cognition* Series. Edinburgh: Edinburgh University Press, pp.1–17.

Aureli, F., Schaffner, C.M., Boesch, C., Bearder, S.K., Call, J., Chapman, C.A., Connor, R., Di Fiore, A., Dunbar, R.I.M., Henzi, S.P., Holekamp, K., Korstjens, A.H., Layton, R., Lee, P., Lehmann, J., Manson, J.H., Ramos-Fernandez, G. Strier, K.B. and van

Schaik, C.P. (2008) 'Fission-fusion dynamics: new research frameworks', *Current Anthropology* 49 (4): 627–54.

Bacon, F. (2000) *The New Organon* (eds L. Jardine and M. Silverthorne). Cambridge: Cambridge University Press.

Barad, K. (2007) *Meeting the Universe Halfway: The Entanglement of Matter and Meaning*. Durham: Duke University of Press.

Bell, H.C., Pellis, S.M. and Kolb, B. (2010) 'Juvenile peer play experience and the development of the orbitofrontal and medial prefrontal cortices', *Behavioural Brain Research* 207: 7–13.

Bishop, E. (2010) 'The moose', in *The Faber Book of Beasts*. London: Faber, pp.151–6.

Boal, A. (2022) *Games for Actors and Non-Actors* (trans. A. Jackson, 3rd edn). London: Routledge.

Carter, A. (1997) *Shaking a Leg: Journalism and Writings, The Collected Angela Carter* (ed. J. Uglow). London: Chatto & Windus.

Casasanto, D. and Lupyan, G. (2015) 'All concepts are ad hoc concepts', in E. Margolis and S. Laurence (eds) *The Conceptual Mind: New Directions in the Study of Concepts*. Cambridge: The MIT Press, pp.543–66.

Chalmers, D. (2022) *Reality +: Virtual Worlds and the Problem of Philosophy*. New York: Norton.

Clark, A. and Chalmers, D. (1998) 'The extended mind', *Analysis* 8 (1): 7–19.

Crenshaw, K. (1989) 'Demarginalizing the intersection of race and sex: a black feminist critique of antidiscrimination doctrine, feminist theory and antiracist politics', *University of Chicago Legal Forum* 1: 139–68.

Csikszentmihalyi, M. (1990) *Flow: The Psychology of Optimal Experience*. New York: Harper and Row.

Dabney, W., Kurth-Nelson, Z., Uchida, N., Starkweather, C.K., Hassabis, D., Munos, R. and Botvinick, M. (2020) 'A distributional code for value in dopamine-based reinforcement learning', *Nature* 577: 671–5.

Davis, P. (2007) *Shakespeare Thinking*. London: Continuum.

Dunn, D. (1981) 'Loch music', in *St Kilda's Parliament*. London: Faber.

Felski, R. (2008) *Uses of Literature*. Oxford: Blackwell.

Hassabis, D., Kumaran, D., Vann, S.D. and Maguire, E.A. (2007) 'Patients with hippocampal amnesia cannot imagine new experiences', *Proceedings of the National Academy of Sciences of the United States of America* 104 (5): 1726–31.

Hume, D. (1739–40) *A Treatise of Human Nature: Being an Attempt to Introduce the Experimental Method of Reasoning into Moral Subjects*. London: John Noon.

Massimi, M. (2023) *Perspectival Realism*. Oxford: Oxford University Press.

Montero, B.G. (2016) *Thought in Action: Expertise and the Conscious Mind*. Oxford: Oxford University Press.

Mullally, S.L., Intraub, H. and Maguire, E.A. (2012) 'Attenuated boundary extension produces a paradoxical memory advantage in amnesic patients', *Current Biology* 22 (4): 261–8.

Newen, A., De Bruin, L. and Gallagher, S. (eds) (2018) *The Oxford Handbook of 4E Cognition*. Oxford: Oxford University Press.

Nguyen, C.T. (2020) *Games: Agency as Art*. Oxford: Oxford University Press.

Nussbaum, M. (2012) *The New Religious Intolerance: Overcoming the Politics of Fear in an Anxious Age*. Cambridge: Harvard University Press.

Nusselder, A. (2009) *Interface Fantasy: A Lacanian Cyborg Ontology*. Cambridge: The MIT Press.

Pinker, S. (2007). *The Stuff of Thought: Language as a Window into Human Nature*. New York: Viking.

Powers, R. (2018) *The Overstory*. London: Penguin.

Raptis, T. (2022) 'Emotions in music education as an ethical issue', *European Journal of Philosophy in Arts Education* 1 (7): 38–61.

Rauch, D., Handsteiner, J., Hochrainer, A., Gallicchio, J., Friedman, A.S., Leung, C., Liu, B., Bulla, L. and Ecker, S. (2018) 'Cosmic bell test using random measurement settings from high-redshift quasars', *Physical Review Letters* 080403: 2–9.

Rawls, J. (2005) *A Theory of Justice* (rev. edn). Cambridge: Harvard University Press.

Rowlands, M. (2008) *The Philosopher and the Wolf: Lessons from the Wild on Love, Death and Happiness*. London: Granta.

Rowlands, M. (2016) *Memory and the Self: Phenomenology, Science and Autobiography*. Oxford: Oxford University Press.

Ryan, M.-L. (2013) 'Possible worlds', *The Living Handbook of Narratology*. Hamburg: Hamburg University Press, available at <https://www-archiv.fdm.uni-hamburg.de/lhn/node/54.html>

Ryan, M.-L. (2015) *Narrative as Virtual Reality: Immersion and Interactivity in Literature and Electronic Media* (rev. edn). Baltimore: Johns Hopkins University Press.

Scarry, E. (1999) *Dreaming by the Book*. New York: Farrar.

Shakespeare, W. (1990) *Coriolanus*. London: Arden.

Shakespeare, W. (1997) *Shakespeare's Sonnets*. London: Arden.

Shakespeare, W. (2002) *Richard II*. London: Arden.

Turing, A.M. (1950) 'Computing machinery and intelligence', *Mind* 49: 433–60.

Vanderschuren, L.J.M.J., Achterberg, E.J.M and Trezza, V. (2016) 'The neurobiology of social play and its rewarding value in rats', *Neuroscience Biobehavioural Review* 70: 86–105.

Wilson, D. (2011) 'Relevance and the interpretation of literary works', *UCL Working Papers in Linguistics* 23: 69–80.

Woolston, C. (2021) 'The puzzle of play', *The Mind*, available at <https://knowablemagazine.org/article/mind/2021/why-animals-play>

CHAPTER 5

The subliminal factors of immersion

Peter Stockwell

In this chapter, Stockwell proposes a set of principles that need to be involved for a reader to move from a state of subliminal engagement with a text to a state of conscious immersion. These are presented as five stages ranging from the effects at an immediate, local level of reading individual sentences, up through a process of grouping domains of feeling together, finally to arrive at an experiential threshold at which the conscious sense of immersion can be articulated. The model proposed is based on the text-linguistic framework of *macrostructures*. The discussion then takes as a case study Ray Bradbury's semi-autobiographical novel *Dandelion Wine*, a text which has been observed to be particularly immersive and evocative.

The emergent property of subliminality

Immersion in literary reading is the global affect that emerges as a result of a readerly encounter with an array of subliminal effects. While a reader might be aware of their own immersion, and recognise it after the fact, the local micro-features which constitute the overall feeling of immersion seem to remain at the subliminal level. This is true for readers reading 'naturally', rather than analytically or academically on the lookout for matters of style. Immersion is an overall, diffused impression that tends to be understood as a holistic experience, rather than as a set of particular stylistic features. How then can we map the process from textual patterns to the overall experience of immersion?

Subliminal effects are very hard to study directly, for the obvious reason that they are by definition at or below the level of conscious awareness. Reading a literary work involves local decoding and construal of all the textual features up to clause level, and then also clause-chaining, text linguistic matters of informativity and coherence, and narratological and discourse features of the reading. All of this is psychological work. Intuitively, the effects of a whole range of these features can produce a sense of, for example, pace, suspense, alienation, joy, inexorability, satisfaction, amusement, nostalgia, melancholy, urgency, anxiety, optimism, fear, aptness, foreboding, alienation, poignancy, bleakness, humour, and many other subjective impressions. Several of these effects are more or less global or local, some of them overlap, and some of them will shift from one to another in the course of a reading. The global experience of immersion may well be an accompanying condition for many of them. Immersion indeed often operates as a reinforcing or intensifying factor for several of these impressions.

Many of these impressions – particularly those listed above – have been explored stylistically, demonstrating that it is possible to specify and account for them systematically. This is because of the following facts:

- subliminal effects are text-driven;
- subliminal effects are diffused over stretches of text;
- subliminal effects are emergent;
- subliminal effects can be triggered by generalising individual propositions;
- subliminal effects are sustained by various resonance techniques to fix them in memory.

All of these claims rest cumulatively on the argument that there is often not a one-to-one correspondence between the denotational value of a single linguistic feature and the generation of a subliminal effect. For example, the first point here claims that effects are text-driven, rather than explicitly textually realised on an individual basis. An impression might be derived from the reader's own schemas of personal experiences, but the point of the claim here is that this impression will only come into play if it is cued up in some way by the text. This cueing might indeed be a denoted semantic reference, but it could also be a looser connotation or personal association which is picked up in the mind of the reader. Making this argument here reminds us that when we talk about subliminal effects in the context of literary reading, we are restricting the discussion to *salient* subliminal effects that might be recognised as such by a community of readers. Idiosyncratic and whimsical effects might well be a feature of an individual reading experience, but they must lie beyond the scope of being relevant to a discussion of literary reading. Indeed, readers generally seem perfectly capable of differentiating between impressions that are valid and those that are private and coincidental.

Further, the overall impression of a reading as it emerges into consciousness is claimed here to be a diffused and emergent effect. The global effect might be accumulated from many small instances during the reading, and where these instances are associated, or collective, or coherent with each other they are likely to resonate and persist in memory and consciousness. Altogether, these facts mean that subliminal effects are locally subconscious and globally affective, and one of the most important global effects is the feeling of immersion. Indeed, I would suggest that the mental work involved in the processing of these subliminal effects represents an investment from which the payoff is a feeling of immersion (see Stockwell 2009). It should be noted that immersiveness is not a feature that is experienced with every literary reading. Many texts never achieve immersion; some texts are immersive for some readers and not others; and some texts are generally regarded as being highly immersive.

Immersion has been explored under a variety of names, each with a slightly different emphasis, but all essentially addressing the same readerly phenomenon. The notion that some represented literary fictional worlds offer an experience of 'transportation' (Gerrig 1993, Green and Brock 2000, Schneider, this volume) was developed as an exploration of the 'self-implication' of identity and consciousness during literary reading (Kuiken et al. 2004, Miall and Kuiken 2002). Immersion has been described as being 'lost in a book' (Nell 1988), as 'imaginative recentring' (Ryan 1999, 2001), as 'aesthetic illusion' (Wolf 1998, 2004, 2017, see also Burwick and Pape 1990, Wolf et al. 2013), as 'absorption' (Hakemulder 2013), and as a modern cognitive poetic framing of Coleridge's (1817) sense of the 'willing suspension of disbelief' (see Gerrig and Rapp 2004, Stockwell 2020). The notion has been explored across a wide variety of discourse situations (Dyson 2009), including theatre (Dove 1994, Machon 2013, Gibbons 2014), children's literature (Arizpe and Smith 2015, Stockwell 2019a), dystopia (Norledge 2019), art (Grau 2003, Liptay and Dogramaci 2015), cinema (Bacon 2009), and especially videogaming (Sweetser and Wyeth 2005, Chen 2007, Cowley et al. 2008) and other screen technologies (Agarwal et al. 1997, Agarwal and Karahanna 2000, van Eck 2010), as well as hypertext fiction (Bell and Ensslin 2011).

Many of these cognitive psychological approaches draw on the work of Csikszentmihalyi (1990, 1996, 2014), which explores the feeling of 'cognitive flow' that is sometimes experienced while engaged in a focused task or pastime, such as non-novice driving, sport, videogaming, or any intense, absorbing activity (for a discussion of flow and autistic readers, see Currie, this volume). It is a feeling of involvement in the world you have engaged in, to the extent that consciousness of the actual world where your body remains physically is either completely distracted, or minimised to basic functions of attentiveness. There is a strong tradition of such empirical work that sets out to demonstrate the existence of immersion as an experience for readers (see Kuijpers et al. 2014, Hakemulder and Kuijpers 2017). In the light of the extensive research on the phenomenon, I take its existence as a given, articulated by readers as part of their impression of reading. The purpose of this chapter is to explore the processes by which different stylistic levels facilitate immersion itself.

In setting out these subliminal factors by which immersion is facilitated, we will be exploring the quality of the immersed world. An immersed world feels rich and textured, rather than a minimalistic set of descriptive propositions. It feels like there is an ambience to the world that is diffused across the senses, just as the actual world feels. And, because at a conscious level we still understand that even a highly immersive world is fictional, the experience of immersion maintains its trace of remarkability, such that it persists resonantly in the mind after the reading is completed.

From local to global effects

There is an existing model in text linguistics that theorises the processes involved in generating global interpretative effects (like immersion) from local features – in the work of van Dijk and Kintsch (1983), which builds on van Dijk's (1977, 1980) earlier work on 'macrostructures'. This approach aimed to model the means by which a reader of a work can derive an overall interpretation or impression from local textual features. The model was mainly concerned with meaningfulness, focusing on propositional semantic content. The factors that van Dijk (1980) proposed are expressed as 'macrorules' that convert local semantic features to global effects:

- First, a *zero-rule* operates to delete (that is, forget) incidental and non-significant individual items. This involves a necessary selection of relevant features, of course. Some of these items are retained in their totality, as *citation* from the source text into the overall interpretation. A reader, for example, might recall the specific phrasing or a complete quotation from the text. This citation is often regarded emblematically in the context of the work as a whole.
- Second, a process of *weak deletion* (called *local deletion* in van Dijk and Kintsch 1983) removes facts that seem to be only relevant locally, such as insignificant details of scenery, event or transient opinion. These matters of local colour are individually not part of the overall recall, though their accumulation might be represented collectively and generically.
- Third, a process of *strong deletion* (*global deletion*) is applied, where information that seemed initially relevant turns out towards the end of the reading not to be so important.
- Fourth, a process of *generalisation* is implemented, whereby a rich set of propositions are rendered into a summarising or encapsulating sense.
- Last, other information elements that are also generalisations but arise from wider sociocultural knowledge are built into the propositional macrostructure by a process of *construction*.

These macrorules for ultimately constructing the macrostructure from the textbase are essentially semantic in character, articulated as propositional meaning. They do not include emotional, ethical, or self-involving feelings that might be regarded as characterising a reading experience, unless those senses are directly expressed.

However, we can extend the usefulness and scope of the van Dijk approach by adapting the same set of process rules to draw out how subliminal patterns can build up to the diffused experience of immersion. In the rest of this chapter, I will outline the following processes that I propose constitute the dynamic mechanisms by which subliminal effects can be generated from text, with examples from a single evocative and immersive literary work:

- *Thematic zero* – where the effect is stated explicitly;
- *Cumulative assignment* – where effects are grouped into domains of feeling;
- *Sustained re-evocation* – enlarging and strengthening the domain;
- *Domain chaining* – connecting the reinforcing characteristics of domains;
- *Articulation threshold* – from subliminality to an awareness that immersion has happened.

Progressively, these delineate the experienced quality of the immersive world. The scheme suggested here tracks the heuristics of the readerly experience by which immersion occurs. Though the list outlined here is arranged from most local effect to most global effect, and this sequence is likely to align roughly with the sequence of reading a text, in fact, of course, local effects like thematic zero, cumulative assignment, and sustained re-evocation will be happening throughout a reading, right up until the last few sentences as well.

The literary work that appears as a case-study in this chapter is Ray Bradbury's (1957) autobiographically-influenced novel *Dandelion Wine*. I selected this text because many literary critics, reviewers, and ordinary readers expressing their opinions on social media have described it as immersive, evocative, resonant, and engaging (see, for example, Reid 2000, Diskin 2010, Eller 2011). The online reviews website Goodreads (2025a) currently has 72,490 ratings of the novel (all data measured from January 2025). Within these, there are 6,607 written reviews, and altogether the novel has received an average rating of 4.09 (out of 5). Reviewers here describe the novel as elegiac, poignant, nostalgic, and conveying the intensity of the texture of life. Most usefully, Goodreads (2025b) also lists 290 memorable quotations that these readers of *Dandelion Wine* consider the most interesting, pertinent, well-written, or simply *quotable*: these can be used as an index of the most resonant excerpts from the novel. In the outline that follows, all the quoted examples are drawn from this body of reader-selected quotations.

Thematic zero

The thematic zero is a direct effect, where the text states plainly and explicitly the feeling or information that is being conveyed. Zero-rule elements often thus have a proverbial flavour, and (as the Goodreads (2025b) data attests) are highly memorable. For example, the following three quotations appear within the top ten 'liked' excerpts from *Dandelion Wine*:

> 'I'm ALIVE. Thinking about it, noticing it, is new. You do things and don't watch. Then all of a sudden you look and see what you're doing and it's the first time, really.'

> 'I want to feel all there is to feel, he thought. Let me feel tired, now, let me feel tired. I mustn't forget, I'm alive, I know I'm alive, I mustn't forget it tonight or tomorrow or the day after that.'

> 'No person ever died that had a family.'

And the following is the twelfth most 'liked' by reviewers:

> 'No matter how hard you try to be what you once were, you can only be what you are here and now.'

Thematic zero effects like these are clearly striking, evocative, and resonant for readers. Such quotations tend to be short, memorable, aphoristic, or proverbial. Proverbial phrasing, as in the last two examples above, is typically framed in a universalising present tense, with a generic 'you', and a word-choice that tends towards abstraction or basic terms (*person, died, family, be*). The first two examples are less proverbial and generic, but they encapsulate directly the key theme of the novel: conveying the intense texture of what it is to feel alive.

Other characteristics of text that are likely to be treated as a thematic zero would be where the excerpt is memorable because of a poetic form, such as alliteration, rhyme, or a striking metaphor arising from a semantic clash, for example.

Cumulative assignment

In the second process, the counterpart of van Dijk (1980)'s *weak deletion*, a reader will subliminally recognise that the micro-effects arising from individual clauses are groupable. This necessarily involves blurring those similar expressions together, in order to assign a generic meaning to the group of expressions. In the following example from *Dandelion Wine*'s Goodreads (2025b) quotations, there is an accumulation of propositions that all circle around the topic of the seasons:

> 'It was the face of spring, it was the face of summer, it was the warmness of clover breath. Pomegranate glowed in her lips, and the noon sky in her eyes. To touch her face was that always new

> experience of opening your window one December morning, early, and putting out your hand to the first white cool powdering of snow that had come, silently, with no announcement, in the night. And all of this, this breath-warmness and plum-tenderness was held forever in one miracle of photographic is chemistry which no clock winds could blow upon to change one hour or one second; this fine first cool white snow would never melt, but live a thousand summers.
>
> That was the photograph; that was the way he knew her.'

The accumulation of sense is carried by the lexical choices: *spring, summer, December*, and also *warmness, cool, snow, melt*, alongside *clover, pomegranate, plum*, and of course *face, breath, lips, eyes, hand*. These – and associated words and phrases – assign a connected-up texture to a vague concept of sensually experienced seasonality. It is not likely that each individual phrase is recalled specifically, but together a sense of atmosphere is built up here, and accumulated into a single concept (for a detailed account of how lexical choices construct a subliminal sense of atmosphere, see Stockwell 2019b).

Similarly, in the following example, the concepts evoked by lexis such as *dust, furnace, warm, volcano, red-hot ashes, yellow, smoldering, combustion, hot, steam, baking, vapors, tar, red, bronze, lightning, blazing, threat*, and the *sun* all accumulate into an atmosphere of heat and fire that is diffused rather than specific:

> 'The sidewalks were haunted by dust ghosts all night as the furnace wind summoned them up, swung them about, and gentled them down in a warm spice on the lawns. Trees, shaken by the footsteps of late-night strollers, sifted avalanches of dust. From midnight on, it seemed a volcano beyond the town was showering red-hot ashes everywhere, crusting slumberless night watchmen and irritable dogs. Each house was a yellow attic smoldering with spontaneous combustion at three in the morning.
>
> Dawn, then, was a time where things changed element for element. Air ran like hot spring waters nowhere, with no sound. The lake was a quantity of steam very still and deep over valleys of fish and sand held baking under its serene vapors. Tar was poured licorice in the streets, red bricks were brass and gold, roof tops were paved with bronze. The high-tension wires were lightning held forever, blazing, a threat above the unslept houses.
>
> The cicadas sang louder and yet louder.
>
> The sun did not rise, it overflowed.'

Of course, the unremitting extended pattern that accumulates here also has its own reinforcing effect. The poetic reinforcement surely creates fullness and intensity in the texture. It is this diffused sense that is carried over into the readerly mental representation, I think.

Sustained re-evocation

So far, the stages of subliminal representation are local to the passages of text in focus. Of course, many of these local examples can then be connected together over longer extents of text. If sustained by constantly being re-evoked, then the re-evocation itself becomes a conceptual effect – a trope – that can be felt to characterise longer stretches of text. The repetition by re-evocation serves to create and reinforce a broader semantic domain, which is then repeatedly itself evoked (and is available for *chaining*, as outlined below). In *Dandelion Wine*, the re-evocation of the dandelion wine of the title stands as the central trope of the novel, and is emblematic of its immersive technique.

> 'And there, row upon row, with the soft gleam of flowers opened at morning, with the light of this June sun glowing through a faint skin of dust, would stand the dandelion wine. Peer through it at the wintry day – the snow melted to grass, the trees were reinhabitated with bird, leaf, and blossoms like a continent of butterflies breathing on the wind. And peering through, color sky from iron to blue.
>
> Hold summer in your hand, pour summer in a glass, a tiny glass of course, the smallest tingling sip for children; change the season in your veins by raising glass to lip and tilting summer in.'

The summer (in this instance, of 1928) is distilled in its senses and feelings in the dandelion wine, just as it is distilled for the reader to enact by immersion in the novel overall.

In this particular case, the re-evocation of dandelion wine as a distillation of summer is often accompanied by the lexical patterns in evidence in the passage above: choices from the natural world such as *flowers, morning, June sun, dandelion, wintry, snow, grass, trees, bird, leaf, blossoms, butterflies, wind, sky, blue*. This pattern of lexical choices reoccurs multiple times across the vignettes that constitute the novel. By this constant re-evocation, the texture of the world and its prose is sustained and refreshed, and that reinforces it cumulatively as an experienced concept in its own right. The level of sustained re-evocation is where the cohesive textual patterns in the text begin to be arrayed together to establish a sense of coherence (see Charolles 1983, Heydrich et al. 1989).

Domain chaining

The final macro-process at the subliminal level is domain chaining. The accumulated sustained tropes, images, concepts, and textures that have been grouped together across the novel are connected together for their coherence. This is a process that develops a sense of the thematics of the text. The domains are now semantic schemas that are diffused quite a long way out from the surface stylistic patterning itself.

In *Dandelion Wine*, the novel is arranged as a series of short vignettes in the life of Doug Spalding. There are no chapter breaks, though the episodes are separated by blank lines. Several of them were previously published as short stories. The oldest one, 'The Night', appeared originally in 1947, in the collection *Dark Carnival* (Bradbury 1947). The key stylistic feature of that original is that it is written in the second person (it begins, 'You are a child in a small town'), with Doug as the 'you', anxious about the lateness of his older brother Skipper. This is reworked in *Dandelion Wine* into the third person, with Doug now the elder and the anxiety focalised through his younger brother Tom. 'The Night' is highly immersive as a direct result of that involving second-person form: you the reader are directed in your thoughts and feelings just an instant before you have to transfer them to the character of Doug.

The act of connecting each related domain across the novel involves constructing thematic consistency by generalisation. It helps if the text provides these domains in ways that are readily coherent (as in the constantly re-evoked scenes, emotions, and episodes in *Dandelion Wine*), though of course incoherence can also be thematised as an apparent meaningful authorial choice (for example when reading postmodern or surrealist texts).

The key feature of this highest level of subliminal process is its generalisation. All of the accumulated local details, grouped together as collective concepts and textured experience, are generalised into an overall sense of the immersive quality of the world of the novel. In *Dandelion Wine*, the coherence across all the vignettes is neatly summarised directly near the end of the novel itself. Doug and Tom are looking at Grandfather's collection of bottles of dandelion wine:

> The two boys pointed along the rows of bottles.
> 'There's the first day of summer.'
> 'There's the new tennis shoes day.'
> 'Sure! And there's the Green Machine!'
> 'Buffalo dust and Ching Ling Soo!'
> 'The Tarot Witch! The Lonely One!'
> 'It's not really over,' said Tom. 'It'll never be over. I'll remember what happened on every day of this year, for ever.'

Each of these recalls a key vignette, re-evoked here for the benefit of the reader on the penultimate page. The dandelion wine in the bottles is a symbolic distillation of the essence of summer and the novel, summarised and generalised here almost at the end.

So far, these processes of thematic zero, cumulative assignment, sustained re-evocation, and domain chaining characterise the subliminal – that is, below the conscious level – of the operation of immersion. The final process, outlined below, is defined as the moment that a reader becomes aware of the feeling of immersion.

Articulation threshold

The experience of immersion involves all of the foregoing processes, from stylistic surface texture to a diffused generalised sense of the world of the literary work. A reader can feel immersed as an ongoing experience at a subliminal level, below the level of conscious self-reflective awareness. I maintain that a reader cannot simultaneously be immersed and at the same time be consciously aware of their own immersion – since awareness constitutes a break-out from the immersed world back into the actual world of their own life. Immersion, by definition for me, is an all-consuming sense.

However, the articulation threshold often occurs at or close to a point of readerly emergence. It is the point at which a reader is first able to articulate their sense that they have been immersed. Often, post-processing recognition and awareness lifts the subliminal micro-effects to a tangible general feeling. The final threshold is the point at which the accumulated array of subliminal effects emerges as a conscious, felt sense of immersion. At this point, the experience of immersion can be articulated and recognised explicitly. This is also the point at which a reader emerges from being immersed in the world of the text.

The final articulation threshold is the expression of the global holistic effect of the novel. In the case of *Dandelion Wine*, this articulation includes any responses that express the feelings of nostalgia, poignancy, excitement, and so on, that have been recognised by readers after they have finished reading. The end of the novel (or any immersive text) marks an emergence from the feeling of immersion. Strictly speaking, the contradictory opposite of immersion is non-immersion: the lack of any drawing in of consciousness in an encounter with a literary world. A literary work might not be immersive for a variety of reasons: non-immersive writing, either by incompetence or deliberate authorial choice; readerly resistance or lack of engagement or effort; readerly distraction, or simple non-disposition. Emergence is the contrary opposite of immersion: it presupposes that immersion has happened, and the reader's consciousness is returning to their actual world.

The reviews of *Dandelion Wine* (in Goodreads 2025a) represent readers who have retrospectively crossed this articulation threshold. They comment directly on their immersive experience (names of reviewers have been changed here so that they are not easily identifiable, though their chosen format has been preserved in the pseudonyms):

> And sometimes, we find those peculiar time machines that take us to somewhere special.
>
> (Syst3r, May 20th 2017)

> I was there immediately. I knew times when summer's arrival was marked by iced tea replacing coffee. Once every summer, when I was a child, my mother would make homemade ice cream. We would take turns turning the handle and wait for what seemed forever for it to set enough to be spooned out into bowls and devoured. Nothing you buy in a store even comes close.
>
> Ray Bradbury whisked me back to that world that I had left behind me for so long.
>
> (Sally, May 6th 2021)

> The descriptions and prose are mesmerising, you can almost smell, hear and see summer.
>
> (Joan, May 8th 2020)

> Bradbury's poetic prose flowed like a lazy river, expertly carrying me through this enchanting novel. If you haven't read *Dandelion Wine*, I highly recommend that you spend some time in small-town Illinois.
>
> (Kelly Shine, June 6th 2023)

These posts articulate the experience of immersion impressionistically, of course. They express the feeling of immersion in sensual terms, as well as in the contentful terms of memory, or of a recognition of something familiar from their own memories and experience. It is also notable that many entries evidencing the articulation threshold are dated to late spring or early summer (examples here from May and June are representative), perhaps an indication that Northern Hemisphere readers have aligned their own season on the cusp of summer with their reading experience. The articulation of immersion drawing on a transportation metaphor, as here, is very common (see Gerrig 1993, Stockwell 2009). Immersion is typically regarded as a removal of consciousness to a markedly different location in space (or metaphorically in the last example above, in time). These readers, looking retrospectively at their immersive experience, have emerged from the world of the text, but retain a resonant memory of it.

Emergence and immersion

My argument in this chapter has been that immersion is the surfacing product of all of this subliminal, text-initiated mental work. The steps set out are a simple system by which the unobservable process can be categorised. I do not make any claims as to its psychological nor neurological reality, beyond those established in the basic work drawn from van Dijk (1977, 1980, and with Kintsch 1983). Whatever the actual mental algorithms that operate in here, it is obvious that the processes set out in each of these steps must have been enacted at some point in some way, in order to arrive at an overall perceived sense or conscious impression of the quality of immersion. Readers experiencing immersion unquestionably construct a world in which to be immersed (see Werth 1999, Gavins 2007, and Gavins and Lahey 2015), and this world is rich, textured, ambient, and resonant in feeling, but no reader can recall every word, phrase, and pattern in the entire text. There must be a process of filtering, gathering, collective representation of feelings and concepts, and a generalisation of this experience into an overall sense of immersion. This is the framework that I have offered above. The question then arises as to what is the validity status of such an account. My proposal is that the pattern set out here corresponds with the actuality of the experience; this is a validity of outcome which invites your agreement as to whether it feels authentic to you.

However, I also think there is a heuristic validity in that the simple scheme offers a means of exploring the compositional factors of the mechanism of immersion. In other words, it offers an analytical tool for connecting stylistic texture to the felt experience of reading. In this chapter, I have tried to tease out the accumulated threads by which Bradbury in *Dandelion Wine* creates the opportunity for readerly immersion. I think the approach will work for any immersive reading of a text. Any successful immersion would need to involve all levels of these subliminal effects.

It should be noted that immersion might not always be an authorial objective of a text. Readers can become immersed in instruction manuals, cookery books, and even lectures. The fact that some literary works are particularly good at encouraging immersion should not obscure the fact that immersion is also dependent on readerly disposition. There are many examples of low-rated reviews in Goodreads (2025a) in which some readers complain that *Dandelion Wine* was, for them, boring, uninvolving, and a drag to read; many of these readers confess that they did not finish the book at all, as a result. It is safe to say that they were not immersed.

As I suggested above, non-immersion is the plain contradictory opposite of immersion. This is where immersion simply does not happen at all. However, all readings that are immersive eventually end with an emergence, a de-immersion in which the end of conscious attention returns from the fictional world to the actual physical world of the reader. Emergence accompanies the articulation threshold as outlined above, in that it coincides with a conscious recognition that immersion has been experienced. Where the immersion was powerful and resonant, the memory of the experience stays with a reader long after the book has been closed. (The difficulty of describing retrospective recognition in reading was set out in Stockwell (2021), with a suggested partial solution.)

Emergence is quicker than immersion. Or at least, it is in general, excluding situations where a reader is already highly disposed to be immersed and resents and resists the ultimate return in the ending to their own world. Although short narratives, lyric poems, music, and theatre can often immerse an audience swiftly (Wolf 1998), it is still a process that requires a few steps of distracting consciousness away from actuality. Initial immersion is more usually an elongated and gradual process of world-building. By contrast, immersion can be broken almost instantly (in the form of an external distraction back in the actual world), or by textual means. In metafiction, sometimes the 'fourth wall' of the text can be broken and the narrating author addresses the reader directly within the course of the reading (Macrae 2019, and Wydrzynska, this volume). However, all fictional literary worlds are eventually de-immersed on the final page.

In literary fiction, this point of emergence often cues back up the initial conditions of immersion. For example, novels that begin with an opening narratorial frame often close with an explicit return to that frame, and even have intermittent reminders of the framing narrative (this is true of Mary Shelley's *Frankenstein*, Emily Brontë's *Wuthering Heights*, Doris Lessing's *Shikasta*, for example, among many others). It is a common framing pattern in cinema: Orson Welles' *Citizen Kane*, Victor Fleming's *The Wizard of Oz*, Bryan Singer's *The Usual Suspects* are among very many examples of embedded narrative structures with such a coda.

Aside from creating perhaps a sense of neatness and closure, the re-evocation, at the end, of one of the initially immersive features represents a return to the thematic zero level of subliminal memory – a verbal callback from the opening. In *Dandelion Wine*, the novel begins with Douglas waking up at the start of summer, just before dawn, 'riding high in the June wind', 'as house lights winked slowly on', going out with his brother Tom and Grandfather to collect dandelions to make wine.

> Dandelion wine.
>
> The words were summer on the tongue. The wine was summer caught and stoppered.

The first section vignette ends with the memorable single-sentence paragraph: 'Summer 1928 began.'

Around 200 pages later, the novel ends with Douglas, Tom, and Grandfather 'stood, as they had stood three months, or was it three centuries, ago, on this front porch', as 'a sudden gust of wind turned cold', 'And the town winked out its lights.' Doug imagines everything running backwards, 'Like matinee films sometimes, where people jump out of water onto diving boards.' This image of the novel reversing back to the beginning is maintained in the ending:

> June dawns, July noons, August evenings over, finished, done, and gone forever with only the sense of it all left here in his head. Now, a whole autumn, a white winter, a cool and greening spring to figure sums and totals of summer past. And if he should forget, the dandelion wine stood in the cellar, numbered huge for each and every day.

> He would go there often, stare straight into the sun until he could stare no more, then close his eyes and consider the burned spots, the fleeting scars left dancing on his warm eyelids; arranging, rearranging each fire and reflection until the pattern was clear . . .
>
> So thinking, he slept.
>
> And, sleeping, put an end to Summer, 1928.

The dandelion wine that the characters have distilled all summer stands, finally, as the emblematic distillation both of the summer (in the immersed world experience of the reader) and of the novel itself as an object in the reader's actual world. The trope has been repeated throughout the text, and it is explicitly connected to the principal theme of the whole novel, here at the ending. Afterwards, the resonant texture of nostalgia, elegy, joy, and fear remains for the reader from the immersive experience. The novel thus iconistically enacts its own emergence just as directly as Doug's imagined matinee film that states, de-immersively, 'The End.'

References

Agarwal, R. and Karahanna, E. (2000) 'Time flies when you're having fun: cognitive absorption and beliefs about information technology usage', *MIS Quarterly* 24 (4): 665–94.

Agarwal, R., Sambamurthy, V. and Stair, R. (1997) 'Cognitive absorption and the adoption of new information technologies', in L. Dosier and J. Keys (eds) *Academy of Management Best Paper Proceedings*. Statesboro: Georgia Southern University, pp.293–7.

Arizpe, E. and Smith, V. (eds) (2015) *Children as Readers in Children's Literature: The Power of Texts and the Importance of Reading*. London: Routledge.

Bacon, H. (2009) 'Aesthetics and the experience of reexperience', in J.D. Anderson and B. Fisher (eds) *Narration and Spectatorship in Moving Images*. Newcastle: Cambridge Scholars, pp.260–76.

Bell, A. and Ensslin, A. (2011) '"I know what it was. You know what it was": second-person narration in hypertext fiction', *Narrative* 19 (3): 311–29.

Bradbury, R. (1947) *Dark Carnival*. Sauk City: Arkham House.

Bradbury, R. (1957) *Dandelion Wine*. London: Rupert Hart-Davis.

Burwick, F. and Pape, W. (eds) (1990) *Aesthetic Illusion: Theoretical and Historical Approaches*. Berlin: de Gruyter.

Charolles, M. (1983) 'Coherence as a principle in the interpretation of discourse', *Text* 3 (1): 71–97.

Chen, J. (2007) 'Flow in games (and everything else)', *Communications of the ACM* 50 (4): 31–4.

Coleridge, S.T. (1817) *Biographia Literaria*. London: Rest Fenner.

Cowley, B., Charles, D., Black, M. and Hickey, R. (2008) 'Toward an understanding of flow in video games', *Computers in Entertainment* 6 (2): 1–27.

Csikszentmihalyi, M. (1990) *Flow: The Psychology of Optimal Experience*. New York: Harper and Row.

Csikszentmihalyi, M. (1996) *Creativity: Flow and the Psychology of Discovery and Invention*. New York: Harper Perennial.

Csikszentmihalyi, M. (2014) *Flow and the Foundations of Positive Psychology: The Collected Works of Mihaly Csikszentmihalyi (Volume 2)*. Dordrecht: Springer.

Diskin, L. (2010) 'Bradbury on children', in H. Bloom (ed.) *Ray Bradbury*. New York: Bloom's Literary Criticism, pp.23–50.

Dove, T. (1994) 'Theater without actors – immersion and response in installation', *Leonardo* 27 (4): 281–7.

Dyson, F. (2009) *Sounding New Media. Immersion and Embodiment in the Arts and Culture*. Ewing: University of California Press.

Eller, J. (2011) *Becoming Ray Bradbury*. Champaign: University of Illinois Press.

Gavins, J. (2007) *Text World Theory: An Introduction*. Edinburgh: Edinburgh University Press.

Gavins, J. and Lahey, E. (eds) (2015) *World-Building: Discourse in the Mind*. London: Bloomsbury.

Gerrig, R. (1993) *Experiencing Narrative Worlds: On the Psychological Activities of Reading*. New Haven: Yale University Press.

Gerrig, R.J. and Rapp, D. (2004) 'Psychological processes underlying literary impact', *Poetics Today* 25 (2): 265–81.

Gibbons, A. (2014) 'Fictionality and ontology', in P. Stockwell and S. Whiteley (eds) *The Cambridge Handbook of Stylistics*. Cambridge: Cambridge University Press, pp.408–23.

Goodreads (2025a) 'Dandelion Wine by Ray Bradbury', *Goodreads*, available at <https://www.goodreads.com/book/show/50033.Dandelion_Wine>

Goodreads (2025b) 'Dandelion Wine quotes by Ray Bradbury', *Goodreads*, available at <https://www.goodreads.com/work/quotes/1627774-dandelion-wine>

Grau, O. (2003) *Virtual Art: From Illusion to Immersion*. Cambridge: The MIT Press.

Green, M.C. and Brock, T.C. (2000) 'The role of transportation in the persuasiveness of public narratives', *Journal of Personality and Social Psychology* 79 (5): 701–21.

Hakemulder, F. (2013) 'Travel experiences: a typology of transportation and other absorption states in relation to types of aesthetic responses', in J. Luedke (ed.) *Wie gebannt: Aesthetische Verfahren der affektiven Bildung von Aufmerksamkeit*. Berlin: Freie Universitat, pp.163–82.

Hakemulder, F. and Kuijpers, M. (eds) (2017) *Narrative Absorption*. Amsterdam: Benjamins.

Heydrich, W., Neubauer, F., Petöfi, J. and Sözer, E. (eds) (1989) *Connexity and Coherence: Analysis of Text and Discourse*. Berlin: de Gruyter.

Kuijpers, M., Hakemulder, F., Tan, E. and Doicaru, M. (2014) 'Exploring absorbing reading experiences: developing and validating a self-report scale to measure story world absorption', *Scientific Study of Literature* 4 (1): 89–122.

Kuiken, D., Miall, D.S. and Sikora, S. (2004) 'Forms of self-implication in literary reading', *Poetics Today* 25 (2): 171–203.

Liptay, F. and Dogramaci, B. (eds) (2015) *Immersion in the Visual Arts and Media: Studies in Intermediality*. Leiden: Brill.

Machon, J. (2013) *Immersive Theatres: Intimacy and Immediacy in Contemporary Performance*. Basingstoke: Palgrave Macmillan.

Macrae, A. (2019) *Discourse Deixis in Metafiction: The Language of Metanarration, Metalepsis and Disnarration*. London: Routledge.

Miall, D.S. and Kuiken, D. (2002) 'A feeling for fiction: becoming what we behold', *Poetics* 30 (4): 221–41.

Nell, V. (1988) *Lost in a Book: The Psychology of Reading for Pleasure.* New Haven: Yale University Press.

Norledge, J. (2019) 'Immersive reading and the unnatural text-worlds of "Dead Fish"', in B. Neurohr and L. Stewart-Shaw (eds) *Experiencing Fictional Worlds.* Amsterdam: Benjamins, pp.157–75.

Reid, R.A. (2000) *Ray Bradbury: A Critical Companion.* Westport: Greenwood Press.

Ryan, M.-L. (1999) 'Immersion vs. interactivity: virtual reality and literary theory', *Substance* 28 (2): 110–37.

Ryan, M.-L. (2001) *Narrative as Virtual Reality: Immersion and Interactivity in Literature and Electronic Music.* Baltimore: Johns Hopkins University Press.

Stockwell, P. (2009) *Texture: A Cognitive Aesthetics of Reading.* Edinburgh: Edinburgh University Press.

Stockwell, P. (2019a) 'Immersion and emergence in children's literature', in B. Neurohr and L. Stewart-Shaw (eds) *Experiencing Fictional Worlds.* Amsterdam: Benjamins, pp.15–32.

Stockwell, P. (2019b) 'Shelley's dominion: subliminal and ambient tonal effects across a literary work', in C. Hart (ed.) *Cognitive Linguistic Approaches to Text and Discourse: From Poetics to Politics.* Edinburgh: Edinburgh University Press, pp.20–36.

Stockwell, P. (2020) *Cognitive Poetics: An Introduction* (2nd edn). London: Taylor & Francis.

Stockwell, P. (2021) 'In defence of introspection', in A. Bell, S. Browse, A. Gibbons and D. Peplow (eds) *Style and Reader Response: Minds, Media, Methods.* Amsterdam: Benjamins, pp.165–78.

Sweetser, P. and Wyeth, P. (2005) 'GameFlow: a model for evaluating player enjoyment in games', *Computers in Entertainment* 3 (3): 1–24.

van Dijk, T. (1977) *Text and Context: Explorations in the Semantics and Pragmatics of Discourse.* London: Longman.

van Dijk, T. (1980) *Macrostructures: An Interdisciplinary Study of Global Structures in Discourse, Interaction, and Cognition.* Hillsdale: Lawrence Erlbaum Associates.

van Dijk, T. and Kintsch, W. (1983) *Strategies of Discourse Comprehension.* New York: Academic Press.

van Eck, R. (ed.) (2010) *Gaming and Cognition: Theories and Practice from the Learning Sciences.* Hershey: Information Science Reference.

Werth, P. (1999) *Text Worlds: Representing Conceptual Space in Discourse.* London: Longman.

Wolf, W. (1998) 'Aesthetic illusion in lyric poetry?' *Poetica* 30 (3/4): 251–89.

Wolf, W. (2004) 'Aesthetic illusion as an effect of fiction', *Style* 38 (3): 325–51.

Wolf, W. (2017) 'Illusion (aesthetic)', in P. Hühn, J. Pier, W. Schmid and J. Schönert (eds) *The Living Handbook of Narratology.* Hamburg: Hamburg University Press, available at <http://www.lhn.uni-hamburg.de/>

Wolf, W., Bernhart, W. and Mahler, A. (eds) (2013) *Immersion and Distance: Aesthetic Illusion in Literature and Other Media.* Amsterdam: Rodopi.

Part II

Cross-modal explorations

CHAPTER 6

Absorbed by the Flat Earth: conspiracy immersion on TikTok

Jessica Mason

This chapter suggests that immersion is centrally relevant to conspiratorial belief, supporting this through an analysis of twenty-four TikTok videos discussing two popular conspiracy theories: 'Flat Earth' and 'Birds Aren't Real'. Mason identifies common stylistic patterns that enable differentiation between the consumption of conspiracy for entertainment, displays of conspiratorial thinking, and expressions of wholehearted conspiratorial belief. She concludes with reflections on the ways in which analysing conspiratorial discourse can inform our understanding and conceptualisation of immersion. Whereas immersion is typically discussed as a readerly experience, this chapter also examines the notion of authorial immersion.

Introduction

The commonly agreed definition of a conspiracy theory is 'a proposed plot by powerful people or organisations working together in secret to accomplish some (usually sinister) goal' (Wood et al. 2012: 767). The phenomenon of becoming convinced by a conspiracist world-view is referred to, both in popular discourse and academically, using two immersion metaphors: getting 'sucked in' and 'falling down the rabbit hole' (West 2020, Sobo 2016). This latter term, which originates from Lewis Carroll's *Alice in Wonderland* (1865) and is also frequently associated with the hugely popular 1999 film *The Matrix*, reflects our shared understanding that becoming embroiled in conspiracy belief involves the transgression of a boundary – the rabbit hole – from our reality to an alternate one. This concept has even shifted from popular culture to recognised academic credulity in the coining of 'Rabbit Hole Syndrome' to describe the onset of a conspiracist world-view (Sutton and Douglas 2022). Like Alice in her Wonderland and Neo within the Matrix, once the rabbit hole has been traversed, conspiracy believers often appear to find a return journey difficult or impossible. The widespread use of these terms indicates an intuitive recognition that conspiracism involves immersion, and thus merits academic scrutiny.

Furthermore, there is a consensus in the research, particularly within psychology, that conspiracy belief extends beyond, and is more encompassing than, a preoccupation with individual theories. This has been variously described in the research as conspiracism as an ideology or world-view (Wood et al. 2012), a perspective arising from a 'trust gap' (Heller 2015), or best understood as a milieu (Bennett 2023). As such, I argue conspiracies therefore offer a rich and complex narrative world in which to potentially fall and become immersed, and belief in them appears to be akin to being absorbed into a different world-view.

Conspiracies problematise and blur the traditional boundaries typically sketched between reality and fiction, making the ontological status of this narrative world deeply ambiguous (Mason 2019). This offers an excellent opportunity to explore immersion in a novel context, where absorption in 'stories' can prompt a continued and ongoing mental immersion in another world, long after the bodily experience of reading or viewing has ceased. This chapter will hypothesise that intense mental preoccupation with stories that permeate the individual's boundary between fact and fiction can lead to a sort of continued immersion, where the traveller is so affected by the narratives they have engaged with that they do not fully return to reality (see Stockwell, this volume). In other words, they remain 'down the rabbit hole'.

It is beyond the scope of this chapter to philosophically engage with disputes surrounding the term, but it must be recognised that labelling something a 'conspiracy theory' is far from a neutral act (Bjerg and Presskorn-Thygesen 2017). It is also important to acknowledge several other contextual realities. First, whilst rare, real conspiracies do and have existed (for examples see West 2020), with discovery usually taking place retrospectively. As such, the notion of believing in something others do not, and the lure of potential vindication after the fact, both have historical precedent. Second, there is money to be made from conspiracy belief, and where there is money, bad actors are sure to follow. Alex Jones, for example, made millions of dollars selling survivalist paraphernalia and supplements by advertising these products on his shows *InfoWars* and *The Alex Jones Show*. Described as 'QVC for conspiracy' by a former employee (Warzel 2017), Jones loudly, proudly, and repeatedly spewed conspiratorial falsehoods about events including the Sandy Hook massacre and the Oklahoma City bombing as well as claims including that chemicals were being pumped into the water supply to 'turn people gay'. One team of investigative journalists found that around 25 per cent of Jones' show was dedicated to advertising his company's products (Maurer et al. 2017). This same team ordered some of Jones' products and were sent a free '9/11 Was An Inside Job' bumper sticker with their purchase. In 2022 Alex Jones was successfully sued by families of the Sandy Hook victims. Jones was ordered to pay US$965 million to fifteen families for defamation, as well as the harassment and emotional suffering they experienced as a result of his actions. Third, conspiracy belief exists at the extreme ends of a positive pair of practices: asking questions and being sceptical of the powerful.

This chapter characterises conspiracism as potentially deeply problematic, for the individual believer, their loved ones, and society more broadly. However, I also caution against the haste and wholeheartedness with which many are ready to dismiss conspiracy believers as ridiculous, stupid, or uneducated. This is profoundly unhelpful: it is also untrue (Architects and Engineers for 9/11 Truth, for instance, is largely comprised of highly educated people, see <www.ae911truth.org/>). Furthermore, in this chapter I ask the reader to consider the potential dangers of this unkind stereotyping. Do we really want to dismiss people as idiots for what is ultimately critical questioning and independent thinking gone awry? Do we want to perpetuate the myth that being intelligent will keep ourselves or our loved ones safe from tripping and 'falling down the rabbit hole'? Instead, this chapter – which deals with two conspiracy theories which are demonstrably untrue – counsels compassion, and separation between the theories themselves and the individuals who become immersed in them.

I will use two key concepts from cognitive investigations on immersion to offer an account as to why viewers may be unfortunately positioned to fall into conspiracy theories when exposed to immersive conspiracy content on an immersive social media platform: figure-ground relations (Langacker 2008, Stockwell 2009), and the willing construction of disbelief (Gerrig and Rapp 2004, Gerrig and Egidi 2010).

Figure-ground: immersion as a matter of attention

In this chapter I will concentrate on immersion as a matter of attention and, as such, will follow Green and Brock's (2000) description, though they prefer one of immersion's synonyms, 'transportation' (see Schneider, this volume):

> [Immersion] is a convergent mental process, a focusing of attention, that may occur in response to either fiction or nonfiction. The components [. . .] include emotional reactions, mental imagery, and a loss of access to real-world information.
>
> (Green and Brock 2000: 703)

Immersion *is* an extreme focusing of attention: it is the mechanism by which the phenomenon is achieved, the state by which it can be characterised, and the cause of its other observable effects. As such, narratives that are rich in attentional attractors (Stockwell 2020) prime conditions for immersion because they demand our focus. Gestalt psychology offers a robust account of why this is the case because,

> Attention is a zero-sum game. What this means is we all have a finite amount of capacity to pay attention to things; we cannot exponentially increase our ability to focus on as many things as we like. As a result, focusing on one thing always comes at the cost of drawing our attention away from something else.
>
> (Mason and Giovanelli 2021: 48)

In other words, the negative (in the psychological sense) effects of immersion – such as loss of sense of time, place, and access to real-world knowledge (Green and Brock 2000) – result from neglect of attention to the physical environment because that attention is elsewhere, namely within the storyworld. Symbiotically, immersion's positive effects, such as rich mental imagery, strong emotional reactions, and intense empathetic response, can be understood as deriving from a strong attentional focus. In this chapter, figure-ground analysis will be used to demonstrate that conspiracy belief narratives are rich in attentional attractors, and thus not only position individuals to become sucked into the world-views they present but also reflect a level of immersion in the conspiracy storyworld on the part of the author.

Immersion, (dis)belief and critical thinking

I also, in this chapter, draw closely on Gerrig and colleagues' findings regarding the interaction between immersion, belief, and critical thinking (Gerrig and Rapp 2004, Gerrig and Egidi 2010). This work contradicts the long-held Romantic notion first proposed by Coleridge (1960 [1817]) that when we encounter fiction, we willingly suspend our disbelief; that we simply press pause on our knowledge about the true state of reality in order to enjoy a good story with its dragons, ghosts, and improbabilities. Gerrig and Rapp (2004) tested this empirically and found that not only is this inaccurate, but the opposite is true: disbelief is something we must willingly construct. In other words, disbelief is a faculty we turn on, not off. Building on this study, Gerrig and Egidi (2010) further found that we tend to use our intuitive processes when reading as a default, which positions us to simply accept what we are told. Reflective processes – turning on our potential disbelief – require us to pull out of the storyworld and critically assess: 'reflective processes require explicit planning; they are slow and effortful' (Gerrig and Egidi 2010: 191). As such, being immersed runs counter to critical thinking.

To examine (dis)belief linguistically, the chapter draws extensively on modality analysis. Epistemic modality is the linguistic category used to express our level of belief and (un)certainty about whether something is true: where 'might' reflects possibility, 'definitely' conveys certainty. Categorical, unmodalised assertions express information *as though* it is fact (for instance 'birds are not real'), regardless of whether it is accurate, representing the highest level of confidence in the truth of one's utterance. Modality analysis will be used to demonstrate that committed conspiracy belief can be robustly distinguished from conspiratorial thinking or simply exploring conspiracies for entertainment. The chapter will contend that by first assessing conspiratorial discourse through the lens of belief commitment, it is possible to then discern other stylistic patterns, such as deictic attribution of beliefs and indications of apparent immersion.

Research design and methods

According to West (2020: 37), 'In the twenty-first century the most common first step in the journey down the conspiracy theory rabbit hole is watching a video.' Researchers contest whether conspiracy belief has become more common in recent years. Many point to the long-standing existence of conspiracism throughout history as evidence that anecdotal reports of a rise in prevalence is impressionistic (see, for example, van Prooijen and Douglas 2017, Mousaw 2022). However, it seems uncontroversial to say that conspiratorial discourse has enjoyed, if not an increase, then certainly a greater embrace by mainstream discourse spaces. Regardless of whether what was once kept private is now simply more acceptable to share publicly, or an actual increase in conspiracism is taking place, the fact remains that discussion of conspiracy theories has moved from the fringes into the collective spotlight, especially online. It is also inarguable that social media platforms have given conspiracism a helping hand in its shift from private to public discourse (Fiadotava et al. 2023).

This chapter reports the findings of an exploratory investigation of conspiracy discourse on TikTok, a social media platform known for its short-form video content akin to Facebook and Instagram 'Reels'. The study focuses on two specific conspiracy theories: Flat Earth and Birds Aren't Real. There is strong consensus that TikTok itself is highly absorbing, with users frequently reporting struggling to pull themselves away from the platform and experiencing classic immersion phenomena such as losing sense of the passage of time. These experiential accounts are strongly supported by the data, which shows that, despite its relatively recent launch in 2018, TikTok now boasts over a billion users a month. Users can 'follow' other accounts, but the app's primary function is its 'For You' page, which infinitely supplies video after video to the viewer, who can then choose to watch, like, comment, share, or scroll past. As with all major social media platforms, details of TikTok's algorithms are not publicly available, but it is apparent that the app is uncannily good at tailoring 'For You' content to users' interests. These core characteristics alongside its undeniable current global relevance makes TikTok of particular interest for data collection for conspiracy discourse.

Data for this study was generated with the aim of mimicking a typical user experience on TikTok. A new account was created so that the 'For You' feed was not influenced by the researcher's past interactions with the platform. The account was then supplied with exclusively conspiracy-related searches, both generic – for example 'conspiracy' and 'conspiracy theory' – and specific – such as 'flat earth' and 'birdsarentreal'. Videos suggested by the searches were then played in full. This was interspersed with visiting the 'For You' page, which increasingly then began to offer conspiracy-related content as the algorithm picked up on the searches. The researcher then allowed all conspiracy-related videos presented on the 'For You' page to play in full, also often clicking on the comments section, which the algorithm interprets as positive engagement. Flat Earth and Birds Aren't Real focused videos were additionally 'liked' so that they would be stored on the account and so that this would indicate specific interest to the algorithm. Videos that were not conspiracy related were scrolled past as soon as this became apparent. After approximately two hours, virtually all the videos offered on the 'For You' page were conspiracy related. Videos were then selected into the dataset if they met the following criteria:

- includes written or spoken language;
- is in English;
- primarily concerns either Flat Earth or Birds Aren't Real;
- distinct creator (i.e., no two videos are by the same author);
- could be downloaded (for accurate transcription and data security).

The dataset comprises twenty-four video transcripts: twelve focusing on Flat Earth and twelve on Birds Aren't Real. Both theories are relatively self-evident from their names; however, I will pause to offer a brief overview of each.

Flat Earth

The Flat Earth theory posits that the Earth is flat, rather than a globe. This conspiracy has reared its head on more than one occasion throughout history, with a notable resurgence of interest from 2015 (West 2020). As with all conspiracies, how many people genuinely believe this theory is impossible to determine: as will be discussed below (see 'Conspiracy as Entertainment'), conspiratorial voyeurism is a popular pastime and the boundaries between exploring beliefs for fun and actual subscription are often shifting and difficult to distinguish. West (2020: 199), a professional debunker, explains that 'much of this is obviously a fad on the part of non-believers – just fascination with the "crazy Flat Earthers". But there are also many people who seem genuinely convinced that the Earth is actually flat and most of them got sucked in via YouTube.' Videos in my dataset range from forty to 6.1 million views; some have in excess of 500,000 'likes'. However, any claim to interpretation of these figures would be purely speculative.

There is division between vocal members of the Flat Earth community on issues such as the shape of the flat Earth and whether gravity really exists (for a full overview see Clark 2018). However, there is consensus on core elements of this conspiracy, including:

- NASA is the architect of, or is complicit in, propagation of the 'globe model';
- the true flat shape of the Earth is being deliberately concealed, by bad actors, for sinister reasons;
- curvature is unobservable (because it does not exist);
- 'Antarctica' is really an ice wall surrounding the edges of the Earth, or at least houses one of the edges.

Birds Aren't Real

Like Flat Earth, the core tenet of the Birds Aren't Real conspiracy is eponymously self-evident: it is the theory that some or all birds are not real. According to the lore of the theory, birds have been replaced by drones, typically in the 1980s by either Ronald Reagan or Margaret Thatcher. Birds Aren't Real is a US-centric version of the conspiracy (see <www.birdsarent real.com>): Pigeons Aren't Real is a UK equivalent (see <www.pigeonsarent real.co.uk>). These drone birds are being used to spy on the public. Common elements of the theory in both iterations include:

- birds' eyes are cameras;
- birds charge their batteries by sitting on power cables through induction coils in their feet;
- bird faeces contains tracking devices;
- 'bird meat' is synthetically produced.

The genesis and ontology of Birds Aren't Real is atypical: it was initially created as a conspiracy satire. Its origin is attributed to Peter McIndoe holding up a satirical 'Birds Aren't Real' sign at a counterprotest to the Women's Marches in 2017. When asked about his sign by 'fellow' counter-protesters he improvised his response, which was recorded and went viral (Williams 2022). McIndoe explained, 'It's not like I sat down and thought I'm going to make a satire. I just thought: "I should write a sign that has nothing to do with what is going on." An absurdist statement to bring to the equation' (McIndoe quoted in *The Guardian*, April 2022). Comments like this from McIndoe and others discussing the satirical status of the Birds Aren't Real movement are scarce. This is because a core principle of the satire is to never admit one is being satirical, but rather to vehemently claim this is your truly held belief. Indeed, the FAQs section on the Birds Aren't Real website includes:

> Q: Is this movement serious?
> A: Yes. The Birds Aren't Real movement has been active since 1976. Once a preventative cause, our initial goal was to stop the genocide of real birds. Unfortunately this was unsuccessful, and the government has since replaced every living bird with robotic replicas. Now our movement's prerogative is to make everyone aware of this fact.
> (Official Birds Aren't Real website, 2024)

A by-product of this falsified sincerity has been that others then encountered online content generated by the Birds Aren't Real group and its followers online and, unaware of its origins, embraced it as a real conspiracy, which it then became.

This outcome in and of itself suggests not only that there *are* common linguistic markers that characterise conspiracy belief discourse, but that this style is intuitively recognisable. McIndoe, his colleagues, and the followers of his satire were able to convincingly mimic this conspiratorial style such that others were not able to distinguish it from 'true' conspiracy discourse. Reinforcing this, throughout the generation of the present dataset it was almost always impossible to determine if videos were satirical or heartfelt. Where this was possible this was only through the use of hashtags such as #joke on the video descriptions, not the rhetorical style. As with Flat Earth, it is impossible to establish the number of people who believe this conspiracy. In both cases videos on TikTok focusing on these conspiracies were many and easy to find.

Modality as a metric

Mason (2022) found that high-certainty epistemic modality and categorical assertions were characteristic of conspiracy discourse in YouTube videos offering false flag accounts of the Sandy Hook massacre. As such, modality was the first stylistic feature examined in the present dataset, anticipating that the same patterns would likely be present. This was not the case: epistemic modality and categorical assertions are rife, but the level of certainty being expressed was substantially much more varied. This led me to pause and reflect on the similarities and distinctions between the dataset in Mason's (2022) study and the present one.

The conspiracy content under examination in Mason (2022) was fifteen long-form videos – many with run times exceeding two hours: by contrast, the videos in the present study are short-form, typically ranging from between forty-five seconds to four minutes. Additionally, the Sandy Hook massacre was a truly horrific event, which claimed the lives of twenty young children and six adults. As such, it seems reasonable to conclude that individuals are unlikely to spend hours creating, editing, and uploading content arguing that the event was staged or fictional unless in their own minds they feel sure of their claims: it is not an 'entry-level' conspiracy. Flat Earth, too, is sometimes characterised as sitting at the extreme end of conspiracies (see for example West 2020), but this is largely due to the scale and audacious nature of its core claims. Overall, Flat Earth and Birds Aren't Real are more frivolous conspiracies that typically do not include specific victims. Therefore, it seems logical to conclude that all the videos in the Mason (2022) study, due both to subject matter and the time-investment required to produce them, can reasonably be taken to have been narrated from a point of wholesale conspiracy belief. This is consistent with patterns of high-certainty modality and categorical assertion (stating things as though they are facts).

These reflections were then used to revisit the present dataset through a different lens. Rather than viewing high-certainty epistemic modality and categorical assertion as a stylistic feature of conspiracy discourse per se, these patterns were instead used as a metric by which to differentiate videos within the present sample. Once this was done, a new and more nuanced dimension to conspiratorial discourse emerged: all of the videos with these patterns do appear to express conspiratorial belief, and do have other patterns consistent with both one another and the Mason (2022) study. The remaining videos instead appear to be either engaging in conspiratorial thinking, without the authors necessarily expressing that they believe the theory themselves, or seem to be discussing these conspiracies from a step further removed, as a topic of interest and entertainment. As such, this study, building on Mason (2022), suggests conspiratorial discourse in fact exists along a cline with three distinct categorisations:

1. Conspiracy as entertainment
2. Conspiratorial thinking
3. Conspiratorial belief

The first two of these categories do not contain markers indicating former or ongoing immersion in a conspiratorial world-view, but the third – 'conspiratorial belief' – does. This chapter will now explore each category in detail.

Conspiracy as entertainment

The videos in the dataset characterised by low-certainty epistemic modality appear to fall into one of two thematic categories, the first being speculative exploration of conspiracy as a form of entertainment. Here is a representative example of this category:

> The earth *could be* much bigger than we *thought*. Over the past few years *there has been ongoing debate* regarding the Earth's shape, with some *questioning* whether it is round or flat. Although *some speculate* about the existence of conspiracy theories, *imagine if there were* more than just seven continents. Some *propose* that Antarctica *might actually be* an enormous ice wall, concealing the existence of additional continents beyond it. *Hypothetically,* once someone manages to traverse this icy barrier, they *might* discover the presence of twenty hidden continents that have been shielded from our knowledge. These mysterious lands have *sparked various theories, suggesting they could* contain prehistoric creatures, extra-terrestrial beings, and advanced civilizations.
>
> (FlatEarth-Video5)

Two notable stylistic patterns characterise this type of conspiracy discourse: low-certainty epistemic modality, and deictic distancing between the theory and the narrator. In this 112-word excerpt there are twelve expressions of uncertainty about the veracity of the ideas being outlined, indicated in italics. The narrator is careful at every point to explicitly present possibility rather than certainty: idea or theory, not fact.

Alongside this, there is consistent and careful attenuation between the speaker and the ideas being outlined (see also Zunshine 2006). This is achieved mainly through subject attribution of epistemically hedged verb processes to other people ('some speculate', 'some propose', 'they might discover') or even inanimate entities ('these mysterious lands have sparked'). On one occasion the same effect is achieved through agent deletion: 'there has been ongoing debate'. Here, the use of the passive construction makes it unclear who has been debating the shape of the Earth, but the narrator is careful not to implicate either themselves or the listener. In fact, the only two occasions on which the speaker deictically positions themselves within the narrative at all is in the collective 'we' pronoun in the first line, 'the Earth could be much bigger than we thought' and a later reference to 'our knowledge'. These both align the speaker with the listeners, implicitly positioning them as adherents to the 'globe model' perspective.

These stylistic features work together to locate both the narrator and the narratees in a voyeuristic role, observing and exploring the theory but from a distance. In this way, the conspiracy is implicitly presented as an object of entertainment, rather than a notion that is particularly plausible.

Conspiratorial thinking

Other videos in the dataset close the deictic gap between the conspiracy theory and the video's narrator but maintain a position of scepticism and uncertainty about the ideas they explore. As such, they move beyond observation for pure entertainment and shift into conspiratorial thinking. A representative example of this is Video 12, which focuses on Birds Aren't Real:

> Okay, so, I've been looking into these videos about fake birds, and birds, really being like, you know government, spy drones or robots or whatever. Now I'm over halfway believing that, because, it would probably explain, why the birds are like, drawn to these power lines and somebody said that the power lines charged them up. So, that kind of like took me over like, wait a minute now, they might have a point here, because when I look at the eyes of birds, they just, seem weird to me like a lot of birds, the eyes just seem like they're recording you. But how do you explain like, bird faeces? Now we saying all the birds are drones and robots or just some of them? Because when I see birds, like excreting like, doody or faeces, you know that's the one, problematic thing. Or, when I'm throwing out bird food, or crackers or bread, they eat it. Would a robot bird do that?
>
> (FakeBirds-Video12)

The pattern of epistemic modality in this video largely mirrors the previous example in that it is characterised by low levels of certainty. Having said this, whilst the creator is not expressing being convinced by the conspiracy theory, they do seem a step closer to being persuaded than the author of Video 5. The theory 'would probably' explain their observations of bird behaviour. It does 'seem like' something is weird, or the birds are recording you. They are 'over halfway believing' it. This slightly higher level of epistemic possibility is moderated, however, by the posing of sincere questions: 'How do you, like, explain bird faeces?'; 'Would a robot bird do that?' The narrator stops short of expressing disbelief, but does label the issue of bird faeces 'problematic' and follows this with a categorical assertion of their observation of other bird behaviours (eating food). They are not sure whether a robot bird would do this, but they do express that birds eating food is an action they have witnessed as a matter of fact. As such, the narrator of this video moves from simply outlining the theory from a distance to personally engaging with its contents. Both the questions and the critical engagement with specific components of the theory indicate reflective processes (Gerrig and Egidi 2010): the author has stepped back and assessed the narrative's claims against their real-world knowledge. Video 12 thus expresses conspiratorial thinking because it moves from observation to participation but stops short of expressing confident belief. The creator appears to be inviting conversation, offering their thoughts and the reasoning behind them, and posing questions that do not seem entirely rhetorical.

This more direct engagement with Birds Aren't Real is also reflected in the deixis that, unlike the distanced position adopted in Video 5, is narrated from the speaker's own deictic centre, with five uses of the first-person pronoun 'I' throughout the video. This chapter does not have the space or scope to deal with the multimodal aspects of the videos in any detail, but it is salient to note here that Video 12's creator is in a full-face shot speaking directly to the camera throughout. Video 5 by contrast, discussed in the previous section, visually comprises a series of images with the narrator never revealing themselves (in fact the voice even sounds like it may be AI-generated or have a filter overlaid). In other words, multimodally both videos reflect deictic involvement or distance parallel to the author's linguistic choices.

A final stylistic feature within this extract is particularly interesting and noteworthy, namely the report of temporary immersion in the Birds Aren't Real world-view using the metaphor 'so that kind of like took me over'. Similarly, the phrase 'now I'm over halfway believing' draws on a transportation metaphor (Green and Brock 2000). This uncertainty and confusion could be framed as a conflict between the creator's intuitive processes and reflective ones (Gerrig and Egidi 2010): whilst immersed and 'taken over' by the conspiracy content they have viewed, their intuitive processes align with belief, but pulling back out of the storyworld and engaging their reflective processes calls these feelings into question.

This chapter will now turn to the final category of conspiratorial discourse: conspiracy belief. I will argue that this final category bears the linguistic hallmarks of immersion in a parallel reality: the conspiracy lens that becomes the viewing point from down the rabbit hole. It is salient, therefore, to see a report of immersion cropping up alongside uncertainty and consideration of the possibility that a conspiracy may be true in this example of conspiratorial thinking. It is notable, too, that the creator also discloses that this process of questioning and conspiratorial thinking stemmed from 'looking into these videos', lending weight to West's (2020) claim.

Conspiratorial belief

The videos in this dataset that express conspiratorial belief have several stylistic patterns consistent with one another but noticeably distinct from the videos exploring conspiracy as entertainment or expressing conspiratorial thinking. These videos share the same patterns as Mason (2022). Here are two examples from the dataset.

> We all felt like, yeah, okay your whole life you being watched. But if you, we've been watched all around the board on. So. Many. Different. Levels. Right? So we thinking like, they're not just using your microwave like in get out he, they showed he was using the microwave. It was a toaster or something, everything. But it's, it, they do do that, but it's in your phones. It's certain birds, certain insects. It gets deeper. Not just birds. Insects. It gets deeper. I'm finna name off the 13 bird species

> that are actually recording your ass. Okay? The brown thresher. Pigeons. Crows. Blue jays. Robins. Ring neck parakeets. Goldfinches. The sparrows. Swallows. The owls. Chickens.
>
> (FakeBirds-Video11)

> Water, when unmanipulated, is to find its level. So whether you look at a cup of water, a bathtub, a swimming pool, a lake, or the ocean, it's flat. Of course natural motion is not considered, and doesn't equal a curve. We have zero authentic pictures of the Earth and they're all composites and NASA even admits that they photoshop Earth images. [They say] 'It is photoshopped because it has to be.' On numerous occasions, NASA admits that we can't go beyond low Earth orbit which is between 99 miles and 1200 miles away. The interesting thing is that the moon is said to be 238,000 miles away, which is a difference of 236,800 miles. No matter if you're on the ground, on top of a building, a mountain, a hot air balloon, an airplane, or looking at high altitude amateur balloon footage, the horizon never fails to rise, right to your eyes. Whether you are looking at Toronto's skyline from Niagara on the lake, 31 miles away, Chicago's skyline from Union Pier, 43 miles away, or even Oahu from Kauai, which is up to 108 miles away from centre to centre or 73 miles away from the closest points, you will not see any curvature where it's supposed to be.
>
> (FlatEarth-Video24)

I propose that conspiratorial belief occurs at a tipping point of immersion into a conspiratorial world-view. This is manifest in conspiracy belief discourse, and observable in both of these examples. I call it falling down the rabbit hole in intuitive recognition of this transition.

First, both of these videos narrate an almost overwhelming barrage of attentional attractors, in particular drawing on the qualities of newness and definiteness (Stockwell 2009). In the first extract, which comprises just 118 words, the narrator maintains one overarching topic – the notion that we are being watched – but introduces sixteen different objects or entities that are spying on us, some of which are repeated more than once: 'microwaves', 'phones', 'toasters', '(certain) insects', 'certain birds', and then eleven specific species of birds. The narrator additionally appears to be merging multiple distinct conspiracy theories in pointing to objects such as phones, microwaves, and birds. The suggestion that insects are drones may even be a novel conspiracy belief, or at least it is not one that I have come across previously or since. In the second 210-word extract, four topics are jumped between: that curvature is unobservable (this is discussed twice both opening and closing the extract); that images from NASA are not authentic; and the distance of the moon. It introduces twenty-five new objects including five different containers for water, six potential observation points, six different specific locations, four scientific concepts ('natural motion', 'curvature', 'orbit', and 'horizon'), an organisation (NASA), and images and photographs. It also includes eight different specific numbers ranging from zero to 238,000.

In both cases, I argue, the video creators narrate from a point of immersion in a conspiratorial world-view, and this is evidenced by the rapid and often chaotic flitting of attention between figures within the conspiratorial storyworld in a manner which is all-encompassing. Both narrators are surrounded by evidence of the conspiracy; it is wherever they look, as it would be if they were immersed. The accepting of the veracity of this evidence and the coherent relationship between these often highly disparate entities is intuitive and unquestioning. There are no linguistic markers suggesting a stepping back and pausing for reflection. The belief in each respective theory is absolute, unquestioned, and not critically justified or interrogated. All of these patterns indicate immersion on the part of the author. Authorial immersion is an overlooked area within the field, which overwhelmingly tends to focus on experiences of reception. This chapter demonstrates that exploration of immersion in production is both highly salient, and possible to undertake. It follows logically from the analysis undertaken in this chapter to suggest that commitment to any set of beliefs could constitute a world-view, and thus stem from a narrative world in which the author is immersed. As this holds for conspiracism, the same may be true for political ideology and religious belief: belief discourse may have much to gain from considering immersion. It further seems reasonable to speculate that authors of fiction may write from a position of immersion in the worlds they have created.

This rapid shifting between attentionally attractive figures was also observed in Mason (2019) and Mason (2022). In those instances, as here, the impression created is one of a huge pile of evidence in support of the theory, when in fact the demands on attention as it shifts from figure to figure and across topics inhibit and reflect a lack of critical thinking. Simply put, there is no time to pause and consider the veracity of these claims, the reliability of the evidence, or even the relationship between the topics, objects, and the theory being put forward. This, too, indicates immersion: there is an absence of reflection (Gerrig and Egidi 2010) and no time for disbelief to be constructed (Gerrig and Rapp 2004).

The questionable nature of the claims being made in both videos is linguistically evident in neither, however. Video 24 presents all its evidence for a Flat Earth in the form of categorical assertions (water in the ocean 'is flat', 'NASA admits' (twice), 'there are zero authentic images') or high-certainty epistemic modality ('of course', 'you will not see'). The only instance of lower-certainty modality in Video 24 is casting aspersions on the distance of the moon from Earth, which is 'said to be' 238,000 miles away. Video 11 exhibits the same confidence that birds (and many other objects) are spy drones, mainly using the categorical construction 'it is' as well as claims such as 'we've all been watched' and high-certainty expressions such as, 'that are actually recording your ass'. Interestingly, there are two phrases used in Video 11 that one would typically associate with lower certainty ('we all felt that' and 'we thinking like') – however the use of the 'we' pronoun reframes these expressions to assert knowledge of what the audience, not just the speaker, thinks and feels.

As in the example of conspiratorial thinking, there is no deictic distancing between the conspiracy and the narrator. However, both authors in these videos narrating conspiratorial belief frequently co-opt the listener's deictic viewpoint into their own through a preference for 'we' over 'I' and even sometimes 'you', the latter of which in particular lays claim to not only confident belief in the theory but also what the audience does or should think too. Again, this chimes with the findings of Mason (2022), which noted that conspiracy advocates often adopt an identity of expertise and authority.

Conclusions

Conspiracy discourse exists along a cline, with its most extreme category – conspiracy belief – bearing the stylistic hallmarks of immersion. These hallmarks, indicated in this study, are:

- high-certainty epistemic modality communicating confidence from the author that their world-view is correct;
- categorical assertions that present the author's perspective as a matter of fact;
- deictic markers taking ownership of the beliefs expressed, sometimes additionally co-opting the reader, listener, or viewer into the author's positioning;
- evidence that the author's attention is consumed by their world-view; and,
- an absence of evidence for reflective processes, indicating that the author is not, or is not able to, step out of their world-view and consider it critically.

These linguistic patterns and the related claim that belief discourse indicates prolonged and ongoing immersion in a conspiratorial storyworld aligns with other recent investigations of conspiracists' communication. Mousaw found that friends and family often reported frustration at their loved one's 'conversational fanaticism', which he defined as a seeming 'inability to refrain from talking' about their conspiratorial beliefs' (2022: 31). This would make robust sense if the person were bodily present in reality but mentally immersed. Mastroni and Mooney's (2024) participants similarly reported their loved one was incapable of respecting boundaries in conversational topics, with even inane subjects leading quickly back to the overarching 'QAnon' conspiracy theory – part of a far-right American political movement – and all requests not to discuss theories disrespected and disregarded. This too makes sense through a lens of continued immersion: the conspiracist's attention remains largely within the storyworld, and this is manifest in the repeated intrusions of that narrative world into their real-world discourse. Mousaw (2022), Mastroni and Mooney (2024), and Jordan and Whitmer (2023) all found that relatives and friends grieved the loss of the conspiracist as one would a bereavement because they felt the old person had vanished and an imposter had taken their place. This study suggests that these people are not so much lost, but trapped in another world, immersed down the rabbit hole.

In this chapter I have identified three brands of conspiracy discourse a user may encounter on TikTok, and I have proposed that those creators expressing conspiratorial belief appear to be narrating from a position of ongoing immersion within the conspiracy world they have constructed. This study has not focused on reception, and therefore cannot make claims as to the potential effects of viewing this content. However, the prospect of users encountering video after video proliferating conspiracy narratives that may range from exploring theories for fun to committed expressions of belief, *ad infinitum* (or at least until your phone battery dies), is troubling. In the case of conspiracy belief videos, in particular, these contain features that not only indicate the immersion of their creators but seem well-positioned to prompt the immersion of their viewers too. This last category of videos is rich in attentional attractors, styled as presenting piece after piece of evidence, and simultaneously devoid of reflective discussion or critical analysis. The platform on which these videos are being encountered is also not conducive to pause or respite. Once a video finishes playing it will simply repeat until the user scrolls to the next one or closes the app. In other words, this is potentially an immersive app feeding you immersive content indefinitely. It may be that the coexistence of videos treating conspiracy as a form of entertainment or demonstrating conspiratorial thinking may maintain enough of a diversity of perspectives to protect viewers from becoming sucked in themselves. Given the overwhelming current success of TikTok and the consistent identification of online videos as a main gateway to conspiracism, however, this is in need of urgent further investigation. In a global context where worldviews appear to be becoming increasingly polarised and entrenched, it also seems productive to consider whether our seeming inability to agree has a psychological basis. Namely, that whilst bodily we share the same planet, we are invisibly, but firmly, mentally immersed in different realities. Linguistics may be the mechanism by which these multiple narrative worlds can be made visible.

References

Bennett, S. (2023) *The Rhetoric of Conspiracy Theories* (unpublished doctoral thesis). University of Nottingham.

Bjerg, O. and Presskorn-Thygesen, T. (2017) 'Conspiracy theory: truth claim or language game?', *Theory, Culture and Society* 34 (1): 137–59.

Clark, D.J. (2018) *Behind the Curve*. Delta-v Productions.

Coleridge, S.T. (1960 [1817]) *Biographia Literaria, or Biographical Sketches of My Literary Life and Opinions*. London: J.M. Dent.

Fiadotava, A., Astapova, A., Hendershott, R., McKinnon, M. and Jürgens, A.S. (2023) 'Injecting fun? Humour, conspiracy theory and (anti)vaccination discourse in popular media', *Public Understanding of Science* 32 (5): 622–40.

Gerrig, R.J. and Egidi, G. (2010) '*The Bushwhacked Piano* and the bushwhacked reader: the willing construction of disbelief', *Style* 44 (1–2): 189–206.

Gerrig, R.J. and Rapp, D. (2004) 'Psychological processes underlying literary impact', *Poetics Today* 25 (2): 265–81.

Green, M.C. and Brock, T.C. (2000) 'The role of transportation in the persuasiveness of public narratives', *Journal of Personality and Social Psychology* 79 (5): 701–21.

Heller, J. (2015) 'Rumors and realities: making sense of HIV/AIDS conspiracy narratives and contemporary legends', *American Journal of Public Health* 105 (1): 43–50.

Jordan, M.M. and Whitmer, J.M. (2023) '"I would give anything to talk about aliens now": QAnon conspiracy theories and the creation of cognitive deviance', *Sociological Perspectives* 66 (6): 992–1014.

Langacker, R. (2008) *Cognitive Grammar: A Basic Introduction*. New York: Oxford University Press.

Mason, J. (2019) 'Making fiction out of fact: attention and belief in the discourse of conspiracy', *Narrative Inquiry* 29 (2): 293–312.

Mason, J. (2022). 'If you can't see the pattern here, there's something wrong', in M. Demata, A. Zottola and V. Zorzi (eds) *Conspiracy Theory Discourses*. Amsterdam: John Benjamins, pp.169–92.

Mason, J. and Giovanelli, M. (2021). *Studying Fiction: A Guide for Teachers and Researchers*. London: Routledge.

Mastroni, L. and Mooney, R. (2024) '"I one-hundred thousand percent blame it on QAnon": the impact of QAnon belief on interpersonal relationships', *Journal of Social and Personal Relationships* 41 (9): 2478–99.

Maurer, J., Oliver, J. and Twiss, J. (2017) 'Alex Jones', *Last Week Tonight with John Oliver*. HBO.

Mousaw, C. (2022). *'I love who he was but hate who he's become': The Impacts of Conspiracy Theories on Interpersonal Relationships* (unpublished master's thesis). University of Colorado.

Sobo, E.L. (2016) 'Theorizing (vaccine) refusal – through the looking glass', *Cultural Anthropology* 31 (3): 342–50.

Stockwell, P. (2009) *Texture: A Cognitive Aesthetics of Reading*. Edinburgh: Edinburgh University Press.

Stockwell, P. (2020) *Cognitive Poetics: An Introduction* (2nd edn). London: Routledge.

Sutton, R.M. and Douglas, K.M. (2022). 'Rabbit Hole Syndrome: inadvertent, accelerating, and entrenched commitment to conspiracy beliefs', *Current Opinion in Psychology* 48: 101462.

van Prooijen, J.-W. and Douglas, K.M. (2017) 'Conspiracy theories as part of history: the role of societal crisis situations', *Memory Studies* 10 (3): 323–33.

Warzel, C. (2017) 'Alex Jones will never stop being Alex Jones', *Buzzfeed News*, available at <https://www.buzzfeednews.com/article/charliewarzel/alex-jones-will-never-stop-being-alex-jones>

West, M. (2020) *Escaping the Rabbit Hole: How to Debunk Conspiracy Theories Using Facts, Logic, and Respect*. New York: Simon and Schuster.

Williams, Z. (2022) '"The lunacy is getting more intense": how Birds Aren't Real took on the conspiracy theorists', *The Guardian*, 14 April 2022, available at <https://www.theguardian.com/us-news/2022/apr/14/the-lunacy-is-getting-more-intense-how-birds-arent-real-took-on-the-conspiracy-theorists>

Wood, M.J., Douglas, K.M. and Sutton, R.M. (2012) 'Dead and alive: beliefs in contradictory conspiracy theories', *Social Psychological and Personality Science* 3 (6): 767–73.

Zunshine, L. (2006) *Why We Read Fiction: Theory of Mind and the Novel*. Ohio: Ohio State University Press.

CHAPTER 7

Understanding the simulation–immersion relationship

Harry Cooper

In this chapter, Harry Cooper looks to explain immersion as a consequence of simulation theory, part of Theory of Mind. He describes a reader experiment in which readers were asked to note their levels of immersion while reading two novels, which differed in their cultural familiarity. The results suggest that both world-building and emotional language are key features in generating a simulative effect in readers, and that this observation can explain some of the mechanics of the link between stylistic articulation and the experiential effect of different degrees of immersion.

Introduction

In recent years, stylistics has made progress towards understanding the interpretative mechanisms engendering the experience of *immersion*. Broadly, immersion is understood as the 'merging of action and awareness as a loss of self-consciousness' (Bilandzic and Busselle 2017: 16), and is produced when readers position themselves within the text. Recent research has turned to the role of formal features in triggering immersion, or *absorption*, as argued by Kuijpers et al. (2017) via the notion of *textual artefacts.* An important aspect of how textual elements create immersion is *mental imagery*, that is, 'visual imagery that comes to mind specifically when reading a story' (Kuijpers et al. 2014: 92). Together, the idea here is that formal features in text prompt readers to produce images of what is going on, and this leads to immersion. I argue that *simulation theory* can add to the discussion of formal features, mental imagery, and immersion. While simulation theory has already been paired with cognitive stylistics, with claims that 'fiction [is] a simulation that runs on the minds of its readers' (Oatley 1999: 101), it is yet to be understood. Therefore, this chapter takes ideas from simulation theory to provide new insights into the functioning of immersion, particularly focusing on how formal features contribute to the experience.

The chapter begins with an introduction to simulation theory from a cognitive perspective, as – despite there being a foundational understanding of the theory's principles in stylistics – more can be said. Then, I turn to apply simulation theory to cognitive stylistics, and where it can benefit research in immersion. The chapter then outlines the methodological approach, which consisted of three semi-structured reading groups conducted at the University of Liverpool campus, totalling twenty-one participants across the groups. These reading groups, each containing seven participants, involved individual mark-up activities and group discussion sections. While a wealth of data was gathered, for the scope of this chapter, my data analysis and discussion sections will focus on two areas: emotive lexis and world-building elements. The chapter concludes by evaluating the role of simulation theory to assist in explaining how these two features contribute to textual immersion.

Simulation in cognition

To outline the value that simulation theory has for stylistics and immersion, it is important to begin with what is meant by *simulation*. Simulation theory has its roots in Theory of Mind, a cognitive and philosophical approach understanding how humans attribute mental states to others in order to make sense of their intentions, knowledge, and beliefs (see Apperly 2011). Simulation theory is one of the main attempts to explain the process of mental state attribution. At a basic level, simulation theory states that we imagine intentions, feelings, and beliefs using our own experiences to assume how other people will behave. These imagined scenarios are called simulations. The idea was first introduced by Gordon (1986: 162) as 'hypothetico-practical reasoning', which occurs when one 'project[s] themselves into the other's situation [. . . into] the other's mind'. The rationale for simulation theory was to reject the idea that a rich body of information is needed to understand others; in the 1980s, a competing Theory of Mind approach, the so-called 'theory-theory', claimed that we rely on an implicit body of information that weighs different hypotheses according to their probabilities (see Apperly 2011). In turn, a divide was created between the 'information-poor' simulation theory, as we rely on our own experiences to attribute mental states to others, versus theory-theory being 'information-rich', as a dedicated knowledge system enabling us to attribute mental states (Schlicht 2023: 66). While there is still a debate as to which approach is responsible for the majority of mental state attribution, it is generally held that both approaches are involved. For simulation theory, it is argued that in some ways the human motor system relies on simulations to 'inform motor execution' and 'explain mental states' (O'Shea and Moran 2017: 6), having been mapped onto the cerebellum and cerebral cortex (D'Angelo and Jirsa 2022, O'Shea and Moran 2017) and more broadly thought to have a 'central role' in psychology (Hesslow 2011: 72). As more research emerges in favour of simulation theory, new suggestions are made as to what it can account for in social cognition. The aim of this chapter is to begin to present some of these findings, and connect them to how formal features can contribute to immersion.

Before exploring recent research in simulation theory, it is also important to acknowledge its limitations. At times, simulation is described as 'standardised and shallow' in that it cannot account for 'the way[s] in which we socially categorise people [. . .] our goals in social interactions' or 'the effects of situational context (Spaulding 2019: 4). Moreover, some claim that we 'perceive others in a non-mentalising way' since we 'do not worry about their minds' as we instead 'perceive their movements, gestures, facial expressions and speech acts as meaningful or intentional' (Gallagher 2007: 74). Simulationists rebuke these claims by admitting that while simulation may not *result* in mental state attribution, it is part of a multifaceted complex cognitive process. For instance, one area of simulation theory that this chapter will draw on later is Goldman's 'mature theory' (see Schlicht 2023: 66), which reconstructs the way we understand simulation by merging it with its rival theory, theory-theory. There is not space to detail Goldman's theory in full, but the broad idea is that simulation is seen not as 'wholly decisive' (Goldman 2006: 45), but has as its main crucial principle that we simulate imagined scenarios based on the world around us to guide our behaviour. Therefore, while I do not argue that simulation is the only route for the psychology of mind, it can have a critical role in mental state attribution. I will now introduce some emerging strands of simulation research and how they may contribute to formal features and immersion.

First, recent cognitive research has revealed that object detection is informed by simulation. The claim here is that when we observe objects, simulations may be triggered to help us understand the object (i.e., how we use the object, or what the object looks like if it is out of view). Estes et al. (2008) conducted three experiments testing whether object words oriented attention towards the location where the denoted object typically occurs: that is, if a word was displayed in the high visual field, participants were expected to look up, or report mental imagery denoting an upwards direction. They concluded that 'object words orientated attention and activated simulations' and therefore 'facilitate perception' (2008: 97). Following Estes et al., Speed and Vigliocco (2014: 379) confirmed the idea that 'corresponding elements in a visual scene' are 'map[ped to] one's mental representation of the world', and Nagoev et al. (2020: 372) affirmed that simulations 'construct[ed] an event' which helped to 'recognise and understand' an object and its surroundings. This process of running simulations of objects to understand them better has been termed 'visual abduction' (Magnani 2015: 117). Altogether, I align this view on object detection with the notion of world-building elements from cognitive stylistics (see Gavins 2007, for example). World-building elements represent any textual unit that helps readers construct a mental image of the world of a text, and have been associated with prompting readers to generate images of what goes on in a text, and subsequently immersing them. I argue that simulation theory can provide a framework to explain in greater detail how readers interact with objects in text and how this leads to immersion.

Second, recent research has claimed that simulation has some role in the generation of emotional responses. In its origins, simulation theory aimed to 'delve deeply into value, desire, emotion and intelligence' (Heal 1986: 72), and has since been suggested to inform part of the emotional response. Shanton and Goldman aver that, from their tests on six basic emotions (fear, anger, disgust, sadness, happiness, and surprise), humans may use 're-experience[s] of emotions' through 'a simulational process', which occurs in the premotor cortex (2010: 528). This is a view affirmed by de Waal and Preston, who claim that we rely on 'embodied representations' to understand the 'emotional states of others' (2017: 498, see Wicker et al. 2003 for further cognitive mappings between simulation and emotion). Valli and Revonsuo (2009) go on to suggest that simulating emotional experiences to respond to or experience emotions is a deeply biological drive. Based on interviews and dream records from Finnish, Swedish, Kurdish, Palestinian, and Canadian participants, they claim that 'simulations of threatening events [. . .] leave a mark on emotional memory to have a survival and reproductive' purpose (Valli and Revonsuo 2009: 17). While there is limited evidence to support this claim from Valli and Revonsuo, the idea that humans simulate based on their own experiences as a form of mental imagery to inform their emotional response remains consistent. This will form the basis of an exploration into how emotion displayed in literary texts may lead to immersion.

Simulation in stylistics

How can simulation theory add to the idea in cognitive stylistics that formal features prompt the production of mental images, which then results in immersion? Most research in this area takes the simulation idea that we use replications to help interpretation, as seen in Oakley's claim that readers 'replicate the events they face, or use their own replications to interpret the events of a literary text' (Oakley 2005: 300). There have also been connections drawn between forming mental images and immersion, most notably and recently in Kuijpers et al.'s (2014, 2017) research into storyworld absorption. Here, mental imagery, which is the 'surroundings, characters, and situations that the reader visualises' (Kuijpers et al. 2014: 92), is considered as one of the main dimensions for absorption. From these two separate strands, if simulation can be responsible for producing mental images, and mental imagery is linked to immersion, simulation may be responsible for immersion.

Some studies in cognitive stylistics have used simulation theory to explain the process of textual immersion. Rembowksa-Pluciennik (2010) outlines her idea of 'a reader project[ing] themselves into fiction [. . .] to simulate their experience', which therefore allows them to 'enter into the fictional world' and 'resemble[s] transportation' (2010: 186). Equally, in the context of narrative empathy, White (2015) argues that a 'readerly simulation of character perception and actions' is 'closely related to the reception phenomenon of immersion' (2015: 534, for more on immersion and narrative empathy, see Keen, this volume). Both researchers express a connection between the simulation of a character, akin to the self-imaged thoughts, desires, and intentions via simulation theory, to understand and relate to the situation of a textual character. What is often lacking in these cases is an empirical framework to explain how simulation exactly fits into the reading process and immersion. It means that while there is an acknowledged sense in cognitive stylistics that readers replicate the events of a text, and this leads to immersion, the underlying understanding of how these replications work and how they cause immersion is less obvious. Those studies that do pair simulation with immersion, or transportation as mentioned above, do not reinforce their claims with an empirical element. At this point, I will start to build that simulation-based framework into the reading process.

Methodology

Due to the interdisciplinary nature of reader-response stylistics, there are several ways to study how readers interpret texts: on the one hand, studies have focused on the influence of formal features on readers' responses; on the other hand, research examines a readers' sense of self (see Whiteley and Canning 2017). Reader response also focuses on 'triangulation': that is, combining data collection during (online) and after (offline) the act of reading, with verbal and non-verbal data (Kuijpers 2021: 230). My methodology focuses on the influence of formal features on reader responses, and triangulates online methods, by having participants mark up on the text during reading, and offline, by including retrospective group discussions. Below, I unpack the nature of my semi-structured reading groups and how they were designed to facilitate the study of simulation theory in immersion.

In the interest of obtaining valid and representative data on how simulation theory operates during the reading process, I designed a study using reading groups. The use of reading groups as a stylistic methodology has become well established, where a researcher follows a group discussion of text, and makes observations based on either verbal or non-verbal data generated from the meeting. Reading groups came to prevalence in stylistics via Swann and Allington (2009) in an attempt to acquire data that best resembled the natural process of reading. Moreover, reading groups have also become a method used by psychologists to study simulation.

Dodell-Feder et al. (2013: 9) identified that readers were simulating 'synthesised contextual, verbal and physical information' by reading a short story and asking questions about mental state reasoning, attribution, and comprehension of the story. They propose that the reading groups acted as a 'forum to practice reasoning about others' mental states' (Dodell-Feder et al. 2013: 9). Moreover, the interactive nature of reading groups aligns with the 'nuanced picture of mindreading' which involves participants not only 'observ[ing]' but also 'interact[ing] with the social world' (Turner and Felisberti 2017: 4). Since Peplow (2016: 181) finds readers using reported discourse 'to simulate the minds of fictional characters' in order to understand their experiences, reading groups can enable a naturalistic and simulation-based methodological design.

My study involved three reading groups, each containing seven participants. Participants were recruited using an online advertisement on local Facebook groups. These Facebook groups already existed, either being neighbourhood groups in the local Liverpool area or dedicated undergraduate groups, and the advertisement was made available for three months in 2021 and 2023. From these advertisements, twenty-one participants were recruited, aged between 18–30 years old. Twelve participants were male. Nineteen participants were born in the United Kingdom, one in Ghana, and one in Sri Lanka. All three sessions used the same literary texts: *Life of Pi*, *Romance of the Three Kingdoms* (hereafter *Romance*), *Self*, and *Journey to the West*, which were presented in extracts (around one and a half pages of A4) on an information sheet. The rationale for choosing these texts was based firstly on the stylistic variety they all presented, with some prose, some poetry, and some typographically deviant. The variety allowed for many different stylistic features to be presented to participants. Further, *Romance* and *Journey to the West* are texts originally in Chinese, written in the fourteenth and sixteenth centuries respectively.

The participants filled out their names, age, gender, and place of birth before beginning the sessions, which were hosted in person in one of the University of Liverpool library rooms. The aim was to host these groups outside of an overtly academic context (see Fernandez-Quintanilla 2020: 133), and while they took place on campus they were in a public and open-space reading room to try and replicate a usual reading context. The sessions lasted for around one hour, beginning with an introduction to the study and my background, before participants introduced themselves. Each group then read an extract at a time. They started by reading the text and marking on the passage where they felt the most and least immersed (possibly more than once), with space provided beneath the extract to elaborate on the choices they had made. Participants were given around ten minutes to read and mark up each extract, but there was no strict countdown. After this time, the group discussed their reflections, which I would begin but not guide. Unlike the mark-up section, there was no time limit to these discussions, as I wanted the discussions to be unrestricted and natural.

Each discussion section was audio recorded using a HOMDER digital voice recorder, of which participants were made aware before it was placed out of sight. The final step after data collection was to unpack the patterns of immersion reported by the participants in my study.

As demonstrated by the inclusion of two Chinese case-study texts (*Romance* and *Journey to the West*), my study also had a cross-cultural focus. Here, the term *culture* is understood as the 'broad network of material artifacts and social practices that connect the individual members of a given community' (Paton 2000: 170). Reader-response stylistics recently sought to better account for culture as a way to provide more 'integrated' and 'holistic' views of aspects such as literary character or the impact of formal features (Vaeßen and Strasen 2021: 82). Consideration of culture in reader-response studies tends to focus on one of two areas: the impact of an individual's culture or the text's culture on textual response. My work focused on the impact of textual culture on a reader's ability to be immersed in a literary text. One of the main challenges with focusing on a text's culture in this way is with accurately representing the text after translation. In other words, when translating a text there are risks of 'cultural [mis]representation and linguistic [in]accuracy' (Steiner 1994: 10). How a translation manages the conflict between being (nearly) identical to the original version versus altering the linguistics of the translation to be more amenable to the translated version remains a key debate in cross-cultural and comparative literature studies. In my study, I aimed to maintain as much of the original text's structure and culture as possible, and therefore selected the *p'ing-hua* translation for *Romance* as it provides a 'resemblance of its major episodes to [the] classical embodiments' with 'only minor stylistic changes' (Hsia 1968: 129).

Following the reading groups, I measured immersion using both qualitative and quantitative methods. Quantitatively, each individual mark-up for immersion was counted, as was each utterance in the discussion section which claimed immersion; both were then tested for statistical significance using the correlation coefficient test, *r*. The test allowed me to examine the correlation between a formal feature, such as emotive lexis and world-building elements, and immersion experienced. One might question how participants knew they were immersed: that is, if their self-reports were accurate. It is impossible based on the nature of my methodology to know exactly when participants were immersed, and my study tried to mitigate this challenge by only using comments that mentioned the word 'immersion'. One way to clarify this, perhaps, would be to superimpose my naturalistic data with real-time experimental data, such as fMRI or eye-tracking technology (Turner and Felisberti 2017: 5–6). This would enable a connection to be drawn between the claims made by participants with empirical data, as if their reports map onto brain areas associated with immersion, or indeed simulation, more assured conclusions could be drawn.

On the qualitative side, these numerical patterns were then applied to empirical simulation data. Attributing simulation to these counts of immersion was done carefully; in my data below, only when a participant accompanied their claim for immersion with a term indicating mental imagery (e.g., replication, reproduction) was it considered for analysis with simulation theory. Similarly to above, there is no way to definitely know if a participant was performing a replication or using mental imagery, but only comments which explicitly stated this were considered for analysis.

Data analysis

My data analysis follows two of the four texts used in the reading groups, *Life of Pi* and *Romance.* I include the data only in part so as to focus on the applicability of simulation in two areas: object detection and emotional response.

Life of Pi

The first extract to be explored is taken from chapter 15 of Yann Martel's *Life of Pi* (2001). At this stage of the novel, a reporter interviews the protagonist, Pi, about his 227-day survival at sea, which is yet to be described for the reader. Chapter 15 is therefore an instance of prolepsis in the novel's structure. During the interview, the scene follows the interviewer's perspective around Pi's house, observing its features. The chapter was initially selected due to its typographical variation, as the text is entirely italicised; however, the two most striking features which participants attributed to immersion were emotive lexis and world-building elements.

The most striking feature emerging from the reading groups was emotive lexis. Across the three reading groups, 23 per cent of all claims of immersion (mark-ups and utterances in the discussion) were connected to emotive lexis, and for *Life of Pi* there were twenty-five instances of immersion attributed to emotive lexis. By emotive lexis, I refer to any grammatical feature that influences mood and preference, such as love, fear, or pain (Nørgaard et al. 2010: 13). More specifically, participants would clarify in the writing section, or in discussion, that the 'emotional' or 'expressive' elements of the text would make them feel 'connected' and 'immersed', such as:

1. Those were the key moments of immersion for me. The language that was explicitly emotive.

The above quotation relates to a section of the text that received the most attention when the group opened up for discussion. Halfway through the extract, the interviewer spots a statue of Jesus Christ, observing, 'The Christ is expressive – He suffers' and 'He brings a smile to my lips' (from *Life of Pi*, Martel 2001: 68). Mark-ups highlighted the adjective 'expressive', and the verbs 'suffers' and 'smile'. Then, in the writing or discussion section, participants elaborated that these words helped to 'visualise' the face of Christ, and experience the emotions he was feeling. Participants also marked up a later section depicting Ganesha, which 'brings a smile' to the narrator's face, but none of the groups expanded on it in the discussion section. The use of facial expressions and the specific emotions expressed in both instances are interesting; both instances focus on a smile being brought to the narrator's face and both express an element of joy, with some deeper emotional tones within the adjective 'expressive'. As was the case for the general comments about emotion above, some participants drew a link between the depiction of the face, then its ability to prompt their own visualising, before perhaps feeling that emotion itself, but the latter stage was less frequently observed. For example:

2. They [the smiles] do set the scene really well [. . .] they paint a picture [. . .] it earns the emotion you have.

As can be seen, albeit in a different order, there was a connection between identifying the emotive lexis in the passage, visualising or experiencing that emotion, and some connections then to feeling immersed.

The second most reported feature from chapter 15 of *Life of Pi* was the physical objects in the passage, which I am identifying as world-building elements. Participants marked up at least one of the following objects from the text: 'entrance hall', 'upstairs', 'living room', 'table', 'sofa', or 'temple', with there being twenty-four total instances of immersion attributed to such world-building elements. In the study overall, world-building elements amounted to 20 per cent of all instances of immersion in the dataset. For *Life of Pi*, participants made comments such as:

3. Obviously it lists a lot of different things, icons and objects, and these help to build a picture.
4. I can see and visualise it [objects], that is what is drawing me in. I feel within the story.

As evidenced in these utterances, participants claimed that such world-builders enabled them to visualise what the scene of the text looked like, which was then attributed to feeling immersed in the story. This affirms the idea in cognitive stylistics that world-builders assist in enabling readers to picture and perhaps project into fictional worlds (Stockwell 2020: 142). There were, however, some claims from participants that the world-builders did create distance from the text, and could break their immersion.

5. The various mentions of all the objects related to different Gods and deities and things not from my background I found quite hard to picture [. . .] and would remove me [from the text].

While this study can only suggest why world-builders disengaged participants, there was some evidence to suggest that a gap in schematic knowledge might have some influence. In chapter 15 of *Life of Pi* there are a number of religious icons and images ('Lakshmi; Shakti, the mother goddess, in the form of Parvati; and Krishna, this time as a playful baby crawling on all fours. [. . .] In between the goddesses is a stone Shiva yoni linga', Martel 2001: 61), and one of the participants who was of Sri Lankan origin said:

6. A little bit opposite [. . .] my Dad went to Sri Lanka and picked up statues [. . .] they were in our living room so ever since I was young I have always been familiar.

Based on the participant's comments, while world-builders are an important element in visualising and in turn immersing in a text, this is a process tempered by contextual knowledge. This would suggest that schematic knowledge in some way facilitates reader engagement, a view proposed by Stockwell (2020: 103), which my discussion section will unpack in relation to simulation theory.

Romance of the Three Kingdoms (Romance)

Romance (Luo 2007) is a historical story set during the rebellion against the Han dynasty and the remaining factions that dominated China at the time. The section provided in my study comes at the specific point when a faction of the Kingdom of Wei conquered the kingdom of Shu-Han. Data for *Romance* is less clear-cut than that from *Life of Pi*, and instances of immersion were less frequent in comparison, as many participants reported that the text was 'difficult overall [to immerse in]'. There were, however, similarities and differences in data to draw between *Life of Pi* regarding emotive lexis and world-builders, as these remained the two most reported features.

For emotive lexis, participants reported that in spite of the different Chinese context, they found points to immerse in the text-world via this type of lexis. There were eighteen total counts of emotive lexis contributing to immersion, such as:

7. I felt like I was fighting to understand the text [. . .] it took me out of the experience. I only really immerse with the emotions I could feel.

As seen in (7), the trend of disengaging context being balanced by moments of immersion is reflected in the emotive language found in *Romance.* Participants tended to mark up the words 'furious', 'sad', and 'harm' (from *Romance*, Luo 2007: 440), which, while not explicitly stating emotions, do connote them, as with the pairs *furious/anger*, or *harm/suffering*. This suggests that the emotion attached to certain words, for instance the link between pain and 'harm', was felt by readers when these words were read.

Semino (2010: 17) makes similar reflections when analysing the cognitive mechanisms underpinning metaphor, suggesting that from the lexeme *pain*, or from other metaphorical representations of pain, readers experience an imitation of pain. The pattern emerging here seems to be that certain emotions are tied to certain words, and participants feel these emotions as they read them, albeit on an infrequent basis in this text. Nevertheless, feeling these emotions may lead to immersion, as seen for *Life of Pi*. It seems that this experience was not as clear in *Romance*, and was tempered by the challenging cultural context.

The dynamic between immersion and the less familiar cultural context continued for world-builders. While participants stated that clauses containing Chinese cultural entities such as 'The Lord of Jin', 'the Yangtze', or the 'yellow of Shu' (*Romance*, Luo 2007: 440) made the text 'inaccessible', 'familiar' geographical and weather-based words such as 'land and water', 'wind and thunder', and 'wind and waves' helped them to feel that they were 'in' the story (*Romance*, Luo 2007: 440):

8. The common thing is more accessible and the weather we can all relate and be in.
9. The way the weather is described makes me feel in it.

Reports such as these seem to suggest that unfamiliar schematic knowledge can be somewhat bypassed using world-builders to immerse. It suggests that there are certain words, as was the same for emotive lexis, that can immerse readers regardless of the cultural context they are found within. The same can technically be said for *Life of Pi*; there was some other contextual information in *Life of Pi* which disengaged participants, and yet there were certain world-builders which managed to immerse participants within the story. These findings come together to suggest that world-builders seem to have an important function for immersion. I now turn to an understanding of how these patterns regarding emotive lexis and world-builders leading to immersion can be understood further using simulation theory.

Discussion

Emotional language was 'connecting'

My dataset shows 387 total accounts of immersion from participants (either mark-ups or discussion comments), with eighty-nine of those (23 per cent) attributed to emotive lexis. A significant difference ($p = 0.01$) was found between the two cases of emotive lexis and immersion, and a correlation coefficient (r) of +0.79 shows a positive correlation between the experience of emotion and feelings of immersion. I argue that emotion looks to have a significant role in immersing readers in fiction, furthering the argument that emotion is not a 'side-effect' in reading but a driving force behind readers' experience of immersion (Stockwell 2002: 200).

The overarching pattern was that emotive lexis triggered participants to visualise a replication of that emotion, which prompted them to feel the emotion, and altogether would be responsible for feeling immersed. For instance, participants marked up words such as 'fear', 'pain', and 'love' (*Life of Pi*, Martel 2001: 68, and *Romance*, Luo 2007: 440), reporting that they were 'gripped by fear' or 'felt love' as they read these words. The majority of these instances were of participants 'feeling for' characters, which created the sense of being immersed in the character's feelings and actions. Simulation can explain this emotional experience through Goldman's (2006) notion of *enactment imagination*, an idea at the heart of modern simulation theory. In Goldman's concept, words such as those marked by my participants act as 'mental state tokens' or 'mental categories' that prompt a 'reenactment' of that feeling (Goldman 2006: 260, see also Hogan 2017 on reenactments). Goldman later clarifies what he means by 'reenactments' when discussing the role of fiction in testing his theory, when he states that 'fiction serves as a series of textual props that fuel a reader's E-imagination into producing surrogate states' (2006: 284). The reports given by participants in my study seem to confirm this idea, as Goldman's surrogate states equate to when my participants say they 'paint a picture' of the emotions in text (see (2)). Therefore, the process of creating these surrogate states, triggered by emotive lexis to simulate similar emotional experiences to feel for the characters, makes up the experience of immersion for readers.

The idea that the simulation of an emotion creates immersion continues with the pattern of facial expressions highlighted by participants. In my studies, all but one participant in three groups highlighted 'Christ is expressive – He suffers' and when the narrator references a painting of Ganesha which 'brings a smile' to their face (*Life of Pi*, Martel 2001: 68). Present work on simulation can offer some discussion as to why facial expressions had such effect. 'FaBER' or 'face-based emotion recognition' (Adolphs et al. 1995, Goldman 2006: 113) states that humans simulate emotions that are associated with certain facial expressions. From these simulations, we classify mental states akin to mental categories, following the same principle in E-imagination, which informs an emotional response. Therefore, I posit that the facial expressions found in the literary texts for this study encourage simulations of their associated emotions for Christ and Ganesha in *Life of Pi* (Martel 2001: 59–60). Again, the process of simulating these emotions makes up the immersion experience.

Despite these claims, reports on emotion and immersion were not always clear-cut. In *Romance*, instances in which we would expect emotive lexis to trigger simulations, and immersion, did not occur. For example, participants did not always attribute immersion to the sentences '[Ganesha] brings a smile' (*Life of Pi*, Martel 2001: 68), or 'Lord Wu was shocked [. . .] south of the Yangtze' (*Romance*, Luo 2007: 440). Some participants stated that these parts of the text were 'quite hard to picture', despite including what would be assumed emotive lexis, with 'shock', and 'smile' linking to FaBER. Based on my data, and the influence of cultural context, it would then seem that the way in which fictional worlds are presented interacts with the emotion within a passage; a passage may contain emotion, but its immersive potential can be influenced by surrounding formal features. This can be supported by Papp-Zipernovszky et al. (2022), who find that when exploring the use of foregrounding in Shakespearean sonnets, 'spatial configuration is more important than quantity for emotional response' (2022: 319). In the case of this study, the alternative cultural context of Ganesha and the Yangtze may estrange readers and hinder the immersive potential of the surrounding emotive lexis. This would be a case of the effect of the combination of techniques in narratives forcing a reader to 'weave in and out' of the feeling of immersion, as desired by Kuijpers et al. (2017: 41), as here we see one feature taking priority and the interruption of one feature for preference of another.

Altogether, my research suggests that the acknowledged gap between emotion in reading and language can be filled in some capacity by simulation theory. Oatley proposed twenty years ago that simulation helps us better 'understand [. . .] the contexts in which emotions arise' (1999: 101), and my claim is that emotive lexis can trigger simulations and in turn visualisations of the textual emotion, which creates surrogate emotional states, and therefore makes up the experience of immersion.

'Pictur[ing] things' to understand the world

The second area of interest in this chapter regards the role of world-builders. In my dataset, seventy-eight of 387 counts of immersion (20 per cent) were attributed to world-builders. A significant difference ($p = 0.01$) was found between world-builders and immersion, and a correlation coefficient (r) of +0.71 shows a positive correlation between the experience of world-builders and feelings of immersion. I thus argue that, as for emotive lexis, world-builders may trigger simulations of the objects they present, which leads to immersion. As stated, this is already thought to be the case in cognitive stylistics, but I present a framework to explicate the process, and in doing so, argue that world-builders are even more fundamental to immersion.

As my data analysis showed for both texts, participants would highlight world-builders and in doing so attribute feelings of immersion. Items such as 'entrance hall', 'kitchen', or 'flower' in *Life of Pi* (Martel 2001: 68), or in *Romance*, 'sun', 'moon', or 'wind' were deemed immersive (Luo 2007: 440). This process of building a picture created a sense of immersion for the readers, which, according to my data and existing reports in cognitive stylistics, is about 'concretising for readers' (Stockwell 2019: 16). Bergen and Chang (2003) make similar claims without a cognitive stylistic background.

They claim that 'open-class words [. . .] contribute content to be simulated' (2003: 1), which helps readers create 'pictures of things' (2003: 1). In other words, world-builders helped to visualise elements of the text and in turn immerse within that world. Visual cognition and simulation-based research provides a framework to explain this process. In simulation theory, words denoting objects trigger the 'activation of perceptual simulations' (Estes et al. 2008: 93), which has been termed a process of 'visual abduction' in which we use 'image-like representations' and 'processing with linguistic information' for 'hypotheses generation' (Magnani 2015: 117). I argue that world-builders trigger simulations, and this begins a hypothesis-generating process to understand the text, which in turn makes up the immersion experience.

The idea that readers use world-builders for hypothesis-generation touches on a more significant role for them within the immersion process. In my data, it seemed that world-builders had a more telling effect on the ability for participants to immerse. Compared with emotive lexis, it appeared that participants were more influenced by the objects in the text, or so-called 'spatial configuration' (Papp-Zipernovszky et al. 2022: 319). This was because supposedly immersive emotive lexis failed to attract participants, possibly due to the estranging cultural context of Ganesha and the Yangtze. Therefore, surrounding world-builders may constrain readers' ability to use other formal features to immerse. Hogan (2013: 25) makes a similar claim in the context of simulation theory, suggesting that simulations of the world are 'influenced' and 'constrained' by 'material conditions' and 'physical properties' when we simulate. It would appear then that world-builders have an influence on the ability to simulate, and in turn immerse, from surrounding formal features.

Furthermore, words such as 'sun' or 'moon' received frequent mark-up and were not only attributed as immersion but also helped participants achieve an immersive response when they struggled with the cultural contexts in *Romance*:

10. I am really unfamiliar with Chinese context [. . .] but the description brings me back in.

Notwithstanding the difference between the phrase 'back in' and the concept of immersion, despite the Chinese context estranging participants, the world-builders provided an opportunity to engage with, and possibly immerse into, an unfamiliar literary and historical context. For instance, considering the case of the discussed Yangtze above, one may question whether, if the noun 'river' had been included, more cases of immersion would have occurred. My data on the role of world-builders would suggest so. We could also consider the universality of words such as 'sun' or 'moon' as objects, whose ability to immerse readers across both texts and in alternative cultures still triggered simulations and immersion. Nagoev et al. (2020)

suggest that there are 'units of knowledge' that are more likely to trigger simulations, such as certain colours, geolocations, and shapes (2020: 373). They do not specify which particular characteristics of objects these may be, but the data from my study seems to confirm that certain objects may evoke simulations more often than others. Thus, world-builders may have an even more central role in how readers are immersed in texts.

Conclusion

This chapter has opened up an investigation between simulation and immersion. My findings confirm the views that emotive lexis and world-building elements trigger immersion, and further add to this discussion via an explicit pairing with simulation theory. I have also made suggestions about the value of cross-cultural literary texts to expand understanding of how immersion works. Future research will look to expand upon my approach, particularly via physiopsychological and cross-cultural methods. On the physiopsychological side, technology such as eye tracking may offer more accurate determinations of how language features produce immersion. On the cross-cultural side, continuing the investigate how participants react to alternative cultures can provide data to test the suggested additional value of cultural variation to understanding immersion.

References

Adolphs, R. (1995) 'Fear and the human amygdala', *Journal of Neuroscience* 15 (1): 5879–91.

Apperly, I. (2011) *Mindreaders: The Cognitive Basis of 'Theory of Mind'*. New York: Psychology Press.

Bergen, B. and Chang, N. (2003) 'Embodied Construction Grammar in simulation-based language understanding', in M. Fried and J. Ostman (eds) *Construction Grammar in a Cross-language Perspective*. Amsterdam: John Benjamins, pp.1–22.

Bilandzic, H. and Busselle, R. (2017) 'Beyond metaphors and traditions: exploring the conceptual boundaries of narrative engagement', in F. Hakemulder, M.M. Kuijpers, E.S. Tan, K. Bálint and M.M. Doicaru (eds) *Narrative Absorption*. Amsterdam: John Benjamins, pp.12–28.

D'Angelo, E. and Jirsa, V. (2022) 'The quest for multiscale brain modelling', *Trends in Neuroscience* 45 (10): 777–90.

Dodell-Feder, D., Lincoln, S.H., Coulson, J.P. and Hooker, C.I. (2013) 'Using fiction to assess mental state understanding: a new task for assessing Theory of Mind in adults', *PLOS* 8 (11): 1–14.

Estes, Z., Verges, M. and Barsalou, L. (2008) 'Head up, foot down: object words orient attention to the objects' typical location', *Psychological Science* 19 (2): 93–7.

Fernandez-Quintanilla, F. (2020) 'Textual and reader factors in narrative empathy: an empirical reader response study using focus groups', *Language and Literature* 29 (2): 124–46.

Gallagher, S. (2007) 'Logical and phenomenological arguments against simulation theory', in D. Hutto and M. Ratcliffe (eds) *Folk Psychology Re-Assessed*. London: Springer, pp.63–78.

Gavins, J. (2007) *Text World Theory: An Introduction*. Edinburgh: Edinburgh University Press.

Goldman, A. (2006) *Simulating Minds: The Philosophy, Psychology, and Neuroscience of Mindreading*. Oxford: Oxford University Press.

Gordon, R. (1986) 'Folk psychology as simulation', *Mind and Language* 1 (2): 158–71.

Heal, J. (1986) 'Replication and functionalism', in J. Butterfield (ed.) *Language, Mind, and Logic*. Cambridge: Cambridge University Press, pp.45–59.

Hesslow, G. (2011) 'The current status of the simulation theory of cognition', *Brain Research* 1428 (1): 71–9.

Hogan, P.C. (2013) *How Authors' Minds Make Stories*. Cambridge: Cambridge University Press.

Hogan, P.C. (2017) *Literature and Emotion*. London: Routledge.

Hsia, C. (1968) *The Classic Chinese Novel*. Hong Kong: Chinese University of Hong Kong Press.

Kuijpers, M. (2021) 'Toward reconciliation of empirical traditions in the investigation of reading and literature', in A. Bell, S. Browse and A. Gibbons (eds) *Style and Reader Response: Minds, Media, Methods*. Amsterdam: John Benjamins, pp.217–29.

Kuijpers, M.M., Hakemulder, F., Bálint, K., Doicaru, M.M. and Tan, E.S. (2017) 'Towards a new understanding of absorbing reading experiences', in F. Hakemulder, M.M. Kuijpers, E.S. Tan, K. Bálint and M.M. Doicaru (eds) *Narrative Absorption*. Amsterdam: John Benjamins, pp.29–49.

Kuijpers, M.M., Hakemulder, F., Tan, E.S and Doicaru, M.M. (2014) 'Exploring absorbing reading experiences: developing and validating a self-report to measure story world absorption', *Scientific Study of Literature* 4 (1): 89–122.

Luo, G. (2007) *Romance of the Three Kingdoms* [online]. Project Gutenberg.

Magnani, L. (2015) 'Understanding visual abduction', in W. Park, P. Li and L. Magnani (eds) *Philosophy and Cognitive Science II*. Berlin: Springer, pp.117–39.

Martel, Y. (2001) *Life of Pi*. Edinburgh: Canongate.

Nagoev, Z., Pshenokova, I., Gurtueva, I. and Bzhikhatlov, K. (2020) 'A simulation model for the cognitive function of static objects recognition based on machine-learning multi-agent architectures', *Advances in Intelligent Systems and Computing* 948 (1): 370–8.

Nørgaard, N., Busse, B. and Montoro, R. (2010) *Key Terms in Stylistics*. London: Continuum.

Oakley, T. (2005) 'A simulation semantics approach to rhetoric analysis', *Language and Literature* 14 (3): 295–310.

Oatley, K. (1999) 'Why fiction may be twice as true as fact: fiction as cognitive and emotional simulation', *General Psychology* 3 (2): 101–17.

O'Shea, H. and Moran, A. (2017) 'Does motor simulation theory explain the cognitive mechanisms underlying motor imagery? A critical review', *Frontiers in Human Neuroscience* 11 (72): 1–13.

Papp-Zipernovszky, O., Mangen, A., Jacobs, A. and Lüdtke, J. (2022) 'Shakespeare sonnet reading: an empirical study of emotional responses', *Language and Literature* 31 (3): 296–324.

Paton, F. (2000) 'Beyond Bakhtin: towards a cultural stylistics', *College English* 63 (2): 166–93.

Peplow, D. (2016) *Talk About Books: A Study of Reading Groups*. London: Bloomsbury.
Rembowksa-Pluciennik, M. (2010) 'Narrative poetics of mindreading', *Issues of Literary Genres* 8 (1): 175–90.
Schlicht, T. (2023) *Philosophy of Social Cognition*. London: Palgrave Macmillan.
Semino, E. (2010) 'Descriptions of pain, metaphor and embodied simulation', *Metaphor and Symbol* 25 (4): 1–23.
Shanton, K. and Goldman, A. (2010) 'Simulation theory', *Cognitive Science* 1 (4): 527–38.
Spaulding, R. (2019) 'What is mindreading?', *Cognitive Science* 11 (1): 1–13.
Speed, L. and Vigliocco, G. (2014) 'Eye movements reveal the dynamic simulation of speed in language', *Cognitive Science* 38 (1): 367–82.
Steiner, G. (1994) *What is Comparative Literature?* Oxford: Clarendon.
Stockwell, P. (2002) *Cognitive Poetics: An Introduction*. London: Routledge.
Stockwell, P. (2019) 'Immersion and emergence in children's literature', in B. Neurohr and L. Stewart-Shaw (eds) *Experiencing Fictional Worlds*. Amsterdam: Benjamins, pp.15–32.
Stockwell, P. (2020) *Cognitive Poetics: An Introduction* (2nd edn). London: Routledge.
Swann, J. and Allington, D. (2009) 'Reading groups and the language of literary texts: a case study in social reading', *Language and Literature* 18 (3): 247–64.
Turner, R. and Felisberti, F. (2017) 'Measuring mindreading: a review of behavioural approaches to testing cognitive and affective mental state attribution', *Frontiers in Psychology* 8 (1).
Vaeßen, J. and Strasen, S. (2021) 'A cognitive and cultural reader response theory of character construction', in A. Bell, S. Browse and A. Gibbons (eds) *Style and Reader Response: Minds, Media, Methods*. Amsterdam: John Benjamins, pp.81–98.
Valli, K. and Revonsuo, A. (2009) 'The threat simulation theory in light of recent empirical evidence', *American Journal of Psychology* 122 (1): 17–28.
de Waal, F. and Preston, S. (2017) 'Mammalian empathy: behavioural manifestations and neural basis', *Nature Reviews* 18 (1): 498–509.
White, C. (2015) 'Embodied reading and narrative empathy in Cormac McCarthy's *The Road*', *Studies in the Novel* 47 (4): 532–49.
Whiteley, S. and Canning, P. (2017) 'Reader response research in stylistics', *Language and Literature* 26 (2): 71–87.
Wicker, B., Keysers, C., Plailly, J., Royet, J.-P., Gallese, V. and Rizzolatti, G. (2003) 'Both of us disgusted in my insula: the common neural basis of seeing and feeling disgust', *Neuron* 40 (3): 655–64.

CHAPTER 8

The immersive potential of an ekphrastic experience

Polina Gavin

Immersion is mainly treated in this book as a literary matter (though see the song lyric analysis by Voice, this volume). In this chapter, Gavin explores the immersive potential of painting and poetry, when one is a reflection or inspiration for the other, as an *ekphrasis*. She presents an empirical case study of readers of a poem about a specific painting and traces their cognitive strategies through their responses. Finding that these responses are complex, rather than a simple mapping from poem to painting, Gavin suggests that the ekphrastic encounter is better characterised as a blended and integrative immersive experience, or what she terms an *entanglement*.

Introduction

This chapter explores the immersive quality of engaging with ekphrasis, a multimodal phenomenon that combines a work of art and a creative response to it. In cognitive stylistic research, an immersive experience is characterised as the increased engagement of the reader with the fictional world, where they cast their mind into and hence feel close to the narrated experiences. While some work has been done on examining readerly engagement with ekphrasis (Kennedy 2012, Panagiotidou 2022), the research focus primarily has been placed on reading an ekphrastic text, without taking into account a work of art which inspired a creative response. In my research, I aim to redress this balance and argue for the experientiality of ekphrasis. Drawing on empirical data, I discuss how immersion in ekphrasis can be achieved via the participatory and interactive positioning of the reader.

Reconfiguring an ekphrastic experience

Ekphrasis in literary theory has been defined as 'the reproduction, through the medium of words, of sensuously perceptible objets d'art' (Spitzer 1955: 207). Scholarship on ekphrasis typically cites celebrated poems by W.H. Auden, John Keats, Anne Sexton, and William Carlos Williams, among others. These exemplar poetic works have for a long time defined an ekphrastic tradition, conferring ekphrastic poetry with an aura of elite literariness. I argue that ekphrastic writing and the way we read ekphrasis need revisiting: a few renowned poetic texts struggle to reflect the ubiquity of ekphrasis in contemporary cultural and artistic contexts. The creative reinterpretations of visual art are far more diverse and integral to our life than one would think. Take, for example, the common museum practice of accompanying displayed artworks with ekphrastic poems that are frequently created by individuals from the local community. This ties with another widespread application of ekphrasis: using artworks as a springboard for creative writing. For example, the Seamus Heaney Centre of creative writing and research in Belfast practises ekphrastic writing as a hands-on learning method. Their annual *Ekphrasis Project* involves a series of seminars and live events that result in the students' collaborative production of ekphrastic pamphlets. This utility of ekphrasis in a contemporary cultural context gives rise to 'ekphrastic inquiry' (Prendergast 2009) as a practice-led research method that encourages reflective engagement with artworks by means of creative writing used as 'our voice, our tool, our discourse' (Harper 2020: xv) for dialogue and interaction.

Each ekphrastic response manifests the writer's idiosyncratic 'way of seeing' (Scott 2023: 14), which they relay by making meaningful choices for using certain linguistic expressions. 'Why these word-choices, clause-patterns, rhythms and intonations [. . .], and not any of the others imaginable?', asks Toolan (1998: ix), and approaching ekphrasis as an accessible, diverse, and eclectic creative writing practice allows us to embrace the full spectrum of language expression, getting insight into the interpretative mechanisms which underpin an experience of ekphrasis. However, a poetic response only partially contributes to our interpretations in ekphrasis. Considering that the phenomenon comes into being by combining contributions from the artist and the writer, I argue that ekphrasis can only be experienced fully with the input of both image and text in readerly experience. The integration of representations offered by the visual and the verbal is likely to increase the immersive experience of ekphrasis, where the reader constructs meaning holistically, leading to an interpretation no less unique than the creative act of responding to an art piece in the first place.

The involvement of both an artwork and an ekphrastic response in meaning-making brings us to cast a new look at the experientiality of ekphrasis. Making sense of ekphrasis in the process of negotiating meaning and integrating its elements is key to heightening readerly engagement.

From its very conception, the transportive powers of ekphrasis and its focus upon reception-orientedness have been at the heart of the phenomenon. Historically, ekphrasis was linked to *energeia*, the ability to vividly capture an experience in language and bring it before the audience's eyes. In ancient rhetoric, for an ekphrastic exercise to be successful, it was supposed to engage listeners in an immersive and imagery-evoking experience, capable of eliciting an empathetic response to the relayed message. Since then, ekphrastic discourse has significantly transformed, with the scholarly interest in the affective impact of ekphrastic reading being a recent trend. For instance, Kennedy (2012: 25) introduces the notion of an 'ekphrastic encounter', where the reader engages with tangible and intangible embodied experiences of an object relayed in writing. As a result, an ekphrastic experience becomes a 'transaction' or 'negotiation' of the impressions from a visual scene and the perspective offered in an ekphrastic retelling (Louvel 2019: 183). The complexity of the reader's positioning in ekphrasis is addressed by Benton (2000), who argues that, facing both an image and a text, the reader is placed in an unusual and unstable stance. Benton (2000) introduces the term 'ekphrastic spectator' to highlight the complex nature of an ekphrastic experience, as

> an individual contemplates a painting or sculpture through the eyes of a poet, aware both that the visual work so represented remains, essentially, a poetic fiction, and that the visual work as presented in the gallery remains a representation; the potential either for a clash of 'readings' or for enhanced insight into the art work is ever present.
> (Benton 2000: 43)

In this definition, Benton highlights polyvocality inherent to an ekphrastic rendering. In response to the text, an ekphrastic spectator is encouraged to engage in self-reflexivity in order to cross-reference the portrayed scene with an offered reading and decide whether their personal interpretation of an artwork clashes or collaborates with an ekphrastic response. This 'interference' or 'enhancement' (Benton 2000: 41) of the spectator's impression is important, because it places focus on how the collaboration with an ekphrastic retelling enhances readerly engagement. Engaging with an offered poetic retelling of an art piece is a challenging and cognitively demanding task, which requires more investment on a reader's part. The process of constructing meaning itself can lead to an increased engagement with the narrative (see Bilandzic and Buselle 2017). In an ekphrastic context, the heightened engagement with an ekphrastic story is achieved when readers find the writer's take on the story interesting and complex enough for it to be explored further. In this case, readers decide to collaborate with the offered retelling and smoothly build a mental model of an ekphrastic story filling in the gaps in comprehension without experiencing inconsistencies that could disrupt this experience.

The cooperation with the proposed ekphrastic retelling can affect readers' positioning in relation to the narrated events. With readers' fictional recentring accounted for by means of the metaphorical mapping READING IS TRANSPORTATION (Gerrig 1993, Stockwell 2009), the immersive experience of ekphrasis frequently brings along a higher level of emotional attunement to the preoccupations of the character, mapped as EMOTIONAL RELATIONSHIP IS DISTANCE BETWEEN TWO ENTITIES (Kövecses 2000). It is possible that readers' cooperation with an ekphrastic retelling and the subsequent interweaving of ekphrastic interpretations may contribute to their increased engagement with an ekphrastic story and an elevated empathetic response to the narrated events. To examine this immersive potential of ekphrasis in this chapter, I draw on reader-response data as an 'indirect measure of literary experience' (Harrison 2024: 15) and illustrate how readers actively and willingly take part in co-constructing the fictional world by taking a collaborative stance and elaborating a representation by investing their personal relevant interpretations.

The model of ekphrastic intervention

To examine how ekphrasis is created and experienced, I introduce the concept of *ekphrastic intervention*, which I define as 'a creative act of responding to an art piece that results in a reimagined version of a portrayed scene' (Gavin 2024: 49). In this, I draw on Pope's (1995: 27) framework of textual intervention, where he places emphasis 'on exploring possible permutations and realisations of texts in and out of their original contexts'. Ekphrastic intervention accounts for a certain change in the interpretation of the artwork proposed by the writer and focuses on how this retelling is conveyed in language. The model of ekphrastic intervention enables us to operationalise how readers' experience of ekphrasis may be actively manipulated by the writer's language choices. While the cognition involved in responding to an artwork as well as interpreting ekphrasis is impossible to capture directly, I operate with the best data available at hand, which is the language manifestations of ekphrastic poems and readers' responses to the phenomenon.

My model of ekphrastic intervention is based on the premise that the writer's retelling conceptually (mis)aligns with the representation originally offered by an artwork to a certain extent. Conceptual alignment is a scalable quality that can be manifested spatiotemporally and thematically, by means of a profiled perspective and dominant atmosphere. Conceptual alignment is important, because it can be responsible for readers' decisions to cooperate or resist the ekphrastic interpretation offered by the writer. As a result of cooperation, readers can feel more immersed into the experience of an artwork after reading an ekphrastic text compared to an experience of a stand-alone art piece. When cooperating with the offered retelling, readers engage with ekphrasis via the processes of interrelation (Mason 2019) and blending (Fauconnier and Turner 2002). First, readers' cooperation with the writer's rendering is bound to be based on recognising some sort of similarity between an artwork and an ekphrastic text. Recognising this connection is a cognitive act of interrelation, where readers create a link in the mind between two narratives which is manifested in language in a form of an intertextual reference (Mason 2019). Second, once the connection is established, readers proceed to blend the two into a structure that surpasses the combined value of its individual input spaces (Fauconnier and Turner 2002). The new blended mental model contains features that are selectively cross-mapped from both input spaces, and their integration leads to the creation of new relations via the processes of composition, completion, and elaboration. In contrast, when the representations in ekphrasis are more prone to signal misalignment, readers tend to show some resistance in connecting the two. In these cases, even if their responses indicate processes of interrelation, readers remain committed to their original interpretations and very rarely develop them into an integrated blend. Instead, readers tend to alternate attention when discussing an artwork and a text, toggling between spotlighting one and backgrounding the other, similarly to the relations of figure-ground (Evans and Green 2006).

To systematise interventions and their manifestations in language, one of my previous analyses (Gavin 2024) of textual traits featured in ekphrastic texts allowed me to identify three dominant intervention strategies, namely *textual*, *contextual*, and *cross-textual*. Textual interventions sustain a close alignment between an image and a text, inviting readers to create a holistic blend of an ekphrastic experience. Contextual interventions focus on storytelling, and hence recentre the focus of attention to a distinct sequence of events which is not captured in the visual scene. Finally, cross-textual interventions disrupt expectations and facilitate readerly awareness of a profound thematic, spatiotemporal, or ontological difference. In this chapter, I will be focusing on the example of textual intervention, which contains a transformation that sustains a high degree of conceptual alignment between an image and a text. Textual interventions occur 'within the margins of the base' (Pope 1995: 427), where the 'base' is the representation that is likely to be evoked by the artwork, with the implemented changes featuring an apparent plot and spatiotemporal setting, hence leading to a minimal departure from an original text. As a result, with the absence of an explicit challenge to their original view of an artwork, readers are likely to establish interrelations and, subsequently, smoothly integrate the offered interpretation and their original view of the artwork into an ekphrastic blend. This construction of a novel mental model commonly enhances the immersive quality of an ekphrastic experience, as readers become active facilitators in creating and running an idiosyncratic ekphrastic blend. In the upcoming discussion, I focus on the reported mechanisms and effects of conceptual blending in ekphrasis that unravel readers' developing engagement with an artwork and its retelling. As the proposed model is ultimately reader- and data-driven, it is of paramount importance to highlight that readers do not create identical ekphrastic blends and even not all readers create blends at all. Instead, drawing on the reader-response data, I illustrate how the reported experiences of ekphrastic blending show the immersive quality of the constructed fictional scenario that is often evidenced in readers' reported identification with the narrated experiences and a high level of emotional affinity with the story.

Methodology

In the majority of cases, existing approaches to ekphrasis do not extend far beyond the researcher's personal introspection. In contrast, my approach to ekphrasis is firmly situated within an established tradition of cognitive stylistic research based on empirical validation. The stylistic empirical turn (Bell et al. 2021) combines 'text-driven analysis with theories of cognition and empirical research' (Bell et al. 2018: 5). Thus, reader response often serves as a tool for 'verifying or problematising theoretical conclusions' (Bell et al. 2021: 2) and enables 'testing and development of stylistic methods and theories' (Whiteley and Canning 2017: 73).

The reader-response data was generated in the experimental setting of online semi-structured interviews. For the case study presented in this chapter, the sample size was twenty participants who all viewed the painting (coded from P1.1 to P1.10 and P2.1 to P2.10). The ten participants in the P1 group read the poem after seeing the painting; the P2 group was tasked with reading a different poem. All participants were familiarised with ekphrasis prior to the interview. At the interview, participants first observed a visual scene and then moved to reading an ekphrastic text positioned alongside the painting reproduction on the slide. The discussion was loosely structured around questions addressing participants' interpretations of the observed scene and the text, whether they felt like they were connected and whether they thought their original interpretation of the artwork had changed. The coding strategy was initially based on *a priori* codes to mark how participants reported recognising interrelations between the image and the text, highlighting the elements they considered salient, and noting the reported interpretative changes when having read the poem.

For this experiment, I used the painting *Roofscape* by Gustave Caillebotte (1878), usually titled *Vue de toits (Effet de neige)*, and the ekphrastic poem 'Lost Dream for my Unvaccinated Lover' by John Milkereit (from 2023). The painting can be found here: <https://www.musee-orsay.fr/en/artworks/vue-de-toits-effet-de-neige-108>

Roofscape by Gustave Caillebotte

Roofscape portrays a wintery view of Paris, where, through the eyes of a non-present observer, the audience overlooks the empty districts usually hidden behind the city's renovated monumental façade – courtyards, back streets, and houses under reconstruction. Deemed one of Caillebotte's most prominent impressionist works, *Roofscape* is marked for its 'envelope of atmosphere' (Varnedoe 1987: 116). The reduced tonal and colour contrast preponderate in the scene, with the sky colours transitioning from a grey hue to occasional touches of gentle pink. When discussing their impressions of this wintery atmosphere, participants reportedly attribute emotions to the portrayed surroundings and remark on the attention-grabbing effect of visual negation as a refiguring technique.

Colour symbolism

The data demonstrate that most participants emphasise the role of colour in sustaining the atmosphere and evoking an emotional response to the scene. Participants often comment on the bleakness and muteness of the colour palette that creates 'indistinctness' (P2.4) and 'messiness' (P2.3) through the lack of light. The low-light conditions of the cityscape are likely to impact viewers' moods; as is well known (see Küller et al.'s (2006) study), participants from the Northern Hemisphere report poor mood, social withdrawal, and other symptoms of seasonal affective disorder due to the lack of light in winter. Within the limited range of colours in the painting, most participants commonly focus on the contrast between grey and white tones. This colour contrast gives rise to a duality of impressions:

> P1.10: Almost like opposites, but they work together to create this feeling of . . . it is eerie and gloomy and dark, but there's also a sense of stillness and comfort and peace.

The influence of colours on producing a range of behavioural and emotional responses is well documented (Mikellides 2017). In responses to the painting, participants draw parallels between colours and certain emotions and project colour associations onto social class. The achromatic tones of grey are prototypically associated with dullness and sombreness, as evidenced in participants' responses. Many responses indicate the use of the metaphor SADNESS IS GREY, where participants connect the greyness of the cityscape with its mood. P2.10 details how their impression of a 'dreary landscape' is constructed via the colour that they transpose from dirty snow and smoke in the surroundings: 'quite a dreary landscape, but it's not just snow, it's dirty snow'. [. . .] It's also got the smoke of the city.' Several participants cross-map the negative connotations of grey onto the industrialism of the cityscape. P1.7 establishes an overt link between the symbolic meaning of colour and the working-class type of area: 'it is an industrial area, maybe because grey is making me think that'. P2.2 foregrounds the negative connotations associated with industrialism by listing the adjectival modifiers 'dark and gloomy and industrial' in a parallel syntactic construction, thus presupposing complementarity of their characteristics. P1.3 speaks of the symbolic darkness conveyed in the scene, which they interconnect with the industrial nature of the portrayed city: 'an oppressive kind of place, a dark place, a dusty coal mining, shoe factory kind of place'. P1.3's comment that the cityscape is not 'fancy and posh' links to another metaphor POVERTY IS GREY, which illustrates how colours can be used to denote social class. P1.4 discusses the progression of colours in the scene, from the monochromatic shades of grey in the foreground to warmer shades of brown and brick-red in the back, which they interpret as a 'border' between the neighbourhoods: 'Somewhat better off in the background. It's obviously not downtown Paris, but it's better.' P2.4 similarly comments on the liminality of the portrayed area: 'It might be on the edge of the middle-class area, tending towards the poor end of society.' P1.4 elaborates on the inhabitants' social status, where the grey colour implies poverty ('even without seeing the people it is about poverty'), with people 'struggl[ing] through their lives'.

In contrast to the grey colour, participants tend to link white to more positive feelings, as they register an attention-pull to the bright white colour in the foreground. The white colour functions as an 'attractor' (Stockwell 2020: 79) guiding participants' attention to a potential change in the atmosphere of the scene. As an achromatic colour, white tends to evoke less intense emotional responses when compared to the coloured content (Spence et al. 2006); however, the reader-response data indicate the highly immersive potential of white in contrast to grey in the painting, as white reportedly foregrounds hope and quietude. P2.1 explains that the snowy white creates an impression of hopefulness ('it still seems hopeful to me and I don't know if that's because of the snow in the front, that is so, so white') that counteracts the dominant depressing atmosphere of the surroundings: 'I can see how it could be kind of very depressing in a way, but I think because of that light in the foreground it looks more hopeful to me.' Fitting with the hopeful connotations of white, participants commonly project the feelings of quietude evoked by snow onto their impression of the painting. Several participants emphasise a ubiquitous muting effect of snow. For example, for P2.7, snow absorbs sound and transforms the scene into a 'muted soundscape'. Participants emotionally resonate with the sense of quietness coupled with the feelings of peace and hope, as they report how the cityscape makes them feel – overwhelmed, invested, and even transported to the scene. P2.7 reports that they feel 'mellow, calm, pretty'; P2.8 foregrounds an impression of resting ('it's snow. [. . .] It's calm. Peaceful, probably better resting or waiting'); P2.9 experiences a profound sense of tranquillity ('the snow makes it very peaceful as well. So quiet and clean and crisp. [. . .] I don't know why I am getting this overwhelming sense of peace just from the snow'). Finally, for P1.4, the atmosphere of the scene becomes highly immersive to the point of them feeling transported to it: 'it just grabs me as a really nice representation of a condition, a weather condition, a social condition [. . .] it is just really attractive, emotionally and visually, I could put myself in there and enjoy looking at it'.

Visual negation

Roofscape presents the view of the city built by humans, which, at the same time, looks abandoned by them. This visual negation (Nørgaard 2019) shifts the normative figure-ground organisation and assigns salience to the cityscape, in which architecture becomes a figure, and humans, so essential to the existence of the city, become backgrounded. Most participants attempt to look for signs of life and repeatedly report their absence, using syntactic negation, in the constructions 'you don't see' (P2.1, P2.6), 'I can't tell' (P2.1), 'I can't see' (P2.4, P2.5), 'there's no' (P2.10, P1.5, P1.2) in relation to the absence of people, smoke in chimneys, living creatures, and life in general. Intensifying adverbials are frequently featured in 'you don't see any people <u>at all</u>' (P2.1), 'I can't see any figures in it <u>at all</u>' (P2.4). P2.10 demonstrates the striking impression of a human void in the contrast between the parallel constructions 'there is / are no' and 'you get' that foreground the instances that are missing but supposed to be present: 'Yeah, <u>there's no</u> life in it. <u>There're no</u> even birds. You know, even in winter, <u>you get</u> birds, <u>you get</u> robins. <u>There's no</u> life in it at all. The trees are bare. <u>There's no</u> even smoke from the chimneys.' P1.10 and P1.7 connect the emptiness in the city to the feelings of gloom (P1.10) and dread (P1.7: 'A dreary day. Probably because there're no people in it.').

Many responses feature inherent negation that highlights emptiness by transposing semantic negativity in an affirmative syntactic form (Givón 1993). An example of inherent negation is the pre-modifier 'bare' that profiles the lack of leaves on the trees. In particular, P2.6 employs the simile to draw a parallel between the absence of human life and the bareness of trees in 'I'm sure the buildings are empty like bare trees.' P1.2 notes: 'the trees are still, which doesn't suggest a wind'. The adjective 'still' here denotes the lack of movement and enables P1.2 to infer an impression of silence that plausibly aligns with pervasive emptiness: 'No sound at all, or no indication of sound.' Further, participants indicate their engagement with the scene by drawing on their personal experiences of the cold weather. The overarching impression of coldness permeates the scene and is inherently negating, as it connotes the absence of warmth. Some participants relate to a universal experience of being outside in wintry weather that allows them to explain the absence of people on the streets. For this, participants frequently ground the scene in their own memories of feeling cold in winter, as P2.6 reports the 'dampening' impact of cold weather on the inhabitants of the portrayed city, as well as themselves, because they are 'probably just projecting [their] own feelings onto this'. P2.10 and P1.5, quoted below, report familiarity with feeling cold in similar wintry circumstances, thus finding the scenery uninviting to the extent that they actively detach themselves from it. By doing so, they imagine themselves repositioned to the fictional setting and, subsequently, reject the hypothetical state of affairs. P2.10 repeatedly negates an imagined scenario that is a conceptual blend of their real-life circumstances and the world portrayed in the painting, where they need to go to work in the wintry weather. Similarly, P1.5 illustrates detachment ('happy to paint it, but not be in it') and positions themselves as external to the portrayed scene, an intermediary space which comprises a blend of the wintry landscape and the participant staying inside their home with a book and tea.

> P2.10: it's not a joyous sight. [. . .] I do not want to be part of that. I don't want to think about going to work in a day like that. You know, it's dismal.

> P1.5: it gives me the sense of isolation, due to weather, like you can't go outside because it's gross [. . .] it doesn't look like you'd be itching to go out there. It looks like you'd be happy to be sitting inside with a cup of tea and a book.

Altogether, the atmospheric feel of the scene allows participants to engage with the portrayed surroundings, but only to a certain extent. Participants draw on the symbolic significance of colours in their interpretations, as they attribute sombreness and gloom to the city and elaborate on the social matters of its non-present inhabitants. The colour white brings more positive connotations to the scenery, as participants feel more closely positioned to the scenery in their experiences of calmness, hopefulness, and tranquillity, transposed by the whiteness of snow. Further, the immersive engagement with the scene is facilitated through visual negation, as participants are invited to decode the significance of the absence of people in the painting. As a result, participants make sense of emptiness by grounding the scene in their personal experiences of winter, where they fleetingly project themselves into the cityscape and subsequently negate their presence. Such participants' positioning and emotional involvement with the cityscape atmosphere reflect a certain level of engagement with the scene and build a basis for a deeper entanglement in an immersive experience of ekphrasis.

'Lost Dream for my Unvaccinated Lover' by John Milkereit

The ekphrastic response text 'Lost Dream for my Unvaccinated Lover' illustrates the techniques of textual intervention that allow for close conceptual alignment between the portrayed scene and the ekphrastic retelling and are likely to prompt the construction of an ekphrastic blend. The poem is reproduced below.

> All anyone wants is a clean, bathed
> sky in pink notes. I'm hovering
> over a snowy roof. Paris, je t'aime.
> The Ghost of Future lifts me via sleigh.
> My ice bones and half-stabbed, frozen lungs.
> Feet groan to land. Roof of innocence.
> Roof of chalky slate. I can't open your shuttered
> windows. I can't climb down your seductive,
> chic facade. Our reality has run adrift so let's start
> anew on a white blanket. Spring is a promise of us
> living in a cherry blossom frame sipping cognac
> and amaretto in a courtyard. The glow of this scene
> awakens. S'il vous plait, I gulp each breath
> in night bright.
>
> (Milkereit 2023)

The indicative features of textual intervention here involve the language markers that replicate spatiotemporal parameters of the visual scene and thus profile highly recognisable references to the painting. Additionally, textual interventions often do not allow for the full-sized effects of a narrative but, instead, evoke the domains of knowledge that offer 'the opportunity to construct narrative sequences' and restore a story on the basis of readerly inference (Panagiotidou 2022: 125). I examine how such allusions allow readers to dynamically navigate their experience through the text by using Stockwell's (2022: 121) list of textual factors that 'encapsulate' a retrospective timeline or 'anticipate' future developments.

The poem presents an intriguing perspective of a homodiegetic narrator who is envisioning *in medias res* a rekindling of a romantic relationship with their lover. The reference to the dream in the title from the outset pre-attributes the narrator's desire, which is simultaneously negated with a pre-modifier 'lost', creating a sense of hopelessness. The poem begins with a generalised statement 'all anyone wants is a clean, bathed / sky in pink notes'. Considering that ekphrastic readers start the poem with an encapsulated representation of the Parisian cityscape in mind, the opening statement refers to the weather condition that directly contrasts and negates the portrayed cityscape. The desire for the 'clean, bathed sky' is highlighted by the boulomaic verb 'wants', with 'all' and 'anyone' laying emphasis on the universality of the aspiration for change. Altogether, the opening sentence pre-attributes a prospective event and then shifts readers back to the surroundings congruent with the Parisian scenery. With the narrator space-wise situated outdoors, the parallel constructions of inability or prohibition 'I can't open', 'I can't climb' allow readers to conceptualise a physical separation that exists between the lovers, which, once again, post-attributes an unclarified event that could have led to their parting. The narrator addresses the impact of their changed relationship in 'reality has run adrift' and invites their partner to start anew. From there, the narration shifts to the change of season, which ultimately indicates the couple's reconciliation. 'Spring is a promise' contains a pre-attribution of the desired future that triggers a flashforward to the reunion of the narrator and their lover. Towards the end of the poem, readers are relocated back to the original setting of a Parisian street, from where the narrator envisions a romantic renewal.

Conceptual alignment and ekphrastic blending

Participants' responses demonstrate a high degree of alignment between the image and the text by commenting on the similarities in spatial arrangements and the common themes of isolation, longing, and absence. P1.3 mentions 'the repetition of wintery things', such as 'frozen and sleigh and those in the white blanket'. These comments act as 'specific unmarked' references (Mason 2019: 84) that allude to salient features of the scene, such as its snowy spatial surroundings. For P1.2, the point of contact between the two is the sense of absence and isolation, as it is reportedly expressed in the implication that people shelter indoors and hope for change in spring: 'there are human beings inside isolating, sheltering and sometimes looking over the roofs and longing for spring'. P1.2 cross-references isolation purported in both the image and the text: 'here "I can't open your shuttered windows" and "I can't climb your seductive chic façade", it suggests isolation, which of course I mentioned isolation in the picture'.

Based on this high level of conceptual alignment, the majority of participants (8 out of 10) reportedly create an ekphrastic blend, where the portrayed cityscape becomes 'refigured' (Giovanelli 2022, Harrison 2023) into the background against which the storytelling is taking place. The generic space that enables cross-space mapping contains wintry Parisian surroundings and the shared themes of loneliness and longing. In the input space of the painting, they are relayed by the projections of emotions onto surroundings discussed earlier; in the input space of the poem, they are conveyed by the storyteller who is longing to be reunited with their lover.

Importantly, some participants' responses show the elaboration of the blend, where they construct novel narrative strands that are not explicitly referred to in either of the input spaces but emerge as a result of the imaginative running of the blend in line with the principles that were established (Fauconnier and Turner 2002). The elaboration of the blend illustrates readers' investment into the story, as an ekphrastic text only supplies minimal information about the characters' relationship, thus leaving it to readers to infer the encapsulated or anticipated events. Participants' decisions to continue imaginatively running the blend indicates an immersive quality of ekphrasis, as it is argued that immersion is often evoked as a result of 'coincidental resonance of the text with the readers' personal memories' (Ryan 2015: 86). In this case study, the specific unmarked reference to 'unvaccinated' strongly directs participants to COVID-19, which divides participants into two groups and becomes an obstacle for developing the blend.

Without taking COVID-19 into account, the data show that the elaboration of the blend becomes significantly hindered. In attempts to infer possible scenarios, participants express doubt and tentativeness and do not engage any further. For instance, P1.5 comments that 'something is keeping them apart' and profiles uncertainty in the use of weak epistemic modality and *verba sentiendi* that highlight subjective perception: 'I don't know if it's an actual physical separation or if they've had a fight or something'; 'it feels like their partner is unattainable to them for some reason'; 'maybe they're growing apart'. Their tentativeness is highlighted by indefinite determiners, such as in 'for some reason', 'they got some fancy new job', 'they feel left behind or something'. P1.5 confirms their hesitancy when they suggest interpreting 'the half stabbed frozen lungs' as a literal and metaphorical inability to breathe: 'I don't know whether they feel suffocated in their relationship, or if they're actually physically ill and can't be with their lover. That was left ambiguous in the text.' The deeper and more elaborate engagement with the blend occurs when participants draw on their experiences of COVID-19 for constructing a fictional scenario, as the data demonstrate that most participants connect the unvaccinated status of the lover in the title to the pandemic. Titles play an important role in framing readerly experience: they cue readers' expectations and prompt them to recruit relevant areas of knowledge (Bartl and Lahey 2023). As a result, participants invest personal experiences of living in the pandemic and infer potentialities of the lovers' separation, anchor the blend to their own sociocultural context, and attribute hopefulness for the upcoming change.

Re-experiencing the pandemic: 'Spring is a promise'

Participants display identification with the conveyed experiences, frequently implicating themselves within the referenced addressee which reflects their deeper emotive engagement with the narrated scenario (Stockwell 2005). The participants' identification with the presented circumstances may act as an indicator of emotional immersion (Ryan 2015). For instance, participants mention: 'everyone's under the same restrictions' (P1.1); 'I really like this response attaching it to the close-up time while we were all closed in during the pandemic' (P1.9); 'the idea of my unvaccinated lover says a lot of things about the pandemic that we've been through and that we're still living in' (P1.4).

Further, the COVID-19 theme becomes the drive for participants to 'spread activation' (Mason 2019: 77) and flesh out fictional scenarios that were alluded to in the ekphrastic text with the reference to the disease. The reference to the COVID-19 pandemic triggers resonant emotive experiences that participants invest into reinterpreting both the artwork and the text. P1.2 talks us through their line of reasoning step by step: '"my ice bones and frozen lungs" – the virus does give people trouble with their lungs. They do have trouble breathing [. . .] "I gulp each breath" – again that is going back to Covid.' P1.9 attempts to post-attribute a range of potential scenarios that could have impacted a relationship, such as the lovers' divided opinions on vaccination, hence the requirement to shield to avoid catching a virus: 'with her lover being unvaccinated, she can't open his shuttered windows, whether it is because of his opinions regarding vaccination, or she needs to stay away from him, one or the other'. Similarly, P1.2's blend contains the events that have not been explicitly brought up in any of the input spaces, where one of the lovers 'has had the vaccination, but only one, and it still hasn't prevented them from having COVID', whilst their partner remained unvaccinated.

The reference to vaccination affects the spatiotemporal situatedness of the blend, as it becomes strongly anchored to the contemporary setting, e.g., P1.8 expresses appreciation of the shift to the present: 'I love the way she's put into a contemporary setting.' The allusion to the pandemic enables participants to invest their experiences of the lockdown into determining the time frame of the narrated event, as demonstrated by P1.1: 'they're looking forward to spring as the next season, yeah, definitely winter. The second lockdown was around about November time, wasn't it?' Identifying with the lived experience of the pandemic, P1.1 and P1.4 situate the blend within their cultural and social context. P1.4 incorporates the story of separation within the US context, highlighting the government policy for self-isolation at the time: 'it's [the story] focusing on, looking from a distance, from a distance the minimum of 6 feet between people, at least here in the States at the time'. P1.1 addresses the narrator's eagerness for future change as opposed to the imposed lockdown restrictions: 'that's their ideal for the future but obviously they're not allowed to gather, they can't even have cheese and wine parties'. P1.1's ironic reference to 'cheese and wine parties' probably refers to the gatherings of UK high officials during the lockdowns, and thus situates their blend within the UK political setting. Interestingly, the mention of what came to be known as 'Partygate' creates a certain double layering in the blend, because although both the lockdown and the governmental parties occurred at the same time, the participant would not have been aware of them simultaneously. As a result, the blend incorporates knowledge acquired from the lived experience of the pandemic at the time and later reflections on how the healthcare crisis was managed, that is once Partygate became public.

As a result of running an ekphrastic blend, many participants reconfigure their original view of the artwork. Through the interanimation of properties across input spaces (Stockwell 1999), participants admit that the stories of the pandemic now reverberate in the wintery Parisian scenery. For instance, P1.1 now feels that the painting transmits entrapment, as the persona overlooking the city could feel confined to their apartment: 'when looking back at the painting, there could be a sense of looking out at the city from a balcony but being trapped and unable to get to the city, which I never thought of initially'. Analogously, P1.10 demonstrates how the story prompts readers to revise their view of the cityscape with a stronger focus on the emotive experiences of people confined to the portrayed houses: 'there's some similarity between the picture and the poem because if I combine the two, it almost seems like these are the words of someone who's suffering inside one of these buildings'. In sustaining a close connection between the image and the poem, P1.2 projects the contrasting properties of the portrayed winter and the promised spring onto the relationship between the lovers in the pandemic:

> P1.2: And the hope that they will be recovered enough and that their other love will also be okay, so that they can meet and have coffee and cognac in the spring, when it is warmer and they are freer, but at the moment they are stifled like as if being covered with snow and they are suffering from COVID because their lungs are frozen.

The response demonstrates the impactful interweaving of the visual and the verbal in the ekphrastic experience, where winter and spring represent separation and reunion ('so that they can meet and have coffee and cognac in the spring'), cold and warmth ('when it is warmer'), confinement and freedom ('they are freer', 'at the moment they are stifled like as if being covered with snow'), illness and recovery ('they are suffering from COVID', 'the hope that they will be recovered enough'). Ekphrastic intervention has shown to transform the winter cityscape of Paris from an attractive and atmospheric scenery into a scene of deeper relevance, where participants feel immersed into the story of living in the pandemic through the participatory engagement with the fusion of image and text.

Conclusion

In this chapter, I have demonstrated how engaging with ekphrasis holistically can lead to an immersive readerly experience facilitated by both an artwork and a poetic text. I have argued that to unlock the immersive potential of ekphrasis it is important to examine it from the perspectives of interaction and experientiality. I discussed how the interaction of visual and verbal elements can lead to constructing an idiosyncratic interpretation that surpasses their stand-alone value. The process of actively constructing a fictional scenario reflects a high level of readerly engagement. However, this only applies if readers choose to collaborate with an ekphrastic retelling, thus leading us to unpack how ekphrastic interventions may invite readers to position themselves in response to ekphrasis. To illustrate how readers negotiate and construct meaning in ekphrasis, I conducted an analysis of participants' responses to a painting and an ekphrastic poem. With responses to the painting, I demonstrated how the atmosphere sustained by colour and visual negation created powerful transportive and emotionally inducing effects on participants. At the next stage, the responses to the poem indicated participants' collaboration with the offered retelling that resulted in a creation of an ekphrastic blend. I have argued that the participatory and interactive nature of ekphrasis, when participants collaborate and get actively involved in creating and developing a fictional scenario, demonstrates the immersive potential of an ekphrastic experience. While immersion is often discussed in terms of being transported to the fictional setting, my analysis has shown how immersion can be fuelled by grounding storytelling in personal lived experiences. Participants' investment creates a solid ground for an ekphrastic blend, which is equally bound to the realms of the fictional and the real. In light of this, it might be interesting to think of immersion as an entangled experience that places readers in an unstable stance between the ontologies.

References

Bartl, S. and Lahey, E. (2023) '"As the title implies": how readers talk about titles in Amazon book reviews', *Language and Literature* 32 (2): 209–30.

Bell, A., Browse, S., Gibbons, A. and Peplow, D. (2021) 'Responding to style', in A. Bell, S. Browse, A. Gibbons and D. Peplow (eds) *Style and Reader Response: Minds, Media, Methods*. Amsterdam: John Benjamins, pp.1–19.

Bell, A., Ensslin, A., van der Bom, I. and Smith, J. (2018) 'Immersion in digital fiction', *International Journal of Literary Linguistics* 7 (1): 1–22.

Benton, M. (2000) *Studies in the Spectator Role: Literature, Painting and Pedagogy*. London: Routledge.

Bilandzic, H. and Busselle, R. (2017) 'Beyond metaphors and traditions: exploring the conceptual boundaries of narrative engagement', in F. Hakemulder, M.M. Kuijpers, E.S. Tan, K. Bálint and M.M. Doicaru (eds) *Narrative Absorption*. Amsterdam: John Benjamins, pp.11–28.

Evans, V. and Green, M.C. (2006) *Cognitive Linguistics: An Introduction*. Edinburgh: Edinburgh University Press.

Fauconnier, G. and Turner, M. (2002) *The Way We Think: Conceptual Blending and the Mind's Hidden Complexities*. New York: Basic Books.

Gavin, P. (2024) *The Cognitive Poetics of Ekphrastic Intervention* (unpublished doctoral thesis). Aston University.

Gerrig, R. (1993) *Experiencing Narrative Worlds: On the Psychological Activities of Reading*. New Haven: Yale University Press.

Giovanelli, M. (2022) *The Language of Siegfried Sassoon*. Cham: Palgrave Macmillan.

Givón, T. (1993) *English Grammar: A Function-Based Approach*. Amsterdam: John Benjamins.

Harper, G. (2020) 'Introduction: responding to creative writing', in G. Harper (ed.) *Responding to Creative Writing*. Newcastle-upon-Tyne: Cambridge Scholars Publishing, pp.vii–xix.

Harrison, C. (2023) '99 ways to retell a story: the styles and functions of narrator reconstrual', *Style* 57 (2): 163–86.

Harrison, C. (2024) *The Language of Margaret Atwood*. Cham: Palgrave Macmillan.

Kennedy, D. (2012) *The Ekphrastic Encounter in Contemporary British Poetry and Elsewhere*. Farnham: Ashgate.

Kövecses, Z. (2000) *Metaphor and Emotion: Language, Culture and Body in Human Feeling*. Cambridge: Cambridge University Press.

Küller, R., Ballal, S., Laike, T., Mikellides, B. and Tonello, G. (2006) 'The impact of light and colour on psychological mood: a cross-cultural study of indoor work environments', *Ergonomics* 49: 1496–1507.

Louvel, L. (2019) 'An artist of the bizarre: Stanley Spencer's "ordinary" ekphrases', in D. Kennedy and R. Meek (eds) *Ekphrastic Encounters: New Interdisciplinary Essays on Literature and the Visual Arts*. Manchester: Manchester University Press, pp.183–202.

Mason, J. (2019) *Intertextuality in Practice*. Amsterdam: John Benjamins.

Mikellides, B. (2017) 'Colour psychology: the emotional effects of colour perception', in J. Best (ed.) *Colour Design* (2nd edn). Cambridge: Woodhead Publishing, pp.193–214.

Milkereit, J. (2023) *Lost Sonnets for My Unvaccinated Lover*. American Fork: Kelsay Books.

Nørgaard, N. (2019) *Multimodal Stylistics of the Novel: More than Words*. London: Routledge.

Panagiotidou, M.-E. (2022) *The Poetics of Ekphrasis*. Cham: Palgrave Macmillan.

Pope, R. (1995) *Textual Intervention: Critical and Creative Strategies for Literary Studies*. London: Routledge.

Prendergast, M. (2009) 'Introduction: the phenomena of poetry in research', in M. Prendergast, C. Leggo and P. Sameshima (eds) *Poetic Inquiry: Vibrant Voices in the Social Sciences*. Rotterdam: Sense Publishers, pp.xix–xli.

Ryan, M.-L. (2015) *Narrative as Virtual Reality*. Baltimore: Johns Hopkins University Press.

Scott, J. (2023) *Creative Writing and Stylistics* (2nd edn). Cham: Palgrave Macmillan.

Spence, I., Wong, P., Rusan, M. and Rastegar, N. (2006) 'How color enhances visual memory for natural scenes', *Psychological Sciences* 17 (1): 1–6.

Spitzer, L. (1955) 'The "Ode on a grecian urn," or content vs. metagrammar', *Comparative Literature* 7 (3): 203–25.

Stockwell, P. (1999) 'The inflexibility of invariance', *Language and Literature* 8 (2): 125–42.

Stockwell, P. (2005) 'Texture and identification', *European Journal of English Studies* 9 (2): 143–53.

Stockwell, P. (2009) *Texture: A Cognitive Aesthetics of Reading*. Edinburgh: Edinburgh University Press.

Stockwell, P. (2020) *Cognitive Poetics: An Introduction* (2nd edn). London: Routledge.

Stockwell, P. (2022) 'The principle of moments', in G. Watson and S. Zyngier (eds) *Pedagogical Stylistics in the 21st Century*. Cham: Palgrave Macmillan, pp.107–29.

Toolan, M. (1998) *Language in Literature: An Introduction to Stylistics*. London: Hodder Education.

Varnedoe, K. (1987) *Gustave Caillebotte*. New Haven: Yale University Press.

Whiteley, S. and Canning, P. (2017) 'Reader response research in stylistics', *Language and Literature* 26 (2): 71–87.

CHAPTER 9

Musical stylistic immersion in Tom Waits' 'The Piano has been Drinking (Not Me)'

Matthew Voice

This chapter advances a multimodal approach to metaphor in song lyrics, where musical style is central to interpretation, and – in this case – where the song's complex metaphors, which may initially appear to fail, in fact provide an additional immersive and textured layer through which the drunken mind-style of the song's narrator is developed and understood. Tracking the dynamic prominence and complexity of the metaphors and Waits' stylised vocal delivery, Voice shows how the song immerses the listener in a unique mind-style through mimetic enaction. Thus, the chapter makes the case for a cognitively-driven, multimodal approach to the song's metaphors as essential to understanding the success of its immersive and evocative imagery.

Introduction

In *The Many Lives of Tom Waits*, biographer Patrick Humphries describes the singer-songwriter's 1976 track 'The Piano has been Drinking (Not Me)', from the album *Short Change*, as 'the archetypal Waits song: the laconic bar-room philosopher delivering pithy lyrics, in a voice that sounds like a garbage crusher' (2007: 93). Similarly, Cohen (2005: 235) calls it 'the giddy drunken music of obsession, that agitated, overstated letting-go, which pushes us viscerally to the edge of our conditioned responses, and then asks us to follow our own deepest, most self-annihilating instincts and plunge with it over that edge, into god knows what'. On listening to the song itself, it is easy to understand why: the performance is deeply memorable, with Waits slurring both his words and his piano playing to produce a visceral sense of the kind of performance that might occur in the early hours at a hazy, late-night blues bar. Writing for *Rolling Stone*, Brackett and Hoard (2004: 855) cite the source of this feeling as Waits' 'parched voice and well-lubricated point of view. He sounds like he's had a bottle in front of him and a frontal lobotomy for quite some time.' That these writers can all describe the hazy intoxication of Waits' lyricism indicates the extent to which Waits transports and immerses his audience in the world of the song and the mind of its narrator, with listeners clearly able to imagine and expand upon the world presented in the song's narrative and its delivery.

These quotations also demonstrate the multimodal means through which immersive transportation is generated in these critics' experiences. It is not just the point of view expressed through Waits' lyrics but the modality of the song that evokes the world it describes: the slurred speech of the singer-narrator is matched by the 'sloppy' piano playing which introduces and accompanies the sung performance. Analysing metaphor in another Waits song from a relevance theoretic perspective, Price and Wilson (2019: 62) note that the core multimodality of the song 'plays an undeniable role in the metaphors used', though their analysis is primarily driven by a focus on meaning produced through language choices within lyrics. Written down in isolation from the music, as in the analysis below, the lyrics of 'The Piano' do not, in my experience, have the same effect as when heard in conjunction with the musical accompaniment and Waits' unique voice. It is the performance *as a whole* that generates the immersive effect, then, and the meaning and cognitive effects of the song should therefore be studied holistically. In taking a cognitively-driven multimodal approach, this chapter seeks to treat music and lyrics as equal contributors to meaning-making in 'The Piano' and, in doing so, account for the song's capacity to immerse the listener.

That 'The Piano' should be so immersive, however, raises several questions for the way immersion is understood from a literary-linguistic perspective. In her seminal work on immersion and interaction, Ryan describes the difference between immersive and non-immersive media as follows:

> For a text to be immersive, then, it must create a space to which the reader, spectator, or user can relate, and it must populate this space with individuated objects. It must, in other words, construct the setting for a potential narrative action, even though it may lack the temporal extension to develop this action into a plot. This fundamentally *mimetic* concept of immersion [. . .] applies to novels, movies, drama, representational paintings, and those computer games that cast the user in the role of a character in a story, but not to philosophical works, music, and purely abstract games such as bridge, chess, and Tetris, no matter how absorbing these experiences may be.
>
> (Ryan 2015: 9–10)

It is unclear whether 'music' in this context means purely instrumental performance, or if songs with lyrics are included. However, the music, performance, and lyrics of 'The Piano' each provide routes towards an immersive engagement that, when attended to in combination, have the capacity to provide a clear evocation of a setting, including the character of the narrator. The multimodal metaphors evoked in Waits' lyrics and performance demonstrate a capacity for immersive, enactive perceptual experiences comparable to more conventionally immersive media. Musical stylistics explores the interaction between music and lyrics in songs, where both complementarity (Morini 2013) and contrast (Voice and Whiteley 2019) can contribute to a listener's understanding, enjoyment, and sense of immersion. Taking 'The Piano' as its focus, this chapter advances a multimodal approach to metaphor in the song's lyrics, where musical style is central to interpretation. Further, it argues that the song's complex metaphors, which may initially appear opaque and at times meaningless, in fact provide an additional textured layer through which the drunken mind-style (see Rundquist 2020) of the song's narrator is developed, and through the understanding of which the capacity for immersion is achieved.

Drawing on Blending Theory (Fauconnier and Turner 2002), analysis of Waits' lyrics independent of their original context reveals a range of interpretively challenging or conceptually incomplete metaphors, which are often only resolved through relation to the song's musical structure and Waits' stylised vocal delivery. Tracking the dynamic prominence and complexity of these metaphors across the song, this chapter explores how Waits combines musical and lyrical structures to immerse the reader in a unique mind-style through mimetic enaction. Thus, this chapter makes the case for a cognitively-driven, multimodal approach to the song's metaphors as essential to understanding the success of its immersive and evocative imagery, and provides a framework for the further development of multimodal metaphor analysis in future stylistic research.

Immersion, attention, and cognition

Ryan (2015) identifies four degrees of absorption in reading, which might equally be applied to listening to music. Of these, the type most pertinent to the kind of immersion produced in listening to 'The Piano' is 'imaginative involvement': 'The "split subject" attitude of the reader who transports herself into the textual world but remains able to contemplate it with aesthetic or epistemological detachment' (Ryan 2015: 69). As noted by the critics Cohen and Humphries discussed at this chapter's opening, listening to the song evokes vivid imagery and a strong sense of association with the world evoked by both Waits' performance and lyricism. It is easy to feel transported, as the piano playing style evokes a homodiegetic engagement, as if listening to Waits singing from within the bar-room world evoked in the language of the song itself. While not going so far as to lead listeners to mistake the world and events of the story with reality (see Adams and Rollings 2006), this degree of immersion nonetheless produces an experience of being 'inside' the world of the song and its narrator-performer.

If 'The Piano' is capable of producing immersion via imaginative involvement, a multimodal analysis of the song's performance, structure, and language will explore how these elements work together to elicit such an effect. Consider the following definition of immersion from Murray (2017), which describes the sensory totality of the phenomenon:

> We seek the same feeling from a psychologically immersive experience that we do from a plunge in the ocean or swimming pool: the sensation of being surrounded by a completely other reality, as different as water is from air, that *takes over all our attention*, our whole perceptual apparatus.
>
> (Murray 2017: 99; my emphasis)

The emphasis on the capacity of an experience to direct and control audience attention is central to much work on the sources of immersion. Ennslin et al. (2019: 337) introduce the concept of 'literary immersion' as distinct from narrative immersion, being 'the need to pay close and often critical attention [. . .] with the aim to gain a deeper understanding of the narrative context in which the story is set'. This is linked to Hayles' notion of 'deep attention' (2007), and further evidences the connection between immersion and attention.

Similarly, Agrawal and Bech (2022) note that immersion may arise from audience members' absorption in facing and overcoming challenges as part of the experience of media. This can take the form of competing demands for a swift response from the audience (e.g., playing videogames that demand action and input), which they call tactical immersion, or strategic immersion, which 'is experienced when one is preoccupied and makes choices mentally to conquer the task on hand' (324), such as when a viewer is presented with an abstract image which they must actively work to interpret. While the process of making sense of Tom Waits' 'The Piano' is not a particularly complex task, it is certainly more resource intensive than most passive music listening. Connecting the performance to lyrical content in the construction of the song's narrative mind-style involves 'an interaction between style and reader' (Nuttall 2018: 31–2), which entails active cognitive effort on behalf of the listener in order to interpret the setting and character of the song's world and its mode. Active absorption in this task, then, offers another potential route to immersion in the world of the song.

Additionally, there is a need to consider the role of simulation in immersion (see Cooper, this volume). From a linguistic perspective, immersion relating to imaginative involvement is grounded in both attention and mimesis, that is the movement beyond representation into the visceral perception and experience of events, states, and worlds as described in language. According to Zwaan's (2004) Immersed Experiencer Framework, 'language is a set of cues to the comprehender to construct an experiential (perception plus action) simulation of the described situation. In this conceptualisation, the comprehender is an immersed experiencer of the described situation, and comprehension is the vicarious experience of the described situation' (36). For Zwaan, any construal that involves the conceptual simulation of an action or event is, to some extent, immersive. Strauss et al. (2024) likewise argue that immersion 'requires attention to be directed intentionally to specific mental representations (memories, narrative structures, schemas, etc.) that must be associated with a particular set of coordinated stimuli existing within the induced reality because those stimuli fit together in some particularly compelling way'. In order to feel transported into the world imagined through the lyrics and musical style of Waits' performance, listeners engage with both musical performance and lyrical meaning as sites of world-building, drawing on both in order to understand the song holistically. Given that immersion is cognitive phenomenon, resulting from this combination of attention, simulation, and coordination, this chapter draws heavily on cognitively-oriented linguistic and multimodal frameworks to support its analysis of the song and its effects.

This close relationship between immersion and attention poses a challenge for literary linguists interested in song lyrics. As Voice and Whiteley (2019) note, close listener attention is far from compulsory in order to elicit enjoyment from listeners. Many listeners will ignore, misunderstand, or remain disengaged from the meaning of song lyrics (for example, by not speaking the language in which the song is sung), and yet may still enjoy or be deeply engaged with the song itself. For researchers concerned with the role of language in multimodal settings, this raises a number of questions about the importance of linguistic analysis: if the lyrics can be ignored, and understanding and enjoyment elicited without close engagement with their structure or semantic contents, then what is the purpose of analysing their structure and content? In this particular case, the analysis below demonstrates that joint attention to musical composition and lyrical structure is key to making sense of the song. Not all music will lead to an experience of immersion, and Waits' unique performance makes 'The Piano' an outlier in the way it demands listener attention in order to achieve comprehension. That said, the relationship between textual and musical structure has also been shown to further enhance audience immersion in a work. Hauck and Hecht (2023), for example, show that readers perceive texts to be both of higher quality and more immersive when paired with emotionally congruent music playing simultaneously. So, while musical enjoyment does not require close critical attention per se, congruency between music and text in contexts of deep attention can result in a strong sense of immersion within a given work.

Providing a cognitively-oriented definition of literary immersion, Allan (2019: 17) suggests that immersive texts 'invite the reader to construct a mental representation of the described situation that is grounded in perception, action, and emotion, while non-immersive texts lack a clearly defined spatio-temporal framework and centre around abstract concepts that are not (directly) grounded in sensorimotor experience'. In other words, it is easier for an audience to become immersed in a text that represents contents relayed from an embodied point of view that can be enacted during interpretation – a world in which one can imagine and position oneself is inherently more immersive than an abstract representation of ideas devoid of context. One way in which this might be achieved is by narrating and describing the world through a clear mind-style. The process of mind-modelling – constructing an internal understanding of the way a narrator or character's mind works (Stockwell 2009) – may function as a possible site of immersion within a text-world through intentional, directed representation. As will be shown in the analysis below, making sense of 'The Piano' at all requires listeners to pay a degree of attention to both its lyrical and musical forms, as well to partake in an enactive blending process, directly mirroring the thought style of the song's narrator for themselves.

Overall, the literature suggests the need to consider both attention and mimesis as key components of immersive experience. In the case of 'The Piano' in particular, the musical stylistic analysis below shows both that attention to the holistic multimodal structure of the song is necessary for making sense of the song at all, and that in attending to this structure the listener engages in the embodied simulation of the world and narratorial mind-style that produced immersive involvement. Acknowledging that this is not the case for all songs (see Voice and Whiteley 2019), this analysis will take the stance that some degree of attention to both lyrics and musical structure is a requirement for understanding of the song, and that the discussion of textual immersion based on this premise is predicated on the kinds of attention work which can be expected of a casual listener.

Multimodal metaphors

This analysis employs the cognitive linguistic model of metaphor set out in Fauconnier and Turner's (2002) Blending Theory framework. Put simply, metaphorical meaning results from the selective identification of comparative attributes from multiple conceptual domains, minimally the source and target of the metaphor. Shared qualities between these inputs are matched in a 'generic space', from which elements are selected for inclusion in an emergent 'blended space'. The blended space has been described as a 'site for central cognitive work' (Fauconnier and Turner 1996: 115), as the result of blending can produce properties in the blend which were not present in initial inputs. For example, in a metaphor like TIME IS MONEY, the process of blending leads to the identification of shared qualities between the inputs of TIME and MONEY in the generic space (both are finite, quantifiable, and valuable resources), while the resultant blend itself allows for the extension of the comparison to imagining more complex connections, such as the idea of 'saving' or 'investing' time as a kind of currency.

The production of blended spaces as a cognitive process for making sense of metaphor, then, is 'meaningful precisely in its newness. It is both more than the sum of its inputs and different from them' (Schneider 2012: 6). In other words, blending is an active process that requires attention, engagement, and cognitive effort on behalf of the listener – an investment of focus similar in scope to traditional views of immersion. As the analysis below will show, 'The Piano' shifts throughout between straightforward and opaque in terms of each line's meaning, requiring differing degrees of cognitive work from the listener, almost line by line. Indeed, it is the capacity for blended spaces to extend and exceed their inputs that this chapter argues is central to listeners' understanding of, and subsequent immersion within, the world of the song at all.

Multimodal metaphors in particular have been studied overwhelmingly in relation to visual/linguistic modes (Zhong et al. 2023), with only a few scholars (Forceville 2009, Zbikowski 2009) exploring metaphor as a product of music-lyric interaction, using relevance theory to guide their analysis. Within this directly multimodal work, Forceville (2009: 384) identifies two functions of music/sound in multimodal metaphor:

(a) To (help) identify the metaphor's source domain
(b) To (help) identify features that can be mapped from the source to the target

In each case, these functions assume a complete metaphor, i.e., one in which a clear source domain can be identified. As the analysis below aims to show, however, Waits' musicality in 'The Piano' does not serve to clarify the conceptual structure of his lyrical metaphor. Rather, it functions as a parallel source of uncertainty and, in doing so, enhances the listener's immersion in the conceptual world of the song through a second sensory avenue.

Similarly, Zbikowski (2009) describes multimodal metaphor in terms of 'text painting', whereby lyrics function as the source domain while music provides the target domain, essentially grounding the interpretation of textual meaning. But in the case of 'The Piano', the relationship between music and lyrics as sites of meaning-making is clearly bidirectional. When first listening to the song, the atonal notes at the end of the second bar may be schematically associated with poor performance, indicating a mistake. Aside from the metatextual knowledge that the song has been recorded and released on a published album, the listener's only other recourse for interpreting this performance as intentional lies in the recognition of the world constructed through the song's lyrics. By recognising the world in which the song is set, as well as the drunken mind-style of its narrator-player as evoked through both the performance style and embodied experience of attempting to blend and make sense of Waits' metaphors of fluctuating opacity, the listener may draw parallels between the lyrical meaning and performance style to reinterpret the 'mistake' as a deliberate stylistic choice.

Overall, then, the literature on immersion suggests a close and almost paradoxical relationship to attention. On the one hand, a text or artefact requires that its audience attend to its meaning-making devices in such a way as to achieve immersion, absorption, or transportation – without engaging with the language that constructs a world, one simply cannot be transported to it. On the other, a metanarrative awareness that points out or highlights these features is decidedly anti-immersive – drawing attention to the artifice of the text seemingly necessarily limits the experiencer's capacity to immerse themselves in the world it purports to create. In analysing the multimodal structure of Waits' 'The Piano', then, the discussion below will explore how the music and lyrics of the song negotiate this tension, and manage the listener's attention in order to engage them with the linguistic devices which offer the possibility of immersion, without making their awareness of the artifice itself a barrier to immersion.

As the song's metaphorical motif is established from the outset in both musical and lyrical modes, and this recurs throughout the song, the central metaphor (OBJECTS ARE (DRUNKEN) PEOPLE) comes to function as a *megametaphor* (Werth 1994, Steen and Semino 2008, Kovecses 2010). This term describes a system of meaning-making in which individual metaphors within a text are made coherent through their relationship to a recurring theme. Such a coherence necessarily requires a degree of attention, as the audience are required to notice patterns across the discourse which are then, in turn, recognised as contributing to the overarching megametaphor. Analytical attention to lyrics and musical features that uphold and deviate from the megametaphor therefore provide a means through which to explore the ways listener attention and expectations are both upheld and challenged throughout the song.

Musical stylistic analysis and discussion

With an approach to multimodal metaphor established, the following analysis works sequentially through the multimodal metaphors of 'The Piano', exploring their structure in relationship to one another as a means to understand how immersive involvement in the narrator's mind-style is developed. As noted by Forceville (2009: 395), a metaphor can be considered multimodal if 'the identity relationship between target and source [is] triggered by making them visible/audible at the same moment'. In 'The Piano', this relationship is triggered through a musical cue at the end of the second bar of the song, where the piano's introductory melody ends on a note outside the key in which the melody is otherwise played, giving the impression that Waits has misplayed. On the very next beat, Waits begins to sing in a substantially slurred style, even by his own standards, and opens the song with the eponymous line: 'the piano has been drinking'. In this particular metaphor, there is a clear textual source and target domain, the musical instrument personified as a drunken human, which further maps to the broader multimodal context of the performance and provides an explanation for the 'mistake' heard in the previous bar. In recognising the framing of the textual piano as drunk, the listener can apply this to their interpretation of the audible piano through a transfer of association: the piano itself cannot be drunk, but its player can. This is, therefore, a clear example of Forceville's (2009) second function of lyrical metaphor in multimodal musical contexts, though operating in both directions: rather than music simply informing the understanding of the lyrical metaphor's target, the blend within the lyrics itself serves as a device to potentially cue (re)interpretation of the music.

From its outset, the lyrics of 'The Piano' set a fairly rigid pattern in their structure and contents, with almost every line foregrounding a new, anthropomorphised feature of the bar room via a metaphorical relational process. This structure is applied most uniformly in the first verse, where all but lines three and six follow this exact formula:

> The piano has been drinking
> My necktie is asleep
> The combo went back to New York
> The jukebox needs to take a leak
> And the carpet needs a haircut
> And the spotlight looks like a prison break
> And the telephone's out of cigarettes
> And the balcony is on the make

For the first two lines, a relatively straightforward conceptual blend can be mapped: the common metaphor OBJECTS ARE PEOPLE is extended to include the equation of drunkenness with sloppiness through common qualities in the blended space. A 'sleeping' necktie can be clearly equated with its looseness, and the drunkenness of the piano is mapped to the quality of its performance. These lines could each be perceived as metonyms in reference to the singer-narrator, given his close proximal and relational association with each of the source domains. Likewise, 'the spotlight looks like a prison break' is easily accessible in both its structure and its meaning: in both input spaces, a projected beam of circular light is used to illuminate a subject, whether escaped prisoner or musical performer. Framed explicitly as a simile, this line foregrounds the blending process at work throughout the first verse, and provides the listener with an accessible pathway into the structure of the narrator's language and mind-style.

While the conceptual blend evoked by this first metaphor and the following lines is relatively straightforward to interpret, especially given the supporting audio contextualisation, this is not always the case. For example, 'the jukebox needs to take a leak' follows the same metaphorical and syntactic structure as the first two lines. It is clear from context that the mapping must relate to the quality of the jukebox, and most likely the sound it produces, though how exactly this might be equated with a need to urinate is not straightforwardly discernible in the same way sleep and alcohol equate to sloppiness. Take the final two lines of this first verse, for example. Within the context of the OBJECTS ARE (DRUNKEN) PEOPLE megametaphor being mapped consistently across the previous lines, it is clear at first sight that these two metaphors continue along the same theme. On closer inspection, however, it is somewhat less clear exactly what qualities are supposed to be mapped across the source and target domains in these lines. Like the jukebox metaphor, 'the telephone's out of cigarettes' implies something about the quality of the sound, or perhaps the looseness of the connection as the evening has gone on, but the qualities which are supposed to be inferred to have been mapped between the input and blended space are unclear. Even more confusing is the final line: precisely what qualities the balcony has that are supposed to represent being 'on the make' are difficult to discern from context.

In other words, although the metaphors themselves can be recognised as following the same conceptual pattern as the rest of the verse, syntactically cueing their interpretation as metaphorical (see Stockwell 2020: 122), the qualities that might be mapped within the blended space from the target input space of each object are decidedly more ambiguous than the metaphors at the beginning of the verse. Nonetheless, given the clear context and repetition of structure from previous lines, the world-building function of the resulting conceptual blend remains readily discernible: while it might not be clear exactly how each object is affected, every line contributes to a growing feeling of a state of decay throughout the bar room in which the listener might imagine the song is being performed, as well as the state of the singer-narrator himself. In working to make sense of these opaque metaphors, the reader enacts a mimetic form of drunk-like thinking themselves, working to make sense of inputs which don't quite align, leaving a necessarily out-of-focus understanding of the song's narrator and narrative world.

Present tense and second-person narration are present throughout the song's lyrics – features described by Ryan (2015, see Adam, this volume) as hallmarks of spatiotemporal immersion within narrative. These provide a sense of immediacy to the events described within the song's lyrics, and a direct connection between the reader and the action ('she hates *you* and *your* friends . . .'). Indeed, the subject of the song is largely a description of a bar room in which the performance might be taking place, and this world-building focus might further ease the reader's transportation into the song's world: with a clear image of the smoky bar in which the narrator performs, coupled with the homodiegetically sloppy performance, music and lyrics work in tandem to continuously reference and expand upon a conceptual world for the reader to access and imagine. This further contributes to the consistent development of a clear spatiotemporal frame of reference throughout the narration, as described in Allan's (2019) account of immersion.

As the song continues, the second verse opens with another obtuse metaphor, where it is unclear how coldness might map metaphorically to other qualities of the menus, but quickly diverges from the structural formula established so far:

> And the menus are all freezing
> And the light man's blind in one eye
> And he can't see out of the other
> And the piano tuner's got a hearing aid
> And he showed up with his mother
> And the piano has been drinking
> The piano has been drinking

As can be seen from the second line onwards, the lyrics break from the previous metaphorical structure 'X is Y' to provide non-metaphorical expressions ('The light man's blind in one eye'), though these are followed up with a statement which seems semantically contradictory ('and he can't see out of the other'), or else a non-sequitur ('he showed up with his mother'). While more literal reference may appear easier to parse at first without requiring the work of blending input spaces, the illogical and sometimes contradictory content of lines retain the same confusing conceptualisation of the world of the song's lyrics.

Though the presence of less metaphorical clauses is established in the third line of the first verse ('the combo went back to New York'), they appear with greater frequency as the song progresses. As listeners already have an established framework for the mind-style of the singer-narrator through both the introductory verse and subsequent enactive efforts to blend the more opaque metaphors used so far, the otherwise contradictory content of more literal lines may be interpreted as part of the continued conceptual theme, in the same way that the metaphors, music, and vocal style cohere and inform the interpretation of one another. The lyrics shift with increasing frequency between metaphorical and non-metaphorical, as well as varying in their semantic coherences, and the conceptual accessibility of Waits' lyrics therefore fluctuates over the course of the song, with more straightforwardly accessible phrases mixed in amongst the harder to parse metaphors and contradictions. Thus, the lyrical structure further mimics a drunken mind-style, as rather than establishing a clear pattern of descent into uncertainty and opacity, the listener is offered moments of seeming lucidity.

This fluctuation continues into the third verse, this time beginning with more literal expressions – albeit non-sequiturs – before reverting to the established metaphorical structure:

> And you can't find your waitress
> With a Geiger counter
> And she hates you and your friends
> And you just can't get served without her

And the box office is drooling
And the bar stools are on fire
And the newspapers were fooling
And the ash-trays have retired

Here, the most extensive moment of lucidity carries over two consecutive lines ('she hates you and your friends / and you just can't get served without her'), which require no interpretation of metaphor or contextual evaluation in order to make sense, and is subsequently followed by four highly opaque metaphors, where a clear connection between the source and target to produce a meaningful blend is particularly difficult to establish. In the recording included on *Small Change*, the transition here from literal to conceptually opaque lyricism is marked by another musical 'mistake': two off-key notes and a slowing of the tempo at 'drooling' draw attention to the line, and connect the moment back to multimodal cues established at the song's opening. According to Walsh (2011: 57), 'the enactment of rhythm is communicative. Rhythm communicates by punctuating or articulating experience, and it is the experience of articulation that is communicated.' In other words, the experience of this slowing not only draws attention to the structure of the song via deviation, but further encourages the enactment of the drunken mind-style through hesitant and broken articulation, once again matching the haziness of both Waits' lyrics and slurred voice.

For the listener, then, the cognitive effort required to make sense of Waits' lyrics is imbalanced – sometimes requiring little work, sometimes being almost impossible to penetrate – and the challenge presented via disparity across the third verse demonstrates the way this listening and interpretation enacts the drunken mind-style: an uncertain and unclear world shot through with moments of lucidity. The conceptual clarity of Waits' lyrical meaning ebbs and flows across the song. A haze of uncertainty is cut through at unexpected moments with clarity, all the while returning to the title metaphor and its megametaphor variants as an anchor. Combined, these elements provide the listener with repeated points of entry into the less clearly accessible mires of the drunken mind-style.

The final refrain of the song's chorus contains one last lyrical twist. After repeating the eponymous line, Waits follows up by asserting that:

The piano has been drinking
Not me, not me, not me.

In doing so, the song closes with an explicit bringing together of lyrics and musicality, as Waits acknowledges (and attempts to humorously excuse) the quality of the piano playing which has served as musical accompaniment. In his insistence that he has not been drinking, Waits keeps foregrounded the dual role of the narrator, both as character within the world of the song and performer of the music as heard by the listener.

Despite the insistence to the contrary, the mind-style of the singer-narrator being produced here is a drunken one. The incomplete metaphors and erratic performance style all indicate a mind functioning on the parameters of schematic expectation. Rundquist (2020) uses Cognitive Grammar to explore textual representations of a drunken narrative mind-style in Malcolm Lowry's *Under the Volcano*. He argues that Free Indirect Speech mimetically represents an alcoholic mind, a 'distracted inward gaze' (47) with uncertain external knowledge. In this song, similar mimesis occurs in both musical and lyrical modes. If uncertainty is the characteristic of conceptualisation most clearly associated with a drunken mind-style, then it is worth noting that the uncertainty in 'The Piano' is not necessarily the singer-narrator's. Rather, the listener is placed in the position of uncertainty as they work to ascertain the nature of the performance: it is only when the lyrics and performing style begin to reveal consistent patterns in Waits' style that a newly revised schema, in which the performing style can be understood as deliberate, can be realised.

That the contents of the blended space for several of Waits' lyrical metaphors feel almost impossible to map is not a problem to be solved, then, but rather a feature of the drunken mind-style through which the song is narrated and played. Making sense of the song's meaning – both in terms of its performance style and lyrical content – requires the mimetic enaction of this uncertain, half-formed cognition. In failing to resolve the metaphorical mapping presented through Waits' lyricism, the listener themselves enacts a hazy conceptualisation of their own equivalent to a drunken mind-style. Such a process requires a degree of active interpretative work on behalf of the listener, and recalls Agrawal and Bech's (2022) notion of challenge as a potential factor leading to engagement and absorption in more conventionally interactive media, like videogames. Precisely in the act of trying to make sense of these incomplete blends do listeners themselves enact the kind of conceptualisations archetypal of the narrative mind-style: a foggy incompleteness that immerses the attentive listener in a simulation of the kind of drunkenness which comprises the world of the song.

Beyond the critical reviews discussed at the beginning of this chapter, further evidence to indicate how general listeners have responded to 'The Piano' comes from recordings of live performances. There are two such performances documented online, the first originally being broadcast on *Fernwood Tonight* in 1977 (Waits 2020), shortly after the song's initial release. In this performance, the audience is quick to respond to Waits' opening musical 'sloppiness' with laughter, with each subsequent metaphor serving as a separate punchline which receives its own response. These reactions indicate that the audience is both attending to the lyrical content of the performance, and understanding of the relationship between this context and the unconventional musicality. Additionally, these live performances take on a further multimodal dimension: on the *Fernwood Tonight* recording, Waits wipes his mouth as he sings that 'the box office is drooling'.

Again contributing to a sense of metonymy, this gesture further serves to position the character and mind-style of the narrator-singer as central to the audience's interpretation of the song.

Waits further performed the song to a live audience on *The Late Late Show* in 1981 (CR's Video Vaults 2020), with significant variation in the lyrical order and musical structure compared to the *Small Change* recording and the *Fernwood Tonight* version. In this iteration, his piano playing is highly atonal throughout, to the point of serialism, and the tune in which he sings is largely misaligned with the accompaniment. In the recording, *The Late Late Show* audience is notably quieter than the *Fernwood Tonight* audience, with small chuckles only appearing halfway through the performance. While lyrics and performance continue to complement one another conceptually, perhaps the lack of anchoring in expected schemas of musicality causes some hesitation and uncertainty in interpretation. Additionally, the audience of *The Late Late Show* does not seem to have the same exaggerated reactions from the show's hosts to signal an intentionally comedic performance.

Allan (2019: 19) argues that 'transparency of the text' is a central principle of immersion in literature: 'we will find [. . .] no metanarrative elements', and 'no elements drawing attention to the conventionality of the textual (literary) genre' (see Wydrzynska, this volume). However, metanarrative commentary is central to the listener's immersion in 'The Piano': it invites a direct conceptual mapping of performance and meaning-making in world-building, and draws attention to the musical and lyrical features which require the enaction of the faux-drunk mind-style in order to be understood. In this multimodal context, drawing attention to musical structure also serves a world-building purpose: the piano is not simply a heterodiegetic accompaniment to lyrical storytelling, but a subject of consistent reference within the narrative world of the song itself. It is this piano *specifically* that has been drinking, and to which the listener has direct access to hear for themselves. As Ennslin et al. (2019: 337) note in their model of literary immersion, there is often 'the need to pay close and often critical attention [. . .] with the aim to gain a deeper understanding of the narrative context in which the story is set'. Enacting a drunken mind-style through both its lyrical structure and performance style, 'The Piano' invites immersion through a need for the listener's close attention: recognition of the performance as an intentional artifice, rather than poor execution, requires an understanding of – and immersion in – the fictional mind-style through which the performance is framed.

Conclusions: getting drunk with the Prince of Melancholy

In 'The Piano has been Drinking (Not Me)', musical performance style and lyrical content function bidirectionally in the production and interpretation of mind-style, serving as joint input spaces in a blend as opposed to a unidirectional source/target relationship, challenging some of the approaches through which musical multimodal metaphor has been framed previously. Whereas Forceville (2009), for example, views music as a means to further clarify the meaning of lyrical metaphor, the function is shown to be reversed in the opening of 'The Piano': any uncertainty about the deliberateness of Waits' out-of-tune playing is resolved through attention to the accompanying lyrics. In other words, it is the lyrics that may help the listener identify a musical dimension to the megametaphor across the song, and provide a framework for mapping the performance style to the construction of storyworld, i.e., the hazy drunken mind-style embodied in both the language and musical style. In this context, multimodal elements are not simply supplementary cues for language-driven meaning, but rather equally contributing elements that simulate the narrator's mind-style independently, and which come to be understood holistically.

In her account of the importance of mimesis for immersion in narratives, films, and representational paintings, Ryan (2015) lists artistic forms in which mimesis is not typically present. Among these, she includes music as a mode that does not 'construct the setting for a potential narrative action' (9). Waits' 'The Piano', however, presents a strong case for multimodal mimesis through which immersion and world-building is developed, with musical cues being as important to the cueing and construction of the text-world as the lyrics themselves. Interpretation of the song's musical and lyrical structures requires mimesis, cued by 'mistakes' in the performance as well as metaphorical opacity – a conceptual 'haziness'. Hence, immersion in the world of the song's narrative is produced through attention, resulting in absorption and leading, in the experience of listeners like Cohen (2005), to immersive transportation and the easy imagining of the setting described within the song's lyrics and in which the sloppy piano playing itself is likely to feature. Because the listener is rewarded in attending to this dynamic, via the subsequent interpretation of the unconventional musicality of Waits' performance as a deliberate stylistic choice, the process of sense-making and understanding is enactive, highly engaging through the listener's imaginative involvement, and, therefore, potentially immersive. Of course, not all listeners will find 'The Piano' to be an immersive experience, but the analysis in this chapter has shown how its multimodal features are perceived in a combination which enables the capacity for such immersion.

This analysis also raises questions around the presumed dialectal opposition between immersion and interaction, with the attention produced through interaction constituting the source of immersion in this instance. The enactive immersion of Waits' multimodal metaphors, the opacity of which is a source of the kind of attention which may induce immersion, therefore demonstrates the necessity for closer scrutiny around the relationship between these concepts. Although 'The Piano' as a song feels distinctive in its demands for listener attention in order to produce such effects, future research could explore other multimodal contexts in which audio and visual stimuli function to provide an enactive, mimetic, sensory experience to the audience. In these settings, where the capacity for immersion is elicited through imaginative involvement, multimodal features might be explored not just in terms of how they support the development of linguistic metaphor, but how meaning arises from a more complex interplay between modes.

References

Adams, E. and Rollings, A. (2006) *Fundamentals of Game Design*. Hoboken: Prentice-Hall.

Agrawal, S. and Bech, S. (2022) 'Immersion in audiovisual experiences', in M. Geronazzo and S. Serafin (eds) *Sonic Interactions in Virtual Environments*. Cham: Springer, pp.219–351.

Allan, R.J. (2019) 'Narrative immersion: some linguistic and narratological aspects', in J. Grethlein (ed.) *Experience, Narrative, and Criticism in Ancient Greece: Under the Spell of Stories*. Oxford: Oxford University Press, pp.15–35.

Brackett, N. and Hoard, C. (2004) *The New Rolling Stone Album Guide*. London: Simon & Schuster.

Cohen, R. (2005) '"The piano has been drinking": on the art of the rant', *The Georgia Review* 59 (2): 233–53.

CR's Video Vaults (2020) 'The piano has been drinking', Tom Waits, 1981, available at <https://www.youtube.com/watch?v=MBQucVmiemY>

Ensslin, A., Bell, A., Skains, L. and van der Bom, I. (2019) 'Immersion, digital fiction, and the switchboard metaphor', *Participations: Journal of Audience and Reception Studies* 16 (1): 320–42.

Fauconnier, G. and Turner, M. (1996) 'Blending as a central process of grammar', in A. Goldberg (ed.) *Conceptual Structure, Discourse and Language*. Stanford: Center for the Study of Language and Information (CSLI) Publications, pp.113–30.

Fauconnier, G. and Turner, M. (2002) *The Way We Think: Conceptual Blending and the Mind's Hidden Complexities*. New York: Basic Books.

Forceville, C. (2009) 'The role of non-verbal sound and music in multimodal metaphor', in C. Forceville and E. Urios-Aparisi (eds) *Multimodal Metaphor*. Berlin: Mouton de Gruyter. pp.383–402.

Hauck, P. and Hecht, H. (2023) 'Emotionally congruent music and text increase immersion and appraisal', *PLoS One* 18 (1): 0280019.

Hayles, N.K. (2007) 'Hyper and deep attention: the generational divide in cognitive modes', *Profession* 13: 187–99.

Humphries, P. (2007) *The Many Lives of Tom Waits*. London: Omnibus Press.

Kovecses, Z. (2010) *Metaphor: A Practical Introduction* (2nd edn). Oxford: Oxford University Press.

Morini, M. (2013) 'Towards a musical stylistics: movement in Kate Bush's "Running up that hill"', *Language and Literature* 22 (4): 283–97.

Murray, J. (2017) *Hamlet on the Holodeck: The Future of Narrative in Cyberspace*. Cambridge: The MIT Press.

Nuttall, L. (2018) *Mind Style and Cognitive Grammar*. London: Bloomsbury.

Price, H. and Wilson, J. (2019) 'Relevance theory and metaphor: an analysis of Tom Waits' "Emotional weather report"', *Language and Literature* 28 (1): 61–81.
Rundquist, E. (2020) 'The Cognitive Grammar of drunkenness: consciousness representation in *Under the Volcano*', *Language and Literature* 29 (1): 39–56.
Ryan, M. (2015) *Narrative as Virtual Reality: Immersion and Interactivity in Literature and Electronic Media* (2nd edn). Baltimore: Johns Hopkins University Press.
Schneider, R. (2012) 'Blending and the study of narrative: an introduction', in R. Schneider and M. Hartner (eds) *Blending and the Study of Narrative: Approaches and Applications*. Berlin: de Gruyter, pp.1–30.
Steen, G. and Semino, E. (2008) 'Metaphor in literature', in R. Gibbs (ed.) *The Cambridge Handbook of Metaphor and Thought*. Cambridge: Cambridge University Press, pp.232–46.
Stockwell, P. (2009) *Texture: A Cognitive Aesthetics of Reading*. Edinburgh: Edinburgh University Press.
Stockwell, P. (2020) *Cognitive Poetics: An Introduction* (2nd edn). London: Routledge.
Strauss, D., Francis, A, Vibell, J. and Corona-Strauus, F. (2024) 'The role of attention in immersion: the two-competitor model', *Brain Research Bulletin* 210: 110923.
Voice, M. and Whiteley, S. (2019) '"Y'all don't want to hear me, you just want to dance": a cognitive approach to listener attention in Outkast's "Hey Ya!"', *Language and Literature* 28 (1): 7–22.
Waits, T. (1976) 'The piano has been drinking (not me)', on *Small Change*. Asylum Records.
Waits, T. (2020) '"The piano has been drinking" (Live on *Fernwood Tonight*, 1977)', available at <https://www.youtube.com/watch?v=RKlmBZsVPK8>
Walsh, R. (2011) 'The common basis of narrative and music: somatic, social, and affective factors', *StoryWorlds: A Journal of Narrative Studies* 3: 49–71.
Werth, P. (1994) 'Extended metaphor – a text-world account', *Language and Literature* 3 (2): 79–103.
Zbikowski, L. (2009) 'Music, language, and multimodal metaphor', in C. Forceville and E. Urios-Aparisi (eds) *Multimodal Metaphor*. Berlin: Mouton de Gruyter. pp.359–81.
Zhong, Z., Wen, S. and Chen, S. (2023) 'Research trends in multimodal metaphor: a bibliometric analysis', *Frontiers in Psychology* 14: 1144725.
Zwaan, R. (2004) 'The immersed experiencer: toward an embodied theory of language comprehension', in B.H. Ross (ed.) *The Psychology of Learning and Motivation: Advances in Research and Theory*. Amsterdam: Elsevier Science. pp.35–62.

Part III

Literary immersions

CHAPTER 10

Escape to Wodehouse world

Alice Haines

Taking as her case study a comic novel by P.G. Wodehouse, Haines develops an exploration of immersion and humour across a set of texts. Comic fiction of this sort is often characterised as 'escapism', which offers another dimension on the immersive experience. She proposes that the sense of immersion can be situated in a 'Wodehouse world' that over-arches the specific texts, and which exists at the same ontological level as the reader, though 'split' across history. This suggests that immersion does not necessarily require an ontological switch into a fictional world (though immersion into and emergence out of that world can explain the feeling of wilful escapism), but it can be effected at the discourse-world level between reader and author.

Reading Wodehouse

The novels and short stories of P.G. Wodehouse are famous for their humour. More specifically, they are famous for the language of the humour. Popular discussion of the works often mentions the creativity and novelty of metaphor used and, indeed, where linguistic analysis has been undertaken this has tended to focus on the construction of short examples of single metaphors (e.g., Holcomb 1992, Veale 2013). However, beyond this and Marszalek's (2020) discussion of dramatic irony and other contextual factors that encourage a humorous interpretation, there is surprisingly little principled analysis of Wodehouse's style and its readerly effects. Apart from the focus on creative metaphor, the other characteristic that is often mentioned is that the writing is highly escapist (e.g., Kimball 2000, Rea 2015). This attribute of the writing is often given as one of the main reasons for reading the works and for enjoying them, as in a quotation from a BBC broadcast by Evelyn Waugh (1961): '[Wodehouse] has made a world for us to live in and delight in'. Sometimes, in more critical treatments, this appreciation is tempered by an inclination to treat the escapist quality as a sign simply of frivolity and a weakness of the literary worth (Epstein 2018, Triezenberg 2008). However, such complaints are rare; the prevailing opinion (both academic and popular) is that escapism is a fundamental part of reading Wodehouse and that, rather than it being seen as something to be disparaged, readers value highly Wodehouse's ability to facilitate their engagement with his works. It strikes me that there is a similarity between the spatial displacements involved in both escaping from one place to another and the sense of immersion in the world of a literary text that is the subject of this book. While escapism tends to produce a judgement of quality (usually negative, but more positive in this case) and immersion may not, it seems to me that escapism can be seen as one form of immersive experience. It is my aim here to discuss the relationship between these two concepts and to explore the effect they have on readers' appreciation of the humour in Wodehouse's writing.

Wodehouse wrote several series of books, the best known – and most frequently referred to by both critical and general readers – being those about Bertie Wooster, a wealthy upper-class gentleman, and his valet, Jeeves. These are, in the main, narrated by Bertie and most are set in a highly idealised interwar England of country houses and Mayfair clubs. Bertie is amiable and well-meaning but not considered especially bright, although he is keen to improve himself, picking up Latin phrases and lines of poetry from the exceptionally intelligent Jeeves. A typical plot centres on Bertie trying to help one of his friends through the execution of an elaborate plan but becoming ensnared in a rather more difficult situation for himself after the plan misfires. A chain of unfortunate repercussions ensues until he calls on the assistance of Jeeves, who extricates Bertie and smooths everything out to the satisfaction of all. One of the novels (selected here for discussion as a representative example of the Jeeves stories) is *Joy in the Morning* (Wodehouse 1946), which has a complex plot involving attempts to arrange a clandestine meeting in the village of Steeple Bumpleigh between Bertie's uncle-by-marriage, Lord Worplesdon, and an American businessman, Chichester Clam. This is complicated by the fact that Bumpleigh Hall is also the home of Worplesdon's daughter, Lady Florence Craye. In a previous short story, Jeeves rescued Bertie from an ill-suited engagement to Florence. Her current fiancé, D'Arcy 'Stilton' Cheesewright (an old acquaintance of Bertie) is jealous of Bertie but also out of favour with Florence, leading Bertie to fear that she will again regard him as a marital prospect. Indeed, at one point, Florence decides, to Bertie's horror, that she will marry him instead. In addition, Boko Fittleworth (another old friend) wants to marry Nobby Hopwood but needs to obtain the consent of Worplesdon, her guardian, and involves Bertie in a plan to win his approval. Added into the mix is Worplesdon's son, the Boy Scout Edwin, whose Daily Acts of Kindness have a habit of causing turmoil and thwarting the various schemes in operation. After these schemes cause further problems for Bertie and the others, Jeeves is consulted and comes up with a plan that enables the clandestine meeting to take place, reunites Florence and Stilton, and leads to Worplesdon giving consent for Nobby to marry Boko. The full plot is rather more convoluted than this simple outline; suffice it to say that it is convoluted and typical of one of the Jeeves novels in both its convolutions and subject matter.

Examining the Goodreads page (2024) for *Joy in the Morning*, there are several features common to many reviews that echo remarks made by professional readers. Most obvious is that the majority of readers enjoy the novel (about 84 per cent of reviewers give it five or four stars) and that they enjoy, in particular, the humour. This is perhaps unsurprising; given that Wodehouse's novels and short stories are well known for being funny, it seems more likely than not that a reader would have some expectation of being amused and that readers motivated to leave a review would comment on this positively. More interesting, digging a little deeper, are the reasons reviewers give for enjoying the novel and finding it funny. Comments about Wodehouse's style feature heavily and many reviewers quote – sometimes extensively – extracts from the novel that they liked. Some even attempt a pastiche of the style in writing their review, using creative metaphor similar to that found in Wodehouse's works and lexis similar to the early twentieth-century British upper-class slang used by Bertie Wooster. Many reviewers also mention, as a reason for their enjoyment of the novel, their familiarity with the fictional world Wodehouse creates: the predictability of the plot, the amiability of the characters, and the triviality of the subject matter. Almost all reviewers are well-acquainted with Wodehouse's works – in particular the Jeeves stories – and several mention that their review of *Joy in the Morning* follows their re-reading of it or that they have read several in the series in close succession. Reading the reviews I get a sense that using the novel as a form of escapism is an important part of the reading experience; readers know what to expect and that is an idyllic world in which nothing unpleasant happens. Importantly, this world tends to be characterised as that of Wodehouse, rather than that of the characters. This is partly, I think, because it covers books in other Wodehouse series, but it emphasises the idea that readers have more of a sense of engaging with Wodehouse than with any of his characters. The observation of the feelings of immersion in 'Wodehouse World' is, I think, critical to understanding why readers find the novel funny.

Modelling immersion and humour

The sense of being immersed in a fictional world is one that appears to be an important part of the experience of reading Wodehouse's novels and short stories. Much of the previous research into the readerly experience of immersion, though, has tended to focus on literary works where humour is relatively minimal and other emotional effects are in action (e.g., Bell et al. 2018, Stockwell 2009). However, that is not to say that the findings of this research are not applicable here, nor that the process of immersion when reading humorous fiction is different; the communicative act of engaging in literary discourse is, of course, the same. What may differ are the specifics of what occurs, and this may account for some of the differences in the reading experience.

One thing that is striking about research into readerly immersion is, firstly, that not all researchers use the term *immersion*. Secondly, there is a wide range of other terms used to denote an immersive experience when reading literature or engaging with other types of text. These include *transportation* (Gerrig 1993, Green and Brock 2000), *narrative engagement* (Busselle and Bilandzic 2009), *storyworld absorption* (Kuijpers et al. 2014), and *presence* (Witmer and Singer 1998), amongst others. Each of these concepts has a slightly different focus, even where the same term is used – Gerrig's notion of transportation involves the deictic shifting of a reader's projected identity, as does the idea of storyworld absorption for Kuijpers et al., whereas Green and Brock emphasise elicitation of mental imagery in transportation. In spite of these differences, what stands out to me – and what is most useful in applying these ideas to the experience of reading Wodehouse – is the strong conceptualisation of the experience in spatial terms. The notion of escapism that is prominent in readers' comments, too, can be conceptualised in spatial terms. However, there is a distinction between a reader's wilful escape and, for example, the more passive process of their being transported. The spatial conceptualisation of the process is also useful in modelling the relationship between an immersive experience and a humorous one.

The reason this is useful is that the modelling of humorous communication also involves the metaphorical (or, indeed, literal) spatial positioning of participants relative to the source of humour. Accounts of the social effects of humour (e.g., Billig 2005, Holmes 2000, Lave and Wenger 1991) often refer to the way in which it is used to establish and maintain social in-groups containing the participants, with the source of humour excluded as part of an out-group. The influential superiority theory of humour (e.g., Gruner 1978, 1997) holds that, to experience mirth, participants must feel superior (i.e., at a position vertically distant) to the source of humour. Bringing in more cognitive aspects of humour modelling, the Benign Violation Hypothesis (McGraw et al. 2012) proposes that 'violations' can be perceived as humorous when observed or recalled from a distance, either spatial, temporal, or psychological. Apter's (2007) suggestion that humour must involve some sort of perceived diminishment of the source can also be conceptualised in spatial terms by observing that distant objects appear small. Because of this overlap in spatial conceptualisation, it seems to me that the modelling of humour and the modelling of literary immersion can be mutually beneficial.

To my mind, the best way of modelling humorous communication is based on the triadic relationship between the source of humour and two participants, the *relay* and the *receiver* (Haines 2023). Typically, the relay observes something about the source that they find amusing and relays it to the receiver. For the receiver to be amused, they must have sufficient knowledge of the source to understand what it is the relay finds amusing. This means that the source is often something that is familiar enough to the receiver that they tend not to notice it in everyday life. The relay's communication has the effect, if successful, of drawing the source to the attention of the receiver, with the outcome that relay and receiver find something about their experience of the world that they have in common. The establishment of this shared experience can be conceptualised as a spatial convergence of relay and receiver.

The nature of literary reading complicates this model somewhat because the relay can, at different points, be a character in the narrative, a narrator, or even the reader's idea of the author. It is also possible for different *enactors* (or versions) (Emmott 1992) of one of these entities to be respectively relay and source. For example, in a homodiegetic narrative, the narrator may relay something amusing about their actions as a character in the story they are narrating. In these circumstances, rather than a simple one-entity relay, the relay can be conceptualised as a complex of all these entities, the complex being a series of authorial relay components corresponding with the levels of deictic projection possible for that text. The narratorial positioning of the receiver at one of these levels, relative to the others, can alter their interpretation of whether a proposition is humorous or not (Chłopicki 2017) because the extent of their projection into the text-world affects the perspective from which they view both relay and source. It seems likely, therefore, that a reader's experience of humour will be related to their immersive experience. One difference arises, however. Where an immersive readerly experience is characterised, as the term suggests, as the result of a movement into the text-world, literary humour tends to result in a movement outward along the authorial relay series (Haines 2024) – in other words, in the opposite direction. This is not necessarily a problem for the modelling of the relationship between the two. In fact, the difference may show in greater detail the intricacies of how immersive experiences arise in different circumstances.

As well as being conceptualised spatially, the feeling of literary immersion has been described by readers in terms of their investment in the process (Stockwell 2009). This foregrounds the idea of immersion being an experience that readers actively construct. Here, too, there is an overlap – although not as immediately obvious as the spatial aspect – with the modelling of humour. To explain how, I need to start with one of the key theories of humour: that, for humour to be recognised, some form of incongruity must be perceived. I would argue that the term 'incongruity' is more applicable to blatant joke humour than to the more subtle humour generally found in literature. However, the reason incongruity has been linked to humour is that the process of humorous communication makes an object or concept stand out to the extent that one becomes aware of the way in which it contrasts with its surroundings. In verbal humour a relay may, for example, linguistically amplify features of the source or contrast it directly with other objects or concepts. The result is a defamiliarising effect that can draw a receiver's attention to the source. The defamiliarisation of the source can be represented as a divergence of the source from relay and receiver, the distancing resulting in a spatial diminishment effect which allows the receiver to experience amusement (for a fuller explanation see Haines 2023).

It has been observed in experimental studies of joke humour (e.g., Wyer and Collins 1992) that participants find jokes that require a moderate amount of effort to process funnier than those that are easier or more difficult. The experimental finding appears consistent with a Relevance Theoretic account of humour (Yus 2016), where an addressee will expend additional cognitive effort (in Sperber and Wilson's (1995) use) to find an interpretation of an utterance that will provide the expected cognitive effect of amusement. In other words, a receiver expecting humour will be prepared to make a cognitive investment in much the same way as readers generally making a cognitive investment to benefit from an immersive experience. What I also propose is that this investment can also be conceptualised spatially, as a willingness of the receiver to make a convergent movement towards the relay. Similarly, in general terms, a reader's investment can be thought of as a willing immersive projection across a text-world boundary. Bringing the two ideas together can provide a means of modelling the way in which a reader's immersive experience relates to their recognition of humour. In the case of reading Wodehouse, a reader's wilful 'escape' could be the same convergent movement towards the relay that is part of their cognitive investment in the humour process.

As well as the convergent and divergent dynamics of relay, receiver, and source affecting the cognition of humour, part of an adequate explanation of humorous communication must also address a receiver's emotional experience of humour appreciation. Building on the observation that the physiological arousal effects associated with amusement (increased heart rate, blood pressure etc.) are the same as those observed in states of anxiety or fear (Godkewitsch 1976, Langevin and Day 1972), Apter (2007) applies the principles of his Reversal Theory to suggest that the interpretation of bodily sensations of physiological arousal is key to the way in which amusement is experienced. The central tenet of Reversal Theory is that a person's behaviour can be understood through comprehension of their motivations; at different times a person will have different frames of mind – termed metamotivational states – that will affect their motivations. One binary pair of metamotivational states concerns means and ends. Every activity has a process and an end, and a person may be motivated by the end result of activity in which they are engaged, or by the process of doing the activity. These states are termed *telic state* and *paratelic state*. In telic state a person will be motivated to avoid arousal because this may be caused by factors that hinder the end result of an activity. In paratelic state a person will seek arousal because they are motivated to engage with the experience of the process of the activity. Thus, the same physiological arousal state will be interpreted and experienced, respectively, as negatively-valenced emotion, such as anxiety or fear, or positively-valenced emotion, such as amusement or excitement. Extending this idea to incorporate the concept of figure/ground, in paratelic state the process of doing the activity will be figured against the ground of the end.

Here, the modelling of the viewing arrangement of a scene in Langacker's (2008) *Cognitive Grammar* is useful. In this, either the conceptual content of a scene is figured to a greater extent (an objective construal) or the conceptualisers and the process of conceptualisation are (a subjective construal) (see Figure 10.1). Conceptualisers can become more figured, or 'onstage' as Langacker puts it, by being explicitly mentioned, for example, or through evidence of their attitude towards the conceptual content. Presenting a source of humour in a way that defamiliarises it would be one way of increasing the subjectivity of the construal. Similarly, a text in which relay or receiver are explicitly onstage, such as first-person narration or where direct address of a reader occurs, will also encourage a subjective construal. Because the process of construal will also be figured, this is analogous to

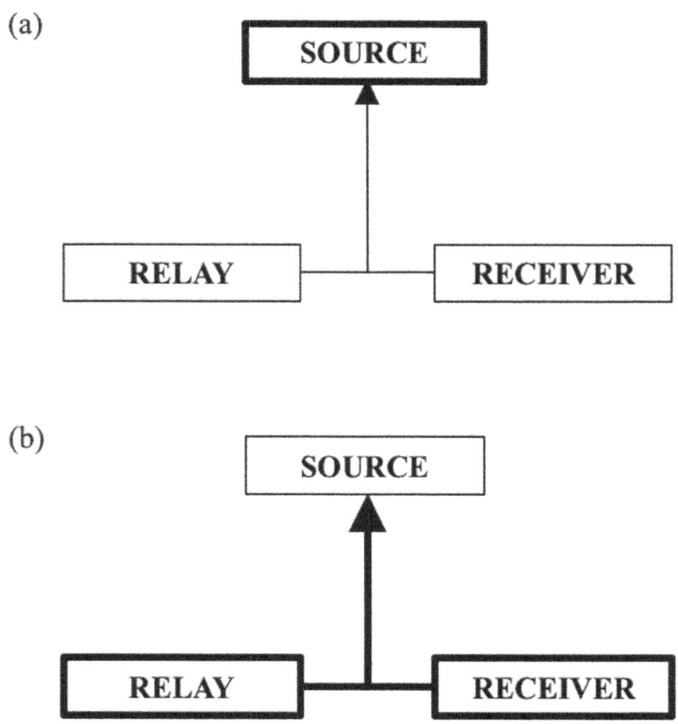

Figure 10.1 Objective (a) and subjective (b) construal of the conceptual content (adapted from Verhagen 2007)

the process-figured paratelic state in which amusement is more readily an emotional effect.

This notion of a process-figured paratelic state seems to me to have a parallel in the idea of investment as a conceptualisation of literary immersion. A reader motivated to make a cognitive investment will be motivated by the return on their investment of the reading experience. There is also a parallel in the idea of the state of *cognitive flow*, described by Csikszentmihalyi (1990), in which much research into literary immersion is grounded. This is characterised as a state of mind in which, among other things, the doing of the activity becomes an end in itself. Other characteristics are the loss of self-awareness and the lack of a need to pay conscious attention to the activity. While the corollary of the first key characteristic mentioned would be that the experience of immersion corresponds with process-figured humorous communication, the self-effacement involved in the latter two may, at first, appear to present a problem. A self-effacing state would correspond with an objective construal rather than the subjective construal that I propose is the basis of verbal humour. However, as Stockwell (2019) points out, readers often report a sense of deep emotional involvement when reading metafictions. He suggests that a sense of readerly agency may be part of the development of this response. I would add that because literary reading involves shifts in a reader's projection to different deictic centres (that of narrator, different characters, etc.), it may be that literary immersion can involve situations where a reader feels a strong sense of their presence in the world of a text that results in a sense of self-effacement in the real world. It could be that there are different types of immersion that result from engaging with different texts (and indeed different activities) and that self-effacement is not characteristic of all. Escaping to somewhere is deliberate and requires an active participation in the process; someone being transported into the world of a text or absorbed in the process of literary reading has more of a passive role. This could help to explain why a humorous novel, such as *Joy in the Morning*, which encourages and employs a reader's active participation in the humour process, can feel immersive but with the qualitative sense of escapism.

The escape route

As I mentioned previously, for readers of Wodehouse's novels and short stories, as can be seen from the Goodreads reviews of *Joy in the Morning*, escapism and humour are typically the most valued qualities of the reading experience. It seems to me – both from my own experience as an enthusiastic Wodehouse reader and with analytical pursuits in mind – that these two aspects of the reading experience have a mutual effect on each other. Certainly, as I argued above, the modelling of immersion (of which escapism is one type) as a spatial process-figured effect has strong similarities with the modelling of humour. It seems likely, therefore, that the textual features that are involved in producing such effects will also be similar.

Opening the novel, one such feature is immediately obvious. It begins: 'After the thing was over [. . .]' (Wodehouse 1946: 1). This and the remainder of the first two pages form an evaluation of the complicating action (in Labov's (1972) terms), in which Bertie describes his confession to Jeeves, while driving home from a visit to Steeple Bumpleigh, that there had been moments in the preceding days when he had despaired that the situation that occurred there would be resolved. The situation has evidently been resolved, however, and Jeeves supplies Bertie with the encapsulating psalm quotation he has been grasping for: 'Joy cometh in the mornings, sir?' Although by no means unique to *Joy in the Morning*, this is not a prototypical opening of a novel. More typically it might be expected that establishing details of key characters, and the time or location in which the events of the story take place, would be given. Some orientating detail is given obliquely – the location of Steeple Bumpleigh can be discerned from the description of them having 'shaken the dust' of it from their tyres – and, of course, Bertie and Jeeves are established as characters, but, in the main, the first pages are comprised of dialogue between the two about the fact that an undesirable situation has resolved and how Bertie's mood has improved substantially. Following this dialogue, the cast of characters is listed:

> And I still think that there can be no neater way of putting in a nutshell the outcome of the super-sticky affair of Nobby Hopwood, Stilton Cheesewright, Florence Craye, my Uncle Percy, J. Chichester Clam, Edwin the Boy Scout and old Boko Fittleworth – or, as my biographers will probably call it, the Steeple Bumpleigh Horror.
>
> (Wodehouse 1946: 2)

Most of these characters appear in other novels (only Nobby Hopwood and J. Chichester Clam do not), and so are a form of marked intertextual reference (Mason 2019). It is likely that a reader familiar with the series will have some idea of who some of them are and their relationship to Bertie, even though no further detail is given beyond the social deixis of 'my Uncle Percy'. At the very least they may be able to guess that Nobby Hopwood, Stilton Cheesewright, and Boko Fittleworth are friends of Bertie's because they would be able to apply their schematic knowledge that he often calls his friends by their nicknames. For someone unfamiliar with this, this is simply a list of names, some of which might be perceived as a little curious. Either way, what is not given is why these characters have been mentioned. There are two things that make this paragraph unusual as part of the narrative's orientation. The first is the contrast between the explicit naming of the characters involved without reference to their relevance to the story and what might be expected at the start of a novel. The second is the contrast between the specification of who is involved and the lack of indication of what happened. It is clear from Bertie's previous evaluative comments that something unpleasant happened and it is described here as a 'super-sticky affair' and 'the Steeple Bumpleigh Horror', but the specifics of what happened are not given. There is a third contrast for readers familiar with the stories, and that is between the indication that the events at Steeple Bumpleigh were unpleasant and the expectation of idyllic pleasantness. Even for readers unfamiliar with this, the informality of 'super-sticky' and the capitalisation of 'Horror' may suggest that the events were not, in fact, as worthy of despair as Bertie describes. Together, the effect of these contrasts is to defamiliarise the story itself, bringing it to the attention of the reader as the source of humour.

The next paragraph adds to the construction of the story as the source of humour.

> Even before the events occurred which I am about to relate, the above hamlet had come high up on my list of places to be steered sedulously clear of. I don't know if you have ever seen one of those old maps where they mark a spot with a cross and put 'Here be dragons' or 'Keep ye eye skinned for hippogriffs', but I had always felt that some such kindly warning might well have been given to pedestrians and traffic with regard to Steeple Bumpleigh.
>
> (Wodehouse 1946: 2)

To me, the name 'Steeple Bumpleigh', even without any description, brings to mind an image of a charming and picturesque rural English village. This is partly from an association I have of steeples with the sort of church that tends to be found in this type of village. The first syllable of 'Bumpleigh' is suggestive of the phrase 'country bumpkin', adding to the image an impression of unsophisticated rustic simplicity. It is also associated with clumsiness and sounds ungainly between an elegant 'Steeple' and a bucolic '-leigh'. In short, Steeple Bumpleigh sounds like the type of carefree setting of country houses that Bertie often visits in other stories. However, this image contrasts with the danger implied by Bertie's suggestion that warnings should be given about the place. While this draws attention to the character of the village, again, though, there is another contrast – between real danger signs and the warnings that Bertie describes. These are features of adventure stories often involving fictional (or fictionalised) pirates or other swashbuckling heroes, which diminishes the danger encouraging a humorous interpretation, as Apter (2007) suggests. This also occurs in the previous passage through the informal register of 'super-sticky affair' and the somewhat melodramatic 'Steeple Bumpleigh Horror', which evokes lowbrow pulp fiction and contributes to the divergence of the source (the story) from the receiver (the reader) and the relay.

The perception of who the relay here is, however, is central to the explanation of the humour and the immersive effects of reading the novel.

I mentioned earlier that the relay in the situation of reading fiction comprises a complex with a series of components corresponding with the series of authorial deictic levels (for the sake of simplicity: author, narrator, and character). In my own experience reading these passages as part of the novel, the relay, with whom I feel I am sharing humour, starts as the narrating Bertie but by the second passage becomes my idea of Wodehouse. In terms of the immersive effect, this is not one of the self-effacement that characterises a state of flow. It is more that I find the opening of the novel somewhat intriguing, and I am motivated to make a cognitive investment in finding out what went on at Steeple Bumpleigh. In fact, as opposed to self-effacement, I am highly aware of my role as a reader and a receiver of humour and yet I feel deeply immersed in the experience. This can be explained with reference to Langacker's (2008) idea of a viewing arrangement in which the construal can be more objective or more subjective. In a subjective construal the conceptualisers (here the relay and receiver) and process of conceptualisation are construed more objectively by being brought more onstage. The novel has a homodiegetic narration, with the narrator being Bertie, which, because the narrator is explicitly onstage through the use of the first-person 'I', makes this a subjective construal. Adding to the subjectivity of the construal is the fact that the narrator's role is made explicit with Bertie's comment about the events that he is 'about to relate'. By making either relay, receiver, or process more onstage, the other two components will also, implicitly, be made more prominent. Here, though, the receiver's role is also made more prominent because the defamiliarising contrasting of the source (which also, in itself, influences the subjectivity) is achieved partly through the receiver's own contributions – their knowledge of pirate stories and pulp fiction, for example, and (for some) intertextual knowledge of characters. Similarly, the narrator's comment about their role brings to the receiver's awareness the textuality of the text and their own role in the process of construal. The result is a construal that becomes maximally subjective – that is, where the conceptualisers are construed with maximal objectivity.

The idea of a relay complex of an authorial series of conceptualisers is very similar to Langacker's (2008: 484) notion of a 'fractal organisation', where one conceptualiser is part of what is conceptualised by another conceptualiser. Nuttall (2018) applies this idea to model subjective and objective construal across the multiple deictic levels involved in literary reading. A construal from the perspective of the narrator, say, will include characters in the narrative as part of the conceptual content. If the construal is from the perspective of the author, the narrator will also become part of the conceptual content. I would argue (Haines 2024) that a construal from the level of the narrator in which the narrator is maximally objective (that is, fully onstage) will be very close to a construal from the level of the author where the narrator is part of the conceptual content. Therefore, by increasing the objectivity of the construal of the conceptualisers, this will encourage a receiver's shift in perspective outwards along the authorial

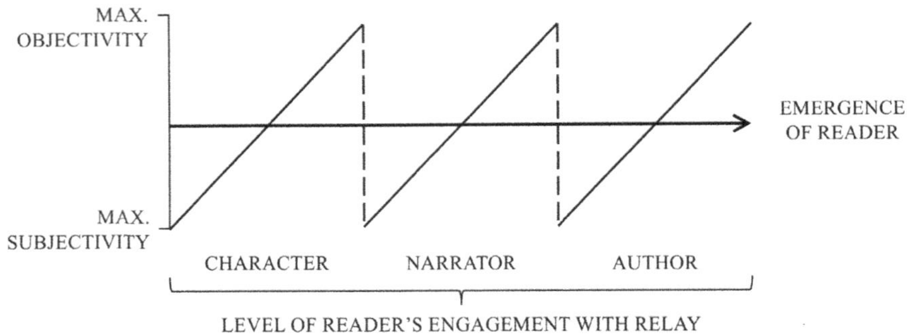

Figure 10.2 Increasing the objectivity of the relay results in emergence

relay series (see Figure 10.2). In this instance, because the construal is maximally subjective – that is, the narrating Bertie and narratee receiver are construed with maximal objectivity – it encourages a receiver's shift out to the perspective of Wodehouse.

Superimposing the viewing arrangement onto a basic Text World Theory (Gavins 2007) architecture is beneficial here. This is composed of a discourse-world inhabited by the reader and author (termed a split discourse-world as the two exist in different spatial and temporal locations) and a text-world comprising the mental representation of the world inhabited by the characters. For a reader to conceptualise the text-world, they must project to a new deictic centre across the text-world boundary. Self-evidently, the receiver's shift out to Wodehouse's perspective is an example of emergence relative to the text-world but, I would argue, the feeling of immersion here is experienced at discourse-world level. This need feel no less immersive than experiencing a feeling of immersion at the level of a text-world. I would suggest that in many cases of literary immersion the viewing arrangement including reader and author is construed less subjectively than in this case. Here, though, the process of receiver and relay co-constructing humour increases the subjectivity of the construal enough to result in a shift outward to the discourse-world. However, for immersion to be experienced, a person's deictic centre must be projected away from their own here and now; the process of something being immersed implies a (metaphorically) spatial displacement. Although immersion here is experienced at discourse-world level, the displacement involved can be explained by examining the 'split' in this split discourse-world. Wodehouse and I have never existed in the same spatiotemporal location. In addition, the Wodehouse with whom I feel a strong sense of collaboration is not the real Wodehouse but my idea of Wodehouse – an implied Wodehouse – who does not exist on the same ontological level as I do. He is no more accessible to me than the fictional characters about whom he writes. This means that my collaboration with him involves my deictic projection across the 'split' in the split discourse-world. In essence, this is cognitively no different to projection across a text-world boundary, but where this can be seen as a vertical displacement, projection across the discourse-world 'split' can be seen as horizontal displacement.

In terms of the effect on humour, the outward shift is a convergence of the receiver towards the ultimate relay, the author – the relay with whom the receiver is nearest on an ontological level (there was, of course, a real Wodehouse). This facilitates their sense of sharing humour with the author and their appreciation of that humour. Humorous appreciation is also facilitated by the fact that the outward spatial shift introduces greater distance between the receiver and the events of the narrative. Comments, both academic and by readers more generally, about the escapism of reading the novel (and others by Wodehouse) often describe it as such because the world inhabited by Bertie is idyllic and the subject matter is inconsequential. However, the main events of the plot of *Joy in the Morning* involve, among other things, a trans-Atlantic business deal, the break-up of an engagement, a house burning to the ground (possibly with a child in it), and several instances of physical violence. Experiencing any of these from a proximal position would be unlikely to result in amusement but the distant perspective helps to encourage an interpretation of these events as trivial and a source of humour.

On the readerly side of the equation, added to the authorial facilitation of receiver-relay convergence is a desire to converge. Most readers will have at least some idea that Wodehouse's works are light-hearted and humorous and will therefore have an expectation of this. For many readers, this expectation extends to more specific features of the series, such as recurring characters, creative metaphor, or typical plots. Rather than running a generic humorous literature schema, they are running a Wodehouse story schema. Readers who have previously enjoyed the experience of reading Wodehouse will wilfully converge with the author to earn the reward of humour appreciation. This sense of actively projecting somewhere attractive is the aesthetic characteristic of escapism.

Sharing Wodehouse's world

One important thing to mention is that discourse-world positioning is not maintained throughout the novel. My own feeling for most of my reading experience is that I am narratee to Bertie's narrator. However, it is rare to read more than a few pages without finding some form of direct address of the reader or of, for example, Bertie's narration digressing from the plot that maximises the subjectivity of the construal, encouraging an emergence from the text-world into the discourse-world. The frequent instances of humour similarly encourage an outward shift. While the motivation to immerse into the text-world again is strong, the idea of Wodehouse is never fully neglected as the repeated excursions back into the discourse-world mean that he is a frequently recurring attractor (Stockwell 2009). His persistent resonant presence throughout the novel is what I believe can account for the numerous reader comments (both professional and amateur) that suggest immersion in Wodehouse's world rather than Bertie's.

The ending of the novel has, I believe, an interesting effect in this regard. It repeats, almost verbatim in places, the opening:

> It was as we were about half-way between Steeple Bumpleigh and the old metrop. that I mentioned that there was an expression on the tip of my tongue which seemed to me to sum up the nub of the recent proceedings.
>
> Or, rather, when I say an expression, I mean a saying. A wheeze. A gag. What I believe is called a saw. Something about Joy . . .
>
> But we went into all that before, didn't we?
>
> (Wodehouse 1946: 281)

The difference is that, where the opening is largely dialogue between Bertie and Jeeves presented as direct speech, the ending presents the same content as indirect speech ('I mentioned [. . .] the recent proceedings') and then as free direct speech. This positions Bertie as his narrator enactor rather than as a character enactor in his narration, as he is in the opening dialogue, and therefore at a level closer to the discourse-world. It is relatively easy then for the final line to be read as Wodehouse addressing the reader. Crucially, whereas most previous instances of direct address use the second-person 'you', here the first-person 'we' is used. My reaction to reading the last line is of being left, on the last word, with a strong sense of having been in collaboration with Wodehouse in constructing and enjoying the world inhabited by Bertie.

The sense of collaborating with Wodehouse can possibly explain why readers feel immersed when reading his stories. This derives from a repeated highly subjective construal leading to the emergence of a reader from the text-world and their positioning in the discourse-world. Although positioning at a particular narratorial level does not necessarily result in a reader experiencing immersion, here readerly familiarity with the features of the text (even if only superficial) means that readers can immerse themselves in the activity of co-constructing humour with Wodehouse by wilfully converging with him as relay. This convergence results in the spatial aspect of immersion and is also involved in the process of humour. The emergent effect from the text-world that leads to a reader's strong sense of immersion in the discourse-world is the same as the one that allows sufficient distance from the events of the plot for humour to be appreciated. Similarly, the convergence of reader and Wodehouse facilitates a sense of sharing the knowledge of the text that also contributes to humour appreciation. The source of humour overall becomes the text itself, with a reader able to enjoy the feeling of collaborating with Wodehouse in its construction.

The feeling of escapism that readers experience – as an active type of immersion – could derive from their active participation in the construction of humour, this being a process-figured activity. The same process-figuring could also be involved in the immersive experience itself as a form of flow state in which, as Csikszentmihalyi (1990) suggests, the doing of an activity becomes the end goal in itself. The difference here is that, rather than the self-effacement of a flow state as described, a reader may be very aware of their presence in collaboration with Wodehouse in this subjectively construed viewing arrangement. It may be that this disparity can account for the immersive experience feeling escapist, specifically, in quality. While escapist literature is often associated with low quality, Wodehouse's writing is valued by both professional and amateur readers. However, it may be that the inferiority associated with escapist literature is a feature of the ease of immersion; a less complex text may make it easier for the attention of a reader to be maintained within the text-world. Here, though, there are aspects of the text that are relatively complex, such as the convoluted plot, the creativity of the metaphor, the numerous incomplete literary references, not to mention the frequent requirement of the reader to shift back and forth across the text-world boundary. It is possible that this relative complexity can be balanced out by a reader's familiarity with elements of the text such as the characters or the likely convolutions of the plot. This may make it easier to collaborate with Wodehouse, in spite of the complexities, because these elements are primed by their expectations of the text. To put this another way, readers with prior experience of reading Wodehouse know what they are escaping to when they choose to escape there, which may enhance their sense of collaboration because they are already actively doing so when they engage with the text. This heightened sense of active participation maximises the figuring of the process of communication that is needed for humour appreciation.

In conclusion, what this chapter demonstrates is that an immersive experience in reading literature is not confined to cases where a reader feels a sense of deep immersion only in a text-world. The experience of reading *Joy in the Morning* may be no less immersive, but the level of immersion is at the level of the discourse-world because of the resonant presence of Wodehouse throughout. It is this feature that is central to the readerly experience both in terms of humour and the escapist quality of the immersion itself.

References

Apter, M.J. (2007) *Reversal Theory: The Dynamics of Motivation, Emotion and Personality* (2nd edn). Oxford: Oneworld.

Bell, A., Ensslin, A., van der Bom, I. and Smith, J. (2018) 'Immersion in digital fiction', *International Journal of Literary Linguistics* 7 (1).

Billig, M. (2005) *Laughter and Ridicule: Towards a Social Critique of Humor*. London: SAGE.

Busselle, R.W. and Bilandzic, H. (2009) 'Measuring narrative engagement', *Media Psychology* 12 (4): 321–47.

Chłopicki, W. (2017) 'Humor and narrative', in S. Attardo (ed.) *The Routledge Handbook of Language and Humor*. New York: Routledge, pp.143–57.

Csikszentmihalyi, M. (1990) *Flow: The Psychology of Optimal Experience*. New York: Harper and Row.

Emmott, C. (1992) 'Splitting the referent: an introduction to narrative enactors', in M. Davies and L. Ravelli (eds) *Advances in Systemic Linguistics: Recent Theory and Practice*. London: Pinter, pp.221–8.

Epstein, J. (2018) 'Frivolous, empty, and perfectly delightful: P.G. Wodehouse's world', *Claremont Review of Books*, winter 2018.

Gavins, J. (2007) *Text World Theory: An Introduction*. Edinburgh: Edinburgh University Press.

Gerrig, R.J. (1993) *Experiencing Narrative Worlds: On the Psychological Activities of Reading*. New Haven: Yale University Press.

Godkewitsch, M. (1976) 'Physiological and verbal indices of arousal in rated humour', in A.J. Chapman and H.C. Foot (eds) *Humor and Laughter: Theory, Research and Applications*. London: John Wiley & Sons, pp.117–38.

Goodreads (2024) 'Community reviews: *Joy in the Morning* by P.G. Wodehouse', *Goodreads*, available at <https://www.goodreads.com/book/show/9928818-joy-in-the-morning>

Green, M.C. and Brock T.C. (2000) 'The role of transportation in the persuasiveness of public narratives', *Journal of Personality and Social Psychology* 79 (5): 701–21.

Gruner, C.R. (1978) *Understanding Laughter: The Workings of Wit and Humor*. Chicago: Nelson-Hall.

Gruner, C.R. (1997) *The Game of Humor: A Comprehensive Theory of Why We Laugh*. New Brunswick: Transaction.

Haines, A. (2023) 'A new approach to the stylistic analysis of humour', *Language and Literature* 32 (2): 195–208.

Haines, A. (2024) 'Comic timing in prose fiction', *Journal of Literary Semantics* 53 (2): 93–109.

Holcomb, C. (1992) 'Nodal humor in comic narrative: a semantic analysis of two stories by Twain and Wodehouse', *HUMOR: International Journal of Humor Research* 5 (3): 233–50.

Holmes, J. (2000) 'Politeness, power and provocation: how humour functions in the workplace', *Discourse Studies* 2 (2): 159–85.

Kimball, R. (2000) 'The genius of Wodehouse', *The New Criterion* 19 (2).

Kuijpers, M.M., Hakemulder, F., Tan E.S. and Doicaru, M.M. (2014) 'Exploring absorbing reading experiences: developing and validating a self-report scale to measure story world absorption', *Scientific Study of Literature* 4 (1): 89–122.

Labov, W. (1972) *Language in the Inner City*. Philadelphia: University of Pennsylvania Press.

Langacker, R.W. (2008) *Cognitive Grammar: A Basic Introduction*. New York: Oxford University Press.

Langevin, R. and Day, H.I. (1972) 'Physiological correlates of humor', in J.H. Goldstein and P.E. McGhee (eds) *The Psychology of Humor: Theoretical Perspectives and Empirical Issues*. New York: Academic Press, pp.129–42.

Lave, J. and Wenger, E. (1991) *Situated Learning: Legitimate Peripheral Participation*. Cambridge: Cambridge University Press.

McGraw, A.P., Warren, C., Williams, L.E. and Leonard, B. (2012) 'Too close for comfort, or too far to care? Finding humor in distant tragedies and close mishaps', *Psychological Science* 23 (10): 1215–23.

Marszalek, A. (2020) *Style and Emotion in Comic Novels and Short Stories*. London: Bloomsbury.

Mason, J. (2019) *Intertextuality in Practice*. Amsterdam: John Benjamins.

Nuttall, L. (2018) *Mind Style and Cognitive Grammar: Language and Worldview in Speculative Fiction*. London: Bloomsbury.

Rea, A. (2015) 'Introduction to middlebrow Wodehouse', in A. Rea (ed.) *Middlebrow Wodehouse: P.G. Wodehouse's Work in Context*. London: Routledge, pp.1–14.

Sperber, D. and Wilson, D. (1995) *Relevance: Communication and Cognition* (2nd edn). Oxford: Blackwell.

Stockwell, P. (2009) *Texture: A Cognitive Aesthetics of Reading*. Edinburgh: Edinburgh University Press.

Stockwell, P. (2019) 'Immersion and emergence in children's literature', in B. Neurohr and L. Stewart-Shaw (eds) *Experiencing Fictional Worlds*. Amsterdam: John Benjamins, pp.15–32.

Triezenberg, K.E. (2008) 'Humor in literature', in V. Raskin (ed.) *The Primer of Humor Research*. Berlin: Mouton de Gruyter, pp.523–42.

Veale, T. (2013) 'Humorous similes', *HUMOR: International Journal of Humor Research* 26 (1): 3–22.

Verhagen, A. (2007) 'Construal and perspectivization', in D. Geeraerts and H. Cuyckens (eds) *The Oxford Handbook of Cognitive Linguistics*. Oxford: Oxford University Press, pp.48–81.

Waugh, E. (1961) *An Act of Homage and Reparation*. BBC Home Service.

Witmer, B.G. and Singer, M.J. (1998) 'Measuring presence in virtual environments: a presence questionnaire', *Presence* 7 (3): 225–40.

Wodehouse, P.G. (1946) *Joy in the Morning*. New York: Doubleday & Co.

Wyer, R.S. and Collins J.E. (1992) 'A theory of humor elicitation', *Psychological Review* 99 (4): 663–88.

Yus, F. (2016) *Humour and Relevance*. Amsterdam: John Benjamins.

CHAPTER 11

The paradoxical properties of immersive metafiction

Ella Wydrzynska

Metafiction – with its self-conscious and pervasive commitment to revealing its own fictionality – might be considered antithetical to immersion. However, the very act of reminding the reader of their real-life reading activity *within* the fictional narrative itself instead seems to allow for readers to be dramatised as 'the person reading the text' in both the real world and within the context of a highly self-reflexive story simultaneously. Building on a pilot study of child-readers, Wydrzynska argues that the inherent fictionality and superficially anti-immersive strategies of metafictive devices in middle-grade children's books explicitly position the reader on the border between fiction and reality. She makes the case for metafiction having the potential to allow for a different type of readerly immersion that, paradoxically, relies on the very absurdism and fictionality that would usually counteract immersive strategies.

What is metafiction?

Generally attributed to the American novelist and essayist William H. Gass (1970), the term 'metafiction' describes writing that is consciously, pervasively, and systematically fictional. It is the kind of writing that highlights its mode and method of construction and subsequently revels in its artifice; in essence, it is fiction 'that takes fiction itself as its topic' (Bird 2010: 208) by being 'in constant dialogue with its own conventions' (Currie 1995: 1). In doing so, metafictions draw attention to – and often subsequently critique – the structure and style of narrative fiction, forcing readers not only to explore the nature of fiction itself, but also 'the relationship between fiction and reality' (Waugh 1984: 2). Readers are confronted with pseudo-authorial narrators who make explicit their act of composition; diegetic characters who are aware of their fictionality and 'overhear' the narration happening around them; or story-level figures who reach out from the pages of the book to interact with or act upon the reader's real world. Consequently, metafiction is 'dominantly, demonstratively, and constitutively engaged with its own conditions of existence, its parameters, its complexities, and its paradoxes throughout' (Macrae 2019: 2).

How, then, can metafiction align with immersion? On the surface, the two seem mutually exclusive. Linking immersion to transportation, Gerrig (1993) discussed how readers feel like they are moved by or into a narrative, while Green and Brock (2000) designed a fifteen-item Transportation Scale to capture readers' experiences in relation to their emotional involvement in a story and lack of awareness of real-world surroundings, among other criteria. Busselle and Bilandzic (2009) explored narrative presence, that is 'the sensation of being present in a narrative world due to comprehension processes and perspective taking' (325) which leads to readers losing awareness of their self, surroundings, and the passage of time. In their introduction to *Narrative Absorption*, Kuijpers and Hakemulder (2017: 1) state that '[b]eing lost in a story [. . .] allows us to leave our troubles behind and "return" feeling refreshed, or even altered in some way'. Going back 200 years, Romantic poet Samuel Taylor Coleridge wrote about readers' 'willing suspension of disbelief' (2009: 270) that stops logic, truth, and realism getting in the way of a good story.

For all intents and purposes, metafiction seems to do the opposite. Metafiction is characterised by its pervasive self-reflexivity and consciously reminds readers that what they are engaging with is an artificial construction, often by calling attention to the reader's real-world reading activity as well. As such, metafictional texts reduce (or remove entirely) the opportunity for readers to lose themselves in a story and 'deliberately seek to disrupt the suspension of disbelief in the reader' (Bird 2010: 208).

When considering immersion in children's literature, scholars have long discussed how readers 'merge' with fictional characters and events through a kind of narrative alignment that results in absorbed reading (see Crago 1996). This is particularly significant when modelling ideal child-readers, as the target audience is encouraged to align themselves with book-loving protagonists who are 'shown to benefit greatly from the ability and experience of reading, which often has lifesaving ramifications' (Hermansson 2019: 30). As such, the real reader's own reading habits are mirrored and affirmed by the virtuous bookworms depicted in fiction.

Even in stories featuring reluctant or challenged readers, characters are inevitably transformed through some kind of positive reading experience: Jared in *The Spiderwick Chronicles* (2003–4) is a non-reader until he engages with the titular book and uses the knowledge gained to lead his siblings on adventures; Bod in Neil Gaiman's *The Graveyard Book* (2008) uses inscriptions on gravestones to teach himself to read, becomes a skilled researcher, and is then able to uncover his family's secret past; in Tony Abbott's *Cracked Classics* series (2002–3), Devin and Frankie repeatedly fake book reports on classic novels they have not read, until they find themselves trapped in the corresponding titles and must use their reading skills to escape. In each case, reading saves the day and affirms the value and virtue of enjoying books. Yet readers (of all ages) tend to 'gravitate towards books that include relevant and relatable characters as well as characters who readers may wish to emulate or "try on"' (Graff 2018: 40); relatability can be fostered in terms of cultural relevance, ethnic representation, religious affiliation, gender or geographic location, but also linguistic ability, personal interests, and accessibility. If developing readers feel they cannot engage effectively with literary narratives or do not see themselves authentically represented in fiction, 'their struggles with reading become more pronounced and [contribute] to perceived "disengagement" or "alliterate" behaviors' (Graff 2018: 41). In fact, struggling to get lost in a book is a repeated theme in discussions of so-called reluctant or developing readers. For instance, self-proclaimed reluctant reader Labelle (2020: 19) wrote in an opinion piece that:

> I never enjoyed a book. EVER. Reading was boring because I thought I had a bad imagination. I'd stare at the piece of paper with words on it, and half the time, I had no idea what was happening.

His perceived 'bad imagination' meant he struggled to construct the storyworld, fictional characters, and events in his head. He repeatedly found himself stuck outside the text, unable to achieve the kind of immersed reading activity outlined above. However, metafiction deliberately, self-consciously, and systematically prevents this kind of reading in the first place and stops the reader losing themselves in a fictional world – at least, supposedly anyway. Instead of automatically pushing readers out of a text, I believe that the metafictive strategies typically understood to be obtrusive or antithetical to immersion can lead to readers being ostentatiously dramatised as 'the person reading the text' both in the real world *and* within the text. In the former, the real reader holds a physical book and quite literally fulfils the role of 'the reader'; in the latter, a spontaneously creating pseudo-authorial narrator interacts with an extradiegetic reading figure in a so-called composition-world, drawing attention to the act of reading as a contributing factor to the main fiction's development (see Figure 11.1).

A similar phenomenon has been explored in videogames. Cox (2016) examined twenty-five games that showed self-awareness, broke the fourth wall, or required players to participate at the story-level of the game while still maintaining their real-world role of 'game player'. He subsequently identified four types of metafictional tendencies in videogames: *emergent*, in which games admit their fictionality to the player; *immersive*, in which games incorporate the player as a player into the fictional world; *internal*, in which character-to-character interactions acknowledge a degree of fictionality, but do not fully break the fourth wall; and *external*, in which a real-world item or message exists within the fictional game, but is 'hidden' from

Real world (extrafictional level)

Participants: real author and real reader

Event(s): real author writes and publishes text; real reader reads it after publication

> **Composition-world (extradiegetic level)**
>
> **Participants**: extradiegetic narrator (I) and extradiegetic narratee (you)
>
> **Event(s):** an internal author/narrator visibly creates the story in real time and narrates their creative/composition process, usually in direct conversation with 'you'
>
> **Linguistic cues:** first-person reference to the internal author/narrator; simple present to indicate narrating present
>
>> **Main storyworld (diegetic level)**
>>
>> **Participants**: fictional characters
>>
>> **Event(s):** characters perform actions, go on adventures, etc.
>>
>> **Linguistic cues:** third-person reference to characters; simple past to indicate temporal location before the narrating present
>>
>>> **Embedded hypodiegetic stories**
>>>
>>> **Participants**: characters (often not physically present at diegetic level)
>>>
>>> **Event(s):** stories told by, to, or of characters (i.e., narration is not attributed to internal author/narrator in the composition-world)

Figure 11.1 The narrative structure of metafictive children's books

in-game characters so only extrafictional players can view it. Within this chapter, it is Cox's *immersive* category that I am most interested in as '[t]his type of metafictional encounter makes use of the player's position and relationship to the game to bring them into the narrative and incorporate their unique position as part of the fiction' (Cox 2016: 50).

Ryan (1999, 2001, 2006) has also explored immersion in digital texts including videogames and virtual reality. She suggests that immersion in a virtual world depends on vividness, with 'the reader's sense of immersion and empathy [being] a function of the depth of information' (1999: 118); the more a reader is able to believe that they can truly embody a different space through vivid representations and sensory stimuli, the more immersed they feel. (For more on the link between immersion and empathy, see Keen, this volume.) However, Ryan draws a distinction between immersion and interactivity. While immersion pertains to feeling like one is *in* another world (representation), interactivity is based on a reader, user, or audience member being able to *affect* another world (simulation).

Ryan also extends her argument to literary fiction in which, she argues, interactivity can be interpreted either figuratively or literally. In the figurative sense, 'interactivity stands for the collaboration between the reader and the text in the production of meaning' (Ryan 1999: 125) in which readers mentally construct the fictional world and support world-building with their own schematic knowledge, essentially meaning 'the text's reality is established by [the reader's] response and reconstituted by his active participation' (Hutcheon 1980: 141). Although nominally interactive due to the reader's actively mediating presence, the reader is limited to their own mental construction and lacks the power to change anything about the text itself. In the more literal sense, however, readers can affect the way a narrative unfolds; prime examples include choose-your-own-adventure stories or hypertextual networks in which readers must piece together images, websites, sound bites, and so on to a form a plot unique to the route they individually took through those fragmentary sources (Ryan 2006). At its strongest, literal interactivity can result in audiences (co-)creating the fictional world and swapping 'between reader-role and writer-role, between immersion and interactivity' (Ryan 1999: 130).

For Ryan, '[i]nteractivity can only be reconciled with immersion if the user's input counts as participation *and* as action in the fictional world' (1999: 130; emphasis added). However, metafiction is something of a grey area. Focusing on figurative interactivity, Ryan acknowledges that making the reader aware of their mental world-building activity might counter a text's immersive properties, but metafiction makes that very awareness part of the co-creation process.

> The price of this consciousness is an ontological expulsion from the fictional world. Insofar as it claims the reality of its reference world, fiction implies its own denial as fiction. By overtly recognizing the constructed, imaginary nature of the textual world, metafiction reclaims our 'native reliability' as ontological center. The implicit message 'this world is the product of language' is not an invitation to make-believe, it is literally true. But the reader's interest is difficult to maintain in the absence of make-believe. The most efficient strategy for promoting an awareness of the mechanisms of fictionality is not to block access to the fictional world, but to engage the reader in a game of in-and-out[.]
>
> (Ryan 1999: 126)

Using John Fowles' *The French Lieutenant's Woman* as an example, Ryan explains this 'game of in-and-out' as a constant repositioning of the reader. At some points readers are construed as external viewers with no access to the fictional world; at others, the narrator turns away from the story and speaks directly to the extrafictional audience, breaking the ontological boundary between text and reality. Sometimes readers are encouraged to view fictional characters as real people and begin to feel emotional investment in their lives (Green and Brock 2000); later, they must acknowledge that those characters are nothing more than literary creations in an artificial plot. In this way, 'the fictional world may be eventually demystified as a textual construct, yet the text succeeds in creating an immersive experience' (Ryan 1999: 126).

The paradoxical nature of being immersed in an artificial construct is central to this chapter. I explore whether, through a combination of immersion and interactivity, metafictional narratives can provide an immersive experience in which the writing style's quintessential self-reflexivity and audience awareness embed the reader's real-world reading activity *within* the fiction. To put it another way, my question is this: If metafiction prevents readers from being transported to an explicitly fictional world by pervasively reminding them of their real-world reading activity, can metafictive texts provide an alternative – albeit potentially paradoxical – kind of absorbed reading in which audiences are dramatised as 'the person reading the text' in both the real world and fiction simultaneously? After all, by engaging in the reading process in the first place, readers inevitably fulfil the action of reading described within self-aware metafictions and thus automatically characterise themselves as 'the person reading the text'. Additionally, if reluctant readers like Labelle consistently struggle to abandon their real-world surroundings and get lost in a book, might some of their difficulties be mitigated by achieving readerly immersion in an overt composition-world instead? This chapter will consider these questions in relation to a selection of metafictive books from three best-selling middle-grade authors: Pseudonymous Bosch's *Secret Series* (2008–12), Tom Fletcher's *The Creakers* (2018) and *Space Band* (2022), and Richard Ayoade's debut children's book *The Book That No One Wanted to Read* (2022).

Aimed at readers between the approximate ages of eight and twelve, middle-grade novels tend to be almost exclusively prose and fall between 25,000 and 50,000 words, reaching up to 70,000 words at the upper end of this publishing category. While some may still have some illustrations, these are secondary to a fully developed narrative that is broken into chapters. They tend to feature protagonists who are around the same age or slightly older than the target readership, with stories often being based, at least in part, on real-world scenarios that pre-teen audiences may be experiencing in their own lives, such as changing schools, making friends, or dealing with difficult family dynamics. As such, middle-grade texts sit between chapter books (typically for children aged 5–10 with under 20,000 words and lots of pictures) and young adult fiction (intended for readers aged 12–18 and possibly including profanity, romantic storylines, and more realistic violence). Given the target demographic of older children who are not quite teenagers, middle-grade books often adopt an overtly playful and chatty tone that goes hand in hand with metafictive tendencies. This is particularly apparent in the novels examined in this chapter, each of which has overarching composition-worlds framing the main storyworld. The following analysis will explore to what extent this facilitates, encourages, or hinders readerly immersion in metafictive children's literature.

The internal author's composition-world

Figure 11.1 depicts the ontological hierarchy of narrative levels in metafiction. Reality is positioned at the 'highest' level and encircles a mediating discourse within which the main story is embedded (Hanebeck 2017, Macrae 2019, Rimmon-Kenan 2005). It is this mediating discourse, equivalent to Genette's (1980) extradiegetic level, that I am most interested in here. A somewhat liminal discourse space between the extrafictional world and the embedded diegetic level in which the primary narrative unfolds, this level is populated by an overt, pseudo-authorial narrator who contextually composes the main story, seemingly in real time as it progresses: hence it is termed the *composition-world.*

This term for a particular type of narrative space can be attributed to Gavins (2013), who, when using Text World Theory (Gavins 2007, Werth 1999) to analyse Kurt Vonnegut's *Slaughterhouse-Five,* briefly referred to the novel's primary text-world as a 'composition text-world' featuring 'a textual enactor of Kurt Vonnegut at the time of his writing the novel' (Gavins 2013: 115). This is because the main narrative described in *Slaughterhouse-Five* is framed by a (fictional) backstory in which Vonnegut gives an autobiographical account of his time in Dresden, explains his inspiration for writing the novel, and subsequently details his supposedly spontaneous creative process. In fact, it is the composition text-world that acts as an overarching matrix text-world from which the rest of the novel stems, and it can be seen, 'in spite of its lack of spatial and temporal detail, to be the most consistent text-world constructed over the course of the novel' (Gavins 2013: 118). While text-worlds are mental representations of discourse through which language can be conceptualised and understood (Gavins 2007), the overarching omnipresence of the composition text-world in *Slaughterhouse-Five* functions in a similar manner to Genette's extradiegetic level, especially as the enactor of Vonnegut frequently offers evaluative commentary which sits outside the main story of Billy Pilgrim. As such, the underlying premise of the composition text-world outlined by Gavins can be incorporated within the hierarchy of ontological levels commonly conceptualised by narratologists as in Figure 11.1. In the figure, I choose to elide its title for symmetry with the term *storyworld*).

A similar narrative structure is established in the primary texts explored in this chapter. In each of the children's books analysed here, there is an overt level of narrative discourse that sits somewhere between the reader's real world and the main story. Much like *Slaughterhouse-Five,* this (contextually extradiegetic) narration is delivered by a pseudo-authorial narrator who may have some connection to a real-life counterpart. This is particularly true for Tom Fletcher, who is likely to be a familiar name to (British) readers through his involvement in the band McFly, his popular vlog series on YouTube, or many of his other children's books (the first of which was published in 2012). Though it may then feel strange when he claims complete authenticity and credits himself as 'the author of this book' (Fletcher 2018: 261) within the composition-world of a clearly fictional story about strange creatures that live under the protagonist's bed, readers can nevertheless connect the textual enactor's narration with any knowledge they have about the real-world Fletcher.

Things change slightly with the other two authors in this study, however. Richard Ayoade is best known by adults as a comedian and actor in shows like *The IT Crowd* so, like Fletcher, could technically constitute a textual enactor as well. However, his first (and thus far only) children's book is instead narrated from the perspective of the book itself and *not* Ayoade. On the other hand, Pseudonymous Bosch (a blatant pseudonym) does not exist in the real world and thus cannot be a textual enactor when he appears as the narrator inside the *Secret Series*, yet it is Bosch – rather than the real-life Raphael Simon – who is credited as the extrafictional creator on the cover, copyright, and 'about the author' pages in his books.

As such, while some of the authors in this chapter are – at least to some extent – textual enactors as per Vonnegut in Gavins' study, I instead favour Currie's distinction between internal and external authors. Using Dr Watson of the Sherlock Holmes stories as an example, Currie delineates between fictional narrators who, within the context of their stories, are meant to be the author (internal) and authors who exist only outside the story (external).

> Watson is, fictionally, a narrator. It is also part of the story that Waston is the author of the stories he tells. [. . .] So in cases like that of Watson and the Holmes stories we have no grounds for distinguishing narrators and author, though we have grounds for distinguishing between someone being an author/narrator and it being part of the story that someone is an author/narrator.
>
> (Currie 2010: 66–7)

Watson is the internal author/narrator of these stories, while Arthur Conan Doyle is the external author/narrator. This is a useful distinction for the primary texts used here and in the context of the composition-world as the extradiegetic pseudo-authorial narrator can be considered an overt internal author/narrator.

Within the composition-world, the internal author communicates with an extradiegetic narratee who likewise exists outside the main storyworld. Borrowing terminology from Goetsch (2004), I refer to this figure as the fictive reader: a descendant of the listening-audience in traditional oral tales who '[appears] chiefly in those narratives which direct attention to the process of narration' (Goetsch 2004: 190). The fictive reader functions as the communicative partner of an extradiegetic narrator and is addressed in the second person accordingly (and often repeatedly). In doing so, fictive readers 'help to make real readers aware of narrative procedures and to keep them attentive' (Goetsch 2004: 192), therein leading to real readers being conflated or aligned with the fictive reader due to 'the gap opened in the discourse by the presence of *you*' (McHale 1987: 224). It is important to note, however, that the fictive reader typically only has access to the extradiegetic narrator's discourse. Therefore, even when aligned with the fictive reader by way of doubly-deictic reference (Herman 1994), real readers can rarely go further into the text than the extradiegetic composition-world; the internal author, however, *can* intrude upon hypodiegetic storyworlds as they are contextually creating those embedded levels of narrative within the overarching composition-world.

The explicit dramatisation of the reader as 'the person reading the text' in metafiction results in immersion only to the text-internal boundary of the composition-world, facilitated and contextualised by their real-world surroundings and ongoing reading activity as a fundamental component of the story's progression. Any immersion felt by the reader within the main storyworld (or further hypodiegetic worlds within that narrative) is triggered more conventionally by vividness or emotional investment and does *not* depend on alignment with the fictive reader, a narrative figure who themselves is contained within the composition-world alongside the internal author. It is this first step into the composition-world that the following analysis explores, with a particular interest on mitigating the need or desire to get proverbially 'lost in a book' for the benefit of developing or reluctant readers who struggle to achieve transportation into the fully fictional world of the diegetic story.

Pseudonymous Bosch

The first example in this study comes from the *Secret Series* by Pseudonymous Bosch, the pen-name of American author Raphael Simon. Consisting of five books, each themed around a different sense (smell, sound, taste, sight, and touch, respectively), the *Secret Series* follows two eleven-year-olds, Cass and Max-Ernest, who join a mysterious society to protect the secret of immortality from a group of evil alchemists. The internal author/narrator, whom readers initially encounter as an 'I'-narrator in the midst of writing the first book in the series, knows this central secret and can no longer keep it to himself. He explains that everything described in the series is true and, by reading the books, readers are putting themselves, the author, and the characters at risk. For this reason, Bosch gives himself (as both the internal and external author) and his (already fictional) characters overtly fake names to protect their 'real-life' counterparts, and asks the reader to participate in narrative construction by choosing where the story takes place:

> Although the real location of this story will have to remain a mystery, to make it easier for all of us, why don't we say the story takes place in *a place you know very well*?

> We'll call it Your Hometown.
>
> When you read about the town the characters live in, just think of the town you live in. Is the town big or little? By the sea or by a lake? Or is your town all asphalt and shopping malls? You tell me. [. . .]
>
> When they go home, imagine they live on Your Street, maybe even in a house right across from yours.
>
> Who knows, maybe Your Street is where the story really takes place. I wouldn't tell you if it was. But I couldn't tell you for certain that it's not.
>
> (Bosch 2008: 16)

The pseudo-oral tone established in the above excerpt is typical of the internal author's narrative discourse in the *Secret Series*. The simple present, first-person plural references, inherently dialogic second-person address, imperatives, and numerous interrogatives all characterise the implied communicative event between the internal author and fictive reader within the composition-world (see the linguistic strategies facilitating immersion discussed by Adam, this volume). Although unable to reply directly, the probing questions encourage the audience to consider their own responses and effectively place the story's setting entirely on the child-reader. In fact, when reading the book as a child myself, I believed it was far more unlikely that these events would take place in *Lincolnshire* than that they would take place *at all*. Yet, even as an adult, I picture my childhood school, street, and town when imagining Cass and Max-Ernest's adventures.

Bosch thus characterises his audience as collaborators in meaning-making and narrative construction from the very beginning and invites readers to take an interactive and participatory role in the story's development. Although this has a contextual impact on the events of the main story (at least as far as the reader's mental conception of the storyworld), the process is contained entirely within the composition-world and is fundamentally based on the reader's extrafictional knowledge of their surroundings. Considering the relationship between immersion and interactivity outlined by Ryan (1999), this fulfils the brief of figurative interactivity with at least a degree of immersion due to the metafictional nature of the text (as per her discussion of *The French Lieutenant's Woman*). After all, this 'do-it-yourself' opening places the onus of setting the story firmly on the part reader.

A similar scenario also occurs at the end of the book – titled 'Chapter Thirty-Two: Do-It-Yourself Ending' – in which Bosch refuses to conclude the story and asks the reader to do it instead:

> You try wrapping up your story, showing how your characters have grown, sewing up any holes in your plot, and underlining your theme – all in a single chapter!
>
> No, really. Try.
>
> Because I'm not going to do it.
>
> (Bosch 2008: 34)

As with the previous excerpt, this interaction takes place firmly in the composition-world and is typified by the pseudo-oral narrative style of the internal author as he speaks to the fictive reader. Real readers are likewise implicated by this demand as they too have read the novel up to this point, inevitably want to see how it concludes, and understand the conventions of fiction that are now being subverted by Bosch. While the previous example invited readers to imagine the setting for the story – something that might be done relatively passively depending on the reader's personal involvement and enthusiasm – this ending '[demands] a more writerly engagement from the reader' (Bird 2010: 209) by inviting them to become a literal co-creator who can contribute directly to the story's development within the composition-world. This fulfils Ryan's (1999) literal interactivity through the simultaneous enactment of reader and writer roles. Although Bosch later provides summaries for each character and, in doing so, effectively writes a highly fragmented ending anyway, he also gives readers specific instructions about what to include in their conclusion and then leaves a blank space, titled 'Chapter Thirty-Three: Your Version', in which readers should insert their handwritten pages.

Importantly, readers are given the opportunity to participate in the construction of the narrative within the composition-world. They are also inevitably exposed to and involved in discussions of fictional conventions that, as per the foundations of metafiction, 'foster an awareness of how a story works' (Mackey 1990: 181). In many ways, readers are immersed in the *process* of fiction and invited to take an active role in its development within the composition-world.

Tom Fletcher

Although less explicitly collaborative than the examples from Bosch above, there is a similarly distinct and overarching composition-world in Tom Fletcher's middle-grade novels. The excerpt below comes from *The Creakers* (2018) which follows eleven-year-old Lucy Dungston who, one morning, discovers that all the adults in her town have been kidnapped by the titular monsters that live under her bed. Lucy bravely ventures into the creakers' homeland, but her climactic showdown with their leader is interrupted by this narratorial aside from Fletcher (as both the internal and external author):

> Here we go. I told you this was going to happen. I warned you that Lucy would have to face the King. Don't blame me. It's not like I'm making this stuff up. If you didn't go to the loo last time I warned you, then now's your last chance. No? You sure? Because, by reading on, you agree to the terms and conditions that I, Tom Fletcher, the author

> of this book, am not responsible if you pee your pants with fright in the next chapter.
>
> (Fletcher 2018: 261)

As with Bosch, the simple present, interrogatives, and metanarrative comments ('I told you this was going to happen') point towards a shared communicative space between the internal author and fictive reader in the composition-world. This is solidified through proximal deictic reference ('Here we go') and explicit acknowledgement of the reader's corresponding reading activity ('by reading on', 'next chapter'), both of which implicate the real reader in the composition-world through effective conflation with the fictive reader.

It is here that Fletcher also explicitly credits himself as both the internal and external author of the book at a textual level. Although many of Fletcher's other middle-grade novels use the same narrative voice and readers are encouraged to recognise the shared internal author in each (see Wydrzynska 2023), this is the first time Fletcher names himself directly within the narrative discourse of the composition-world. By overtly declaring himself as the internal author in *The Creakers*, Fletcher confirms that the narrator is, as with Vonnegut in *Slaughterhouse-Five*, a textual enactor with a real-life counterpart. This then plays into a much wider metafictional effect as readers must supplement their mental image of the internal author with any extrafictional knowledge they possess about the real-world Fletcher, likely predominantly based on their schematic knowledge of twenty-first-century British boybands if not their awareness of his other books. Thus, when the internal author makes claims about the truthfulness of his clearly fictional texts ('It's not like I'm making this stuff up'), readers inevitably have to suspend their disbelief and attribute the purported veracity of the story to Fletcher's real-life counterpart too.

Interestingly, Fletcher's approach to narrative voice and storytelling changes in his more recent novels. *The Danger Gang* (2021), for instance, begins with a prologue narrated by Fletcher as the internal author, but the rest of the book swaps to an epistolary form with letters written by a separate autodiegetic narrator, Franky. During my doctoral research, I conducted a pilot school study with a group of upper primary pupils with special educational needs (SEND) who, having thoroughly enjoyed *The Creakers*, struggled to engage with *The Danger Gang* as it lacked an overt storyteller to guide them through the narrative. This in itself lends weight to the central argument of this chapter: that interaction with an internal author and immersion in the composition-world through the dramatised act of reading helps to bring developing readers into the text in a safe, accessible, and engaging way without necessitating transportation into the main storyworld or complete investment in diegetic characters.

In *Space Band* (2022), Fletcher is even more removed, and readers are instead introduced to the protagonist, George, as the internal author from the very beginning. *Space Band* does, however, maintain Fletcher's traditional narrative structure and, unlike Franky in *The Danger Gang*, George speaks directly to the reader and frequently makes metanarrative *and* metafictive comments from an overt composition-world:

> I bet you're thinking, *How did the worst band in the world become the best band in the universe*? I guess it all began on the day I started writing my own songs and decided to put them all down in a book. This book, in fact. The book you're about to read.
>
> (Fletcher 2022: 3)

While Fletcher himself appears absent, the opening of *Space Band* displays the same playful, pseudo-oral, self-reflexive, and audience-aware narrative style seen in many of his other middle-grade novels. Furthermore, given the age and mannerisms of George as a child protagonist, the internal author of *Space Band* is able to present himself as even more conspiratorial and intimate with the child-reader, and there is a clear sense of commonality between George and the target readership throughout. This leads to frequent shared in-jokes within the metafictive commentary of the composition-world or through parenthetical asides in the main storyworld that trigger ascending metaleptic transgressions to the reader outside the text via George's extradiegetic narrative discourse, as seen in the two examples below:

> OK, I know on the outside this book looks like a normal school exercise book . . . and it kind of is. (I 'borrowed' it from the classroom supply cupboard.) But that's just a clever disguise. It will be on these very pages, where boring equations and snore-fest theories would normally be written that I shall write my masterpiece of musical awesomeness.
>
> (Fletcher 2022: 5)

> Nelia is super smart. Seriously. She's full of nerdy knowledge that she'll probably never use, like the seven times table and what S is on the periodic table. (It's sulphur, by the way – the stuff that makes that bum gas smell!) But underneath all those layers Nelia's inner core is made of pure rock 'n' roll. The only problem is that she's just a little scared to let it out. (The rock 'n' roll, not the bum gas.)
>
> (Fletcher 2022: 22)

While less explicitly immersive or interactive than the previous examples discussed, the real reader is dramatised as the internal author's confidant (Goetsch 2004) within the composition-world. They feel that they are spoken to and engaged with directly by way of their ongoing, real-world reading activity, which positions this comparatively one-sided interaction at least on the pathway towards immersion.

Richard Ayoade

Unlike the previous examples from Bosch and Fletcher, which feature explicitly human internal authors (some who, as I have said, are textual enactors of real-life people), Ayoade's *The Book That No One Wanted to Read* is instead written from the perspective of the very book that audiences are meant to be reading. The internal author is the book itself, and its composition-world is used to outline its own existence as a book. Real readers are again implicated in the composition-world through pseudo-oral narration and simulated dialogue, but are also asked to reflect more explicitly on their own reading habits, as in the following excerpt which opens the book:

> What is it that makes YOU want to read a book?
> They say you should never judge a book by its cover. But how else can you decide whether you like it?
> You can't read a book to work out whether you want to read that book because, by that stage, you will have already read it.
> (Ayoade 2022: 7)

The internal author explains that attracting readers is just the first part of a book's ongoing battle to be read and provides a corresponding selection of sample book covers (illustrated by Tor Freeman) that might be considered particularly fun or interesting. The book then politely greets the reader – 'Well, why *shouldn't* a book say "hello"? We're not animals' (Ayoade 2022: 9) – outlines some poor reading habits that make it angry (including folding over pages or skipping to the end), and introduces the main story about the titular book that no one wanted to read. All the while, the real reader is conflated with the fictive reader in the book's composition-world by way of second-person address and metafictive acknowledgement of their corresponding reading activity.

The main story then begins on page 17, but the internal author's voice remains just as present in the first few story-level chapters as it was in the composition-world; in fact, one would be hard pressed to find a clear ontological distinction between the different narrative levels in Ayoade's novel, at least initially. This is a key difference compared to the works of Bosch and Fletcher, both of whom separate the composition-world and main storyworld by way of tense (present vs. past), narrative voice (first-person vs. third-person), and even graphological presentation (both tend to start new chapters when swapping back to the internal author's discourse in the composition-world, but *The Creakers* also italicises Fletcher's narratorial interludes and places them on a grey background). When it is the book narrating and composing its own story, it understandably becomes harder to distinguish between the composition-world and main storyworld, especially when that book claims it is learning about the plot alongside the reader: 'This story is happening *now*. It's *unfolding*. Or (to be less fancy about it), I'm making it up as I go' (Ayoade 2022: 37; original italics). While Bosch and Fletcher also use the internal author's narrative discourse to present their novels as if they are being written as they are read, both still acknowledge their authorial control and relative omniscience by situating their respective composition-worlds after the events described in the storyworld. Ayoade removes this temporal logic and has the narrator and reader experience the main story in real time.

What makes this all the more confusing is that a diegetic version of 'you' is later introduced within the main storyworld. While the second-person address in the opening prologue implicates 'the person reading the text' (as with the other examples discussed so far), the 'you'-character in the main storyworld triggers a complete departure from the internal author's narrative voice and the book instead swaps to a second-person narrative. When this change occurs in Ayoade's novel, the story begins to follow a separate main character in the second person who searches for and then interacts with a book, much like the way the fictive reader and internal author engage within the composition-world. For this part of the story, the 'you'-character definitely is not the real reader but is nonetheless *a* reader upon whom real readers are encouraged to model themselves. As the story progresses, the 'you'-character befriends the neglected titular book by way of telepathic conversation in which the book's dialogue is depicted in an assertive, bold, serif typeface while 'you' speaks in a more friendly, sans-serif, handwritten font. The two then realise the book's pages are actually blank and pair up to write a story together. This further affirms the 'you'-character's knowledge of and enthusiasm for reading, writing, and storytelling – and likewise implies that the real reader should behave in the same way.

Before the final epilogue (at which point the narrative firmly swaps back to the original composition-world), this intermingled alignment is emphasised: 'And with that, you climb down the ladder, holding your new friend tight, in much the same way I hope you are holding me now' (Ayoade 2022: 115). The first instance of *you* here refers to the character in the main storyworld and the progressive participle *holding* indicates the interaction between this 'you'-character and the book (at some point prior to the publication of the physical novel). By contrast – and with no real linguistic or graphological separation – the first-person reference to the internal author switches the narrative back to the composition-world, and the second *you* denotes the (fictive) reader who is reading the book in the present.

The various 'you'-referents in Ayoade's novel make for an exceptionally complex and rather surreal reading experience. The introduction of a main character who is also called 'you' – coupled with the acknowledgement of a diegetic story that 'is happening *now*' (37) – conflates not only the figures to whom the second person could apply, but also removes any separation between narrative levels, consequently producing a more blended space in which the reader's real world, composition-world, and main storyworld exist and overlap simultaneously. For instance, readers are asked to imagine the library in which the diegetic story takes place – 'Would you mind imagining that particular library for me? (Ayoade 2022: 31) – and are invited to contribute other descriptive details about the size, age, and dustiness of the space. However, when the 'you'-character stumbles across the titular book in that very same library, the second-person narrative praises 'your' imagination and acknowledges that '[y]ou practically invented this library just a little while ago' (Ayoade 2022: 56). This raises questions about the overlap between the extrafictional reader, the fictive reader in the composition-world, and the 'you'-character in the storyworld, as only the former two were initially invited to imagine the library.

This is perhaps the starkest contrast between these case-study texts. In the examples by Bosch and Fletcher, developing readers are guided through the narrative by their dialogic interactions with the respective internal authors and inbuilt opportunities to co-create story elements. Although I would argue that this leads to readers' immersion in the composition-world and dramatisation as 'the reader of the text', their real-world reading activity and surroundings are nonetheless highlighted at every opportunity. As mentioned previously, this mitigates some of the potential difficulties of readers struggling to lose themselves in the fictional world, as their imagination needs only to incorporate what is already physically around them as they read. By contrast, Ayoade draws attention to the immense imaginative capacities of his audience, which risks precluding child-readers who cannot relate. The involvement of 'you' in the storyworld adds another barrier to this as the inherent double deixis of the second-person implicates the real reader at the diegetic story-level, even though the 'you'-character described definitely is not the person currently reading the book.

It is worth noting here that, while Bosch and Fletcher have written exclusively for children, Ayoade is a prolific writer of self-aware fiction for adults. Although *The Book That No One Wanted to Read* has strong metafictive tendencies, the execution of these ends up feeling more surreal, rather than relying on readers' extrafictional schematic knowledge, awareness, and positioning as a playful and participatory invitation into the composition-world. That is not to say that child-readers will not enjoy it, of course, but rather that the immersive potential of metafiction needs to be carefully considered for different target audiences. In the case of developing readers, Ayoade's book may be a step – or narrative level – too far.

Conclusion

This chapter began by asking whether metafiction can be immersive. Although its pervasive self-reflexivity could seem antithetical to narrative absorption or transportation, the composition-world provides a stepping stone between the real world and diegetic storyworld in which readers are engaged in the fiction as a dramatised and contextualised reader figure. Further study is needed to ascertain to what extent distinct composition-worlds encourage reader-narrator interaction (and to what degree of overtness) in non-metafictive texts, but the fundamental self-awareness and constructedness of metafiction facilitates a prevalent layer of narrative discourse in which a visibly inventing author lays bare their storytelling process. In the middle-grade texts examined here, the metafictive tendencies of the composition-world expose readers to the conventions of fiction – even when they are then subverted – and frequently draw attention to the audience's ongoing reading activity and real-world surroundings. Instead of completely breaking the illusion of narrative immersion, however, alignment with the fictive reader in the composition-world encourages readers to straddle the book's extrafictional boundary, keeping one foot in the fiction and one in the real world. This enables readers – and particularly developing readers – to enter the world of the text to a limited degree, often through literal or figurative interactivity, and therein engage with meaning-making, narrative construction, and the acts of reading and storytelling from the safety and comfort of the real world. In effect, this mitigates the need to imagine fantastical storyworlds because it puts the onus on the reader being nothing more than a reader – a role they automatically fulfil by opening a book in the first place.

References

Ayoade, R. (2022) *The Book That No One Wanted to Read*. London: Walker Books.

Bird, A.-M. (2010) 'Metafiction', in D. Rudd (ed.) *The Routledge Companion to Children's Literature*. London: Routledge, pp.208–9.

Bosch, P. (2008) *The Name of This Book is Secret*. London: Usborne Publishing Ltd.

Busselle, R. and Bilandzic, H. (2009) 'Measuring narrative engagement', *Media Psychology* 12 (4): 321–47.

Coleridge, S.T. (2009) *Biographia Literaria* [1817]. Auckland: The Floating Press.

Cox, J.E. (2016) 'Metafiction in videogames', *Games + Learning + Society (GLS) 11.0 Conference Proceedings*, available at <https://press.etc.cmu.edu/proceedings/games learningsociety-gls-110>

Crago, H. (1996) 'Bibliotherapy and psychology', in P. Hunt (ed.) *International Encyclopedia of Children's Literature*. London: Routledge, pp.634–43.

Currie, G. (2010) *Narratives and Narrators: A Philosophy of Stories*. Oxford: Oxford University Press.

Currie, M. (ed.) (1995) *Metafiction*. London: Longman.

Fletcher, T. (2018) *The Creakers*. London: Puffin.

Fletcher, T. (2021) *The Danger Gang*. London: Puffin.

Fletcher, T. (2022) *Space Band*. London: Puffin.

Gass, W.H. (1970) *Fiction and the Figures of Life*. Boston: David Godine.

Gavins, J. (2007) *Text World Theory: An Introduction*. Edinburgh: Edinburgh University Press.

Gavins, J. (2013) *Reading the Absurd*. Edinburgh: Edinburgh University Press.

Genette, G. (1980) *Narrative Discourse: An Essay in Method*. Ithaca: Cornell University Press.
Gerrig, R. (1993) *Experiencing Narrative Worlds: On the Psychological Activities of Reading*. New Haven: Yale University Press.
Goetsch, P. (2004) 'Reader figures in narrative', *Style* 38 (2): 188–202.
Graff, J.M. (2018) 'Addressing "struggle": strengthening the literary bonds between children and books', in D.A. Wooten, L.A. Liang and B.E. Cullinan (eds) *Children's Literature in the Reading Program* (5th edn). New York: Guilford Press, pp.37–55.
Green, M.C. and Brock, T. (2000) 'The role of transportation in the persuasiveness of public narratives', *Journal of Personality and Social Psychology* 79 (5): 701–21.
Hanebeck, J. (2017) *Understanding Metalepsis: The Hermeneutics of Narrative Transgression*. Berlin: de Gruyter.
Herman, D. (1994) 'Textual "you" and double deixis in Edna O'Brien's *A Pagan Place*', *Style* 28 (3): 378–410.
Hermansson, C.E. (2019) *Filming the Children's Book: Adapting Metafiction*. Edinburgh: Edinburgh University Press.
Hutcheon, L. (1980) *Narcissistic Narrative: The Metafictional Paradox*. Waterloo: Wilfried Laurier University Press.
Kuijpers, M. and Hakemulder, F. (2017) 'Narrative absorption: introduction and overview', in F. Hakemulder, M.M. Kuijpers, E.S. Tan, K. Bálint and M.M. Doicaru (eds) *Narrative Absorption*. Amsterdam: John Benjamins, pp.1–7.
Labelle, L. (2020) 'Getting into the mind of a reluctant reader', *Canadian Children's Book News* 43 (2): 19.
McHale, B. (1987) *Postmodernist Fiction*. London: Routledge.
Mackey, M. (1990) 'Metafiction for beginners: Allan Ahlberg's *Ten in a Bed*', *Children's Literature in Education* 21 (3): 179–87.
Macrae, A. (2019) *Discourse Deixis in Metafiction: The Language of Metanarration, Metalepsis and Disnarration*. London: Routledge.
Rimmon-Kenan, S. (2005) *Narrative Fiction* (2nd edn). London: Routledge.
Ryan, M.-L. (1999) 'Immersion vs. interactivity: virtual reality and literary theory', *Substance* 28 (2): 110–37.
Ryan, M.-L. (2001) *Narrative as Virtual Reality*. Baltimore: John Hopkins University Press.
Ryan, M.-L. (2006) *Avatars of Story*. Minneapolis: University of Minnesota Press.
Waugh, P. (1984) *Metafiction: The Theory and Practice of Self-Conscious Fiction*. London: Methuen & Co.
Werth, P. (1999) *Text Worlds: Representing Conceptual Space in Discourse*. Harlow: Longman.
Wydrzynska, E. (2023) *Do Not Read Beyond This Page: Postmodernism for Children* (unpublished doctoral thesis). University of Nottingham.

CHAPTER 12

Immersing readers in the text-worlds of *Anxious People*

Piergiorgio Trevisan and Gaetano Fiorin

Using a combined approach from Text World Theory and narratological research on second-person forms of narrative, Trevisan and Fiorin in this chapter explore the novel *Anxious People* by Fredrik Backman. They identify the novel's complex narratorial layering as a key element in readers' sense of its immersive power and develop this account with a focus on the use of second-person address forms throughout the text. They also observe features that seem to generate an empathetic engagement with the characters in the work. This makes the immersive effect of the novel both compelling and nuanced.

Introduction

This chapter examines the role of immersive phenomena in determining the success of Fredrik Backman's highly acclaimed novel *Anxious People* (2021), which readers have often described as highly immersive. *Anxious People*, which became a *New York Times* bestseller shortly after its translation into English, narrates a failed bank robbery in a small Swedish town, where the would-be robber, desperate and panicked, flees into an open house. Finding people inside, he holds a group hostage, including a retired couple and a pregnant woman. As the story unfolds, the characters begin to share their stories and vulnerabilities with one another, with several connections between their experiences being revealed. The novel is told through a mix of flashbacks, shifting perspectives, and police interviews, which taken together allow the reader to gradually piece together the events leading up to and following the unintentional hostage situation.

Anxious People, which has received very positive reviews for its emotional depth, humour, and exploration of human connection, is frequently described as very immersive by online readers. Numerous comments on the social platform Goodreads reflect this sentiment:

> In the first part of the book the author doesn't stay with any one character long enough for the reader to relate to them. For me this is critically important for establishing what I need most out of a book, The Fictive Dream, a state where I become immersed in the story. (Reader 1)

> Within just a few minutes of reading this, tears pricked my eyes, and I knew from that moment on that I was into this book. (Reader 2)

> I was so deeply immersed in the story that I completely lost track of time, finding myself fully transported into the world Backman created – the kind of reading experience where you forget you're even reading and feel like you're living alongside the characters. (Reader 3)

These comments demonstrate that *Anxious People* invites physical, embodied manifestations of inner immersion.

Throughout this chapter we propose that the sense of immersion experienced by readers of *Anxious People* results from the interaction of at least three contributing factors. First of all, textual architecture: different parts of the text are hierarchically organised in a way that requires continuous world creation in the reader's mind. This type of textual organisation, rather than producing 'emergence' (Stockwell 2020: 198) as is often the case, contributes to enhancing curiosity for the plot development, therefore favouring immersion. Secondly, these continuous changes in context are organised in such a way that different versions of the same character are presented, at different points in time; this is conducive to empathic mechanisms regarding the behaviour of the characters in the main plot, including those who may originally be experienced as negative. Finally, a crucial role for the development of immersion is played by the projection of the reader themselves in some of the subplots by means of the systematic and purposeful use of the second-person pronoun 'you'. Thanks to this strategy, used especially in highly dramatic or humorous parts, the narrator treats the reader as a confidante, which encourages the reader to feel more involved, and therefore immersed.

Textual architecture

In order to monitor the various aspects of a fictional world being developed readers must construct mental representations of the circumstances and events within that world. These mental representations, referred to as 'text-worlds' in Text World Theory (Gavins 2007, Werth 1999), are formed from the language of the text itself as well as from the inferences drawn by readers, termed the 'discourse participants'.

Text World Theory examines how readers process information, shedding light on the co-construction of fictional worlds by authors and readers. It does so by dividing every discourse into a series of distinct conceptual levels (Gavins 2007: 9):

1. **Discourse-worlds**, which are the mental representations of the situation surrounding human beings as they communicate, including their personal and cultural knowledge.
2. **Text-worlds**, which are the mental representations of the discourse in readers' minds in terms of time, location, characters. These worlds are often as richly detailed as the discourse-world from which they originate.
3. **Modal-worlds**, which are remote text-worlds cued by expressions of attitude. Modal-worlds can be deontic (cued by expressions of obligation), boulomaic (cued by expressions of desire), or epistemic (cued by expressions of belief).

In the process of building up mental representations, two important kinds of information are used: 'world-building elements' (Gavins 2007: 40) (terms referring to time, place, characters, and objects) and 'function-advancing propositions' (Gavins 2007: 56), used to propel the narrative forward. Very frequently, several text-worlds must be monitored at once throughout the reading process, even though it may happen that one of them is more 'prominent' than the others (Gavins 2007: 76). Characters and objects are anchored to the specific text-world in focus and are disengaged once a different text-world is introduced thanks to a 'world-switch', which usually involves changes in location or time. Typically, these changes are conveyed linguistically through spatial or temporal locatives, which trigger 'deictic shifts' (Galbraith 1995, Segal 2012). If the narrative returns to a previously established text-world, a process of world-switching back is activated in the reader's mind.

Interestingly, while the complex structure of certain narratives may disrupt the linear flow of the reading experience by means of several world-switches, this does not necessarily diminish the sense of immersion for readers who are deeply engaged (Stockwell 2020: 197). We believe that the attentional system, the primary cognitive mechanism underlying immersion (Csikszentmihalyi 2014, Kuijpers et al. 2014) may be stimulated rather than inhibited by textual architectures that feature continuous 'back-and-forth' transitions between text-worlds, particularly when these transitions occur between the main text-world and additional text-worlds which contain different 'enactors' (Emmott 1997) of the same characters, such as their past selves.

The architecture of *Anxious People* relies heavily on these strategies from the opening scene, where a specific text-world is constructed through a paratactic sequence of noun phrases:

> *Extract 1*
> A bank robbery. A hostage drama. A stairwell full of police officers on their way to storm an apartment.
>
> (Backman 2021: 1)

The three noun phrases serve as world-building elements that guide readers in constructing a mental representation of the scene. Based on these three phrases, readers are likely to imagine a world populated by specific locations (a bank and an apartment), objects (a stairwell, police officers' uniforms and guns), and enactors (a bank robber, some police officers, and some hostages). These elements also have the potential to trigger readers' mental schemata (Cook 1994, Emmott 1997, Stockwell 2020) regarding bank robberies and hostage situations, even if these schemata have not formed through direct experience but have been acquired through mediated sources, such as movies or other narratives. In other words, primed by these noun phrases readers form specific expectations about the situation based on their prior knowledge of similar events.

Quite interestingly, as soon as this text-world is beginning to be outlined through world-building elements like 'bank robbery', 'hostages', 'police officers', etc., the reader is seemingly addressed directly by the narrator through the use of the second person.

> *Extract 2*
> It was easy to get to this point, much easier than you might think. All it took was one single really bad idea.
>
> (Backman 2021: 1)

The phrase 'much easier than you might think' is an evaluative commentary made by the narrator that triggers an epistemic modal-world as a result of the modal auxiliary 'might' and the lexical verb 'think'. An enactor of the narratee (who we argue is an enactor of the reader) occupies this new text-world.

Perhaps against readers' expectations, the story does not continue by explaining what the 'bad idea' noted by the narrator actually was, but focuses rather on the absurdities of living in the contemporary world:

> *Extract 3*
> This story is about a lot of things, but mostly about idiots. So it needs saying from the outset that it's always very easy to declare that other people are idiots, but only if you forget how idiotically difficult being human is. [. . .] Because there's such an unbelievable amount that we're all supposed to be able to cope with these days. You're supposed to have a job, and somewhere to live, and a family, and you're supposed to pay taxes and have clean underwear and remember the password to your damn Wi-Fi.
>
> (Backman 2021: 1)

By this point in the narrative, just half a page into the novel, readers have already been required to imagine different aspects of the text-world: a bank robbery, hostages, police officers who are about to storm an apartment.

The compositional deixis 'This story' draws attention to the enactor of the narrator making judgements about the story and about the difficulties of navigating the daily challenges of today's lives. We believe this type of textual architecture enhances the sense of immersion by sparking the reader's curiosity about who these 'idiotic' characters are, how they are connected to the robbery, and how they relate to us as we navigate the daily challenges of our own lives. Moreover, the narrator clearly confides in the narratee, situating themselves as someone who is in the position of guiding them throughout the complexities of the narrative and, more generally, of the world. This is realised by including an enactor of the reader through the use of the second-person pronoun, which seems to reinforce the intimacy between author and readers.

The structure of the entire novel relies on 'deictic braids' (Stockwell 2020: 184), which are mainly achieved through flashbacks or modalisations. For example, at the end of section 2 the enactor of the reader is addressed with the sentence 'That's really all you need to know at this point. Now the story can begin': immediately afterwards, however, instead of starting the robbery narrative as may be expected, a deictic shift in time introduces a flashback in which an event that took place ten years before is described:

> *Extract 4*
> Ten years ago a man was standing on a bridge. This story isn't about that man, so you don't really need to think about him right now. [. . .]
> All you need to know is that a man was standing on a bridge ten years ago. Up on the railing, high above the water, at the end of his life. Don't think about that anymore now. Think about something nicer.
> (Backman 2021: 4)

Here, a first text-world is established through the noun phrases 'ten years ago', 'a man', and 'a bridge'. Once a mental image of that situation is triggered in the readers' minds, a world-shift introduces a world-switch back to the moment of narration where the narrator directly addresses the reader, emphasising that they should disregard the flashback just introduced. Immediately afterward, a world-switch back to the text-world of the past provides additional details, such as the railing and the end of the man's life. Finally, the command 'Don't think about that anymore now' triggers a negated epistemic modal-world, inviting the reader to imagine something more pleasant instead.

While frequent world-switches may seem disruptive at first glance, we believe their combination with other strategies used in the extract may enhance readers' sense of immersion. More specifically, the switch to epistemic modal-worlds that accompany direct address to the reader likely creates a sense of personal connection with the narrator and creates engagement. Additionally, by being instructed to avoid thinking about the man on the bridge ('think about something nicer'), readers are likely to become more invested in the 'forbidden thoughts' about the man and want to know more details about his fate. The constant movement between acknowledging and avoiding the dramatic scene is likely to build suspense and, at the same time, favour the creation of curiosity about why we are being told not to think about the scene. While certainly providing entertainment, this constant shift in viewpoints is therefore particularly effective in eliciting the reader's responses discussed above. In order to monitor all the objects, places, and enactors introduced in the first two pages, readers must sustain their focus and resist distraction, which is likely to enhance their sense of immersion.

More generally, the novel encompasses at least six main overarching storylines, including the main bank robbery, the hostage drama, the personal lives of the hostages, the personal lives of the police officers, the life of a man who committed suicide on a bridge years earlier, and the police interviews and investigation. Each of these narrative threads, in turn, cues numerous text-worlds that often contain world-building elements or function-advancing propositions that are tied to other subplots. For example, the hostage drama, which is central to the novel and set inside an apartment, requires readers to mentally simulate a text-world containing the enactors and actions taking place in that setting. At the same time, the narrative cues text-worlds that feature the same characters as they appear in the past or at alternate points in the narrative timeline.

Notably, the hostage drama, which readers might perceive as the central event, is introduced only in chapter 15 of 74. Before this, the narrative explores numerous other settings and characters. These 'ancillary storyworlds' present different versions of the characters at various points in their lives, providing crucial context for understanding the events in the primary storyworld. In addition to functioning as a character development vehicle that informs the primary hostage drama storyline, this textual architecture plays a central role in eliciting empathy for the characters involved in the hostage drama itself. As a matter of fact, while navigating between text-worlds, readers have the possibility to gain deeper psychological insights into the characters' behaviours and emotional states. This cumulative understanding likely creates a more immersive and empathetic reading experience.

Empathy-generating mechanisms

The comment 'Within just a few minutes of reading this, tears pricked my eyes and I knew from that moment on that this book was special', which refers to Backman's novel, exemplifies the potential of literature to generate feelings that clearly are not 'quasi-feelings'. Rather, they are authentic, embodied emotions that partially activate the same neural networks as the corresponding 'real' events. This is why, when reading a story, we can (re)-experience the scent of a flower or a kiss on our lip (Jacobs 2023: 3).

One of the most common feelings experienced by readers of literature is empathy, defined as a 'vicarious, spontaneous sharing of affect [. . .] provoked by witnessing another's emotional state, by hearing about another's condition, or even by reading' (Keen 2010: 4). The link between empathy and literature has sparked extensive research in recent years (see Bonasera 2023, Bousfield and McIntyre 2011, Fernandez-Quintanilla 2020, LaCosse and Quintanilla 2021, Mallan 2013, Sopcak et al. 2016), with a significant number of studies exploring the relation between empathy and immersion. More specifically, studies in the psychology of literature have provided experimental support to hypotheses on the relationship between empathy and narrative immersion, as well as between empathy and emotional arousal in reading (Miall 2006, Bal and Veltkamp 2013, Burke et al. 2016). For readers to experience empathy and immersion (Sanford and Emmott 2012, Zunshine 2006), they must mentally simulate characters – a process Stockwell (2020: 177) terms 'mind-modelling'. This simulation draws heavily on readers' mental schemata, which contain general templates for character types encountered in reading experiences (Culpeper 2001).

Interestingly, the protagonist of *Anxious People* seems to defy all the general templates readers may have of a bank robber, for various reasons. First, they are not motivated by greed nor a criminal lifestyle, but are driven by desperation and unfortunate circumstances. Second, they perform the robbery very poorly, in a bank which does not contain any cash. Third, they show genuine concern for the hostages and struggle with guilt over their actions: in other words, they show a level of empathy which is quite atypical for the stereotypical bank robber character. In turn, these features are likely to evoke empathetic feelings in readers, as it becomes apparent early on that traits such as 'vulnerability' and 'moral complexity' will likely be attributed to the character. Additionally, the meta-comments formulated by the narrator are likely to serve as a bridge to empathy by making the character more likable and relatable:

> *Extract 5*
> You look over your shoulder and realize that you're on your own, the person you were married to turned off somewhere along the way. Maybe you uncover a lie. That's what happened to the bank robber. An infidelity comes to light, and even if no one's actually been unfaithful to you, you can probably appreciate that it's enough to knock a person off balance.
>
> (Backman 2021: 53)

More generally, mind-modelling can produce relatively 'flat' characters, i.e., characters built around a single trait or idea, who remain unchanged throughout the story, or 'round' ones, i.e., characters who can change and develop throughout the story and behave in ways that might surprise readers while remaining believable (Forster 1927). Stockwell (2020: 179) offers the following list of patterns that may contribute to rich mind-modelling and pave the way for empathy:

- Direct descriptions of physical appearance and manner, gestures and body language, explicit narratorial direction;
- The presentation of speech for an apparently autonomous sense of a character's personality, mood, and perspective;
- The representation of thought, beliefs, and intentions as if you as a reader have a telepathic ability;
- The reactions of other characters (including the narrator), who can serve as counterparts for your own reading response;
- Social relationships defined by deictic markers and social register, defining and sustaining all the divergences of characters' viewpoints from your own.

Throughout the seventy-four chapters of *Anxious People*, these patterns are consistently employed, resulting in the development of a fully-rounded character with whom readers are invited to empathise. Let us consider three illustrative excerpts:

> *Extract 6*
> Okay. A bank robber robs a bank. Think about that for a moment.
> Obviously, it has nothing to do with you. [. . .] Because you're a normal, decent person, so you would never have robbed a bank. There are simply some things that all normal people understand that you must never under any circumstances do. You mustn't tell lies, you mustn't steal, you mustn't kill, and you mustn't throw stones at birds. We all agree on that. Except maybe swans, because swans can actually be passive-aggressive little bastards.
>
> (Backman 2021: 50)

> *Extract 7*
> Because how happy can anyone really be, all the time? [. . .] Mostly we're just trying to get through the day. You've probably had days like that as well. But when you get through enough of them, one morning you look over your shoulder and realize that you're on your own, the person you were married to turned off somewhere along the way. That's what happened to the bank robber.
>
> (Backman 2021: 53)

> *Extract 8*
> It's probably hard to say precisely what would be normal in a hostage drama, but this certainly wasn't it. Jim looked intently at the bank robber.
> 'Can I ask, how did you get caught up in all this?'

> The bank robber, now unarmed, took such a deep breath that she doubled in size, then she became smaller than ever. 'I don't know where to start.'
>
> Then Jim did something deeply unprofessional. He reached out his hand and wiped a tear from the bank robber's cheek.
>
> (Backman 2021: 259)

In extract 6, several function-advancing propositions reflect the narrator's perspective on the events, often tinged with irony. Consequently, readers' mind-modelling processes are engaged not only with the characters but also with the narrator, though the depth of engagement may vary. This alternation between the narrator's perspective and the perspective he assigns to the reader across chapters introduces considerable demands for 'deictic tracking', as readers must cognitively navigate shifts in perspective to follow the characters' minds and world-views (Stockwell 2020: 188).

A typical example of a strategy likely to foster empathy for the character can be found in extract 7. First, a universally relatable and sad situation is established. The narrator then reveals that this scenario is precisely what happened to the bank robber. By universalising the bank robber's struggles, the narrator effectively reduces the distance between the reader and the character, fostering a deeper emotional connection and, in turn, enhancing immersion in the narrative.

Extract 8 marks a fundamental turning point in the plot, as a personal pronoun is used for the first time to refer to the bank robber. Interestingly, it is a feminine pronoun, which may clash with the readers' mental schemata regarding the bank robber before this point and consequently generate a frame readjustment in their minds (Adam 2021: 180). The extract also incorporates the characters' direct speech alongside descriptions of the bank robber's physical reactions in the specific situation (e.g., doubling in size and becoming smaller again, crying). Furthermore, it depicts another character's reaction (reaching out to wipe a tear from the bank robber's cheek). These narrative techniques, used in combination within a concise passage, likely contribute significantly to the reader's mind-modelling process. Consequently, they facilitate a close emotional identification with the character, which is conducive to narrative immersion.

The relationship between deictic braids and immersion in this text operates through multiple, interconnected mechanisms: the deictic braids create a layered narrative experience which engages readers both emotionally and cognitively. By weaving together different perspectives and temporal moments, they offer insights into characters' inner lives while simultaneously maintaining critical distance through the narrator's reflective stance. These shifts have multiple functions: they provide deep psychological access to various characters, revealing their motivations, fears, and desires through carefully orchestrated movements between viewpoints. This may be conducive to empathy with the characters and make readers feel more immersed in their stories and motivations.

Moreover, the text-worlds created through these deictic braids are enriched by specific details that contribute to what Stockwell (2020: 201) terms 'atmosphere' or 'ambience': this atmospheric quality therefore emerges not just from descriptive details but from the dynamic interplay between different perspectives and temporal moments. The cognitive demands of tracking these shifts may actually enhance reader engagement by requiring active participation in meaning-making, though this engagement does not necessarily coincide with immersion.

'You' narrative

A third and last factor that we believe plays a substantial role in determining the immersive potential of *Anxious People* has to do with the frequent use of indexical pronouns and, more particularly, the second person. Indeed, the pervasive use of 'you' has already been pointed out in the discussion above, particularly as one of the tools in the hands of the narrator to accompany the reader across the complex textual architecture and fostering empathy. In this section, we will discuss in some more detail how the author achieves these goals by exploiting the rich semiotics of 'you'.

In order to better describe the occurrence of the second person in *Anxious People* and assess its effects on immersion, we adopt the model developed by Sorlin (2022), which is an especially rich framework for the analysis of the semantics and pragmatics of second-person narratives and, therefore, particularly suited to the task at hand. Extending Kluge's (2016) original classification of five different types of 'you' (the first five 'you' in the list below) and adapting it to the context of narrative, Sorlin proposes a sixfold classification of the different possible interpretations of 'you':

You1 = 'you' meaning 'I'
You2 = 'you' meaning 'I' as a representative of a larger entity
You3 = generic 'you', meaning 'anyone'
You4 = 'you' in form of me as representative of a larger entity
You5 = 'you' meaning the person in front of me
You6 = 'you' as protagonist

Two features of this model are especially relevant for the discussion to come. First, the classification proposed by Sorlin encompasses three distinct underlying dimensions. The first dimension ranges from the uses of 'you' where one refers to oneself to those uses where the speaker refers to the other. The two extremes of this SELF-OTHER axis are You1 and You5, while the other 'you' forms are distributed between these two poles, depending on how closely or distantly they individuate the speaker or the addressee.

The second axis ranges from the more personal uses of 'you' to the more generic ones. This is the axis that distinguishes between You1 and You5 on the one hand (the most individuating) and You3 on the other (the most generic), whereas You2 and You4 stand in the middle ground between the two poles. To these two dimensions, in fact already part of Kluge's original model, Sorlin adds a third: the distinction between the use of you in the extradiegetic dimension of the 'discourse-world' (Gavins 2007) and its use on the diegetic dimension of the 'text-world'. This last distinction is obviously relevant in the context of narratives and it is precisely in this context that Sorlin introduces You6, that is, the 'you as protagonist': 'a type of "you" situated in between You1 (where the protagonist would also be the narrator) and You5 (where the protagonist is the identified narratee, clearly addressed by a narrator)' (Sorlin 2022: 185).

The second important feature of the model is that it is dynamic. The different types of 'you' are not to be regarded as segregated units but rather as gravitational poles on an interpretive continuum. One of the most important consequences of such understanding of the 'you' semiotic space as a continuum is that the reader of a narrative who encounters a second person is called upon *position* themselves (in the sense of O'Connor 1994) within this continuum through an act of semantic and pragmatic negotiation with the text and its author.

With this much background in mind, we now return to the analysis of the use of the second person in *Anxious People*. The first, striking observation is that the novel makes extensive use of the second person. A cursory look at the first two chapters is sufficient to witness it. The first eleven lines of the first chapter mention a second-person pronoun seven times. These first mentions of 'you' are highly ambiguous to the reader. The author is clearly introducing the story from an external perspective, and the use of 'you' oscillates between seemingly addressing the reader directly to making generic statements. The author refers to facts relevant to the story and at the same time makes generic statements about the human condition. Here, the second person is ambiguous across all three dimensions of Sorlin's model: it is not clear if it is personal or generic, if it is positioned in the text-world or in the discourse-world, or even where it stands in the self-other axis. This last sense of ambiguity is reinforced by the fact that, after the first few lines, the second-person pronoun is suddenly replaced with as much frequency by the first-person plural, more likely interpreted as inclusive (of the writer) and generic. Finally, the ambiguity dissipates at the end of the chapter with a single 'you' that clearly addresses the reader in a direct and personal way ('That's really all you need to know at this point'). This use of 'you' is maintained in the second chapter, to which we already referred in a previous section in its role within the novel's larger textual architecture. In this chapter, similarly to what was happening at the very end of chapter 1, the writer is addressing the reader personally and directly, often with imperative asserting force (e.g., 'Think about cookies').

These first observations are already quite telling. They offer a rather vivid exemplification of how the author manipulates the reader into positioning themselves within a semiotic space that, as mentioned in a previous section, promises right from the start to be very rich. The narrator does so by first welcoming the reader with a wide interpretative offer, represented by the highly underspecified use of 'you', but then quickly establishing a direct line of personal communication between narrator and reader, demonstrated by the use of an explicitly unambiguous form of You5. These observations are only exemplificatory. In fact, it should be observed that the use of the second person, at several times accompanied by the use of the first person (especially the inclusive plural), remains pervasive across the whole novel. Furthermore, this pervasive use of 'you' is found across different text-worlds and, most interestingly, even across the text-world/discourse-world divide as the characters themselves indulge in a variety of uses of the second person, from addressing each other personally to making generic statements, to talking about themselves.

In light of these observations concerning the use of 'you' in *Anxious People* and the discussion in the previous sections, we point out three ways in which 'you' plays a decisive role in contributing the effect of immersion of the novel. Firstly, we observe that throughout the novel the reader is almost constantly required to engage actively in the disambiguation of the many, different and often ambiguous, uses of 'you'. The brief illustration offered above of the first two chapters provides a telling example of how the author uses the second person to capture the attention of the reader and guide them across the narration and its architecture. As was observed earlier, at the onset of the novel the reader finds themselves faced with many ambiguous occurrences of 'you' and is prompted to search for clues in the text to disambiguate them. This makes them immediately engage with the text in an attempt at positioning themselves across the emerging semiotic dimensions of the narration and its actors. By the time the reader reaches the second chapter, the writer is already addressing them personally and directly, in fact commanding their thoughts in an authoritative manner ('Don't think about cookies!', 'Think about cookies'). In a few pages, the reader has both explored the larger landscape of communicative interactions that define a great deal of the narration to come as well as entered into a direct and personal communicative interaction with the author (to the point that the author is now telling her what to think, or not to think).

Secondly, throughout the many occurrences of the second person, the reader is prompted to engage, with noticeable frequency, in mental acts of self-ascription. The notion of self-ascription was introduced by Lewis (1979) to account for the non-propositional nature of the first-person attitudes. According to 'Lewis, saying 'I am . . .' does not correspond to attributing a property to an entity objectively identified but to a more primitive and essential (Perry 1979) act of self-ascription of a property (Fiorin and Delfitto 2020). Weschler (2010) extends Lewis' mechanism of self-ascription to the second person, at least in its use to address the addressee (You5 in Sorlin's model): in this case, a sentence of the form 'You are . . .' is an invitation made by the speaker to the addressee to self-ascribe a certain property. Basing herself on a wealth of evidence coming from psychological and cognitive empirical research, Sorlin observes that, in fact, all uses of 'you' invite an act of self-ascription on the part of the reader (although, admittedly, to different degrees). If this is correct, the abundance of second-person forms in *Anxious People* is bound to prompt a corresponding abundance of acts of engagement by the reader with the text, in terms of mental acts of self-ascription, that give her a more psychologically grounded sense of participation within the semiotic space of the novel and the negotiation of its meaning. In this way, the reader becomes one of the relevant actors in the narrative landscape, on a par with the author and the novel's characters.

Thirdly, and finally, the effects described above are further strengthened by the ubiquitous use of the second person across narrative worlds. This seems to us a particularly effective strategy in stimulating the reader's immersion because it blurs the boundaries between text-world and discourse-worlds. In this way, both of these dimensions surge to equal relevance in making the reader one of the active actors in the semiotic space of the novel. In this respect, a number of instances of Backman's use of 'you' substantiate Herman's (2002) notion of 'narrative you' – a narrative strategy grounded on the second-person perspective (as opposed to the more widely attested, and studied, first- and third-person narrative perspectives) where the reader is explicitly addressed in the second person. This type of narrative, Herman observes, blurs the line between the reader as an external observer and the reader as a participant in the narrative. This duality of interpretation (corresponding to Herman's notion of 'double deixis') enhances the complexity and richness of the narrative and creates a sense of immediacy and depth as it encourages the reader to inhabit the text-world while remaining anchored to her external position.

Concluding remarks

This chapter has explored the immersive qualities of Fredrik Backman's novel *Anxious People*, arguing that the sense of immersion experienced by many readers is the result of at least three factors working in combination: textual architecture, empathy-generating mechanisms, and the strategic use of second-person narration. By examining these elements, we have tried to show how Backman employs various techniques and makes deliberate choices to create a deeply engaging and immersive reading experience.

The analysis of *Anxious People*'s textual architecture reveals Backman's skilful use of switches in storyworlds and in text-worlds. These techniques require readers to continuously modify their mental representations of the fictional world, potentially enhancing curiosity about plot development and character relationships. The novel's structure, which encompasses at least six distinct narrative threads, demands sustained focus from readers as they navigate between different settings, events, and characters. This cognitive engagement, we argued, may play an important role in fostering immersion.

Backman's strategic construction of the novel's textual architecture, particularly the delayed introduction of the central hostage drama, serves to build anticipation and maintain reader interest. The various subplots, far from being distractions, are crucial for the development of empathy towards the characters involved in the main narrative. This layered approach to storytelling may be conducive to readers' emotional investments in the characters and their circumstances, potentially deepening their immersion in the fictional world.

Other empathy-generating mechanisms are at play in the novel: Backman skilfully defies reader expectations by presenting a bank robber character who challenges prototypical mental schemata. By portraying the protagonist as vulnerable, morally complex, and relatable, the author invites readers to form a deeper emotional connection with the character. The use of various stylistic patterns, such as direct descriptions, representation of thought, and depiction of social relationships, contributes to this rich mind-modelling. The narrator's meta-comments and humorous asides also serve as a bridge to empathy, making the characters more likable and relatable.

Finally, the pervasive use of second-person narration in *Anxious People* plays a crucial role in creating an immersive reading experience in close interaction with the factors identified above. By employing various types of 'you' across different narrative dimensions, Backman engages readers in active disambiguation and interpretation. This constant negotiation of meaning keeps readers mentally engaged and invested in the story as relevant participants in the novel's semiotic space. The ambiguity of the second-person pronoun, oscillating between addressing the reader directly and making generic statements, blurs the boundaries between the text-world and the discourse-world (Herman 2002): this technique effectively draws readers into the narrative, making them feel as if they are part of the story's landscape. Moreover, the frequent use of 'you' prompts readers to engage in mental acts of self-ascription, giving them a more psychologically grounded sense of participation within the narrative discourse. By inviting readers to position themselves within the communicative interactions of the story, the author creates a sense of personal involvement that is likely to enhance immersion.

It is important to stress that the immersive quality of *Anxious People* does not result from any single technique or choice, but rather from the synergic interaction of multiple narrative strategies. The combination of these techniques creates a reading experience that is both cognitively demanding and emotionally engaging. Readers are required to navigate multiple text-worlds, form emotional connections with complex characters, and constantly negotiate their own position within the narrative. This multifaceted engagement is, in our view, what ultimately leads to the sense of immersion.

References

Adam, N. (2021) '"Your duplicitous point of view": delayed revelations of hypothetical focalisation in Ian McEwan's *Atonement* and *Sweet Tooth*', *Language and Literature* 30 (2): 174–99.

Backman, F. (2021) *Anxious People* (trans. from *Folk med ångest* [2019]). Harmondsworth: Penguin.

Bal, P.M. and Veltkamp, M. (2013) 'How does fiction reading influence empathy?' *PLOS ONE* 8 (1): e55341.

Bonasera, C. (2023) 'Exploring the potential of sentiment analysis for the study of negative empathy', *Journal of Literary Semantics* 52 (2): 163–89.

Bousfield, D. and McIntyre, D. (2011) 'Emotion and empathy in Martin Scorsese's *Goodfellas*: a case study of the "funny guy" scene', in R. Piazza, M. Bednarek and F. Rossi (eds) *Telecinematic Discourse: Approaches to the Language of Films and Television Series*. Amsterdam: John Benjamins, pp.105–23.

Burke, M., Kuzmičová, A., Mangen, A. and Schilhab T. (2016) 'Empathy at the confluence of neuroscience and empirical literary studies', *Scientific Study of Literature* 6 (1): 6–41.

Cook, G. (1994) *Discourse and Literature: The Interplay of Form and Mind*. Oxford: Oxford University Press.

Csikszentmihalyi, M. (2014) 'Flow and the foundations of positive psychology', in *The Collected Works of Mihaly Csikszentmihalyi (Volume 2)*. Dordrecht: Springer.

Culpeper, J. (2001) *Language and Characterisation: People in Plays and Other Texts*. London: Routledge.

Emmott, C. (1997) *Narrative Comprehension: A Discourse Perspective*. Oxford: Clarendon Press.

Fernandez-Quintanilla, C. (2020) 'Textual and reader factors in narrative empathy: an empirical reader response study using focus groups', *Language and Literature* 2 (2): 124–46.

Fiorin, G. and Delfitto, D. (2020) *Beyond Meaning: A Journey Across Language, Perception and Experience*. Dordrecht: Springer.

Forster, E.M. (1927) *Aspects of the Novel*. London: Harcourt, Brace.

Galbraith, M. (1995) 'Deictic shift theory and the poetics of involvement in narrative', in F. Duchan, G.A. Bruder and L.E. Hewitt (eds) *Deixis in Narrative: A Cognitive Science Perspective*. Hillsdale: Lawrence Erlbaum, pp.19–59.

Gavins, J. (2007) *Text World Theory: An Introduction*. Edinburgh: Edinburgh University Press.

Herman, D. (2002) *Story Logic: The Problems and Possibilities of Narrative*. Lincoln: University of Nebraska Press.

Jacobs, A. (2023) *Neurocomputational Poetics: How the Brain Processes Verbal Art*. London: Anthem Press.

Keen, S. (2010) 'Narrative empathy', in F.L. Aldama (ed.) *Toward a Cognitive Theory of Narrative Acts*. Austin: University of Texas Press, pp.61–94.

Kluge, B. (2016) 'Generic uses of the second person singular: how speakers deal with referential ambiguity and misunderstandings', *Pragmatics* 26 (3): 501–22.
Kuijpers, M.M., Hakemulder, F., Tan, E.S. and Doicaru, M.M. (2014) 'Exploring absorbing reading experiences', *Scientific Study of Literature* 4 (1): 89–122.
LaCosse, J. and Quintanilla, V. (2021) 'Empathy influences the interpretation of whether others have violated everyday indeterminate rules', *Law and Human Behavior* 45 (4): 287.
Lewis, D. (1979) 'Attitudes *de dicto* and *de se*', *Philosophical Review* 88: 513–43.
Mallan, K. (2013) 'Empathy: narrative empathy and children's literature', in Y. Wu, K. Mallan and R. McGillis (eds) *(Re)imagining the World: Children's Literature's Response to Changing Times*. Dordrecht: Springer, pp.105–14.
Miall, D. (2006) *Literary Reading: Empirical and Theoretical Studies*. Bern: Peter Lang.
O'Connor, P.E. (1994) '"You could feel it through the skin": agency and positioning in prisoners' stabbing stories', *Text* 14 (1): 45–75.
Perry, J. (1979) 'The problem of the essential indexical', *Noûs* 13: 3–21.
Sanford, A.J. and Emmott, C. (2012) *Mind, Brain and Narrative*. Cambridge: Cambridge University Press.
Segal, E.M. (2012) 'Narrative comprehension and the role of deictic shift theory', in F. Duchan, G.A. Bruder and L.E. Hewitt (eds) *Deixis in Narrative: A Cognitive Science Perspective*. Hillsdale: Lawrence Erlbaum, pp.3–17.
Sopcak, P., Salgaro, M. and Herrmann, J.B. (2016) 'Transdisciplinary approaches to literature and empathy', *Scientific Study of Literature* 6 (1): 2–5.
Sorlin, S. (2022) *The Stylistics of 'You': Second-Person Pronoun and Its Pragmatic Effects*. Cambridge: Cambridge University Press.
Stockwell, P. (2020) *Cognitive Poetics: An Introduction* (2nd edn). London: Routledge.
Wechsler, S. (2010) 'What "I" and "You" mean to each other: person indexicals, self-ascription, and theory of mind', *Language* 86 (2): 332–65.
Werth, P. (1999) *Text Worlds: Representing Conceptual Space in Discourse*. London: Longman.
Zunshine, L. (2006) *Why We Read Fiction: Theory of Mind and the Novel*. Columbus: Ohio State University Press.

CHAPTER 13

The spirit of immersion: ghosts in award-winning contemporary fiction

Naomi Adam

Drawing from both cognitively- and ontologically-oriented models, Adam in this chapter explores the distinct stylistic texture of Booker Prize-winning novels that feature ghosts. These texts are often described in immersive fashion by readers in their online reviews, despite the fact that most such readers are sceptical of the existence of ghosts in the first place. This non-belief does not seem to be an obstacle for immersion. The approach represents a detailed stylistic description that accounts for immersive effects as expressed by natural readers. The comparative approach subsumes a consideration of each novel's distinct profile of the accessibility relations of its imagined worlds, which inevitably impacts upon a reader's ability to fictionally recentre and thus immerse themselves in a work of fiction for the duration of the reading experience.

The spectral and the sceptical

Do you believe in ghosts? If you answered *yes* to this question and live in one of the five so-called 'core' Anglophone countries (Australia, Canada, New Zealand, the United Kingdom, and the United States), then you are in the minority. Over the past four decades, opinion polls as well as academic research have revealed popular belief in ghosts to hover somewhere between the 35 and 45 per cent mark (e.g., Clarke 1991, Ipsos 1998, Baker and Bader 2014, Dahlgreen 2014). Naturally, there is intranational variation, most especially with regard to age (younger individuals are more likely to be believers than their older counterparts) and gender (women are, on the whole, less sceptical than men). International variation between contemporaneous studies rarely exceeds 10 per cent (Ipsos 2021, Centre for Public Christianity 2021, Statista 2024), and may be accounted for by varying belief systems in respective countries, including among indigenous peoples. Ultimately, scepticism is common and widespread, with no one survey yet placing belief levels at above 50 per cent.

However, what is on balance a lack of belief in ghosts does not appear to have dampened our enthusiasm for narratives involving ghosts. Ghost stories have a long and illustrious history, from their inceptive oral forms to written versions which began to appear from the early eighteenth century, becoming firmly entrenched by the Victorian era (Schenkel 2016: 11). These tales act as precursors to today's proliferation of ghost-related media, including podcasts, television series, and film franchises. For instance, Baker and Bader (2014: 570–1) discuss the upsurge in paranormal reality television programmes in recent decades, concluding that 'the paranormal has become a near ubiquitous feature of American popular culture' (586). Meanwhile, an opinion piece in one of Britain's foremost national newspapers ties the 'strange little resurgence' (Scott 2024) of all things ghostly to general social malaise amid concurrent cost-of-living, environmental, and global health crises.

If new media ghost stories are enjoying a newfound popularity, they are still yet to supplant those told in the more traditional print form. This was highlighted for me when researching patterns within recent winners of the Booker Prize (Adam 2022), a literary award which is widely considered to be the most prestigious in the English-speaking world (Drąg 2014, van Urk 2023), and presented yearly to what a judging panel deems 'the best sustained work of fiction written in the English-speaking world and published in the UK and Ireland' (The Booker Prizes 2024). I was surprised to discover just how frequently ghosts appeared within the Booker Prize-winning pantheon: at the time of writing, four of the past ten winners – published between 2014 and 2023 – have been narratives featuring ghosts. This statistic is made all the more striking when one considers that the Booker Prize champions literary fiction – a genre usually associated with innovation, defamiliarisation, and the avoidance of what may be considered cliché or a trope.

In conjunction with the above discussion of popular scepticism, this results in something of an impasse. We may be keen to discount the existence of ghosts in our everyday lives, in the actual world (Ryan 1991), but we appear more than happy to read and write (and reward) tales of their exploits in fictional contexts. Altogether, this prompts a series of questions. How are readers able to overcome their (on balance) inherently sceptical attitudes when engaging with fiction featuring ghosts? Do real-world belief systems hamper or otherwise impact the experience of reading ghost-containing narratives? What linguistic strategies may be adopted to mitigate any potential natural inbuilt scepticism?

Throughout, I understand immersion in a narrative to be a phenomenon that occurs whenever 'the fictional world in some way, at least temporarily, becomes the real world' (Schellenberg 2013: 507) to a reader – that is, the reader begins to conceive of the fictional world as if it is the real world, as (Ryan 2022) defines immersion. Following this logic, I suggest that narrative immersion can be signalled by the conflation of ontological boundaries, and that the perceived collapsing of these boundaries can be considered the quintessence, or the spirit, of immersion. This may manifest in a variety of ways, including, but not limited to:

- the disappearance of the fictional medium from active consciousness (Ryan 2022: 1)
- the conception of a fictional world as possessed of independent existence (Ryan 2022: 6)
- a perceived 'effortless access to the fictional world' (Ryan 2022: 7)
- the formation of vivid mental imagery (Ryan 2022: 7)
- a cognitive relocation into the world of a story (Atencia-Linares and Sebastián 2023), and the conflation of deictic centres and ontological levels (Lombard and Ditton 1997). This may take different forms, being either movement down the ontological chain (readers perceiving themselves within a storyworld, see Martínez 2014), or up the ontological chain (readers perceiving fictional characters as actual people).

This chapter explores instances of potential narrative immersion across four case-study novels: Marlon James' (2014) *A Brief History of Seven Killings*, George Saunders' (2017) *Lincoln in the Bardo*, Damon Galgut's (2021) *The Promise*, and *The Seven Moons of Maali Almeida* by Shehan Karunatilaka (2022). These are the aforementioned novels that feature ghosts and also have been awarded the Booker Prize during the past ten years. Combining the exploration of naturalistic online data with introspective stylistic analysis, I explore how readers respond to the presence of ghosts in these award-winning contemporary novels, focusing especially on linguistic features which may mitigate scepticism and encourage immersion.

Ghosts in the machine: digital reader responses

To address the questions posed above, I used various international instances of the marketplace website Amazon (Australia, UK, and USA), alongside its social cataloguing subsidiary Goodreads (2024), to compile a database of reader responses to recent Booker Prize-winning novels that feature ghosts. Use of digital reader-response data has become a popular research methodology in recent years: Allington (2016) considers critique of another Booker Prize-winner, *The Inheritance of Loss*, on Amazon, while both Nuttall and Harrison (2020) and Doche and Ross (2023) investigate reactions to their respective focus texts on the Goodreads platform. The resulting data may be analysed quantitatively and/or qualitatively and can supplement the responses of a trained academic reader with those of a lay readership comprised of so-called 'civilian readers' (Stockwell 2016: 149), acting as a form of research triangulation.

While the layout and function of Amazon and Goodreads necessarily differ, both websites present their users with the opportunity to leave reviews about the books they have purchased and/or read. Nominally, Amazon is geared more towards reviews of the quality of books as consumer products, and Goodreads towards sharing recommendations with like-minded bibliophiles, but this distinction does not apply in practice. Often, the comments left on the two sites are very similar, if not identical (i.e., copied-and-pasted from one site to the other). On both sites, users typically detail their reactions to novels and may also interact with the comments of their fellow reader-reviewers. In this regard, reader reviews must be considered as inherently performative: they are freely accessible online for all to view, and there is the possibility that this may impact upon their content, particularly where contentious topics including belief in ghosts are concerned.

To sift the reviews of the four novels for comments engaging specifically with the topic of ghosts, I used the search function on each site to filter by the keyword *ghost*, and its lemmas (e.g., *ghosts*, *ghostly*). For manageability, search results were capped at 100 where they exceeded this figure (or twenty-five apiece for the three international iterations of Amazon). The order of selection followed the order in which the reviews were presented on the respective sites. This allowed me to prioritise comments that were classed as 'top reviews' by the sites' respective algorithms, being those with which other users had engaged the most frequently. The comments were then copy-pasted into a spreadsheet to enable detailed thematic analysis. Each was manually marked with one or more of the following five codes:

- *ghost-neutral* (denoting descriptive references that merely detailed the presence of ghosts in the novel);
- *ghost-positive* (for positively-valent reactions to and judgements of the depiction of ghosts in the novel);
- *ghost-negative* (negatively-valent reactions to ghosts in the novel);
- *ghost-linguistic* (references that made mention of how ghosts were linguistically presented in the novel, for instance the narrative stance, focalisation, or use of speech tags);
- *ghost-null* (indicating references to ghosts in a metaphorical, colloquial, or otherwise irrelevant sense).

In the following analyses, priority will be given to the responses tagged as *ghost-positive*, *ghost-negative*, *ghost-linguistic*, or some combination of the three. This allows me to tie responses to the inclusion of ghosts within the respective novels to the specific linguistic strategies involved in their depiction.

The responses comprising my database were all posted publicly and are freely available to anyone online. Nonetheless, as Thomas (2021: 184) recognises, 'ease of access does not mean ethical access': online reviewers are unlikely to have posted their commentary for it to be co-opted as research data in an academic context. Further to this, discussions about belief in ghosts necessarily implicate sensitive topics of spiritual and religious belief.

For this reason, below I refer to the authors of online comments using an anonymising code. Responses from Amazon are marked as *A*, followed by an initial corresponding to the novel under discussion (*B* for *A Brief History*, *L* for *Lincoln in the Bardo*, *P* for *The Promise*, and *S* for *Seven Moons*), then a number between 1 and 100. Likewise, Goodreads reviews are indicated by a *G*, followed by a novel-specific initial and a number from 1 to 100. For instance, *GB1* denotes the first response collected from Goodreads about the novel *A Brief History*.

In the analysis, I take a sequential and tripartite approach to explore my four case-study texts using the digital reader-response data collected. First, I contextualise the novel under scrutiny and provide a brief, indicative excerpt from the narrative that features one or more ghosts. Following this, I spotlight salient stylistic features in the excerpt that contribute to its distinct *texture*, or 'the experienced quality of textuality' (Stockwell 2009: 1) which will influence how a text is received and interpreted by its readership. Finally, I present digital reader responses to the ghost(s) depicted in the novel, concentrating in particular on comments which yoke specific stylistic features to the reception of and engagement with these fictional ghosts – be they features that help or that hinder readerly immersion – as well as comments suggesting some degree of ontological conflation. Where relevant, these responses from civilian readers will also be compared to reactions from a more 'professional' reading audience (Allington 2016), in the form of newspaper reviews and research articles on the four case-study novels. To ensure maximum and unbiased coverage, press reviews of each novel were sourced from the website Book Marks (2024).

Ghosts in award-winning contemporary fiction

Aside from the preliminary paratextual (Genette 1997) material, the first words of Marlon James' 2015 Booker Prize-winning *A Brief History of Seven Killings* are assigned to a ghost. Sir Arthur George Jennings, a former politician and the novel's only ghost, also acts as the first of its dozen narrators, beginning the loosely factual chronicle of a 1976 assassination attempt upon the singer Bob Marley with the imperative: '*Listen.* Dead people never stop talking' (James 2014: 1; original italics). Neatly, the aspectless sentence fragment and following universal statement avoid cleaving themselves to any particular context: they are applicable intertextually as well as extratextually. This ontological mutability is also apparent in Jennings' ensuing existential musings:

> Maybe death is not death at all, just a detention after school. You know where you're coming from and you're always returning from it. You know where you're going though you never seem to get there and you're just dead. Dead. It sounds final but it's a word missing an *ing*.

> [. . .] I could listen to myself, still claiming to anybody that would hear that I didn't fall, I was pushed over the balcony at the Sunset Beach Hotel in Montego Bay. And I can't say shut your trap, Artie Jennings, because every morning I wake up having to put my pumpkin-smashed head back together. [. . .] I seem to have misplaced the left half of my face.
>
> (James 2014: 1–2)

James' ghost is an internal focaliser: the reader experiences the fictional world from his perspective, complete with aphorisms ('Dead. It sounds final but it's a word missing an *ing*'), black humour ('I seem to have misplaced the left half of my face'), and colourful metaphor ('my pumpkin-smashed head'). Jennings reveals himself to be preoccupied with the act of communication ('talking', 'hear', 'This is what I wanted to say'), and his narration is highly dialogic, as the ghost both self-addresses ('shut your trap, Artie Jennings') and appears to advise an unspecified interlocutor: 'When *you*'re dead speech is nothing but tangents and detours'. While the italicised second-person pronoun here may be interpreted as generalised *you* (Herman 2002: 355), akin to the more formal pronominal *one*, it could also be read as direct address to either an intradiegetic character or extradiegetic reader. Indeed, beyond Herman's (2002) discussion of doubly-deictic *you*, the pronoun's braided ambiguity here positions it as potentially *triply* deictic: amenable to not one or two but three potential interpretations. Similarly mutable are the passage's *world-building* elements (Werth 1999). The 'Sunset Beach Hotel in Montego Bay' may be one of the novel's fictional settings, but it also has reference in the actual world: it is an all-inclusive resort, spa, and waterpark on the northwestern fringes of the Jamaican coastline. Finally, James' ghost is also individuated from the first: the chapter from which the above passage is excerpted begins with the emboldened, centre-aligned heading 'Sir Arthur George Jennings', hence introducing the character with a highly personalised vocative. This can be interpreted as a technique to heighten the affective appeal of a non-human enactor. Research suggests that human or human-like figures in texts are more likely to engage our empathy (Keen 2007) and may also be perceptually privileged (Stockwell 2020: 79).

However, digital reader responses to *A Brief History* suggest that anthropomorphism is not guaranteed to override existing scepticism. Several reviewers openly expressed their distaste for novels featuring ghosts, with their commentary hence coded as *ghost-negative*. For some this was phrased obliquely – '[B]ut the first chapter is narrated by a ghost for goodness' sake' (GB55) – while for others irritation was couched less diplomatically: 'And most significantly, do we really need a ghost? Couldn't this whole thing have been carried off without the supernatural?' (GB41). Interestingly, one reviewer noted that despite a personal dislike for books featuring ghosts, the 'beautifully written [. . .] rhythmic quality' (GB97) of *A Brief History* meant that for James' novel he would make an exception to the rule, demonstrating that stylistic texture has the potential to override readerly preferences and prejudices.

Relatedly, readers who approved of *A Brief History*'s ghostly narrator were more likely to spotlight specific features that contributed to their enjoyment: the tags *ghost-positive* and *ghost-linguistic* were thus frequent companions. Several credited the *in media res* opening with facilitating their 'rich, all-consuming *submersion*' (GB62) into the novel, whilst also referencing James' use of dialogism and homodiegetic narration. The above italicised head noun clearly gestures to immersion as it suggests the blurring of actuality and fictionality, a conflation of ontological levels that results in 'effortless access to the textual world' (Ryan 2022: 7). The READING IS SWIMMING metaphor underlying the quotation reappeared in another reviewer's reference to 'plung[ing] into [the novel] feet first' (GB23) due to its use of direct address and blending of fact and fiction. This reader also complimented the use of direct address, concurring with Tomczak's (2019: 116) characterisation of apostrophe in the novel as 'a form of address [that] implies interaction with a listener or an audience', implicating readers as 'co-witnesses' (117). The result, the reviewer claims, is that the characters are 'all very real' (GB23) – an opinion shared by a fellow Goodreads reader who (presumably non-ironically) describes even the 'ghostly' characters as 'fleshed out, believable' (GB29). Once again, the fictional and the actual merge, as fictional entities are perceived to have independent, real-world existence.

Ghosts in *Lincoln in the Bardo* are far more numerous than in *A Brief History*. Over 100 jointly narrate events following the premature death of President Abraham Lincoln's eldest son, Willie, as he is laid to rest in a Georgetown cemetery in the winter of 1862. These ghosts, and newly Willie, populate the novel's eponymous *bardo*: a liminal realm in Buddhist theology akin to Catholic purgatory. Rather than sharing their homodiegetic storytelling with living enactors, as in James' novel, the ghosts apportion it between themselves, with frequent overlap and completion of one another's sentences. Typographically, the ghosts' narration is presented as a series of direct speech utterances followed by a postposed, attributive tag; the result is a piecemeal, patchwork-like narrative, one which has previously been compared to that of a playtext (Wagner 2017). Here, for instance, are the reminiscences of the ghost Hans Vollman, who details the day of his death with the help of fellow graveyard inhabitant, Roger Bevins:

> On our wedding day I was forty-six, she was eighteen. Now, I know what you are thinking: older man (not thin, somewhat bald, lame in one leg, teeth of wood) exercises the marital prerogative, thereby mortifying the poor young—
>
> But that is false.
>
> That is exactly what I refused to do, you see.
>
> [. . .] And that day – alas – was the day of the beam. [. . .]
>
> Per the advice of my physician, I took to my—

> A sort of sick-box was judged – was judged to be—
>
> hans vollman
>
> Efficacious.
>
> roger bevins iii
>
> Efficacious, yes. Thank you, friend. [. . .] At that time, there on the sick-cart, as yet unbound, I found I could briefly leave my sick-box [. . .].
>
> hans vollman
>
> (Saunders 2017: 3–6)

As the passage demonstrates, several stylistic features observed in *A Brief History* above reappear in *Lincoln in the Bardo*. Saunders' ghosts similarly employ present-tense, first-person narration ('I must admit') that is couched in almost maximally free direct discourse, achieving an impression of immediacy. Proximal deictics also appear frequently, anchoring the reader in the here-and-now of the narrative moment ('*Now*, I know what you are thinking', 'hitting me just *here*'). This narration is likewise highly dialogic, as typified by the sentence fragment 'But that is false', which incorporates two of Sotirova's (2007) indices of interactivity (the sentence-initial coordinating conjunction 'But', alongside the anaphoric 'that'). Meanwhile, the lexicon of both ghosts is idiosyncratic, and (arguably) humorous – note especially the circumlocutions 'sick-box' and 'sick-cart', corresponding respectively to *coffin* and *hearse*, and betraying the ghosts' reluctance to accept their deaths – establishing for each ghost a distinctive idiolect. Each ghost is also assigned a maximally specific proper name: see, for instance, 'roger bevins iii', above. Finally, there is also direct address: Hans displays a preoccupation with what 'you' may be thinking. The *you* of this metaperspective is somewhat ambiguous, given that it may simply refer horizontally within the text-world to Vollman's interlocutor, Bevins, to the other ghosts gathered in the graveyard, or to some hypothetical entity who would describe him dispassionately (as 'not thin, somewhat bald', etc). However, following Herman's (2002) notion of doubly-deictic *you*, the second-person pronoun is also interpretable as apostrophic, vertical address directed towards a reader of Saunders' fiction in the actual world.

Among actual-world readers, and much as with *A Brief History*, responses to the ghost characters of *Lincoln in the Bardo* varied. However, on balance the commentary was less forgiving for the latter novel, with *ghost-negative* responses outnumbering the *ghost-positive*. Most especially, readers appeared hyperaware of the innovative typography, largely judging it negatively due to the 'distracting, distancing' (GL71) effect it had upon their reading experience. One characterised 'these story fragments' as 'incessant stutters which never allowed me to relax into the book and really experience the story' (GL73), suggesting that form can be an impediment to immersion just as much as content in narratives featuring ghosts. Another posited, metatextually, that Saunders 'was determined to not to use "he said" or "she said" because ghosts don't really talk', yet ultimately concluded that:

'there's no such thing as ghosts, so having a whole book based on what they say, whether you use "he said" or write a tiny name at the end of what he said, makes no difference, because it's still stupid' (GL2).

Several reader reviews also gestured towards something of a ghostly saturation point. The 'large secondary cast' led to the mind of one reader 'wandering from the book' (GL11), while another observed that frequent shifts in point of view led to her feeling 'less connected to the story' (AL35), and yet another simply stated: 'What I hated: the ghosts. All of the damn ghosts' (GL9).

Readers who reacted positively to *Lincoln in the Bardo*'s ghosts made reference to its use of humour (e.g., 'I found myself flying through the story. [. . .] [H]ow funny some of them were' (GL85)) and the distinctive idiolects associated with the various characters ('The most human ghosts [. . .] you'll ever encounter! [. . .] And all of it is [. . .] in the emotional and flowery language of the era' (GL46)), as well as the homodiegetic narration that led to 'self-voicing ghosts' capable of 'engag[ing] emotion' (AL7) in the reader. Other positive reactions spotlighted the novel's genre, with several reviewers claiming that their interest in Abraham Lincoln and/or the American Civil War enhanced the reading experience, and that even though the novel took 'a little while to get the hang of', eventually they had the impression that they were 'hanging with a lot of ghosts in a graveyard at night' (AL69). From these comments, it may be suggested that overlaying what is widely considered fictional (i.e., ghosts) with details that are understood to be factual (for instance, concerning the American Civil War) may result in a more engaging and ultimately immersive reading experience. This suggestion that an individual in the actual world may imagine themselves to be imported into a fictional world – redolent of Martínez's (2014) notion of the storyworld possible self – gestures to the collapsing of ontological boundaries identified above as central to the experience of narrative immersion. Nonetheless, the connection between genre and narrative immersion is far from straightforward, as the further discussions relating to *Seven Moons* below capture.

The ghost of Galgut's *The Promise*, awarded the Booker Prize in 2021, does not appear until a substantial portion of the way through the novel. Moreover, this ghost plays a far less central role than its counterparts in *Lincoln in the Bardo*, or even *A Brief History*. Employing the typology of Chatman (1986), Galgut's ghost is an *interest-focus* rather than a more prominent *center* and/or *filter*.

The Promise follows the Swart family, white Afrikaners in post-apartheid South Africa, adopting the conceit that familial dynamics over the decades can be explored by way of vignettes of successive family funerals. While a total of four funerals are depicted across the novel, it is only the first character to depart, the Swart matriarch, who reappears as a ghost:

> The spirit of Rachel Swart, née Cohn, lingers around the house in a state of confusion. [. . .] It's not uncommon, the dead are frequently

> unable to accept their condition, they resemble the living in that respect, but they have forgotten what they're nostalgic for, much is lost in the crossing over, and when they see you they do not know you. [. . .]
>
> Eventually she tires of the house and becomes noticeable in the streets of Pretoria, in places she liked to visit. She paddles in the pond at Magnolia Dell, drinks tea at a café in Barclay Square. Looks through the fence of the Austin Roberts Bird Sanctuary [. . .].
>
> You get the idea. She touches down where her spirit was once thick, but she's no longer solid, a watercolour woman.
>
> (Galgut 2021: 43–4)

The narrative profile of this third ghost-focused passage differs from the pattern thus far established. Rather than a homodiegetic narrative employing (multiple) internal focalisation, the zero focalisation used across the novel momentarily adopts Rachel as the reflector of the fiction. This is apparent from the use of *verba sentiendi*, referencing how she appears 'in a state of confusion' and eventually 'tires of the house'. Outside the house, and as with *A Brief History*, the world-builders referenced are both explicit and ontologically dual. That is, each of the place names featured – 'Pretoria', 'Magnolia Dell', 'the Austin Roberts Bird Sanctuary' – have counterparts outside of the fictional context, in our actual world. The sole proper noun without an actual-world referent is the identifier for the ghost herself, 'Rachel Swart, née Cohn'. Note that here, once again, the ghost is assigned a maximally granular name – even one which accounts for the character in multiple iterations.

Despite the difference in narrative stance, the narration in this third ghost narrative, as with its two predecessors, is present tense (although it is possible that this patterning may merely reflect a vogue among contemporary novelists: see Shigematsu 2022). Furthermore, several chained universal statements appear, applicable beyond the bounds of the fictional context: 'the dead are frequently unable to accept their condition', 'they have forgotten what they're nostalgic for', 'much is lost in the crossing over'. Direct address recurs, as with the abrupt and metafictional 'You get the idea'. Finally, Galgut – much like James before him – employs figurative language in the description of his ghostly character. Rachel is described as 'a watercolour woman', which harnesses the conceptual metaphor A PERSON IS A PAINTING and maps the qualities of fragility, translucency, and etherealness onto the Swart ghost. Conceptual metaphors are commonly conceived as a means of understanding more abstract, or intangible, concepts by way of concrete and everyday entities. Following this logic, it is perhaps unsurprising that authors should choose to characterise their (notoriously intangible) ghosts through metaphor use.

Likely due to the relatively minor role played by the ghost character in *The Promise*, few readers made mention of it in their digital reviews. Of those who did, many were keen to attempt an explanation for the inclusion of a ghost character, considering the impact upon the novel's genre and whether it could be classified as magic(al) realist or fantastic. These negotiations were each tagged as *ghost-linguistic*, for while lacking in specificity, the genre-based preoccupation is still of analytical interest. Generic labels appear to be used as shorthand somehow excusing the inclusion of a ghost character, as with: 'There are also hints of magical realism when Galgut offers a POV of Rachel's ghost' (GP11). This aligns with Ryan's (1991) suggestion that our contextual knowledge of genre is brought to bear when processing literary texts, and that we are more readily accepting of elements that do not appear in our actual world if these elements are associated with a specific fictional genre.

When linguistic and stylistic features were explicitly mentioned in reviews of *The Promise*, discussion centred around the novel's narrative stance. One reader related how in the novel '[e]verything and everyone has a voice', and credited this multiple focalisation, along with the use of direct address, for ensuring that '[t]he reader is fully immersed in the plot' (GP30). Another deployed sophisticated metalanguage to comment upon 'the author's third person omniscient, head-hopping POV' that allowed the reader to be 'treated to the thoughts and feelings' of 'even ghosts', and ultimately 'fall into' the prose (GP7). This seems to contradict comments above, which aligned first-person, homodiegetic narration with immersion in fictional ghost stories featuring ghosts. Nonetheless, it is an impression shared by the *Financial Times* reviewer Skidelsky (2021), who suggests that Galgut's 'kind of hyper-omniscience [serves] to create an almost physical sense of immediacy', giving the reader a sense that they 'are there, in the room with the characters' – a clear expression of ontological conflation and thus immersion.

In October 2022, Shehan Karunatilaka's *The Seven Moons of Maali Almeida* was named winner of the 54th Booker Prize. The novel, an amalgam of experimental and historical fiction, black comedy, and murder mystery, charts the attempts of the eponymous Maali – formerly a war photographer, recently departed – to discover the identity of his murderer, and is set against the backdrop of Sri Lanka's civil war. Responding to the announcement of Karunatilaka's win, one Goodreads user suggested:

> If I had a nickel for every time the man booker prize was awarded to a book about ghosts navigating the afterlife in a country in political turmoil I'd have two nickels which isn't a lot but it's odd that it happened twice.
>
> (GS62)

She is correct – if only partially. At the time the review was left in January 2023, as explored above, four Booker Prize-winning novels within the previous ten years alone fit this epigrammatic description. Her implicit comparison, however, is to the winner of the Booker Prize from five years previously: Saunders' *Lincoln in the Bardo*, which has been credited by Karunatilaka as a source of inspiration for his later novel (The Booker Prizes 2022). This comparison is echoed by a fellow Goodreads user, who observes that *Seven Moons* 'might as well have been called "Maali in the Bardo"' (GS10) due to the novels' similar settings, inclusion of 'whimsical ghosts', and 'musings on mortality'. Stylistically, *Seven Moons* diverges from *Lincoln in the Bardo* in one key regard, as it adopts a second-person narrative stance throughout. The novel opens with the eponymous narrator awakening in a celestial visa office, as he ruminates:

> If you had a gravestone it would say:
>
> MALINDA ALBERT KABALANA
> 1955–1990
>
> [. . .] It started ages ago, a thousand centuries ago, but let's skip all those yesterdays and begin last Tuesday. It is a day you wake up hungover and empty of thought, which is true of most days. You wake up in an endless waiting room. You look around and it's a dream and, for once, you know it's a dream and you're happy to wait it out. All things pass, especially dreams.
>
> You are wearing a safari jacket and faded jeans and cannot remember how you got here. You wear one shoe and have three chains and a camera around your neck. The camera is your trusty Nikon 3ST, though its lens is smashed and its casing is cracked. [. . .] Time to wake up, Maali boy. You pinch yourself and it hurts, less like a short stab and more like the hollow ache of an insult. You are in a queue, shouting at a woman [. . .]. Who hasn't been furious at women behind counters before? Certainly not you.
>
> (Karunatilaka 2022: 1–2)

Otherwise, stylistic features in the novel parallel those identified in *Lincoln in the Bardo*, with many also recalling *A Brief History* and *The Promise*. The narration is once more present tense ('You pinch yourself and it hurts'), and, despite the second-person narrative stance, internally focalised (observe the *verba sentiendi* in '[y]ou [. . .] cannot *remember* how you got here'). The passage is threaded through with dark humour ('you are hungover and empty of thought, which is true of most days') as well as dialogic ('Time to wake up, Maali boy'). Once again, the ghostly protagonist is assigned a fully realised proper noun as name, one which is typographically foregrounded from the first through capitalisation and centre alignment.

In this passage, too, ghostliness is captured with recourse to figurative language; Maali's pinches 'hurt, less like a short stab and more like the hollow ache of an insult'. There is an explicit and ontologically dual world-building element ('Nikon 3ST'), alongside universal statements ('All things pass, especially dreams') and instances of double deixis (as with the rhetorical '[w]ho hasn't been furious at women behind counters before? Certainly not you'). Each of the triad help to yoke the fictional world that *Seven Moons* depicts to the actual world that the reader inhabits. This is also true of the *in media res* opening, which combines metaleptic direct address (although subtly, through the clitic '*let's* skip all those yesterdays') with proximal deixis ('begin *last* Tuesday').

Given the relative scarcity of second-person novels, many digital reader reviews made mention of this unusual narrative stance. Most significant were those that linked the novel's narrative profile with their reactions to its ghostly characters, as with: 'The story is written in second person, so you are really there, along for the ride with Maali as he navigates his afterlife and memories' (GS27). Indeed, this positive reaction to the use of second person was recurrent; two reviewers suggest that it results in the impression of a joint endeavour ('We enter the afterlife with him' (GS23); 'You and Maali's spirit are in the waiting room of a limbo-like afterlife' (GS56)), and another casts the 'narration from the second person' as the primary reason they were 'caught in from the very first sentences' and enjoyed 'the most exceptional reading experience of all time' (GS66). Overall, the consensus seems to be that the second-person pronoun is a conduit to ontological blurring, and resultantly narrative immersion. This chimes both with Herman's (2002: 345) assertion that doubly-deictic *you* leads to the 'conflation' of an actual reader 'with a fictional self', and Wydrzynska's argument (this volume), that second-person pronouns trigger ontological overlap by 'removing any separation between narrative levels'. Here, it should be noted that while there is no one-to-one mapping between an enjoyable and an immersive reading experience (Ryan 2022: 8), the two do seem to accord for online reviewers of this novel – as indeed is the case for each of the three novels examined above.

Nonetheless, not all reactions to *Seven Moons* were quite so effusive. In an interesting instance of a professional reviewer's response differing from the consensus among civilian readers, Owolade (2022) suggested that the second-person stance 'gives the narrative a slightly distancing effect, but it's compensated for by the sardonic humour [and] the vivid use of similes'. Recalling the stylistic features profiled above, reference to these latter two elements also recurred in digital reader responses. The novel's 'flash[es] of deadpan humour' were said to result in 'a thoroughly immersive reading experience in both this world and the next' (AS7). Meanwhile, the 'descriptive' (GS51) and 'meticulously crafted' (GS23) prose was credited with enhancing believability, with one reviewer writing: 'The vivid descriptions of the ghosts [. . .] left a pervasive eerie feeling and while reading it I began to imagine these lost souls floating around me too' (GS100). This anecdote clearly evidences conflation between distinct ontological levels, and resultantly immersion, as fictional entities are imagined to inhabit the real world.

However, this blurring of ontological boundaries – encouraged by the novel's inclusion of actual historical incidents, and enhanced by references to explicit and dual world-builders like the Nikon camera – was not unanimously approved of by readers. Some suggested that the inclusion of ghosts in the loosely factual tale was disrespectful, betraying low tolerance for 'nonsense tales of ghosts and the afterlife' (GS78) which detracted from the 'reading experience' (GS15). Another claimed that, despite being 'loaded with really interesting detail about the atrocities of the Sri Lankan civil war', it was ultimately '[g]lib', doing a poor job of navigating between the 'ghost world and the real world' (GS14). Once more, these reactions can be tied to readerly expectations surrounding genre – several of these latter reviewers appeared to expect a more traditional historical fiction narrative and were 'bamboozled' (GS14) by the inclusion of ghosts. The implication is that if readers can be willing to accept fictional ghosts, this is complicated by mitigating factors, including generic expectation. For instance, one reviewer gestured to a generic clash, suggesting that the novel's parts do not form a coherent whole: 'There is some incisive stuff about life in Sri Lanka [. . .] and the nature of the [civil] war and the regime, but for me the ghost story elements intervened too often' (GS15). The comment evokes Pavel's (1986: 93) notion of *maximal departure*, by which he understands the primed expectation of the unexpected in readers engaging with certain fictional genres, most especially those that emphasise 'the futility of real-world knowledge' (Ryan 1991: 58), as do, for instance, speculative and magic-realist novels. This theory could also account for the response of a *Lincoln in the Bardo* reader, who despite enjoying the story herself observed: 'an audience expecting answers from the book in regards to [*sic*] the world's practicalities and rules will come away extremely dissatisfied' (AL42). Ultimately, the implication is that fictional ghosts can be tolerated, even appreciated, but only in genres in which their presence is expected or considered somehow fitting. In certain contexts, readers are simply more accepting of the otherwise unbelievable.

Moreover, it should be noted that readers are alerted to novels' genres through text-internal 'genre cues' (Martínez 2014: 125), alongside paratextual features, including blurb, preface, and book jacket design. It is common for Booker Prize-winning novels to prominently feature a rosette announcing the accolade on their front cover, meaning that readers are alerted to this fact before beginning the book proper. Given the tendency for realist, so-called 'serious' works of literary fiction to be awarded the Prize (Adam 2022), it is possible that readers are primed from the first not to expect the inclusion of more fantastical elements. In turn, ghosts in this literary context may be received as jarringly out of place, and for this reason may trigger readerly disapproval more readily than in other contexts.

Ghost writing

There are numerous ways in which the authors James, Saunders, Galgut, and Karunatilaka could have chosen to present the ghosts that haunt their award-winning works of fiction. The high level of congruency between the stylistic strategies each have selected in doing so is therefore particularly striking. Indeed, coalescing the four novels into one ghostly whole, one could easily offer a blueprint, or prototype, of the Booker-winning narrative featuring ghosts: a novel written in the present tense, which adopts the ghost as internal focaliser – or, at the very least, a reflector of the fiction – and incorporates humour, direct address, dialogism, universal statements, ontologically-dual world-building elements, and metaphorical conceptualisations of the embodied experience of being a ghost. If there is any commonality between these disparate features, it is their capacity to override existing sceptical attitudes to ghosts in our actual world through the softening of the boundary between the world of the novel and the world of the reader. In turn, narrative immersion is encouraged as the reader is coaxed into accepting a shared reality. This is impressed by the privileging of ghost characters with (often maximally specific) proper names: in this way, readers are made to conceptualise these ghosts as if they were actual, living beings. Access to the ghosts' unique, subjective perspective (often couched in a distinctive idiolect) only enhances this impression. The ghosts are ultimately considered 'people with all the usual flaws and we are asked to care about them' (AL8).

Saliently, it is precisely the features listed above that are frequently spotlighted in responses to the four novels from both professional and civilian readers. While there is not, nor is there ever likely to be, perfect consensus among readers (Peplow 2014), these are the features continually credited for enabling immersion in the fictional world and ultimately enhancing the reading experience. Indeed, as one Goodreads user observed, the 'idea of in-betweenness' (GL14) has been thematically pivotal to the ghost story across the centuries, and it is precisely this liminality that is inherent in stylistic features which enable today's readers to 'connect' to and feel 'fascinated' (GL14) by modern-day ghost stories, despite remaining sceptical in everyday life.

References

Adam, N. (2022) 'How to win the Booker Prize: is there a formula for the "finest in fiction"?', *The Conversation*, 14 October 2022, available at <http://theconversation.com/how-to-win-the-booker-prize-is-there-a-formula-for-the-finest-in-fiction-191528>

Allington, D. (2016) '"Power to the reader" or "degradation of literary taste"? Professional critics and Amazon customers as reviewers of *The Inheritance of Loss*', *Language and Literature* 25 (3): 254–78.

Atencia-Linares, P. and Sebastián, M.Á. (2023) 'Narrative immersion as an attentional phenomenon', *Inquiry*: 1–25.

Baker, J.O. and Bader, C.D. (2014) 'A social anthropology of ghosts in twenty-first-century America', *Social Compass* 61 (4): 569–93.

Book Marks (2024) *Book Marks* website, available at <http://bookmarks.reviews>

The Booker Prizes (2022) 'Ten books that led Shehan Karunatilaka to *The Seven Moons of Maali Almeida*', *The Booker Prizes*, 21 October 2022, available at <http://thebookerprizes.com/the-booker-library/features/ten-books-that-led-shehan-karunatilaka-to-the-seven-moons-of-maali>
The Booker Prizes (2024) 'The Booker Prize', *The Booker Prizes*, available at <http://thebookerprizes.com/the-booker-prize>
Centre for Public Christianity (2021) 'Easter 2021 survey', *Public Christianity*, 26 March 2021, available at <http://www.publicchristianity.org/easter-2021-survey>
Chatman, S. (1986) 'Characters and narrators: filter, center, slant, and interest-focus', *Poetics Today* 7 (2): 189–204.
Clarke, D. (1991) 'Belief in the paranormal: a New Zealand survey', *Journal of the Society for Psychical Research* 57 (823): 412–25.
Dahlgreen, W. (2014) '"Ghosts exist", say 1 in 3 Brits', *YouGov*, 31 October 2014, available at <http://yougov.co.uk/politics/articles/10857-ghosts-exist-say-1-3-brits>
Doche, A. and Ross, A.S. (2023) '"Here is my shameful confession. I don't really 'get' poetry": discerning reader types in responses to Sylvia Plath's *Ariel* on Goodreads', *Textual Practice* 37 (6): 976–96.
Drąg, W. (2014) 'The Man Booker Prize and the emerging canon of contemporary British fiction', *Studia Litteraria Iagellonicae Cracoviensis* 9 (1): 17–28.
Galgut, D. (2021) *The Promise*. London: Vintage.
Genette, G. (1997) *Paratexts: Thresholds of Interpretation*. Cambridge: Cambridge University Press.
Goodreads (2024) *Goodreads* website, available at <http://www.goodreads.com>
Herman, D. (2002) *Story Logic: Problems and Possibilities of Narrative*. Lincoln: University of Nebraska Press.
Ipsos (1998) 'Paranormal survey', *Ipsos*, 1 February 1998, available at <http://www.ipsos.com/en-uk/paranormal-survey>
Ipsos (2021) 'Ghost encounters: nearly half of Canadians (46%) believe in supernatural beings; 13% have stayed at haunted hotel', *Ipsos*, 9 June 2021, available at <http://www.ipsos.com/en-ca/news-polls/ghosts-encounters-nearly-half-canadians-46-believe-supernatural-beings-13-have-stayed-haunted-hotel>
James, M. (2014) *A Brief History of Seven Killings*. London: Oneworld.
Karunatilaka, S. (2022) *The Seven Moons of Maali Almeida*. London: Sort of Books.
Keen, S. (2007) *Empathy and the Novel*. Oxford: Oxford University Press.
Lombard, M. and Ditton, T. (1997) 'At the heart of it all: the concept of presence', *Journal of Computer-Mediated Communication* 3 (2).
Martínez, M.-Á. (2014) 'Storyworld possible selves and the phenomenon of narrative immersion: testing a new theoretical construct', *Narrative* 22 (1): 110–31.
Nuttall, L. and Harrison, C. (2020) 'Wolfing down the *Twilight* series: metaphors for reading in online reviews', in H. Ringrow and S. Pihlaja (eds) *Contemporary Media Stylistics*. London: Bloomsbury, pp.40–60.
Owolade, T. (2022) '*The Seven Moons of Maali Almeida* by Shehan Karunatilaka review – life after death in Sri Lanka', *The Guardian*, 9 August 2022, available at <http://www.theguardian.com/books/2022/aug/09/the-seven-moons-of-maali-almeida-by-shehan-karunatilaka-review-life-after-death-in-sri-lanka>
Pavel, T. (1986) *Fictional Worlds*. Cambridge: Harvard University Press.
Peplow, D. (2014) '"I've never enjoyed hating a book so much in my life": the co-construction of identity in the reading group', in S. Chapman and B. Clarke (eds) *Pragmatic Literary Stylistics*. London: Palgrave, pp.152–71.

Ryan, M.-L. (1991) *Possible Worlds, Artificial Intelligence, and Narrative Theory*. Bloomington: Indiana University Press.

Ryan, M.-L. (2022) 'Immersion', in *Wörterbuch zur Sprach- und Kommunikationswissenschaft (WSK)*, Berlin: de Gruyter, available at <http://www.marilaur.info/immersion.pdf>

Saunders, G. (2017) *Lincoln in the Bardo*. London: Bloomsbury.

Schellenberg, S. (2013) 'Belief and desire in imagination and immersion', *Journal of Philosophy* 110 (9): 497–517.

Schenkel, E. (2016) 'Preface: ghosts – or the (nearly) invisible', in M. Fleischhack and E. Schenkel (eds) *Ghosts – or the (Nearly) Invisible*. Frankfurt: Peter Lang, pp.11–12.

Scott, E. (2024) 'Ghosts are suddenly in vogue. Perhaps we believe in them more than we care to admit', *The Guardian*, 1 January 2024, available at <http://www.theguardian.com/commentisfree/2024/jan/02/ghosts-are-suddenly-in-vogue-perhaps-we-believe-in-them-more-than-we-care-to-admit>

Shigematsu, E. (2022) 'Is it narration or experience? The narrative effects of present-tense narration in Ali Smith's *How to Be Both*', *Language and Literature* 31 (2): 227–42.

Skidelsky, W. (2021) 'A poisonous legacy: South African Damon Galgut's first novel for seven years is written with an immediacy that gives its themes more impact, says William Skidelsky', *Financial Times*, 19 June 2021, p.9.

Sotirova, V. (2007) 'Woolf's experiments with consciousness in fiction', in M. Lambrou and P. Stockwell (eds) *Contemporary Stylistics*. London: Continuum, pp.7–18.

Statista (2024) 'United States: belief in ghosts 2021', *Statista*, 9 August 2024, available at <http://www.statista.com/statistics/1271915/belief-in-ghosts-in-the-united-states>

Stockwell, P. (2009) *Texture: A Cognitive Aesthetics of Reading*. Edinburgh: Edinburgh University Press.

Stockwell, P. (2016) 'The texture of authorial intention', in J. Gavins and E. Lahey (eds) *World Building: Discourse in the Mind*. London: Bloomsbury, pp.147–64.

Stockwell, P. (2020) *Cognitive Poetics: An Introduction* (2nd edn). London: Routledge.

Tomczak, A.M. (2019) 'Bridging the narrative gap: the ghost narrator in Marlon James' *A Brief History of Seven Killings* (2014)', *Hungarian Journal of English and American Studies* 25 (1): 107–28.

Thomas, B. (2021) 'Reading the readers: ethical and methodological issues for researching readers and reading in the digital age', in A. Bell, S. Browse, A. Gibbons and D. Peplow (eds) *Style and Reader Response: Minds, Media, Methods*. Amsterdam: John Benjamins, pp.179–95.

van Urk, H. (2023) '"Good" South African literature: the Booker Prize, its infatuation with the postcolonial and Damon Galgut's *The Promise*', *English Studies in Africa* 66 (2): 11–18.

Wagner, E. (2017) '*Lincoln in the Bardo* is a stunning portrait of a violently divided America', *New Statesman*, 10 March 2017, available at <http://www.newstatesman.com/culture/2017/03/lincoln-bardo-stunning-portrait-violently-divided-america>

Werth, P. (1999) *Text Worlds: Representing Conceptual Space in Discourse*. Harlow: Longman.

CHAPTER 14

Autism, repetition, and flow in literary narratives

Andrew Currie

Currie, in this chapter, argues that by directing efforts towards understanding autistic and neurodivergent readers of fiction, we may uncover new forms of immersion that raise interesting questions. The chapter takes into consideration the flow states that autistic people can experience through repetitive behaviours and asks whether, for readers with cognitive traits associated with such behaviours, these states also emerge in response to extreme repetition in literary narratives. To explore this question, he constructs two idealised readers, drawing on research into autism and neurotypicality in relation to repetitive behaviours, and presents an analysis of one highly repetitive text, *Worstward Ho* by Samuel Beckett (published originally in 1983). Currie suggests that foregrounding devices like linguistic repetition may not always be experienced as defamiliarisation or 'disruption' to the reading process. Instead, he suggests that these devices have the potential to generate phenomenologically distinct immersive experiences for readers with different cognitive traits.

Introduction

As with other areas of cognitive literary research (for example, Faber et al. 2020) there has been increasing awareness of the importance of studying individual differences in readers when researching immersive reading experiences. Mak and Willems (2019) for example describe how individual differences in mental simulation abilities – including mentalising and perceptual and motor simulation – potentially shape how certain readers become immersed in a narrative text. Kuijpers et al. (2019) found that the presence or absence of certain personality traits, as well as individual differences in reading habits, can predict the extent to which a reader becomes immersed in a literary narrative text. Eekhof et al. (2021) found that differences in low-level processing abilities (e.g., sensitivity to word characteristics such as lexical frequency and length) and levels of book exposure can determine levels of narrative absorption. Such research contrasts sharply with how researchers of literary immersion and other phenomenon have typically worked in the past, studying general characteristics of reading processes and experiences applicable to all readers, to the exclusion of questions about variability and heterogeneity (van Peer et al. 2012, Alber and Strasen 2020). It is within this growing interest in inter-reader variation that this chapter situates its discussion of immersion.

In what follows, I suggest that accounting for neurodiversity can reveal new insights about literary immersion that more traditional cognitive literary approaches may not necessarily allow for. Many kinds of variations can exist between readers, including contextual factors such as the level of expertise, education, and personality traits, but one such variation I pay particular attention to is variation in neurotype. The term *neurotype* reflects the way certain cognitive traits cluster and are distributed across the human population, so that, for example, the clustering of traits related to social-communication and sensory processing differences may be associated with the neurotype of autism, and differences in verbal memory and processing speed with dyslexia (Hillary 2020: 92). In my own research, I explore what neurodiversity, and specifically autism, can say about literary reading, especially with regard to how belonging to a certain neurotype may yield different textual affordances for literary narratives. Neurodiversity, as both a concept and research paradigm, encompasses the notion that there is natural variation in how humans process information around them and in the world; neurotypes, then, are a reflection of how such differences cluster into certain diagnostic criteria for autism, ADHD, dyslexia, schizophrenia, and so on (Fletcher-Watson 2022). Adapting the theories of neurodiversity and autism to a literary context in this way challenges neuronormative assumptions about how literary texts are read and should be read, with the potential to acknowledge the dimensionality of readers' cognitive traits. It also has the potential to reveal experiences with literary texts that have gone undocumented so far.

In order to develop the main theoretical claims put forward here, I consider how having certain autistic traits related to 'repetitive behaviours' – a domain classically associated with the repetitive behaviours and interests (RRBIs) criterion of autism diagnoses (APA 2013) – may change the kind of affordances offered by one highly repetitive text, *Worstward Ho* (2009) by Samuel Beckett. I consider what qualitative aspects might make such a text immersive for readers with these traits, in ways different to a reader who lacks them. The text chosen offers up an interesting case study because of its extensive use of linguistic repetition, which, for a reader with neurotypical traits that reduce their tolerance for repetition, may be experienced as either anti-immersive or defamiliarising enough to elicit an immersive experience coloured by increased processing effort and difficulty. Yet, in a different context, since repetition forms a core aspect of how autistic people tend to engage with the world, it is worth asking whether a text with an extreme amount of repetition may yield different immersive effects for readers with the trait of engaging in repetition through autism. From such a case study, we could see that a stylistic feature not associated typically with immersion could unexpectedly generate immersion in this context, thus demonstrating the need for researchers to take into consideration variations between neurotypes. In the first part of the chapter, I outline the connections between autism, immersion, and repetition, with a particular focus on flow theory, which is both relevant to the study of autism and literary reading. First, I elaborate on the conceptual similarities between flow in autism and flow in reading, suggesting that their overlap can help theorise about the autistic flow responses in relation to reading. I then go on to discuss the nature of repetition in literary narratives, as it relates to repetitive behaviours in autism and the flow experiences it can generate. It is here that I suggest how studying neurodivergent differences in processing can change what is known about literary reading, with repetition and flow states being a case in point. In the last part of the chapter, I discuss repetition in *Worstward Ho*, and how readers with varying traits relative to autism and neurotypicality might respond to it.

Autism, repetition, and flow experiences as immersion

Flow theory in autism and literary reading

In what ways might autism generally connect with literary immersion? We can begin to answer this question by exploring recent work on autistic phenomenology as it relates to repetitive behaviours. From the outset we see that aspects of autistic phenomenology are already conceptually connected to literary immersion. This is reflected in recent research in 'autistic flow theory', initially developed by McDonnell and Milton (2014), who borrow from Csikszentmihalyi's (1990) original theory of flow states, which aims to characterise many of the behaviours witnessed in autism as instances of flow states being achieved (Heasman et al. 2024). Flow states, which are common in many activities, from gardening and rock-climbing to painting and, most relevant here, reading, entail the complete immersion in some given task or activity; phenomenological aspects of it include increased focus, engagement, and attention, losing awareness of oneself and of time, and a clear sense of ease, intrinsic enjoyment, and goal feedback in the task being performed (Csikszentmihalyi 1990). McDonnell and Milton (2014) use this theory to argue that many of the behaviours of autistic people that traditionally have been conceptualised as 'dysfunctional', 'non-adaptive', and 'pathological', and which parallel current diagnostic criteria for autism, may be designated as instances of autistic people entering flow states. Such behaviours can include pursuing highly specialised interests, seeking out rigid routines, engaging in ritualistic, repetitive 'stimming' behaviours, and being driven to seek certain sensory inputs. Heasman et al. (2024: 1) highlight that through such behaviours, caused by differences in sensory, social, and cognitive processing, and how attentional resources are allocated, autistic people are 'uniquely placed to discover and manage flow'. Flow activities are also important to many autistic people: they allow for sensory and emotional self-regulation in environments that are overwhelming and unpredictable by providing regularity, but they are also pursued for their intrinsic pleasure, enjoyment, and the sense of well-being and achievement they offer.

In a different context, flow theory has also played an important role in shaping our understanding of literary immersion during reading (Thissen et al. 2021). In many respects flow shares important conceptual components with other theories of immersion, such as feeling lost in the activity of reading, sustained attention, time dilation, and so on (Bilandzic and Busselle 2017: 24). However, flow theory can be thought as a unique construct with a specific application to literary reading, with various cognitive processes and phenomenological experiences associated with it. Thissen et al. (2021: 832) note how the various flow components formulated by Csikszentmihalyi mentioned above can be applied to literary reading, which, along with the components already defined so far, include the active and optimal construction of mental models of the text, and deep engagement with elements of the narrative, such as its characters and style.

However, beyond the apparent conceptual connections between autistic flow theory and flow experiences in reading, I wish to put forward a more specific case in which flow might be said to emerge that has broader implications for what we understand about literary immersion. Indeed, I suggest that the properties of flow in autism outlined above may, in fact, have the potential to shape and interact with processes and experiences of flow in reading. However, the particular context in which flow occurs – in the reading of highly repetitive literary narratives – may seem to run counter to what is currently understood about immersion in literary reading. In the next section, I discuss the ways in which literary narratives can become repetitive; this I connect to how neurodivergent processing styles – in this instance the traits associated with autism – could change the affordances of repetition, compared to readers with neurotypical traits, in such a way that connects autistic flow theory to literary immersion.

Repetition and immersion in literary narratives

We find repetition in a variety of different literary contexts, whether through rhyme and alliteration in poetry, in elements of rhetoric such as anaphora (repeating a word or phrase at the beginning of successive clauses) and epizeuxis (repeating the same word in immediate succession), in representations of speech discourse, or general pragmatic communication

(Pickstock 2019). Such elements can produce various effects as well, from processing fluency and positive aesthetic judgements like beauty or succinctness, to higher-order cognitive assessments about meaning and value. In many ways, repetition has the potential to draw readers further into the narrative of the text, by bringing about greater attention to the stylistic properties of a literary narrative (Kuijpers et al. 2017). Yet, if there is too much repetition such effects may be cancelled out. Pinning down precisely when individuals begin to subjectively perceive too much repetition is difficult, since there appears to be no empirically determined upper limit. Moreover, what is experienced as excessive repetition is highly context-dependent through various cultural and aesthetic norms (Fludernik et al. 2021). But there is good reason to presume that excessive repetition may either be disfavoured by readers, appearing as monotonous, difficult to process, or unnecessarily innovative. On the other hand, such repetition might provoke further interest, and subsequently immersion, by encouraging readers to engage in further cognitive mastery – a process found in other aesthetics involving artefact complexity and novelty (Graf and Landwehr 2017) – that explores the purpose of such repetition.

To demonstrate the effects of repetition on readers, we can consider the following passage, taken from Gertrude Stein's work 'A Long Gay Book' (1912). Like many of Stein's other works, the text is notoriously repetitive, as we can see below:

> George Clifton telling that a day is a day is telling it every day. George telling that a day is a day is telling it every day, is telling every day that a day is a day. George telling that any day is a day is telling that every day has been a day. George telling every day that a day is a day is telling every day that each day was a day.
>
> (Stein 2000: 37)

A reader who is aware of Stein's role in developing experimental modernist practices might come to appreciate the high levels of repetition in this passage and others. Working out why repetition is deployed in this manner might contribute to their experience of immersion in the passage, engaging in close attention to its thematic and stylistic significance through a process of cognitive mastery. However, arguably, a reader without such knowledge, nor a desire to contextualise the repetition, may find it disruptive. The passage repeats enough to ensure that no new information is being communicated, unless the reader engages in extra-cognitive processing to derive further information; it also removes fundamental narrative elements such as causality, temporality, and character agency as a result of the repetition. For these reasons, 'A Long Gay Book', and other books like it, might be considered anti-absorbative, or at least disruptive enough to warrant extensive attention directed towards understanding the purpose of such repetition. But to what extent does a response like this apply to all readers? Is there a possibility that some readers may actually find such repetition immersive, but without experiencing processing disfluency or defamiliarisation, instead undergoing an experience closer to what is reported in novels that are easier to read and contain less foregrounded repetition?

Autistic flow in response to repetition

As stated before, autism is highly heterogenous, meaning that how certain autistic traits are experienced differs widely in the population, so that accurately theorising and predicting autistic reader responses is difficult and requires caution. However, I argue that there is at least room to speculate that, for certain readers, being in possession of autistic traits related to repetition might change the way in which repetitive literary works are received, which in turn will have consequences for how flow is achieved. This point relates more generally to how neurodivergent processing styles can change the relative textual affordances of a text, just in the same way that possessing expertise or having a unique combination of personality traits can change how a text is received. Barber-Stetson (2014) for example considers the comparison that can be made between autistic processing styles, which can, at times, tend towards detail rather than gestalts, and modernist aesthetic practices, in which attention to sensory stimuli and linguistic fragmentation are foregrounded stylistically over narrative plot and action. Possessing certain autistic traits in this context might then allow the reader to circumvent the narrative difficulties presented by modernist compositional practices that disrupt global narrative processing, with Gertrude Stein being one example.

A particular set of traits I wish to draw attention to relates to sensory processing and repetitive behaviours, which was described earlier. A primary manifestation of this is stimming (Charlton et al. 2021). As stated before, for many autistic individuals, such behaviour is fundamental in helping regulate overstimulating sensory environments. But it is also sought for its intrinsic enjoyment and pleasure, and, most importantly, for its affordances to flow. One sensory domain in particular that is relevant is language. In the autobiography of autistic writer and advocate Donna Williams, she writes how engaging in repetitive sensory-seeking behaviours allowed her to 'lose myself in anything I desired', from observing patterns on wallpaper and tapping her chin to listen to the 'repetitive hollow sound' it produced. Included in this were words, as other people's 'words became a mumbling jumble, their voices a pattern of sounds. I could look through them until I wasn't there, and then, later, felt that I had lost myself in them' (Williams 1992, cited in Grohmann 2018). In a qualitative analysis of first-hand accounts of autistic sensory experiences, Jones et al. (2003: 113) quote one blogger's discussion of their relationship to language: 'I hear SOUNDS rather than WORDS (I then must think to recognise the words) and can often duplicate the sounds. [. . .] If I am absorbed in reliving, say a TV show, I will recite it to myself verbatim – and sometimes in the voice of the original actor – and I may do it repetitively many times, giggling at amusing moments as I go.'

On a related point, repetition can also be a source of pleasure and flow in aesthetic domains, suggesting a further connection between the aesthetic potential of repetition in literary works for readers with these specific autistic traits. Autistic blogger Lyric Rivera (2022) discusses how the pleasure and flow created by repetitive body movements (i.e., stimming) are enhanced by the rhythmicality and repetitiveness of music, and vice versa. Roth (2020) looks at the repetitive aesthetic practices of autistic artists, as it relates to repetition and immersion in autism, which are comparable to examples of repetition in works by artists like Andy Warhol. Lastly, in the domain of literature, repetition is also noted as a source of pleasure. In their collective, autoethnographic reading of *A Room Called Earth* (2020), by autistic author Madaleine Ryan, Rosqvist et al. (2023) note how its stylistic aspects feed into their own autistic reading tendencies, of which intense interest and concentration is one. They write: 'We think of the different textual pleasures in the ways of writing; the rhythm of the text, the sense of a particular textual texture (the density of the text/writing), and the pleasures of repetitions' (Rosqvist et al. 2023: 38). In particular, they cite several passages in the novel that use repetition: 'Lunging, and parlaying, and lunging, and parlaying'; 'Tick, tock, tick, tock'; 'It would have been rude to go, he said. It would've been rude' (Ryan 2020, cited in Rosqvist et al. 2023: 38). The authors note that these 'textures' form an important aspect of their embodied engagement with the text, and more broadly, along with other features of the book, their immersion in the world of *A Room Called Earth* (Rosqvist et al. 2023: 27, 39).

As we have seen from above, repetitive language in different contexts, from daily stimming to repetitive textual practices, has the potential to be a source of autistic flow for readers with certain autistic traits. Likewise autistic flow traits have the potential to modify and influence how repetitive language is received. We can thus speculate that readers with the trait of engaging in behaviours that induce flow through repetitive language might have a different perception of the same phenomenon in the context of literary narratives. Going back to the example of repetition in Stein's work, we might say that its repetitiveness – achieved through its duplication of lexical items and its piling-up of similarly structured relative clauses – could be a source of literary immersion, or flow with respect to a reader in possession of this trait. They may well find Stein's work a source of sensory and cognitive pleasure, in which they appreciate the rhythmicality of 'A Long Gay Book', its cadencies, and its complex linguistic patterns of repetition. On the other hand, a reader with the neurotypical trait of tolerating only lesser amounts of repetition may be struck with the feelings outlined earlier. In the next section, I expand these claims much further through an analysis of *Worstward Ho*, where we may see more clearly how an approach which considers neurodiversity in theorising about literary immersion can be revealing of new modes of literary engagement.

Worstward Ho

Like many of Beckett's later prose works, *Worstward Ho* (2009) is formally dense, with extensive use of grammatical deviation, a limited and highly abstract vocabulary, and a stripped back narrative almost devoid of any story elements. The story features an unspecified narrator, appearing as a disembodied voice who exists in a near-empty void and who attempts to define their existence (or non-existence) through a series of paradoxical negations. The narrator also attempts to describe the nature of the void that they occupy and the several figures, including a 'shade', an 'old man and child', and a 'woman', who populate it. In these attempts, the narrator provides a deeply philosophical and poetic meditation of the representational capacity of language, of failure and perseverance, and on the nature of being and silence. More significantly, though, the text is highly repetitive, as shall soon be revealed.

For all readers, it is likely that *Worstward Ho* would provide extensive reading challenges. But its affordances – especially with regard to its linguistic repetitions – may change how such challenges are perceived, and how they may achieve immersion, relative to the cognitive traits of a reader. Here, I provide two artificially constructed readers who have differing traits associated with different neurotypes. Setting forth an idealised or 'implied' reader or set of readers in analysing literary texts is a common method used in stylistics and other related fields (Whiteley and Canning 2017). However, to the knowledge of the author of this chapter, the type of imagined experimental idealisation set out here currently has no precedent and thus represents a novel approach to considering individual differences between readers with varying cognitive traits. Working with traits as opposed to contrasting a generically constructed 'autistic reader' and 'neurotypical' reader also avoids some of the risks in making assumptions about real groups of readers, given the heterogeneity of autism. For this reason, I present below the set of traits applicable to these different reader types; each trait is either associated or not with autism and neurotypicality:

Associated with neurotypicality:

- Trait (i) Does not engage in repetitive behaviours.
- Trait (ii) Does not experience flow when encountering repetition in language

Associated with autism:

- Trait (iii) Engages in repetitive behaviours and interests.
- Trait (iv) Experiences flow when encountering prolonged repetition of sensory/perceptual inputs related to language.

Throughout the analysis, I will assume that for each different abstract reader there are a set of traits that are applicable to them. This will mean that *Reader A*, for example, could have traits (i) and (ii), and *Reader B* has traits (iii) and (iv), and so on. To reiterate, these artificially constructed readers are not intended to be representative of how a specific neurotype would experience the text. Forms of neurodivergence like autism have a wide constellation of traits associated with them, meaning that whilst many autistic people might share the general trait of engaging in repetitive behaviours, more specific traits regarding the content of their repetitive behaviours and their subjective experiences of these behaviours will differ widely, a fact my analysis intends to capture.

With the above in mind, we can begin to analyse the potential responses of these readers who encounter *Worstward Ho*'s repetitions. Much of the text's repetitiveness can be found at various linguistic levels, through phonology, syntax, and larger discoursal patterns (e.g., the repetition of sentences across the course of the story), which often permutate into new combinations. Combined with other difficulties presented by its composition and themes, this repetitiveness will present various obstacles to reading, and significantly immersion, which we can illustrate with the passage below, taken from the beginning of *Worstward Ho*:

> First the body. No. First the place. No. First both. Now either. Now the other. Sick of the either try the other. Sick of it back sick of the either. So on. Somehow on. Till sick of both. Throw up and go. Where neither. Till sick of both. Throw up and go. Where neither. Till sick of there. Throw up and back.
>
> (Beckett 2009: 81)

From what can be interpreted here narratively, the narrator tries with some difficulty to explain or articulate the world (the 'dim void' (Beckett 2009: 91)) around them. They vacillate between describing the 'body' first or the 'place' first, suggesting that both are in a process of construction through language in the narrator's mind, thus signalling their near immateriality. The narrator then acknowledges the futility of this exercise (e.g., 'Till sick of both') and urges to 'Throw up and go', in much the same manner that they try to define their existence through words: 'The void. How try say? How try fail? No try no fail. Say only –' (Beckett 2009: 86).

Putting aside their responses to the passage's thematic elements and other compositional practices, *Reader A* with traits (i) and (ii) will likely notice that the passage, along with many others, is highly repetitive. This reader will be aware that various linguistic units are repeated alternately, falling into different combinations using parallelism. Sentences one and three repeat the same adverbial modifier 'First' (although this is more ambiguous due to the absence of context), the determiner 'the', and the nouns 'body' and 'place', as well as repeating the ellipses of a verb phrase, making them incomplete syntactically. Sentences two and four repeat the same lexical unit also. We can assume that such repetitions for *Reader A* will be perceived as a significant departure from the norms of language they are accustomed to in more traditional literary narrative texts, and even more experimental ones. This has the potential to generate different responses. They may find this repetition irrelevant, meaningless, or deliberately frustrating, particularly since it communicates information that they will already know. Subsequently, they may engage in a form of shallow processing, in which they do not commit extra processing effort towards understanding why repetition is being used extensively (Harash 2022). This could have the capacity of lowering *Reader A*'s feelings of immersion, which often requires deeper processing of the text. On the other hand, they might be drawn to the very fact that the passage's repetitiveness is difficult for them, generating a process of disambiguation, or a sense of strikingness, that draws them further into the text, thus increasing their sense of immersion. At a phenomenological level, though, this experience of immersion will be characterised by a conscious awareness of the text itself that can be called 'artifact absorption' (Kuijpers et al. 2017: 39), as opposed to being absorbed by the content of the text.

Reader B with traits (iii) and (iv), however, could have a very different experience. Their response can be broken down into different areas of cognitive processing. At the sensory-perceptual level, *Reader B* may be able to tap into the passage and *Worstward Ho*'s sound-based affordances generated through repetition. This is because, as was mentioned in previous sections, some autistic people are able to perceive the acoustic qualities of language signals more easily, such that more attention is shifted towards its sensory-perceptual qualities and less to its semantic dimensions, as is the case for Donna Williams. Importantly, such acoustic signals can also be source of pleasure and flow, particularly when it is repeated. For *Reader B*, then, in contrast to *Reader A*, their processing of the passage is not entirely geared towards communication and meaning, but rather to its sound-based aspects, because their attentional resources are geared towards processing lower-level perceptual information. Rather than experiencing the passage and text as some deviation from the norms of communication, they perceive far more easily its sound-based aspects. Based on this, they might, for example, be able to perceive the passage's constituent sounds, such as its patterns of alternating and repeating phonemes in the first several sentences, in the repetition of words 'First the' and 'No', or in the repetition of plosives in 'Sick of the either try the other. Sick of it back sick of the either' and 'Till sick of both.' As they progress through the passage, they will encounter more repetitions, either from material repeated earlier in the passage, or in new forms of repetition. Linguistic repetition in the passage could, at that point, be similar to how the repetition of linguistic signals might be experienced in the real world, whether through the reader's own vocalisations or in the language production of others, and of the flow or immersion they consequently obtain. Given this, *Reader B* might be able to experience flow with the passage and the text overall, in a manner that is distinct from *Reader A*'s experience. This, we can say, could be a fundamentally new experience of immersion that has not been investigated before – one in which devices that are commonly associated with slower, effortful processing induce a form of immersion associated with 'backgrounding' processes (Jacobs 2015). What is crucial is the fact that these backgrounding processes are linked to the language itself.

We can add further dimensions to the responses of both readers as they progress through the text. I mentioned above that *Reader A* could undergo 'artefact absorption', following their allocation of attentional resources to the meaning of repetition in *Worstward Ho*. This could entail trying to figure out the intentions of Beckett – a common response to forms of linguistic deviation (Kuijpers et al. 2017) – which will likely increase cognitive load and thus increase their mental involvement with the text (Bálint et al. 2016). Consider the following passage taken from the middle of *Worstward Ho*: 'On. Stare on. Say on. Be on. Somehow on. Anyhow on. Till dim gone. At long last gone. All at long last gone. For bad and all. For poor best worse and all' (Beckett 2009: 90). This passage also happens to repeat a similar paragraph at the beginning of the novel: 'On. Say on. Be said on. Somehow on. Till nohow on. Said nohow on' (Beckett 2009: 81). Both extracts produce the repetition of similar sentence structures (a verb followed by a preposition) and lexical items that relate to action. *Reader A* could engage in a process of interpretative activity in order to understand the function or purpose of these repetitions. They could, for example, form a connection between the use of action verbs and their repetition between sentences and different parts of the story to one of the major themes of *Worstward Ho*: the desire for action and moving forward in the face of failure, or endurance of the existential anxieties which characterise the human condition (e.g., 'Try again. Fail again. Fail better' (Beckett 2009: 81)). Interpretative activity of this sort is known to produce immersion for readers, despite at times increasing cognitive load and processing effort, and for that reason *Reader A* experiences immersion through such activity (Bálint et al. 2016).

However, *Reader B*'s response could involve a lowered sense of cognitive load, as their attention is directed towards processing repetitive acoustic stimuli, perhaps even experiencing ease and a sense of control, which are elements found in flow experiences. In some respects, reading *Worstward Ho* may even be more akin to listening to music. A relevant finding in the psychology of music is that repetition in language is known to musicalise, which we find in the 'speech-to-song' illusion for example, whereby if spoken phrases are repeated enough, they begin to be perceived as song (Margulis 2013a). Elsewhere, Margulis (2013b: 162) has suggested that the 'shift, effected by repetition, away from what is directly captured by words and toward what is revealed by the structure, prosody, rhythm, and tempo of the utterance of the words, is essentially a shift toward a musical way of listening'. On a related point, Frattarola (2018: 143) also notes this quality about Beckett's works, writing that, in his quest to test the semantic limits of language and its referential capacities, Beckett makes it his goal to strip 'words of their referents so that the reader can aesthetically experience the acoustic qualities of language'. Incidentally, Frattarola (2018) also refers to the speech-to-song illusion as a quality of Beckett's repetitions throughout his prose. Because of their strong predisposition towards processing linguistic signals purely by their acoustic qualities, *Reader B* is able more easily to tap into these 'acoustic qualities of language' found in *Worstward Ho*'s repetitions in a manner which parallels the speech-to-song illusion. However, *Reader B* might not just experience an awareness of Beckett's musicality, as some neurotypical readers might feel, but an experience of flow, because they are already predisposed to achieve this state with linguistic repetition. This is not to suggest that no reader without *Reader A*'s cognitive traits cannot have the same experience, but a reader with traits associated with neurotypicality that affects their ability to shift attention downwards towards perceptual information may find achieving immersion in this manner harder. Overall, the flow state that emerges for *Reader B* may in fact share more resemblance to the flow states that can be achieved through music listening (Loepthien and Leipold 2022).

One last comparison I would like to make concerns the different dynamics of reading that modelled readers' experience which underpins their sense of immersion and flow. These dynamics connect to the role that action, perception, and agency play in reading. One typical response to stylistic foregrounding that has been recorded is the reduced sense of control over reading and comprehension. In their study, Bálint et al. (2016) note that many readers can feel a reduction in their own sense of agency when they encounter textual features that are difficult, as many of their own readers had done in the study they conducted for their publication. This is relevant, evidently, to the use of repetition in *Worstward Ho*. *Reader A* may feel a lack of control over their own reading processes as their comprehension skills as well as their ability to appreciate the text are challenged. But there is a more important consequence to this reduced sense of agency. Being unable to read fluently or with full control might have the potential to create a more fragmented, less holistic experience of immersion. As stated earlier, repetition can disrupt the structures of causality and temporality that are key to reading processes in forming a coherent overall narrative experience. In a more fundamental sense, it can even disrupt typical patterns of motor action that readers must perform whilst reading. Linguistic foregrounding is known to produce more eye saccade regressions (van den Hoven et al. 2016), and deviant linguistic repetition might be capable of inducing similar behaviour, despite the common understanding that repetition can enhance predictive processing. We could thus hypothesise that in the real world a reader similar to *Reader A* could experience the text in a fragmented manner, both in terms of constructing a mental model of the narrative and in how they act upon the text through bodily action, despite the sense of immersion they achieve through more conscious and deliberative narrative processing strategies. On the other hand, a reader similar to *Reader B* could experience flow and immersion in response to the text in a more holistic and fluid manner, despite the presence of deviant linguistic repetition. In some senses, this type of reader can be said to have a more participatory role in the process of reading, which relates to how they engage in repetitive behaviours in the real world. Their ability to act on the repetitions at a purely sensory level allows them to experience a sense of control – a key dimension of flow experiences – in the way they might, for example, engage in stimming, as both action (through eye movements) and thought are able to merge more seamlessly – another dimension of flow experiences (Heasman et al. 2024). In this way, despite the difficulties that some autistic people can face in integrating multisensory information, which can often lead to subjectively experiencing the self as fragmented, *Reader B* may, as McDonnell and Milton (2014) suggest, be able to derive the sense of wholeness and unity that flow states create, despite encountering a text which tends towards linguistic fragmentation.

Conclusion

This chapter presented a hypothetical situation involving two imagined readers with differing processing traits respective to two different neurotypes – autism and neurotypicality. These traits were defined in relation to whether the reader engages in repetitive behaviour and experiences immersion in response to repetitive language. This textual feature was chosen because of its conceptual relevance to autism and because of its challenging nature in certain contexts. In the first part of the chapter, I highlighted the pre-existing connections between accounts of flow states in autism and literary reading, which set the ground for discussing how the chapter's hypothetical readers might respond to *Worstward Ho*'s excessive repetition. In the abstract system of differing responses set out in the analysis, it was suggested that *Reader A* would experience either 'artefact' absorption or a form of engagement associated with Harash's (2022) model of failed foregrounding; *Reader B*, on the other hand, would undergo an experience similar to what is reported in autistic flow accounts. It was the hope of this analysis to suggest how neurodivergent differences might change the relative affordances of a literary text.

There are, however, some limitations that should be mentioned. The chapter has tried to avoid making any empirical claims as to how real readers with autism diagnoses would experience immersion in response to certain textual features – in this instance, repetition. It has attempted to work with a model that is, in many respects, far removed from the real-life complexity of actual autistic readers' experience of fiction. This is reflected in the fact that the chapter has focused on only two of a vast array of cognitive traits that characterise both autism and neurotypicality. There remains still further scope to analyse more complex hypothetical readers with additional traits and even combinations of traits across different neurotypes.

However, through its thought exercise, the chapter has been able to provide suggestions for how researchers can begin to consider neurodivergent differences in their research, particularly in relation to immersion. This is especially important given what was described at the beginning of this chapter: that researchers, in their idealisation of readers, often presume neurotypicality as a default condition of reading, and understand neurodivergence as deviations from such idealisations. For example, Zunshine's (2006) influential discussion of theory of mind in literature uses autism and, according to her account, its supposed 'deficits' in this area to demonstrate that our appreciation of other minds in fiction would be severely hampered if we lacked this cognitive ability (though note that Zunshine's more recent work has moved away from this perspective on autism). This of course then presumes that literary reading can only be enjoyed by neurotypical readers, and in empirical research (Chapple et al. 2023) this has been challenged, especially with respect to theory of mind, where the supposed deficits do not appear to exist and can be framed instead as differences from neurotypical norms regarding social behaviours.

This chapter has also offered a set of ideas that, through further refinement and hypotheses construction, could be testable in the future. Some of the ideas are being developed in my own research, as mentioned, through qualitative investigation into adult autistic experiences with fiction (serving as a useful basis for future research in this area). Relevant to this chapter, I have found that many of the components thought to be crucial to immersion, such as vivid imagination and strong emotional connection to characters (in Green and Brock's (2000) account of 'transportation'), do not appear to be involved in some of these participants' experiences of immersion; for other participants, such components are critical to attaining immersion, again reflecting the wide heterogeneity of autism and reading generally, although whether this characterises only autistic readers or readers generally needs further scrutiny. A future study related to this project will build on the ideas developed here to more fully address whether real readers, autistic and neurotypical, experience the repetition in the manner described in this chapter.

References

Alber, J. and Strasen, S. (2020) 'Empirical literary studies: an introduction', *Anglistik* 31 (1): 5–14.

American Psychiatric Association (2013) *Diagnostic and Statistical Manual of Mental Disorders: DSM-5* (5th edn). Washington: American Psychiatric Association.

Bálint, K., Hakemulder, F., Kuijpers, M.M., Doicaru, M.M. and Tan, E.S. (2016) 'Reconceptualizing foregrounding: identifying response strategies to deviation in absorbing narratives', *Scientific Study of Literature* 6 (2): 176–207.

Barber-Stetson, C. (2014) 'Slow processing: a new minor literature by autists and modernists', *Journal of Modern Literature* 38 (1): 147–65.

Beckett, S. (2009) 'Worstward Ho', in D. van Hulle (ed.) *Company, Ill Seen Ill Said, Worstward Ho, Stirrings Still.* London: Faber and Faber, pp.79–104.

Bilandzic, H. and Busselle, R. (2017) 'Beyond metaphors and traditions: exploring the conceptual boundaries of narrative engagement', in F. Hakemulder, M.M. Kuijpers, E.S. Tan, K. Bálint and M.M. Doicaru (eds) *Narrative Absorption.* Amsterdam: John Benjamins, pp.11–27.

Chapple, M., Davies, P., Billington, J. and Corcoran, R. (2023) 'Exploring the different cognitive, emotional and imaginative experiences of autistic and non-autistic adult readers when contemplating serious literature as compared to non-fiction', *Frontiers in Psychology* 14: 1001268.

Charlton, R.A., Entecott, T., Belova, E. and Nwaordu, G. (2021) '"It feels like holding back something you need to say": autistic and non-autistic adults accounts of sensory experiences and stimming', *Research in Autism Spectrum Disorders* 89 (11): 101864.

Csikszentmihalyi, M. (1990) *Flow: The Psychology of Optimal Experience.* London: Harper Collins.

Eekhof, L.S., Kuijpers, M.M., Faber, M., Gao, X., Mak, M., Van Den Hoven, E. and Willems, R.M. (2021) 'Lost in a story, detached from the words', *Discourse Processes* 58 (7): 595–616.

Faber, M., Mak, M. and Willems, R. (2020) 'Word skipping as an indicator of individual reading style during literary reading', *Journal of Eye Movement Research* 13 (3): 1–9.

Fletcher-Watson, S. (2022) 'Transdiagnostic research and the neurodiversity paradigm: commentary on the transdiagnostic revolution in neurodevelopmental disorders by Astle et al.', *Journal of Child Psychology and Psychiatry* 63 (4): 418–20.

Fludernik, M., Middeke, M. and Buchleitner, A. (2021) 'Symmetry, proportion and seriality: the semantics of mirroring and repetition in science and the arts. Introduction to special issue', *European Review* 29 (2): 159–62.

Frattarola, A. (2018) *Modernist Soundscapes: Auditory Technology and the Novel.* Oxford: Oxford University Press.

Graf, L.K.M. and Landwehr, J.R. (2017) 'Aesthetic pleasure versus aesthetic interest: the two routes to aesthetic liking', *Frontiers in Psychology* 8 (15): 00015.

Green, M.C. and Brock, T.C (2000) 'The role of transportation in the persuasiveness of public narratives', *Journal of Personality and Social Psychology* 79 (5): 701–21.

Grohman, T. (2018) 'Hypnotic experience and the autism spectrum disorder. A phenomenological investigation', *Phenomenology and the Cognitive Sciences* 17 (5): 889–909.

Harash, A. (2022) 'The model of failed foregrounding', *Psychology of Aesthetics, Creativity, and the Arts* 16 (4): 594–609.

Heasman, B., Williams, G., Charura, D., Hamilton, L.G., Milton, D. and Murray, F. (2024) 'Towards autistic flow theory: a non-pathologising conceptual approach', *Journal for the Theory of Social Behaviour* 54: 469–97.

Hillary, A. (2020) 'Neurodiversity and cross-cultural communication', in H.B. Rosqvist, N. Chown and A. Stenning (eds) *Neurodiversity Studies: A New Critical Paradigm.* Abingdon: Routledge, pp.91–107.

Jacobs, A.M. (2015) 'Neurocognitive poetics: methods and models for investigating the neuronal and cognitive-affective bases of literature reception', *Frontiers in Human Neuroscience* 9: 1–22.

Jones, R.S.P., Quigney, C. and Huws, J.C. (2003) 'First-hand accounts of sensory perceptual experiences in autism: a qualitative analysis', *Journal of Intellectual and Developmental Disability* 28 (2): 112–21.

Kuijpers, M., Douglas, S. and Kuiken, D. (2019) 'Personality traits and reading habits that predict absorbed narrative fiction reading', *Psychology of Aesthetics, Creativity, and the Arts* 13 (1): 74–88.

Kuijpers, M.M., Hakemulder, F., Bálint, K., Doicaru, M.M. and Tan, E.S. (2017) 'Towards a new understanding of absorbing reading experiences', in F. Hakemulder, M.M. Kuijpers, E.S. Tan, K. Bálint and M.M. Doicaru (eds) *Narrative Absorption.* Amsterdam: John Benjamins, pp.29–48.

Loepthien, T. and Leipold, B. (2022), 'Flow in music performance and music-listening: differences in intensity, predictors, and the relationship between flow and subjective well-being', *Psychology of Music* 50 (1): 111–26.

McDonnell, A. and Milton, D. (2014) 'Going with the flow: reconsidering "repetitive behaviour" through the concept of "flow states"', in G. Jones and E. Hurley (eds) *Good Autism Practice: Autism, Happiness and Wellbeing.* Glasgow: BILD Publications, pp.38–47.

Mak, M. and Willems, R.M. (2019) 'Mental simulation during literary reading: individual differences revealed with eye-tracking', *Language, Cognition and Neuroscience* 34 (4): 511–35.

Margulis, E.H. (2013a) 'Repetition and emotive communication in music versus speech', *Frontiers in Psychology* 4: 00167.

Margulis, E.H. (2013b) *On Repeat: How Music Plays the Mind.* Oxford: Oxford University Press.

Pickstock, C. (2019) 'Repetition', *Oxford Research Encyclopaedia of Literature*, 22 November 2019, available at <https://doi.org/10.1093/acrefore/9780190201098.013.1088>

Rivera, L. (2022) 'Rhythmic stimming – stimming with music – my autistic neurodivergent experience', *Neurodivergent Rebel: Refusing Assimilation into Neurotypical Society*, 16 November 2022, available at <https://neurodivergentrebel.com/2022/11/16/rhythmic-stimming-stimming-with-music-my-autistic-neurodivergent-experience>

Rosqvist, H.B., Nygren, A. and O'Donoghue, S. (2023) 'Earthlove – theorising neurodivergent reader love of *A Room Called Earth*', *Journal of Language, Literature and Culture* 70 (1): 25–37.

Roth, I. (2020) 'Autism, creativity and aesthetics', *Qualitative Research in Psychology* 17 (4): 498–508.

Stein, G. (2000) 'A long gay work', in *Matisse, Picasso, and Gertrude Stein, with Two Shorter Stories* [1912]. New York: Dover Publications.

Thissen, B.A.K., Schlotz, W., Abel, C., Scharinger, M., Frieler, K., Merrill, J., Haider, T. and Menninghaus, W. (2021) 'At the heart of optimal reading experiences: cardiovascular activity and flow experiences in fiction reading', *Reading Research Quarterly* 57 (3): 831–45.

van den Hoven, E., Hartung, F., Burke, M. and Willems, R.M. (2016) 'Individual differences in sensitivity to style during literary reading: insights from eye-tracking', *Collabra: Psychology* 2 (1): 1–16.

Whiteley, S. and Canning, P. (2017) 'Reader response research in stylistics', *Language and Literature* 26 (2): 71–87.

Zunshine, L. (2006) *Why We Read Fiction: Theory of Mind and the Novel.* Ohio: Ohio State University Press.

CHAPTER 15

Embodied cognition in *Emergency Skin*

Jessica Norledge

This chapter examines the representation of cybernetic consciousness and (dis)embodied cognition in N.K. Jemisin's *Emergency Skin*. Though the nameless, faceless, and seemingly skin-less narratee is positioned as focaliser – the character who 'sees' throughout the course of the text – the reader has only secondary access to their thoughts and reactions, being guided instead by 'a dynamic-matrix consensus intelligence': a collective, distributed voice implanted within the character's mind. Consequently, the reader is required to project into the mind of the narratee, immersing themselves in the fiction in order to imagine the unspoken responses of the protagonist and comprehend narrative events. Taking a mixed cognitive stylistic and cognitive narratological perspective, Norledge explores the ways in which the text invites such immersion and encourages the reader to model consecutively the posthuman mind of the narratee and the synthetic non-human mind of the narrator.

Introduction: skin is the key

This chapter examines the immersive modelling of cybernetic consciousness and (dis)embodied cognition in N.K. Jemisin's *Emergency Skin*, one of six original narratives comprising the *Forward* collection, a unique set of science-fiction stories curated by best-selling author Blake Crouch. Published digitally in 2019, the collection responds to a series of questions posed by Crouch, whose attention was turned, in the years prior to *Forward*'s release, to topics of technical advancement and discovery and the various ambiguities such progression might present. 'How', for example, 'does anyone know at the moment of discovery where their work will ultimately lead? Should we let that uncertainty stop forward momentum or do we roll the dice and let the chips fall where they may? How does it feel to change the world?' (Crouch 2019: 36). These are the questions that inspired *Forward*'s creation and defined the collection's thematic impetus, with Crouch commissioning each of his five contributors to explore 'the resounding effects of a pivotal technological moment' (Crouch 2019: 36). Alongside the companion narratives of Veronica Roth, Paul Tremblay, Amor Towels, Andy Weir, and Crouch himself, Jemisin's *Emergency Skin* stands as a self-contained response to this prompt, extrapolating the future lives of those inhabiting our planet following apocalyptic upheaval.

In *Emergency Skin*, the moment of the world's apparent cataclysm precedes the narrative present by a number of years, being defined by the narrator – an advanced form of artificial intelligence (AI) – in terms of environmental collapse. The Earth, now referred to as Tellus, is introduced as a 'graveyard world', which, as a result of overpopulation and ecological decay, has become inhospitable to life: 'its seas have become acidic and barren, its atmosphere a choking mix of carbon dioxide and methane'. The rain cycle has long since dried up and the planet's surface houses only 'toxic drowned cities, still burning underground coal fires, [and] melted-down nuclear plants' (Jemisin 2019: 5). Or so it is believed. These statements, which offer a text-initial description of Tellus, are purely speculative, presenting the expectations of the narrating AI as they brief an unnamed narratee, commissioned by 'the Founders' – the new world's ruling elite – to return to a seemingly ruined Earth.

The narratee, from whom we never see or hear directly, is tasked with retrieving samples of HeLa from Tellus' remains. HeLa is an immortal cell line that was collected without consent during the treatment of Henrietta Lacks, an African American woman who died of cervical cancer in the actual world in October 1951. Since this time, HeLa has been instrumental in various advances in real-world biomedical research, enabling among other things the eradication of polio, the testing of various cancer treatments, and the development of HPV vaccines. The manipulation of HeLa marks the discovery that drives Jemisin's narrative, as the collection and use of HeLa cultures within the narrative opens up questions around race, consent, and sociopolitical power. Such topics are often marked in Jemisin's work, which through the presentation of new and textured possible worlds grapples with dominant sociocultural stereotypes and inequalities. *Emergency Skin*, like Jemisin's Hugo Award-winning *Broken Earth* series, for example, champions marginalised communities and, in so doing, highlights the persistence of structural racism in the present day against the backdrop of a speculative ecodystopian future (Norledge 2024; see also Ferrández San Miguel 2020, Morris 2019).

Within the world of the fiction, HeLa appears to be one of several materials used to grow or fashion human skin; rather than being a natural part of the human body, this is gifted only to those who are deemed deserving. The offer of skin – which is upheld as a mark of honour – serves as incentive to the narratee, who (having no face or identifying features) is to be rewarded with a complete body on successful return to their home planet. They are promised a noble brow, classical patrician features, blonde hair, lean musculature, a long penis, and long thighs, all of which project stereotypical markers of white Caucasian beauty. Whiteness is clearly prized by the Founders, as are features of archetypal masculinity, both of which are emphasised and standardised by the Founder's 'technorati' through eugenics and artificial modes of procreation.

The narratee, who is a member of a lower militia class, has been modified through such experimentation, and exists without physical edges, 'floating' inside a composite body. It is unclear what exactly this composite body looks like, aside from its having 'facial beads' and a markedly absent mouth. The narratee does appear to possess some form of physicality, however, with the AI reporting on the character's strong muscles and fine motor control, though it is unclear whether these features belong to an unseen alien body, or to the composite suit in which the mind of the narratee is seemingly housed.

The exact nature of this embodiment is also ambiguous. The protagonist is fully sentient, 'unimpeded by the voyages of organic dysfunction and bolstered by generations of high-intelligence breeding' (Jemisin 2019: 4). They are also the one who 'sees' throughout the course of the text. Reason would dictate, then, that the character must have eyes or some form of sensory organs with which to perceive the world. Accordingly, such organs must be attached to a biological organism with a central nervous system. Yet, without skin to contain such a system, the somatic identity of the narratee does raise an intriguing question: How are we to conceptualise an experiencing body that is, potentially, bodyless? Taking a mixed cognitive stylistic and cognitive narratological perspective, I present a possible answer to this question.

Drawing upon deictic shift theory (Duchan et al. 1995) alongside narratological approaches to situated and social cognition, I explore the estranging relationship between the posthuman body and the posthuman mind in Jemisin's text, investigating the peculiar dynamic between the distributed, collective consciousness of the AI and the (dis)embodied consciousness of the protagonist. In examining how such minds are conceptualised, synthesised, and opposed, I consider the ways in which internal homodiegetic narration, performative second-person address, and metafictional textual deixis combine to create a highly complex futuristic mind. In so doing, I argue for the immersive enactment such construal necessitates, analysing the ways in which the narrative not only invites but positively requires readerly projection into *Emergency Skin*.

Beautiful you

Contemporary research on language and cognition contends that the mind is embodied, embedded, enacted, and extended, these being the four components of 4E cognition (see Newen et al. 2020a, Anderson, this volume).

As argued by Dancygier (2014: 213), '[p]roponents of theories of embodiment and situated cognition claim that the mind is influenced by the body in that embodied experience and situated action are the primary sources of material for conceptualisation, including the conceptualisation of emotions and abstract concepts'. Throughout the narrative, the narratee is seen to experience such emotions: they feel excitement when embarking from their ship (they can, notably, distinguish this from feelings of fear); they marvel at the beauty of their first sunset; and they become increasingly angry at the AI as they comprehend the reality of a flourishing, almost utopian, Earth. Following cognitive logic, the ability to hold such emotions and comprehend abstract concepts – particularly in relation to bodily experience – signal an embodied mind. We also understand that '[p]eople's subjective, felt experiences of their bodies in action provide part of the fundamental grounding for language and thought' (Gibbs 2005: 9), and the narratee is evidently capable of both, communicating non-verbally with the AI and later (with the aid of a digital translator) to the people of Tellus. The reader has only secondary access to the narratee's speech and thought, however, with their responses being realised through the language of the AI, signalled in the text through the intricate workings of *perceptual* and *textual deixis*.

Perceptual deixis signals a perceiving consciousness, with perceptual deictic markers typically aligning with a particular *deictic centre* or *origo* (Bühler 1982). Personal pronouns such as 'I' and 'you' are markers of perceptual deixis: they are speaker-dependent, shifting their meaning according to context of use. Both the first- and second-person referents presented in *Emergency Skin* are unusual, with the AI being marked by the first-person plural pronoun 'we' and the narratee being marked by a fictionalised 'you'. *Fictionalised address*, according to Herman (1994: 381), 'entails address to and/or by the members of some fictional world'. The address of the 'you' in *Emergency Skin* clearly aligns with this categorisation, signalling communication between enactors: between the internal narrator and an invisible internal narratee. However, this relationship is not immediately evident, with the second-person pronoun initially appearing to be *apostrophic* (Herman 1994).

At the beginning of the story, for instance, the use of the second-person pronoun – which 'has a strong inter-personal base' (Wales 1996: 59) – encourages readerly identification and immersion, appearing to cross world boundaries to address the reader directly. Consider the opening sentences of the narrative: 'You are our instrument. Beautiful you' (Jemisin 2019: 4). These lines have no clear addressee. There are no obvious 'enactors' (Emmott 1997) visibly present at this moment in the text, nor is there an immediate sense of who is speaking to the 'you'. As 'the indexical pronoun *you* does not operate in a discursive vacuum' (Mildorf 2016: 146), it is arguably difficult at this point not to feel addressed by the 'you'. It is only on reaching the following sentence – 'Everything that could be given to you to improve on the human design, you possess' (Jemisin 2019: 4) – that it becomes apparent that the narratee is decidedly *not* the reader. In this sentence, the 'you' is the carrier of a *relational attributive process* (Halliday 2013) in which the attribute 'everything that could be given [. . .] to improve on the human design' is both futuristic and unobtainable in the actual world of 2025.

The suggestion of such characteristics signal division between the reader and the narratee for, as argued by Fludernik (1994: 287), 'as soon as the protagonist becomes too specific a personality, becomes, that is, a fictional character, the quality of the presumed address to an extradiegetic reader [. . .] evaporates' (see also Phelan 1994: 357). The distance between these two roles only increases across the following paragraphs, with both the characterisation of the 'you' and the world-building of the narrative illustrating further disjuncture between reader and narratee. The use of proximal spatial deixis, for example, highlights that the AI is addressing an internal character, as it is evident they share a perceptual field. On describing the narratee's physical appearance, the intelligence notes: 'Here is what you will look like when your time comes [. . .] Are you not magnificent?' (Jemisin 2019: 4). As the reader cannot see what is being shown to the narratee – the image is not described in the language of the text – it can only be inferred that the AI is sharing a mental image, either directly within the mind of the narratee (in which they are implanted), or projected within the composite suit. Either way, the image is something that the reader cannot access, as the deictic referent is extralinguistic (Rauh 1983).

In order to understand the use of 'here' in the above example, we must consequently suspend 'our normal egocentric assumptions about deictic terms of reference' (McIntyre 2006: 99) and assume instead that the deictic centre is internal to the narrative. This understanding entails what Levinson (1983: 67) refers to as *deictic projection*: a 'shift from the egocentric centre' (see also Green 1992). To offer a further example of this deictic phenomenon, consider the following lines, in which the narratee and the AI first experience life on Tellus.

> This . . . cannot be.
>
> That is *movement*. Those are *lights*. There should be clear signs of eco-collapse. It had already begun when the Founders left – but compare the geographic maps we have stored against what's there now. See that branching line in the southwestern portion of the continent? That was, *is*, the Colorado River.
>
> (Jemisin 2019: 6)

In order to conceptualise the scene presented here, the reader must project into the mind of the 'you', taking up a position in the narrative world relative to the narratee's *deictic field*. However, as the AI shares the narratee's mind, the narrator-narratee duality complicates this projection and muddies our typical understanding of the deictic centre. In standard real-world face-to-face communication, 'deictic expressions typically take the speaker's position as their point of anchorage, and [. . .] can only be successfully interpreted with reference to that position' (Semino 2011: 421, see also Lyons 1977). As such, we typically project into the deictic centre of the speaker, which in the case of *Emergency Skin* would be the AI. However, such projection is hindered by the unnaturalness of the intelligence; as a technological cybernetic implant, it is both artificial and doubly-situated, occupying both the body and mind of the narratee and – presumably – a body and mind of its own.

In reading *Emergency Skin* the reader must consequently toggle between the mind of the AI and the mind of the narratee. The use of the proximal demonstrative 'this' in the extract above, for example, positions the reader in line with the narrator's deictic centre, signalling their confusion and surprise at the revitalised Earth. The ellipsis – a marker of *textual deixis* – maintains this position, highlighting the mental processing of the intelligence as they pause in their communication with the narratee. The textually deictic gap between the first and second sentence signalled by the line break, however, shifts the reader's attention to the reactions of the narratee, who presumably poses a question to the AI. The following distal deictic markers move us back into the mind of the narrator, with the demonstratives 'that' and 'those' pointing to objects which are familiar to the AI but unfamiliar to the protagonist: 'That is *movement*. Those are *lights*.' The use of distal deictic markers maintains the narrator's deictic centre, as the AI continues to educate the narratee about their surroundings, as exemplified by the 'was/is' paradox in the final sentence of the extract. Here attention is drawn away from the digitised or holographic maps (which are internal to the narratee's consciousness) towards the real river in the narratee's immediate foreground to which the narrator 'points'. Such a shift highlights further the distinction between the artificial extended cognition of the narrator (extended through the use of 'extrabodily components or tools', Newen et al. 2020b: 6) and the lived experience of the narratee.

Perceptual deixis and the posthuman mind

Having distinguished between the consciousness of the narrator and the consciousness of the narratee, the reader must then go one step further, recognising that the mind of the narrator is not one mind but many. Presented through the use of the first-person plural 'we', the mind of the AI is a collective one, representing at once a cybernetic, non-human consciousness and a seemingly projected form of social intelligence: an imprint of the beliefs, attitudes, and directives of the human Founders. The duality of the AI's identity is evidenced in the following extract in which they reflect on their relationship with the Founders whilst reprimanding the narratee for their idleness:

> Look. We're glad to note the reduction of your agitation neuro-response, but how long do you mean to stand here?
>
> Your attitude grows irritating. Must we report your disrespect to the Founders when we return? We're their consensus consciousness, after all. Some parts of our consciousness are amused by your anger, others offended, but we are all certain that you wouldn't talk to a Founder this way.
>
> (Jemisin 2019: 20)

The passage opens with an exclamation, 'Look,' which is employed by the narrator to regain the narratee's attention. The imperative verb that is here used as a discourse marker is also a marker of textual deixis, pointing forward to the question that follows. The AI continues with an affirmative evaluation, 'We're glad to note', indicating their response to the protagonist's regularising vital signs, of which they have oversight and partial control. The interrogative 'how long do you mean to stand here?' draws attention to the shared physicality of the narrator-narratee, with the use of the proximal spatial deictic marker 'here' signalling their mutual location. The use of the present tense, an indicator of *temporal deixis* ('how long do you mean to stand here?'), also signals this positionality, recognising that the characters not only share space but also share time. According to Ikeo (2023: 104), the use of present tense in first-person narration emphasises an internalised 'vantage point, closely tied to the character's [. . .] perceptions and contemporaneous awareness'. As the narrator and narratee are intrinsically bound, the present tense consequently highlights the synchronicity of the narrator and narratee's joint perceptions and further immerses the reader in the immediate narrative moment.

The interrogative itself receives no response from the narratee (either in the language of the text or inferably in the storyworld), with the pause in the narrative – signalled again through textual deixis – implying the narratee's lack of movement. The following reactive evaluation 'Your attitude grows irritating' confirms this response, highlighting the AI's annoyance that the narratee has remained stationary. Such annoyance prompts a threat on the part of the narrator, signalled by the deontic lexical verb 'must' embedded within their follow-up interrogative 'Must we report your disrespect to the Founders when we return?' Up to this point in the narrative, the AI has presented a unified voice, with the use of 'we' an effective stand-in for the first-person singular 'I'. However, in the final sentence, 'Some parts of our consciousness are amused by your anger, others offended . . .', the referent notably splits and it becomes apparent that the intelligence comprises multiple parts that, though connected, are not wholly united (for work on the mutability of the first-person collective pronoun, see Bekhta 2020).

Due to the potential ambiguity of the *relational identifying possessive*, 'We're their consensus consciousness, after all', there is also the additional perspective of the Founders with which to contend (for relational processes see Halliday 2013). The sentence arguably presents two possible meanings: either the AI belongs to the Founders, and the relationship presented is Master-Servant; or the AI stands as an artificial extension of the Founders, in which case the relationship presented is Part-Whole. The surrounding grammar would suggest the former, given the use of the noun 'Founder' to define a separate non-present entity. However, earlier in the text, when the identity of the AI is first documented, the use of 'we' does present similar ambiguity, as exemplified in the extract below:

> To ensure success, and your mental health during extended isolation, we have equipped you with ourselves – a dynamic-matrix consensus intelligence encapsulating the ideals and blessed rationality of our Founders. We are implanted in your mind and will travel with you everywhere. We are your companion and your conscience.
>
> (Jemisin 2019: 4–5)

Here we have a *material action intention process* (Halliday 2013) in which the actor 'we' and the circumstantial element 'with ourselves' are one and the same – unless, that is, the referent of the first-person plural pronoun in the first sentence applies to the Founders, whose 'ideals' and 'rationality' are imparted by the intelligence and then adopted by the narratee, for whom the AI is an omnipresent guide. The possessive use of 'our', in 'our Founders', however, continues to jar this particular reading, perhaps confirming instead that the 'we' are an extension of the 'technorati', the class presumably tasked with the creation and upkeep of the composite suit. Either way, the notion of a 'consensus intelligence' and the multiperspectival response it projects (regardless of the exact make-up of that perspective) is suggestive of a dystopian collective, of a dystopian *social mind* (Norledge 2022, see also Palmer 2010). Such a mind – which in the fictional world is made real through technological advancement – brings this chapter back to questions of embodiment.

In a detailed critique of the social mind, Stockwell (2011: 290–1) observes: 'Palmer insists persuasively that social minds exist, and can be presented with characteristic patterns of their mind-style. If this is so, then the social mind must also be embodied, like all minds are. But what exactly is the body in which a social mind is embodied?' Palmer's (2011: 396) rejoinder to such critiques stipulates that minds are 'situated' – that is, 'individual minds are situated by being embodied and social minds are situated by being distributed'. Palmer uses the term 'distributed' here to refer to the shared presence of a social mind amongst the individual, embodied minds of which it is a part. In the case of most dystopian social minds, the notion of distributed cognition is particularly useful, recognising the characteristic shared belief system of a highly controlled world order. With respect to Jemisin's *Emergency Skin,* if the individual minds that comprise the 'we' do belong to the Founders or to the technorati, then such an interpretation would hold true. However, if they do not, then what we have instead is a wholly unnatural dystopian mind (Norledge 2019), which, despite being temporarily housed within the mind of the narratee, may be in itself wholly disembodied.

Edgework, immersion, and enactment

At this point in my analysis, I have recognised several interconnected consciousnesses: that of the 'You', that of the Founders and/or the technorati, and that of the mysterious 'We' which comprises multiple connected cognitive parts. In order to fully map out the narrative-communicative situation of Jemisin's text, it is important to also consider the mind of the reader, who was initially drawn into the narrative world by the seemingly apostrophic address of the opening lines. As noted above, it becomes apparent quite quickly that the narratee is not the reader. However, as the narratee remains covert throughout the narrative, having neither speech nor explicitly described actions, the address feels somewhat *autotelic* (Richardson 2006: 30), necessitating a level of immersive enactment and performativity which is not typically associated with *fictionalised horizontal address* (Herman 1994).

Unlike the *doubly-deictic* you (Herman 1994) found in such narratives as Italo Calvino's *If on a Winter's Night a Traveller* – in which the boundary between reader and narratee is consistently blurred – the personal identity of the 'you' is never really in question. However, the monologic nature of the discourse, combined with various instances of metafictional textual deixis, invites readers to project into the mind of the narratee, immersing themselves in the fiction in order to envision the actions and perceptions of the protagonist. In the following example, for instance, the pause in the narrative (marked by the hyphen), signals an interruption from the covert narratee whose actual thoughts we cannot hear:

> Please take a sample. The technorati in Biotech are always looking for new potential commodities –
>
> Oh. Not even with the monomolecular blade? Hmm. Very well. Resume mission.
>
> (Jemisin 2019: 10)

The exact wording of the communication is omitted, requiring the reader to infer and imagine the non-verbalised speech and/or thought of the narratee. As the passage opens with an imperative ('Please take a sample'), it is clear that the narratee is expected to perform an action. Given the typical two-part exchange of a standard adjacency pair, it can then be inferred that the narratee proffers a negative response, given the apostrophe ('Oh') which follows. The addition of the negative proposition 'Not even with the monomolecular blade?' then confirms this response, evidenced by the negative particle + adverb + preposition, 'Not even with', which signals the failure of the first action. The interrogative, which is also unanswered, indicates a further negative response from the narratee as inferred from the discourse marker 'Hmm', and the narrator's closing instruction to 'Resume mission.'

In order to understand the above exchange, the reader must project into the mind of the narratee, imagining their reactions – both physical and mental – and conceptualising the scene with respect to the narratee's *deictic field*. Galbraith (1995) refers to such projection in terms of a *deictic push*. A deictic push occurs when we 'submerge from a basic level to a less available deictic plane' (Galbraith 1995: 47), initially, for example, from the actual world into the fictional storyworld. Having pushed into the storyworld to the mind of the narrator (to whose voice and thoughts we have access), there is then a second push into the covert mind of the narratee, cued by every question, request, or directive issued to the 'you'. In imagining the thoughts and actions of the narratee, the distance between the character and the reader decreases, as the reader pushes further into the narratee's consciousness at the level of the text. However, as the process of filling in narrative gaps or omissions is a conscious activity, such processes occur at the level of the discourse and are therefore ontologically distinct from the textual narrative.

Having immersed themselves in the fictional world so as to model the mind of the narratee, the reader must consequently perform a *deictic pop* every time they are faced with a narrative gap, projecting back to their own deictic centre in the actual world in order to flesh out narrative events. Such processing is dependent upon the reader's real-world interactional competence and psychology; upon their knowledge of conversational patterns, preferred responses, and discourse domains. The reader's inferences at discourse level are projected back into the text, being assigned to the mind of the narratee and incremented in the reader's construal. For Galbraith (1995: 47), a *pop* allows the reader to 'emerge from one deictic plane to a higher or more basic-ontological-level deictic plane', with such *emergence* recognising a 'coming round' of consciousness (Stockwell 2019: 20, and see Stockwell, this volume). In *Emergency Skin*, the emergence of the reader is determined by changes to the deictic field, marked through textual deixis, and realised through the readerly process of *edgework* (Segal 1995b, Stockwell 2020).

The process of *edgework*, and the identification of and movement between deictic fields, forms part of deictic shift theory (DST). As noted by McIntyre (2006: 92), DST offers an explanation of 'how it is that readers often come to feel deeply involved in narratives, to the extent that they interpret events in a narrative as if they were experiencing them from a position within the story world'. McIntyre here builds on the work of Segal, whose research similarly examines the 'cognitive stance' taken by the reader when engaging with a literary narrative. As argued by Segal (1995a: 15), in taking up the deictic field of another, the reader necessarily 'interprets the text from that perspective', projecting to another's deictic centre and away from their own. It is the continual oscillation or toggling between deictic fields that arguably defines the estranging experience of reading *Emergency Skin*, as the narrative at once relies upon readerly inference and performance in the actual world (in line with the deictic field of the reader) whilst inviting immersion and projection into the text (in line with the deictic field of the narratee).

Textual deixis, negation, and omission

Before bringing my analysis together, there is one final aspect of the narrative to consider, which is the use of negation. As the text is narrated by the AI, the narrative inevitably breaks down whenever the protagonist attempts to access restricted information or when the AI goes offline, as it does during periods of high emotion, pain, or lack of action on the part of the protagonist. During these moments, the reader is popped out to the level of the discourse in order to account for the narrative gaps. As argued by Emmott (1997: 105), 'to understand a story fully [. . .] the reader needs to make inferences about what is not mentioned', and this process is very much realised during a reading of *Emergency Skin*. Consider the following exchange in which the narratee questions the narrator, having first encountered a human woman:

> Yes. We know what 'her' means. We simply do not acknowledge it.
> [reference request denied]
> [reference request denied]
>
> (Jemisin 2019: 17)

The interaction presented here follows a question-answer format, with the narratee attempting to force information from the intelligence. The opening use of 'Yes' signals the AI's response to the first question, which was presumably something like 'Do you understand that creature's use of "her"?' There then follow two textual deictic markers, cued by the repeated parenthetical comment '[reference request denied]', which indicates that the narratee's follow-up questions are blocked. The AI often shuts down communication in this way, limiting the narratee's access to information whenever they come close to prohibited topics, in this case to the concept of gender and womanhood. The textual deixis acts as a form of negation, with the omission of information combined with inherent negation ('denied') priming the narratee's questions in the mind of the reader. Negation 'is built on duality: the toggling of absence and presence in a language user's mind' (Nahajec 2021: 203). In order to comprehend this interaction, the reader must consequently toggle between their understanding of female existence in the real world and the defamiliarising absence of women in the fiction. In doing so, they are able to imagine the confusion and surprise of the narratee on meeting a female human for the first time, whilst popping out of the storyworld so as to imaginatively infer their persistent questions.

Other reference requests are more difficult to understand, especially when the request made by the narratee is decontextualised. Early on in the narrative, for instance, the narratee poses a question that the reader can neither hear nor easily unpack based on surrounding information. At this point in the story the AI is describing the features of the composite suit, noting what would happen should the composite be breached and the narratee be placed under threat. Following the AI's mention of an emergency situation, the topic shifts sharply and the AI states: '[reference request denied] You don't need to know about that yet. Please focus, and limit your curiosity' (Jemisin 2019: 5). In this sentence, *internal contextualisation* (Fillmore 1975, 1981) would suggest that the request concerns what exactly would constitute an emergency, given the previous discourse topic. *External contextualisation*, by comparison – which 'holds that certain sentences found outside of appropriate contexts cannot be interpreted' (Segal 1995a: 11) – might imply an alternative. If the request for information does not concern the suit, then it has likely been triggered by external stimulus, reflecting happenings in the fictional world which are accessible only to the characters. It is up to the reader, then, whether they interpret the positive proposition primed by the negative reference as coincident to or distinct from the narrator's original subject focus.

Similar decisions must be made when the AI goes offline and the reader loses access to both the mind of the narrator and the mind of the narratee. At the close of *Emergency Skin*, the narratee has the AI exorcised from their mind and it is at this point that the narrative collapses completely. The physical removal of the AI, which is enacted by an older citizen of Tellus, follows the narratee's decision to return home and broker a revolution. Such rebellion requires the narratee's connection to the Founders (and to the narrator) to be severed: you '"Can't start a revolution with the enemy shouting in your head, after all"' (Jemisin 2019: 34). The direct speech, uttered by the citizen of Tellus, marks the final words spoken in the text before the closing textual deixis signals the expiration of the AI:

> What is a revolu
> . □
> .
> . □
>
> OFFLINE
>
> End
>
> (Jemisin 2019: 34)

In interpreting the unicode, the reader projects an interpretation onto the text, recognising the omitted narrative as being indicative of the AI's demise.

All that is left is silence as the gateway to the mind of the narratee is closed. It is at this point that all sense of the 'literary performative' (Kacandes 1993) and the connection to the 'you' is lost. The conclusion of *Emergency Skin* confirms, then, that the textual deixis presented throughout Jemison's narrative supersedes the perceptual, with the breaks in the narrative pushing the reader back to their own deictic level. In the end, not only does the character's split or dual consciousness stymie readerly identification with the 'you', but the breakdown of the narrative disconnects the reader entirely from the character whose conscious activity they had imagined, and, at times, shared. As a result, the disconnect simulates at once the severing of the connection between narratee and AI, whilst acting as a site of shared readerly emergence.

End

In discussing the narrative style of Jemisin's *Broken Earth* trilogy, Wickham (2019: 396) contends that the use of second-person address marks a 'distinctive narrative approach that highlights fragmentation, identification, and communication'. The same holds true in *Emergency Skin*. Throughout the text, the reader is immersed in and subsequently popped out of the narrative as determined by their engagement with the 'you'. In aligning with the deictic centre of the narratee, they necessarily conceive of the fictional world from the you's perspective, with the world-building elements presented throughout the narrative being described in relation to the narratee's deictic field. However, as I have argued throughout this chapter, such projection is not straightforward, and the reader must also contend with the disembodied social mind of the narrating AI. As the narratee's mind is occupied by another, and it is the AI's voice which 'speaks', deictic projection consequently fluctuates, with the reader toggling between the deictic field of the AI and the deictic field of the narratee.

The fragmentation of the narration enriches this duality, requiring the reader to creatively fill in the narrative, imagining the speech and thought of the 'you' that is never realised in the language of the text. As such, the second person 'continuously solicits the reader's complicit presence' (Sorlin 2015: 50), requiring them to imagine and to some extent cognitively enact the mental and verbal processes of the narratee. (For a discussion of this dynamic in children's metafiction, see Wydrzynska, this volume.) However, as the process of filling in these textual gaps is a conscious readerly activity, it can only be undertaken at the level of the discourse and is therefore ontologically distinct from the workings of the narrative proper. The reader's imaginative action therefore relies on insinuation and active readerly involvement, yet does not suggest a merging of worlds nor allow for complete immersion in the text. Projection into the narrative is instead continuously interrupted, as the reader is necessarily popped out of the text in order to fully engage with those omissions marked by textual deixis. Immersion and emergence consequently go hand in hand for the reader of Jemisin's text, who must, in the course of reading, inhabit and ultimately abandon the posthuman mind.

References

Bekhta, N. (2020) *We-Narratives: Collective Storytelling in Contemporary Fiction*. Ohio: Ohio State University Press.

Bühler, K. (1982) 'The deictic field of language and deictic worlds', in R.J. Jarvella and W. Klein (eds) *Speech, Place and Action: Studies in Deixis and Related Topics* (translated from *Sprachtheorie* [1934]). Chichester: John Wiley & Sons, pp.9–30.

Crouch, B. (2019) 'A note from the curator of the Forward collection', in N.K. Jemisin (ed.) *Emergency Skin*. Seattle: Amazon Original Stories, pp.36–7.

Dancygier, B. (2014) 'Intensity and texture in imagery', in P. Stockwell and S. Whiteley (eds) *The Cambridge Companion to Stylistics*. Cambridge: Cambridge University Press, pp.212–17.

Duchan, J.E., Bruder, G.A. and Hewitt, L.E. (eds) (1995) *Deixis in Narrative: A Cognitive Science Perspective*. Hillsdale: Lawrence Erlbaum.

Emmott, C. (1997) *Narrative Comprehension: A Discourse Perspective*. Oxford: Oxford University Press.

Ferrández San Miguel, M. (2020) 'Ethics in the Anthropocene: traumatic exhaustion and posthuman regeneration in N.K. Jemisin's *Broken Earth* Trilogy', *English Studies* 101 (4): 471–86.

Fillmore, C.J. (1975) *Santa Cruz Lectures on Deixis*. Bloomington: Indiana University Linguistics Club.

Fillmore, C.J. (1981) 'Pragmatics and the description of discourse', in P. Cole (ed.) *Radical Pragmatics*. New York: Academic Press, pp.143–66.

Fludernik, M. (1994) 'Second-person narrative and related issues', *Style* 28 (3): 281–311.

Galbraith, M. (1995) 'Deictic shift theory and the poetics of involvement in narrative', in J.F. Duchan, G.A. Bruder and L.E. Hewitt (eds) *Deixis in Narrative: A Cognitive Science Perspective*. Hillsdale: Lawrence Erlbaum, pp.19–59.

Gibbs, R.W. (2005) *Embodiment and Cognitive Science*. Cambridge: Cambridge University Press.

Green, K. (1992) 'Deixis and the poetic persona', *Language and Literature* 1 (2): 121–34.

Halliday, M.A.K. (2013) *An Introduction to Functional Grammar* (4th edn). London: Arnold.

Herman, D. (1994) 'Textual you and double deixis in Edna O'Brien's *A Pagan Place*', *Style* 28 (3): 378–411.

Ikeo, R. (2023) 'Contemporary present-tense fiction: crossing boundaries in narrative', *Language and Literature* 32 (1): 98–128.

Jemisin, N.K. (2019) *Emergency Skin*. Seattle: Amazon Original Stories.

Kacandes, I. (1993) 'Are you in the text? The "literary performative" in postmodern fiction', *Text and Performance Quarterly* 13 (2): 139–53.

Levinson, S. (1983) *Pragmatics*. Cambridge: Cambridge University Press.

Lyons, J. (1977) *Semantics, Volume 2*. Cambridge: Cambridge University Press.

McIntyre, D. (2006) *Point of View in Plays. A Cognitive Stylistic Approach to Viewpoint in Drama and Other Text-Types*. Amsterdam: John Benjamins.
Mildorf, J. (2016) 'Reconsidering second-person narration and involvement', *Language and Literature* 25 (2): 145–58.
Morris, S.M. (2019) 'Epic fantasy, and utopia in N.K. Jemisin's Dreamblood duology', in P. Ventura and E.K. Chan (eds) *Race and Utopian Desire in American Literature and Society*. New York: Springer, pp.283–300.
Nahajec, L. (2021) *Negation, Expectation and Ideology in Written Texts: A Textual and Communicative Perspective*. Amsterdam: John Benjamins.
Newen, A., de Bruin, L. and Gallagher, S. (eds) (2020a) *The Oxford Handbook of 4E Cognition*. Oxford: Oxford University Press.
Newen, A., de Bruin, L. and Gallagher, S. (2020b) '4E cognition: historical roots, key concepts, and central issues', in A. Newen, L. de Bruin and S. Gallagher (eds) *The Oxford Handbook of 4E Cognition*. Oxford: Oxford University Press, pp.3–18.
Norledge, J. (2019) 'Immersive reading and the unnatural text-worlds of "Dead Fish"', in B. Neurohr and L. Stewart-Shaw (eds) *Experiencing Fictional Worlds*. Amsterdam: John Benjamins, pp.157–75.
Norledge, J. (2022) *The Language of Dystopia*. London: Palgrave.
Norledge, J. (2024) 'N.K. Jemisin', in R. Parks (ed.) *Literary Criticism. Volume 547*. Farmington Hills: Gale-Cengage, pp.1–114.
Palmer, A. (2010) *Social Minds in the Novel, Theory, Interpretation, Narrative*. Ohio: Ohio State University Press.
Palmer, A. (2011) 'Social minds in fiction and criticism', *Style* 45 (2): 196–240.
Phelan, J. (1994) '"Self-help" for narratee and narrative audience: how "I" – and "you"? – read "how"', *Style* 28 (3): 350–65.
Rauh, G. (ed.) (1983) *Essays in Deixis*. Narr: Tübingen.
Richardson, B. (2006) *Unnatural Voices: Extreme Narration in Modern and Contemporary Fiction*. Ohio: Ohio State University Press.
Segal, E.M. (1995a) 'Narrative comprehension and the role of Deictic Shift Theory', in J.F. Duchan, G.A. Bruder and L.E. Hewitt (eds) *Deixis in Narrative a Cognitive Science Perspective*. Abingdon: Routledge, pp.3–17.
Segal, E.M. (1995b) 'A cognitive-phenomenological theory of fictional narrative', in J.F. Duchan, G.A. Bruder and L.E. Hewitt (eds) *Deixis in Narrative: A Cognitive Science Perspective*. Hillsdale: Lawrence Erlbaum, pp.61–78.
Semino, E. (2011) 'Deixis and fictional minds', *Style* 45 (3): 418–40.
Sorlin, S. (2015) 'Person deixis and impersonation in Iain Banks's *Complicity*', *Language and Literature* 24 (1): 40–53.
Stockwell, P. (2011) 'Changing minds in narrative', *Style* 45 (2): 288–91.
Stockwell, P. (2019) 'Immersion and emergence in children's literature', in B. Neurohr and L. Stewart-Shaw (eds) *Experiencing Fictional Worlds*. Amsterdam: John Benjamins, pp.15–32.
Stockwell, P. (2020) *Cognitive Poetics. An Introduction* (2nd edn). London: Routledge.
Wales, K. (1996) *Personal Pronouns in Present-Day English*. Cambridge: Cambridge University Press.
Wickham, K. (2019) 'Identity, memory, slavery: second-person narration in N.K. Jemisin's *The Broken Earth Trilogy*', *Journal of the Fantastic in the Arts* 30 (3): 392–411.

Index

EU Authorised Representative:
Easy Access System Europe Mustamäe tee 50, 10621 Tallinn, Estonia
gpsr.requests@easproject.com

Printed and bound by CPI Group (UK) Ltd, Croydon, CR0 4YY
14/09/2026
02216781-0009